SEX & CRIME

Sara Miller McCune founded SAGE Publishing in 1965 to support the dissemination of usable knowledge and educate a global community. SAGE publishes more than 1000 journals and over 800 new books each year, spanning a wide range of subject areas. Our growing selection of library products includes archives, data, case studies and video. SAGE remains majority owned by our founder and after her lifetime will become owned by a charitable trust that secures the company's continued independence.

Los Angeles | London | New Delhi | Singapore | Washington DC | Melbourne

SEX & CRIME

ALEXANDRA FANGHANEL

EMMA MILNE

GIULIA ZAMPINI

STACY BANWELL

MICHAEL FIDDLER

Los Angeles | London | New Delhi
Singapore | Washington DC | Melbourne

Los Angeles | London | New Delhi
Singapore | Washington DC | Melbourne

SAGE Publications Ltd
1 Oliver's Yard
55 City Road
London EC1Y 1SP

SAGE Publications Inc.
2455 Teller Road
Thousand Oaks, California 91320

SAGE Publications India Pvt Ltd
B 1/I 1 Mohan Cooperative Industrial Area
Mathura Road
New Delhi 110 044

SAGE Publications Asia-Pacific Pte Ltd
3 Church Street
#10-04 Samsung Hub
Singapore 049483

Editor: Natalie Aguilera
Editorial assistant: Eve Williams
Production editor: Sarah Cooke
Marketing manager: Susheel Gokarakonda
Cover design: Francis Kenney
Typeset by: C&M Digitals (P) Ltd, Chennai,
Printed in the UK

Library of Congress Control Number: 2020938336

British Library Cataloguing in Publication data

A catalogue record for this book is available from the
British Library

ISBN 978-1-5264-9113-8
ISBN 978-1-5264-9112-1 (pbk)

At SAGE we take sustainability seriously. Most of our products are printed in the UK using responsibly sourced
papers and boards. When we print overseas we ensure sustainable papers are used as measured by the
PREPS grading system. We undertake an annual audit to monitor our sustainability.

For all those who hustle under the grip of normativity

Contents

About the authors

Alexandra Fanghanel

Senior lecturer in Criminology at the University of Greenwich

I am a queer, non-monogamous, femme. I am a middle-class, cisgender, white European, who does not consider herself to have any disabilities. I share the care of my two young children with my partner.

I research fear of crime, security, sexuality and sexual practice in public space. I use queer, feminist, post-structuralist and anti-colonialist approaches to analyse power and to strive for social justice.

I see education as a tool through which to become free and to begin to undo the injustice of the world; that is why I am so committed to radical, critical pedagogy. When I was a student, I was encouraged to read promiscuously, and that is what I try to do, and to encourage in others: be gone, disciplinary borders.

My book, *Disrupting Rape Culture: Public Space, Sexuality, and Revolt* (Bristol University Press, 2020) is a riot.

Emma Milne

Assistant Professor in Criminal Law and Criminal Justice at Durham University

I am a white, middle-class, dyslexic, queer woman. I am an activist for women's rights, specifically reproductive rights and justice. I am a feminist. My research is informed by and uses feminism, intersectionality and post-structuralism. My approach to law and legal research is from Feminist Legal Theory and Critical Legal Studies perspectives.

My research and teaching are interdisciplinary, focused on criminal law and criminal justice responses to women who are deemed to be criminal or deviant, specifically those suspected of newborn-child killing and foetal harm. The wider context of my work is social, cultural and legal controls and regulations of all women, notably in relation to motherhood, pregnancy, sex and reproduction. I am the author of *Criminal Justice Responses to Maternal Filicide: Judging the Failed Mother* (Emerald, 2021) and co-edited *Women and the Criminal Justice System: Failing Victims and Offenders?* (Palgrave, 2018).

Giulia Federica Zampini

Senior lecturer in Criminology at the University of Greenwich

I am a feminist, cisgender woman. I am Italian, bisexual and middle-class. I practise ethical non-monogamy. On the UK ethnicity classification forms, I tick the box 'any other white background', but people call me 'olive-skinned' and usually cannot tell where I am from.

My formal academic studies span across history, politics, social policy and socio-legal studies, but I am also interested in anthropology, ethics and moral psychology. I am attracted to a variety of theoretical and epistemological positions, including – but not limited to – feminism standpoint theory, critical theory and critical realism.

My research interests centre around evidence and policy on drugs, prostitution, morality, harm reduction, decriminalisation and prison education. Recently, I have become obsessed with hierarchies and have been reflecting on their naturalisation.

I am dedicated to research, activism and advocacy for harm reduction across drug policy and prostitution policy, and committed to enabling platforms for marginalised communities, including people who use drugs and people who are incarcerated.

My current ongoing project, 'People and dancefloors: Narratives of drug-taking', involves team-based participatory action research through film.

Stacy Banwell

Principal lecturer in Criminology at the University of Greenwich, programme leader: MSc Criminology, Gender and Sexualities, University of Greenwich

I am a cisgender, middle-class, heterosexual woman of colour. I am a vegan and a supporter of the climate movement.

My background is in Criminology and Criminal Justice. My current research interests are:

- Gender and the violence(s) of war and armed conflict, including the relationship between war/armed conflict and climate insecurity.
- Gender and economic foreign policy, specifically US foreign policy on abortion. I am currently reviewing the impact of President Trump's revised global gag rule (GGR) and the defunding of UNFPA in humanitarian and war-affected settings.

These topics are addressed in my monograph *Gender and the Violence(s) of War and Armed Conflict: More Dangerous to be a Woman?* (Emerald Publishing, 2020). This work draws on Critical, Feminist and Visual Criminology; International Relations, Security Studies (including environmental security), Post-colonial Studies and Gender Studies.

I am a feminist who aligns herself with postcolonial and transnational feminism. My research practice is informed by feminist standpoint theory (which I apply to both human and non-human animals) and participatory action research.

Michael Fiddler

Associate Professor of Criminology at the University of Greenwich

I am a cisgender, white, middle-class man. My background is in Criminology.

My research has explored prison architecture, as well as the ways in which the 'gothic' and 'uncanny' can be applied to representations of imprisonment and violence. My current project is focused upon 'Ghost Criminology' and unpacking the ways in which the conceptual metaphors of haunting and spectrality can be applied to crime and punishment.

Acknowledgement

We conceived and created the project of this book as a quintet and were fortunate enough to be so numerous as to be able to support each other in the writing of it. We would like to thank Dr Sarah Rybczynska-Bunt and the helpful anonymous reviewers who commented on earlier drafts of parts of this text. Special thanks go to our students, who are a constant source of inspiration; particularly Alex's 2019/20 cohort of Sexuality, Culture and Criminality who test-ran a number of the ideas that feature prominently in this book. Thanks also to students on Stacy's Women, Power, Crime and Justice, and Michael's Crime and the Media modules. Finally, we would also like to thank the usual suspects who support us in our writing projects and help us create space to make it possible. We hope they know who they are.

Part 1

Encountering Sex and Crime

1

Introduction

The issues and controversies of sex and crime are intimately intertwined. In this book, we will explore the ways that **sexuality**[*] and **sexual practice** interact with crime and **deviance**, and the ways that understanding this interaction enriches our understanding of criminology and **social justice** more broadly.

In many ways, the regulation of sexuality through the law is something that we all experience, every day of our lives. As we will see in Chapters 3 and 5, sexuality and sexual practice have been controlled by law for centuries. Certain sexual practices are legislated against (such as sex with children), while others have had changing legal status (for example, anal sex). Other expressions of sexual desire or of sexual preference may be legal, but can bring with them shame and stigma (such as bondage, domination and sadomasochism (BDSM), pornography addiction, cybersex); thus, they are also regulated by social mores and accepted sexual etiquette.

In this book, we examine a range of ways that institutions of control interact with sex and sexuality. The book is broken down into four sections: the first part, 'Encountering sex and crime', helps you to get on board with the key concepts and ideas crucial to understanding sex, crime and control; the second, 'State, sex and crime', explores how the nation state both controls and facilitates crime related to sex. The third, 'Sex, cultures and crime', outlines how 'cultures' of sexuality and sexual practice interact with the state, and how and why sex is controlled and regulated; and, finally, 'Future sex' is where we reflect on how laws, controls, cultures and society may develop in relation to sexual practice. In our final chapter, we suggest ways to put your learning into practice.

By the end of this chapter, you will understand more about:

- key and fundamental ideas that will help you engage with this topic
- how you might read this book
- the type of learning you are going to do as you engage with this material.

Why is sex such a big deal?

One of the reasons why sexuality, sexual practice, crime and law are so heavily intertwined is because controlling sexuality is a way of controlling the population and creating a **nation**; nation-building is something that preoccupies nations all over the world. We see more of this in Chapter 3. As Michel Foucault (1998[1976]) has argued, when everyone follows the rules – is an obedient citizen – society functions as desired by those with **power** and control.

---

[*]The definitions of words in bold can be checked in the glossary.

The regulation of populations and nations is a big project, so many different tools are used to do this; the criminal law – and the **state** in general – is but one of them. The family, the education system, multinational corporations, **public health** messages, and religion are all examples of ways that sexuality is policed and controlled. The implications of this for criminology will become apparent in this book. As such, we will be talking about power and control a great deal throughout the book, thinking about who holds it and how it shapes behaviour and practice.

A content note

Before we embark on this project, we would like to offer a note about the content of some of the chapters. One of the implications of reading a book about sex and crime is that you will inevitably come across discussion of topics that are unpalatable, difficult, even traumatic. They may trigger something in you that upsets you. We have tried to present each issue in as sensitive a way as possible, but we know that we may not have anticipated all instances in which specific issues may be traumatic for a reader. As you read this material, pay attention to how it makes you feel. Take breaks from the book. Come back to it later if you want to. Stay in touch with your friends and family; do things that make you feel better; rest; speak to your lecturers and university support services if you want extra support. We have offered advice and support groups who might be able to help your further in Chapter 15.

BOX 1.1

As we begin these discussions, we ask you to think about the ways in which you are aware, in today's context, that sexuality and sexual practice are policed and controlled:

- What examples of illegal sexual practice and behaviour can you think of?
- What examples of **deviant** sexual practice and behaviour can you think of?
- Can you think of any other ways that sexuality or sexual practice is controlled?

What is clear is that attitudes towards crime, law, sexuality and sexual practice emerge in social and cultural contexts that are specific to the time and place in which they occur. As far as possible in this book, we have tried to situate the examples that we use to tell the stories of sex and crime in the temporal and geographic context in which they are relevant. This helps us not only to understand that there is no one 'truth' about sex or crime, or when sex is criminalised, and when it is not (for example, child marriage or the publishing of pornographic stories), but also to consider that our understanding of what is going on when sexual practice or sexuality is criminalised (or is not) can only ever be partial and limited by our own positionality (or the place from which we speak). It is our job as criminologists to enquire after the parts of the story that we do not know; to ask awkward questions that address this partial knowledge, in order to gain a better understanding of the politics, morality or exercise of power that work to normalise the specific control of sexuality. It is also our job to be curious about why we think what we do about a specific issue. What is it about us/our lives/our upbringing/our society that leads us to think the way that we do about sex and crime? As authors, we have outlined our own positionalities in the opening pages of this book.

Alongside examining the complex relationship between crime and sex, we intend to help you to acquire the tools to do this awkward questioning and this critical thinking. We will do this by exploring some of the many ways that sex and crime are linked and, using case studies to illustrate what we are saying, invite you to ask, and to answer, probing questions about the scenarios we are asking you to think about.

The following four tools will come in handy for you when you are doing this work.

1. Understanding what we mean by normative and non-normative sexuality

The word 'normative' is used in the social sciences to describe something mainstream or commonplace. For instance, in most of the world heterosexuality is mainstream and normative; much policy planning, news reporting, educational material, and law are created with heterosexual people and heterosexual coupling in mind. The word **heteronormative** is used to describe a world created for heterosexual lifestyles. Other things are normative too: marriage, monogamy, having children, living in a family unit, working, staying fit and healthy, obeying the law ... and it is not only heterosexual people who do all these things. People who identify as lesbian, gay, bisexual or **trans (LGBT +)** can also live normative lives, just as some heterosexual people may refuse to live a normative lifestyle. Nonetheless, normativity is often a word used to describe the way certain dominant modes of living – and in this context having sex – have become mainstream. We sometimes use the word 'normativity' critically because the mainstreaming of certain lifestyles necessarily comes at the expense of others. Minority groups are usually excluded from what is normative. For instance, same-sex relations are criminalised in 70 countries around the world and carry the death penalty in seven. In England and Wales, it was only in 2011 that the census started collecting data for same-sex households. In the USA, the census of 2020 will be the first to collect these data. And, even despite now counting gay and lesbian couples, these records of the population do not count bisexuals, trans people or gay/lesbian people who are not living in a couple. What do you think the implications of missing this population might be?

We also use the word 'normative' to describe a desire for the way life 'should' be, or 'could' be. We might say that we want social justice to be normative, meaning that we want it to be mainstream that we live in a socially just world. We might say that the fact that, as of 2019, same-sex marriage is recognised in 26 countries worldwide means that gay marriage is becoming normative.

In the context of sexual practice and the law, Gayle Rubin's (1984) analysis of the so-called 'charmed circle' of sexuality also helps us to better understand normativity. Rubin suggests that, in public policy, law and morality, there is 'good' and 'bad' sex:

> Only sex acts on the good side of the line are accorded moral complexity. For instance, heterosexual encounters may be sublime or disgusting, free or forced, healing or destructive, romantic or mercenary. As long as it does not violate other rules, heterosexuality is acknowledged to exhibit the full range of human experience. In contrast, all sex acts on the bad side of the line are considered utterly repulsive and devoid of all emotional nuance. (Rubin, 1984: 152)

The circle of the 'sex hierarchy' that Rubin has created situates sex that is monogamous; married; procreative; non-commercial; coupled; in a relationship; 'vanilla' (meaning not engaged with non-normative or unusual – we might say kinky – sexual practices); taking place at home; without pornography; between heterosexuals of a similar age; using just their bodies (and no sex toys), as 'good sex'. 'Bad sex' – sex which is condemned, criminalised or otherwise deviant or 'non-normative' – is kinky sex; using objects; taking place in public; using pornography; non-procreative; queer; anonymous; promiscuous; commercial (paid for); inter-generational; unmarried; casual; alone; or in a group. In this way, Rubin's sex hierarchy helps us to understand the difference between 'normative' and 'non-normative' sex. We will use these concepts a lot in this book because normativity is so important in the context of crime and of designating how deviant sexuality or sexual practice is approached.

The charmed circle:
Good, Normal, Natural, Blessed Sexuality

Heterosexual
Married
Monogamous
Procreative
Non-commercial
In pairs
In a relationship
Same generation
In private
No pornography
Bodies only
Vanilla

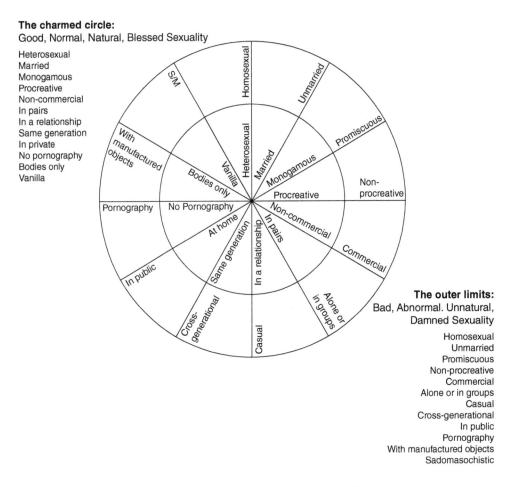

The outer limits:
Bad, Abnormal. Unnatural,
Damned Sexuality

Homosexual
Unmarried
Promiscuous
Non-procreative
Commercial
Alone or in groups
Casual
Cross-generational
In public
Pornography
With manufactured objects
Sadomasochistic

Figure 1.1   The sex hierarchy: the charmed circle vs the outer limits

---

BOX 1.2

Rubin's schema was created in 1984:

- Do you think it still applies now?
- What is similar?
- What is different?
- Are there now any practices that you would add or remove from the circle?
- How can the concept of 'good' and 'bad' sex and 'sexual hierarchies' help us understand sex and crime?
- Who do you think gets to decide what counts as 'good' and 'bad' sex?

2. Practising loving perception and world travelling

In this book, we will talk about issues that you may sometimes find difficult. Paedophilia, rape as a weapon of war, so-called 'revenge porn', sex trafficking, online harassment, sexual violence: all of these issues are highly emotive and sometimes controversial. You, or someone you know, may have personal experience of some of the things. Indeed, it is likely that in your class, at least one person will have some experience of these sorts of crimes. According to the 2017 Crime Survey of England and Wales, one in five women and 4 per cent of men have experienced some type of sexual assault since the age of 16. According to the United Nations, in North Africa and the Middle East, 40–60 per cent of women have experienced street-based sexual harassment. In 2017, of the women in the world who were intentionally killed 58 per cent were killed by intimate partners or family members (UN Women, 2019a). In the first three months of 2019, nearly 2,000 women and girls received treatment for female genital mutilation (FGM) in England (NHS Digital, 2019). Sexual violence and sex crimes are not rare.

When we talk about issues in this book, and as you explore them in your classes, we bear in mind the different trajectories that people have taken to come to study these questions (see also the section on intersectionality and positionality below). Some people may need to spend more time than others on some topics in order to fully work with them. For some people, the material may just be unbearable, or not-yet-bearable.

When encountering difference in this book, and with other people with whom you talk about the topics in this book, we suggest that you consider adopting a praxis (that is, a practical action) that Maria Lugones (1987) refers to as 'loving perception' and 'world travelling'. It may seem counter-intuitive to be asked to encounter violent crimes like FGM and child sexual abuse with 'love', and here we are not suggesting that you should try to love or like these crimes. Instead, we are offering loving perception as a tool to understand *why* they happen, so that from this position of understanding, we can better act against them. We discuss this more in Chapter 15. We appreciate that it is somewhat unusual to reflect on topics such as these in this way and you may find this challenging, odd or unsettling.

Lugones (1987: 5) contrasts loving perception with arrogant perception. Arrogant perception is one that refuses to 'travel' to the perspective of another person or to try to see a situation or understand a concept from their perspective. Arrogant perception thinks that nothing anyone else has to say is of interest if it does not agree with them. Arrogant perception tries to erase differences of opinion, or worse, silence them. The tool of world travelling helps us to practise loving perception. A 'world', in this context, is someone's flesh-and-blood reality. It may be their past, it may be their imagined past, it may be the imperfect present: it is a life experience that informs a world view.

Thus, even if some of the material we talk about shocks you, or disgusts you, or you cannot understand why people would do it, try to adopt a loving perception – an openness to difference – towards this issue. Think about the fact that people in your class may have been affected by the issue at hand, or may disagree with you that they are shocking or disgusting things. Adopting a loving perception recognises difference and allows a plurality of opinions about a topic to be held together. That is how we better understand the world, and ultimately make it more just: by better appreciating the opinions that other people hold, and understanding why they hold them (we talk more about this in Chapter 15). It also helps in your project of critical engagement, reflexivity and intellectual curiosity; of reflecting on why you hold the opinions and perspectives you do about an issue.

BOX 1.3

Take a moment to think about the following sexual practices and consider using the praxis outlined by Lugones:

- sexting with a person you do not know
- taking stimulants or other chemical substances to change the experience of sex
- having a sexual relationship with a sibling
- paying someone to engage in sexual behaviour.

What would arrogant and loving perception look like for each? What questions would you ask or consider if you were doing some 'world travelling' in order to understand this issue?

---

3. Understanding intersectionality and positionality

The concept of intersectionality is one that has received increased traction in popular **discourses** in recent years. Positionality – accounting for where you are speaking from and how it is influenced by the experiences you have encountered – and intersectionality often go hand in hand. The concept of intersectionality itself is not new and is borne out of **Black** feminist praxis. Kimberlé Crenshaw developed the term of intersectionality in 1989 in response to the erasure of Black women's experiences within the feminist and anti-racist movements. She argued that feminist approaches which demand that women unite behind issues of gender, or that Black women unite behind issues of 'race', without attending to the specific experiences that some women have as Black women, 'contributes to the marginalization of Black women in feminist theory and in antiracist politics' (Crenshaw, 1989: 140). Often, anti-racist debates would be dominated by men, while feminist fights would centre around issues that were prioritised by white women. Crenshaw argues that 'the intersectional experience is greater than the sum of racism and sexism, any analysis that does not take intersectionality into account cannot sufficiently address the particular manner in which Black women are subordinated' (1989: 140).

We can develop this further than the axes of 'race' and gender here in our study of sex and crime. Teenage pregnancy, while not a crime, is still considered to be 'deviant'. The extent to which teenage pregnancy is considered deviant will also depend on the **ethnicity** and **class** of the pregnant teenager, and on whether or not the teenager has a disability. Police attitudes towards children who have been trafficked for sex may also depend on the family background the child is perceived to have – their class and ethnicity – if they are trans, if they are care-leavers, if they have a history of drug or alcohol use. Similarly, people who have been raped or sexually assaulted may not report their experience to the police if they are from communities which have historically been harassed or attacked by the police; travellers, immigrants, trans, queers, members of **BAME** communities. On the other hand, white, middle-class women who have never been bullied by the police may not hesitate to go to the police to report the same crime. All of this is to demonstrate that there are multiple axes of identity that inform people's experiences, politics and perspectives on the world. We need to consider how positionality and intersecting identities impact on experiences of sexual practice, crime and control. Such critical analysis helps us to make sure that our analysis of the relationship between sex and crime is as complex and nuanced as it needs to be to make pertinent, inclusive analyses that make sense in the real world and which call into question all the ways in which intersectionality is obscured in contemporary criminal justice.

This is not to suggest that only the most marginalised can speak, nor is intersectionality about claiming victimhood, or a 'race to the bottom' of disadvantage. Some people *are* multiply marginalised, but the picture is rarely as straightforward as this. Some, like Caitlyn Jenner, may be marginalised in some contexts – as a trans woman, for instance – but in others benefit from their **whiteness**, their able-bodiedness, and from enormous wealth and influence. In other contexts, white, heterosexual, working-class men might benefit socially, economically and culturally from their ethnicity and gender, but men are also the group which is most likely to commit suicide in England and Wales, according to the Office for National Statistics (ONS, 3 September 2019), and are the most under-represented group in higher education institutions (Hillman and Robinson, 2016).

BOX 1.4

Thinking about your own positionality (where you are coming from) and trying to appreciate that of other people, including the way in which it influences the world, is not easy. Here is an exercise you can use to try to visualise your own positionality. All you need is some space (a large room or an outdoor space would be best), a bin and a ball. Position the bin at one end of the room, and position yourself in the middle of the room, holding the ball. Once you are there, read out each of the following statements to yourself. Each statement will ask you to take a step forward (closer to the bin) or to take a step back (away from the bin):

1. Step forward if you identify as male.
2. Step back if you've been cat-called/whistled at in the street.
3. Step forward if you didn't need to take a loan to go to university.
4. Step back if you sometimes feel you are expected to wear makeup to be presentable.
5. Step forward if you're never asked to speak for all the people in your ethnic group.
6. Step back if you have had someone in a position of authority (such as your teacher, boss, supervisor) come onto you or flirt with you.
7. Step forward if you don't identify as having a disability.
8. Step back if you've been mocked for an aspect of your identity.
9. Step forward if your citizenship and your country of residence align (e.g. you are an Australian citizen living in Australia).
10. Step back if you've ever felt inadequate due to your bodily features.
11. Step forward if you identify as heterosexual.
12. Step back if you're a primary caregiver.
13. Step forward if you are monogamous (are married to, or in a relationship with, just one person at a time).
14. Step forward if you've never been burdened by the cost of sanitary products (tampons, sanitary towels, menstruation cup).
15. Step back if you had 'less than enough' growing up as a child, however you define enough.
16. Step forward if you feel safe walking home alone at night.
17. Step back if you were expected to do housework chores as a child.

(Adapted from Österman et al., 2018)

Now, wherever you are, try to throw the ball in the bin. Did you dunk the ball? Perhaps you are a talented basketball player, yet distance will inevitably affect your chances of a slam dunk.

Your position in relation to the bin will be influenced by your positionality in society, at the intersection of different identities which are influenced by structural categories of gender, 'race' and class, but also disability, sexuality, age and sexual orientation. Some identities endow people with certain privileges, making it easier to 'score', while others make it harder.

4. Reparative, rather than paranoid, thinking

Eve Sedgwick (2003) articulates two ways in which contemporary critics, theorists and activists (we might also add critical criminologists) tend to think about contemporary social problems – through paranoid thought or through reparative thought.

Paranoid readings are, according to Sedgwick, analyses of contemporary social issues or phenomena (the *Love Island* TV show, for instance, or Pride marches, or gay marriage), which seek to reveal a 'dark truth' about the phenomenon that nobody else has seen, or that prove the false consciousness we live under (that TV shows are racist, or that Pride has been commodified by **capitalism**, or that gay marriage is homonormative). To an extent, critical criminology must do some of this questioning work, but to do it in a way that, as Sedgwick says, is 'paranoid' is to occlude any sort of transformation, or way out. If the project of criminology is to understand why crime happens and also to work towards a position which advocates for justice (and we may not agree on what justice looks like), then it must be necessary to move beyond paranoia towards 'reparation'. A reparative reading of a social phenomenon is one which seeks to repair the damage that a paranoid reading may have identified, by formulating or seeking out an outcome beyond outright condemnation or rage (though this is not to say that rage does not have its place in a social justice project; see Chapter 15) (Sedgwick, 2003: 128).

Rather, then, than analysing the world and finding fault all over the place and leaving our analysis there, Sedgwick urges us to think reparatively about social issues: to ask, 'what can we do now?'. This does not mean being complacent or naïve about the world (Ball, 2016: 65); rather, it means to turn our critique into an active practice of bringing about social change, or what Paolo Freire (2017[1970]) refers to as developing a praxis.

Praxis is not only about activism. It is also about adjusting ways of thinking and perceiving the world; about working to be curious, critical and perceptive. We have already talked about world travelling and loving perception as a way to do that. Analysing the world from a reparative perspective is another way of doing this.

Consider how reparative readings and paranoid readings might operate in the story in Box 1.5.

BOX 1.5

In 2009, the singer Rihanna was beaten in a car by her then-boyfriend Chris Brown. The pictures of her swollen face were released online two weeks afterwards,

(Continued)

confirming the viciousness of the attack and making the case notorious. The attack happened on the eve of the Grammys in Los Angeles, USA. Both artists had been due to perform at the Grammys, but neither of them did as a result of this incident and the subsequent global attention that it received. Brown, who had turned himself into police after the attack, pleaded guilty to a felony assault and was sentenced to 180 hours of community service and a five-year suspended sentence. Rihanna was also granted a restraining order against Brown. Brown's public appearances were cancelled. His 2012 album *Fortune* was targeted by protesters who placed stickers on it, reading 'Warning: Do not buy this album! This man beats women'. Every one of Brown's collaborations and singles has been negatively reviewed in left-wing newspapers like *The Guardian* in the UK, who specifically cite his violence against Rihanna as the reason why they slate his music. And yet, in 2013, Rihanna announced that she was once again in a relationship with Chris Brown (which lasted six months). Before they reunited, she had appeared on the Oprah show and, crying, told the chat show host that after the attack:

> I lost my best friend – like everything I knew switched in a night, and I couldn't control that. So, I had to deal with that and that's not easy for me to understand, interpret and it's not easy to interpret on camera, not with the world watching.

Her decision to get back together with Brown a year after this interview drew huge criticism from her fans and supporters. Rihanna told *Rolling Stone* magazine that 'if it's [getting back together with Brown] a mistake, it's my mistake'. Celebrity blogger, Perez Hilton commented:

> Okay, Rihanna, we really felt for you when this whole mess erupted. But you're sort of making it hard to continue to love you!!!!!!!!!!!!!!!!!!!!!!!! First, we hear you're back together with your abuser, Chris Brown … And, now we're hearing that you don't want to speak in court if asked to testify … Oh come on, Rihanna! You're setting a bad example!!!!!!!!!!!!!!!!!!!!!! (Hilton, 13 March 2009)

The notion that not only would she not help to incriminate Brown in court, but that she was also intimate with him again, was too much for some onlookers to bear.

How might a paranoid reading of this case go?

A paranoid reading might suggest that Rihanna is a classic victim of intimate partner violence, lacking the self-esteem to leave an abusive relationship. Some critics have called her decision 'dumb' (see Bierria, 2011), but a paranoid reading would suggest that she is in fact unaware of her own victimisation; maybe her huge celebrity and her worldwide fame make her feel less anchored and secure than other people. As other commentators have noted, the presentation of Rihanna's sexuality is of one erotic Islander from Barbados; the figure of the 'island woman' is one whose sexuality is figured through an erotic attachment to violence (Fleetwood, 2012). Rihanna had an abusive and neglectful childhood. Indeed, some of Rihanna's songs are about BDSM, and many feature nihilistic, bondage-orientated themes and images. After being attacked, Rihanna then collaborated with a number of male artists, which can be interpreted as unfeminist. She eroticises violence, which is also unfeminist, and therefore has no real choice but to be in a violent relationship. She does not know, or want, anything else.

How might a reparative reading of this case go?

A reparative reading of the same incident might note that Black women have a history of antagonistic relationships with the police and the criminal justice system. Rihanna's decision not to engage with the criminal justice system to convict Brown may stem from a rejection or, or refusal to engage with, systems of oppression which have historically (and currently) been engines of racist violence. Rihanna may indeed like bondage and BDSM. She has reportedly confirmed this (Fleetwood, 2012: 429). And why should she not? It should be noted that participating in, and enjoying, BDSM is not equivalent to accepting abuse within an intimate relationship, and to elide the two in a way that a paranoid reading might, is very dangerous. bell hooks (1994) and Audre Lorde (1978) tell us that the erotic has power. Erotic power is, for Audre Lorde (1978), feminine power that has been suppressed in all realms but that of sex, that has been approached with suspicion. Lorde (1978: 55) explains that 'the very word erotic comes from the Greek word eros, the personification of love in all its aspects – born of Chaos, and personifying creative power and harmony'. Erotic power is 'replenishing' and 'provocative'; it allows women to find pleasure and love in all realms of the world. This is why it is dangerous in a **patriarchal** world. Here Lorde suggests:

> Beyond the superficial, the considered phrase, 'It feels right to me,' acknowledges the strength of the erotic into a true knowledge, for what that means is the first and most powerful guiding light toward any understanding … In touch with the erotic, I become less willing to accept powerlessness, or those other supplied states of being which are not native to me, such as resignation, despair, self-effacement, depression, self-denial. (1978: 56)

Bringing Lorde's conceptualisation of erotic power into this reparative reading of Rihanna's actions in the aftermath of being attacked by Brown, we can come to understand Rihanna's decision to record songs with men as an appropriation, or incorporation, of their perceived power. Rather than being unfeminist, her decision to do what 'feels right' to her by getting back together with Brown is an expression of erotic power and a refusal of the victim-blaming that is latent in critiques of her decisions. It is also a refusal of her status as 'role model' – hinted at by Perez Hilton – and the discourses about personal responsibility (responsibilisation discourses) that accompany this.

(Continued)

A reparative reading, in a sense, is one that pushes the paranoid further and which also seeks to find some sort of way out, or some sort of response beyond simply saying that everything is dreadful. It opens up dialogue and permits ways of being curious as well as critical. Be under no illusion; sometimes some of the issues that we cover in the context of sex and crime are distressing, unfair and astounding. Criminologists need to do the critical work to excavate understanding of all of the ways that the relationship between sex and crime are intertwined; then, in the words of Freire (2017[1970]: 25), they must develop a praxis or the skills to 'reflect *and act* upon the world in order to change it' (emphasis added). In this book, we take you along some of these paths and point you in the direction of others.

How to read this book

Each chapter in this book is structured around particular issues that are illustrated with case studies to ask you to think about the way that sex and crime interact with each other in practice. They each start with an outline of what you can expect to learn about in each chapter. Task boxes offer questions and exercises that we really urge you to stop and think about/complete. One of the reasons why we ask these questions is to highlight that the issues we explore in this book are not straightforward. There is no right or wrong answer to many of the things that we think about. Doing a reparative reading, and using loving perception to understand our own trajectory, and our own way of thinking as well as those of other people in different situations, require us to ask difficult questions. Therefore, we encourage you to take the time to complete the tasks, either on your own in preparation for teaching and learning sessions, or in groups as part of seminars, workshops or group study sessions.

As we have argued above, in addition to knowledge always being incomplete, it is also contextual, and is influenced by the time and place it is written in. So much criminological scholarship is written from a white person's perspective, telling stories from the **Global North** which present poorer parts of the world as exotic, strange places, or which ignores them entirely. We have tried to challenge such a presentation of knowledge in this book.

Finally, as you will see, if you do not realise already, the potential field of study in the context of sex and crime is enormous. We have chosen cases that interest us, that we think will interest you, and that we think are important. We have been comprehensive, but we cannot be complete. This is why we end each chapter by sending you off into other directions in this book which are also relevant and interesting but which are beyond the scope of the chapter, so, as you prepare your classes and your assignments, you can move around the book, following ideas, exploring new ones and coming up with ideas of your own.

2

Theory: How to think about sex and crime

Understanding theories of crime helps us to do two things. It helps us to look for things that we may not see at first glance, or that we may not have thought about looking for; and it helps us to understand the priorities and biases of dominant theories. Theory runs through all of what we know about sex and crime, so it might seem strange for us to have created a standalone chapter about it. We have chosen to do this in order to demonstrate how theories which are key to our understanding of sex and crime can be applied to particular problems in order to understand them better. In this chapter, we summarise six different theoretical approaches that we think are helpful, and then apply these approaches to a case to demonstrate how each theoretical approach can help us see the same story, idea, occurrence or practice in several different ways.

By the end of this chapter, you will understand more about:

- six different theoretical approaches which help us in our study of sex and crime
- how to critique using theory
- how to apply different theories to a single problem.

Feminism

Feminism – or the political practice of establishing **gender** parity – is fundamental to our understanding of sex and crime. The history of feminism is exciting, controversial and important. It is beyond the scope of this book to talk about the story of the feminist movement, though there are many excellent texts we would recommend, each examining how feminism has evolved and providing examples of feminist politics in action (see, for instance, Adichie, 2017; Brownmiller, 1975; Daly, 1990[1978]; Fausto-Sterling, 1993; Firestone, 1970; Haraway, 1991; Levy, 2005; Lorde, 2007[1984]; Smith, 2013[1989]; Solnit, 2016; Young, 1990). In this section, however, we focus on how and why feminism helps us in these criminological analyses.

Feminism is the 'political and philosophical devotion to ending the oppression of people on the basis of gender and sex' (Hirschmann, 1998: 348). At its heart, feminism is the study of the world through a **gendered** lens. That means that feminist theory provides a gendered analysis of contemporary phenomena. It also highlights the injustices of the contemporary world. For instance, following the global economic crisis of 2008, many countries – especially in Europe – adopted an austerity economic agenda which meant that they cut budgets for public spending (for example, in education, public transport, in the provision of benefits and other welfare measures). While at first glance these policies might appear to apply equally to men and women, and living under austerity politics may seem to have little to do with gender, feminist research demonstrates how these equally applied policies have unequal effects, and how women are dis-proportionately disadvantaged by austerity compared to men. Women rely more on public services than men because they tend to be more likely to look after children compared to men, and they live longer than men, thus needing more care when they are older. More women than men work in public ser-vices (health care, local authorities, nursing, social work and education) which are sectors where budgets are cut, and, in order to plug the care gaps left by budget cuts, women are more likely to be called upon by their families to pro-vide unpaid support (Ginn, 2013; Reis, 2018). It is for the same care-orientated reasons that women are disproportionately disadvantaged by climate change. Again, this is an issue which at first glance appears to have little to do with gendered issues and affects men and women equally, but has demonstrably more impact on women's lives (Aguilar et al., n.d.; Denton, 2002). Women dominate agricultural production among the world's rural poor, and so suffer first when climate change causes flood, drought and crop failure. After natural disasters, women and girls take second place to men and boys in rescue efforts. In Syria, following drought, and in the context of the ongoing war, women (as the heads of the household in the absence of their husbands) resort to survival sex work in order to provide food and shelter for their families (Banwell, 2020). We are able to see this because of the gendered analysis of climate change that feminism enables. One of the key facets of feminist thought is that due to the structural disadvantages faced by women because of their gender, treating men and women the same often does not result in equal treatment. In fact, it often results in severe disadvantages for women.

Patriarchy – a system in which men hold **power** and women are excluded from power – is what feminisms works to dismantle. Patriarchy has long framed public policy, the rule of law, and other **institutions**. Patriarchy is hierarchical, which means that not all men – or even just men – benefit from it in the same way. It turns upon an axis which is inflected by – in the **Global North** at least – wealth, **whiteness**, able-bodiedness and education. Patriarchy normalises the dominance of men and the subordination of women. It is because of patriarchy that high-profile sex offenders, like Donald Trump, Louis CK and Kevin Spacey, are able to get away with sex crimes (as yet) untouched by law. By specifically referring to patriarchy as a structure, femi-nists focus on the structural causes of oppression and discrimination, rather than necessarily focusing on individual men who hold power and control.

In the context of crime, feminist analyses, often falling under the banner term 'feminist criminology', have drawn attention to the way that the criminal justice system treats female offenders. It has enabled us to have debates about whether or not women offenders who have young children should be impris-oned (Baldwin, 2020). It enables us to have discussions – and to voice outrage about – the short sentences that rapists have received in high-profile cases such as the rape of Chanel Miller by the wealthy, white, Stanford University student, Brock Turner. Thanks to feminist activism, the treatment of rape and sexual assault victims by the police is now more sympathetic, but recent moves by the police in the UK to scrutinise the social media and mobile phone records of women and men who have been raped also need to be criticised, and feminist activists are doing so (see Bowcott, 23 July 2019). The criminalising of marital rape, of upskirting, of stalking; campaigns to challenge rape myths held by juries, police and judges; campaigns to promote awareness about intimate partner violence and abuse; campaigns to prevent child sexual exploitation; and campaigns which ask us to recognise that men as well as women, the young and the elderly, can be victims of sexual violence, whatever they are (not) wearing, are all legal and political changes that feminism has brought about.

So, feminism brings a gendered analysis to social issues, even if they do not initially appear to be related to gender. Almost every social issue has a gendered implication. Sometimes the reason why this is hard to perceive is because the systemic injustices which structure everyday life are entirely taken for granted. This is played out in, for instance, **heteronormative** dating scripts such as 'he has to make the first move; she has to play hard to get'. Systemic patriarchy accounts for part of how these inequalities emerge in such an ordinary and banal way.

Feminism has been criticised from a number of directions for being complicit with systemic power because it is dominated by **cisgender**, heterosexual, white, middle-**class** voices (Crenshaw, 1989; hooks, 1984; Lugones, 1987). Feminism is at its most powerful when it deals with these intersectional issues, and engages with the different ways in which the contemporary world diminishes those who are not held up by contemporary patriarchal structures.

Intersectionality, which we met in Chapter 1, is not a new concept, as women of colour have long been highlighting that they face discrimination and oppression beyond gender (for example, the speech given by Sojourner Truth in 1851, *And ain't I a Woman?*). Kimberlé Crenshaw's (1989) work has had a powerful impact on feminist thought. The purpose of intersectionality is not a race to the bottom of the oppression ladder, nor to attempt to demonstrate that your own position is worse than others. Instead, Crenshaw provides the helpful analogy of attempting to climb through a small hatch in the ceiling above you. The intersections of different aspects of your identity impact on how closely you are positioned to the hatch and how easy you will find it to pull yourself up through the hatch. So, for example, a white, middle-class, professional, heterosexual, able-bodied, British woman in the UK may find that her ability to get through the hatch is hindered by her gender, due to levels of discrimination such as those we have outlined above, but other aspects of her identity will assist her to lift herself up to the floor above. The key aspect of the 'hatch' analogy is that it is never impossible for someone whose multiple components of their identity will potentially result in discrimination from getting through the hatch, it is just made harder for them. By using this analogy, we can appreciate how people who hold an identity that often experiences oppression can reach powerful positions, while still acknowledging the structural barriers to the wider social group – for example, Barack Obama becoming President of the United States of America in 2008 does not mean that there is no longer racial discrimination in the USA. Indeed, **Black** men continue to face extreme forms of discrimination, have some of the worst work and health prospects in the USA, and continue to face harsh responses by criminal justice, including police violence (see the campaign *Black Lives Matter*). President Obama pulled himself up through the hatch in spite of incredible levels of racial discrimination, undoubtedly assisted by his educational level, professional success, his gender and **sexuality.**

Though there is no universal voice of feminism, and debates between feminists about the proper object of feminist interventions rage on, it is thanks to the gendered lens of analysis that feminism enables, that a field of masculinity studies has emerged (see Connell and Messerschmidt, 2005), that **trans** rights – and trans prisoners' rights – are being properly fought for. Knowledge about female genital mutilation (FGM), about male rape, about reproductive rights, about 'gaslighting' abuse, and beginning proper conversations about what counts as sexual consent have become possible thanks to feminist politics and action, wherever that feminism might come from. Be under no illusion: debates and differences within feminism are no walk in the park to navigate, but what feminism brings is a questioning of what we take for granted when it comes to power and dominance, and an energetic activism against private, institutional and international gendered abuses of power.

Queer theory

The premises of queer theory are not easy to identify because of the elusive and fluid nature of the theory. Indeed, as Annamarie Jagose (1996: 3) states, its 'indeterminacy [is] one of its widely promoted charms'. Historically, queer theory has been most loudly appropriated by gay and lesbian theorists and activists to challenge the normative and heterosexist assumptions that structure aspects of contemporary society. Jagose suggests that 'queer' has become an 'umbrella term for a coalition of culturally marginal sexual self-identifications' (1996: 1). In a passionate defence of Foucaultian queer subjects, David Halperin (1995: 62) argues that there is 'nothing in particular to which [queer] refers', it is a 'positionality', not a 'positivity', and describes 'whatever is at odds with the normal, the legitimate, the dominant'. Certainly, it is undesirable, and it would be inaccurate to quantify 'queer' in any more certain terms than this. Its breadth of interpretation renders queer more liberatory, if problematic, for those who adopt the approach. However, it is possible to suggest that queer theory is built on a Foucaultian understanding of **discourse,** where power and knowledge are constructed in, and constituted by, networks of power relations which operate in flux on the body to discipline and regulate it (Foucault, 1998[1976]: 94). These knowledges tend to operate around sex and sexuality in an attempt to control and discipline 'licit and illicit' sex and sexuality or 'the way that each individual [makes] use of his [sic] sex' (Foucault, 1998[1976]: 37, 28). We saw some of this in our discussion of normative and non-normative sexuality in Chapter 1. Foucault illustrates his argument by pointing to the creation of the homosexual as a 'species', the prohibition of 'consanguine marriages' (incest) and the establishment of the 'marital obligation' (reproductive sex) as means of promoting **heteronormativity** (Foucault, 1998[1976]: 37–43). Queer theory uses this **(de)constructionist** understanding to destabilise and subvert these established heteronormative discourses.

To 'queer' is to question the mainstream. To be queer is to exist outside of normativities. To be 'queer' has historically been used as a slur or an insult, so when queer theory reclaims this word as a label for itself, it subverts – queers – the very power structures that designate who or what has rights, legitimacy or access to justice, among other issues. Whatever queer is, it is arguably at its most potent and its most subversive when conceptualised as a verb (something which I do) rather than as a noun (something which I am). Queer is not simply an alternative identity category in the way that male/ female or non-binary/gay/bi/lesbian is. It is rather a political position from which to generate action and alternative thought.

Lauren Berlant and Michael Warner (1998: 552) emphasise that heteronormativity – that is, privilege acquired through sexual hegemony – is not the same as heterosexuality. Indeed, heterosexuality is not 'a thing': not a coherent ideology. Heteronormativity, on the other hand, is produced at every level of societal life to maintain this 'tacit sense of rightness and normalcy' (Berlant and Warner, 1998: 554). Additionally, Halperin (1995: 62) argues that the 'positionality ... [of queer] is not restricted to lesbians and gay men' and can encompass the identities of people who feel marginalised by their **sexual practices**, including, he suggests, 'married couples without children'. We might add trans people, polyamorous people, people living with HIV, abstinent people or asexual people.

In the context of criminology, scholars have begun to engage with the potential of queer to understand justice (Buist and Lenning, 2015; Dwyer et al., 2016). By using the analytical potential inherent in queer approaches which challenge the construction of knowledge and power, queer criminologists work to bring to the fore not only the experiences of **LGBT +** people in the criminal justice system, as victims, as offenders, or as professionals, but also the importance of challenging or critiquing the way that the law operates, and the normativities which underpin it. Analyses of police violence, of hate crime, of prison cultures from a queer perspective enable criminologists and professionals who work in these fields to see old problems differently, and to understand crime and **deviance** in more nuanced and complex ways.

At the same time, queer theory and queer criminology have come in for some criticism. Halperin argues that the term fosters a 'false impression of inclusiveness' (Halperin, 1995: 64). It suggests that the divisions between gays and lesbians have been 'triumphed over', when, in fact, in dismantling identity categories, queer is accused of effacing the different lived experiences of gay men and lesbian women (Halperin, 1995: 64). Sheila Jeffreys (1994) criticises queer and the postmodernist movement more widely, which, she argues, are flawed because they are based upon gay male thought (like that of Foucault) rather than on the work of early feminists (like Mary Daly, Shulamith Firestone or Audre Lorde). A further criticism of queer theory is that it is androcentric (centred on male experiences) and ethnocentric (centred on Whiteness). Elizabeth Grosz and Anne Marie Smith illustrate this in the context of the invisible lesbian (Grosz, 1994) and 'dangerous Black gayness' (Smith, 1992). When used to focus on the experience of gay and lesbian individuals, queer is susceptible to conflating 'lesbian and gay' to the erasure of the lesbian entirely (Jagose, 1996: 116). Lesbianism has never been recognised as a crime in legal discourse in the same way that gay men's sexual practices have been legally regulated and (un)sanctioned (Grosz, 1994: 146; Smith, 1992: 204). Smith calls for an acknowledgement of lesbian experiences of sex, and for lesbian sexual practices to be discussed with the alacrity of gay men's sexual practices (Smith, 1992: 210–11).

For Derek Dalton (2016: 18), one of the problems of queer theory is that the focus on the **deconstruction** of categories and its, at times, lurid complexity, means that it becomes difficult for a criminologist to see what they might usefully glean from such a theory (though brilliant, Judith Butler's work is an example of such dense prose, e.g. 1990). Criminology, with its focus on real-life examples, involving real people, with real problems, demands something that it can use – a praxis (see Chapters 1 and 15 for our discussions of praxis), if you will. Some queer approaches resolutely refuse to offer one because to point to a path of action would be somewhat 'unqueer'. Some approaches do not hold that a path of action is necessary, or possible, preferring what Dalton (2016: 19) refers to as a 'negativity thesis' (see Edelman, 2004).

Vocal criticisms of contemporary queer theory also come from African queer scholars who are roundly invisible in contemporary queer literature (Ekine and Abbas, 2013). Indeed, Douglas Clarke (2013) notes that contemporary queer theory, which comes predominantly from North America, dominates debate about what 'counts' as queer. Queer theory is written 'with the white homosexual in mind', with Black homosexuality only emerging through a Euro-American gaze (Clarke, 2013: 176–7). With this bias, this means that mainstream queer theory reinforces the objectification, silencing and hierarchies that it seeks to dismantle elsewhere.

Queer theory, and the approach that it has taken, has opened up debates around other marginalised groups and their experiences. Trans theory, for instance, draws on Butler's work (1990) of the instability of the sexed body and performativity to articulate transsexualism in the contemporary world (though, for critique, see Audrey Mbugua, 2013). As with queer, crip theory, which explores disability through queerness, has adopted the 'reclaiming' of offensive words used to insult disabled people. In the same way that queer critiques heteronormativity, crip approaches draw attention to the injustice of a world created for bodies which are temporary-abled (see Chapter 10 for more discussion of what it means to be temporary-abled) (McRuer, 2006). These theories helpfully encourage us to look with new eyes at what we have taken for granted: an important task when dealing with questions of justice.

Critical race theory

Critical race theory (CRT) is also a practical and theoretical approach that emerged in the 1970s in the USA and the UK. CRT centralises '**race**' in its analyses and holds that, just as feminism applies a gendered lens to better understand (in)justice in the world, so too do racialised analyses help us to understand more about (in)justice. CRT emerged out of recent developments in the 'legal leftist' movement known as critical legal studies. This movement critiques the liberalism that underpins contemporary legal ideologies and structures. CRT, in response to critical legal theorists' focus on class, developed a mode of analysis that centralises the lived experience of 'race' and racism in contemporary social life.

CRT is, in many ways, both a straightforward theory to grasp and a difficult one for many people to stomach. One of the main tenets of CRT is that racism is normative. That is, racism is everywhere, and it is normalised. Rather than one-off instances of aggression that we all agree are aberrant, racism is so ordinary – so much a part of the landscape of everyday life – that it appears natural (Rollock and Gillborn, 2011; also see Delgado and Stefancic, 2000). The idea that racism is 'normal' can be difficult for some people to accept, especially those who are not usually on the receiving end of it.

For CRT scholars, this refusal, or inability, to see racism is an expression of White supremacy. White supremacy, like patriarchy, reinforces unequal power relations. It is what sustains the subordination of Black people. White supremacy and White ideology are taken for granted in everyday life. CRT is spearheaded by Black scholars (Crenshaw's understanding of intersectionality, for instance, interacts with CRT, and Crenshaw is a key CRT scholar), but white people working with CRT can use their own experience of 'race' privilege, and their reflections on their own racism, to bring a critical race analysis to their own work and to their own ways of doing/being White (Ware and Back, 2002).

In many ways, the anti-**colonialism** that is espoused by Franz Fanon (1952, 2001[1963]) can be understood to interact with CRT as a way of transforming the bases upon which knowledge is constructed. As with queer theory, and with feminism, anti-colonialism is presented as a politics which seeks to transform the very structures of socio-economic dominance, not merely by rejecting them, but also by reconceptualising what it is to live with these structures and to construct a world outside of them. One of the ways that CRT does this is through story-telling and constructing subjective narratives which put at the centre the experiences of marginalised story-tellers themselves.

Derrick Bell's (1992) allegorical story *The Space Traders* is an example of this sort of practice and of the tenets of CRT more broadly. The story concerns a scenario where aliens arrive in the USA and decide to offer wealth and various technological advances to the USA in exchange for the USA handing over all of its Black citizens. Following a referendum and lots of negotiation, including eliminating the objections of protesters, the **State** agrees to the trade. The point of the story is to show how, in contemporary life, if such a situation arose, it is likely that the majority of white Americans would vote for this trade; they would put their interests ahead of the **human rights** and the human status of Black Americans. Of course, such a theory cannot be tested, but the story is intended to provocatively ask its reader to reflect on the insidious way that something initially outrageous becomes, through sleight of hand, normalised.

Using story-telling in this way, CRT scholars trouble the dominance of conventional ways of debating, of framing arguments or of doing politics. Yet, this method is one of the reasons CRT is contested and potentially controversial. Critics object to a theory which does not apparently deal in **objective** analysis, that is avowedly partial. They argue that it is impossible to enter into a debate with material like this. Conservative ideologies dislike the emphasis on **subjectivity** and on **experiential knowledge**, which is considered to be lacking in rigour. They dislike the rejection of meritocracy that CRT espouses. Left-wing thinkers, too, find CRT difficult to accept. CRT scholars also receive so-called 'friendly fire' from 'progressive' thinkers 'who publicly avow their commitment to advancing equity but object to CRT's bold decision to put "race" and racism at the forefront of their analysis' (see Gillborn, 2018). The premise that racism is normal, and that white people only help eradicate racism and fight for the rights of minorities when it suits them (when there is 'interest convergence'), is perhaps too unsavoury a reality (Rollock and Gillborn, 2011).

Yet, notwithstanding the backlash, CRT theory has also fostered the development of a number of offshoots that centre differently marginalised groups in the analysis of social and political justice. DesiCrit centres the experiences of South Asian people in the judicial system in the Global North. From being racially misrecognised, to profiling when travelling, to being characterised as a 'model minority', the specific experience of being South Asian is one that has received specific focus through a DesiCrit lens (Harpalani, 2013). TribalCrit and LatCrit also centre the experience of Indigenous and Latinex people in the USA in the context of their interaction with the institutions of law and control (Brayboy, 2005), while a branch of theory that examines the intersection of disability and 'race' (DisCrit) also has at its origins the political work of CRT (Annamma, 2012).

The principles of CRT emerge out of a North American and European context, so it might be argued that CRT cannot function in the same way in the Global South as it does in the North. Certainly, racism operates everywhere, but the structures that CRT responds to – namely unproblematised Whiteness – are also produced in part by neoliberal **post-industrialist** socio-cultural contexts, as well as being hangovers of coloniser pasts.

Neoliberalism

Not a theory in itself, but more a buzzword of our time, this concept is useful to understand our global political economic system. We currently live under neoliberal **capitalism**, a political economic system where wealth, or capital, is in the hands of private owners, rather than the State, or the people, for the purposes of capital creation and wealth accumulation. The *neo* in neoliberalism stands for a resurgence of classic liberal ideas and practices after a period of experimentation with other political economic systems, including communism, or versions of state capitalism (where the State owns the means of production; Cliff, 1974) and social democratic capitalism (where ownership is shared between the State and the private sector, and the State owns most public services and invests in them; Harvey, 2007).

Liberalism has been the dominant **Western** political ideology since the eighteenth century. In a sense, liberalism was about challenging traditional social and political hierarchies, which, up to the end of the eighteenth century, saw the monarchy, aristocracy and clergy at the top and the rest at the bottom, with little to no opportunity to 'climb the social ladder'. Early liberals like Adam Smith and Jean Baptiste Say were all white middle-class men trying to consolidate their social, political and economic power. They did not stand for equality among 'races' or genders. They were, like most men at the time, what we would now consider to be racist and **misogynist**. As such, three centuries of liberalism in the West have produced societies where white men tend to be socially and politically advantaged through law, institutions and social norms. This means that social, economic and political power is unequally distributed in liberal societies *by design*.

Liberalism is an ideology and not a natural state of affairs (Harvey, 2016). Political ideologies are made up of many different, sometimes contradictory, ideas that pertain to the individual, society, the economy and the relationships therein (Freeden, 1994). While liberalism has evolved into both right (conservative) and left (social democratic) incarnations, its essence is about protecting and furthering individual freedom. For this purpose, government is necessary to protect the individual, but too much government can threaten freedom. Thus, liberal doctrine has long been concerned with discussing where government is necessary and should intervene in the lives of individuals, and where it is not, and should therefore be kept at bay. In his famous work 'On Liberty' (1892), liberal commentator J.S. Mill argued that the State and government should be concerned with protecting individuals from **harm**, whether that comes from others (through the criminal justice system), disease (through health provision) or war (through defence). This principle was broadly supported by other liberal commentators including John Locke and Adam Smith (Berlin, 1969). The pursuit of individual freedom is connected to increasing individualism, which means putting individual self-advancement, goals and needs over and above the shared goals and needs of community and society. Our age of liberalism is said to be characterised by increasing individualism (Elliott and Lemert, 2005).

So, what is new about neoliberalism to deserve its name? Stuart Hall (2011) talks of the neo in neoliberalism as standing for neoconservatism, or the right-wing governments spearheaded by Margaret Thatcher in the UK and Ronald Reagan in the USA in the 1980s. Other commentators identify a resurgence of ideas that used to be popular in the nineteenth century, but lost popularity in the middle of the twentieth century during the golden age of social democracy and European welfare states (Grewal and Purdy, 2014; Harvey, 2007). These ideas include reverence to the **free market** and *laissez faire* economic liberalism, or the lesser involvement of the State in directing and regulating markets. This entails such economic policies as privatisation of services, austerity and cuts in public spending, and generally increasing the roles and responsibilities of the private sector, curtailing the role of the State and the public sector in the economy and society (Peters, 2012). Does this sound familiar? Think about the UK context (or a context that you are familiar with). Are policies such as privatisation and cuts in public spending popular? Increasing individualism and the lessening role of the State and the public sector have translated into a political strategy where individuals are made to feel solely responsible for their own conditions (Peters, 2017). Shifting the burden of responsibility away from government and the State and towards the individual has serious implications for people's lives, from health through work to criminal justice. Here is an example:

> Marion, a Black single mum with two children, lives in London, UK. She is a British national. She works early morning and night shifts as a cleaner in an office in the city; she may also have another job during the day on top of her cleaning position. Her work has been outsourced to an agency, so that the company that owns the office does not have to be responsible for her health and occupational rights. She works for this company, but she does not have a contract with said company. The employment agency that contracts her gives her a zero-hours contract paid at the minimum wage, so she needs to work long hours to make ends meet and cannot afford to be sick, or miss work, or her children will go hungry. Given that her salary is low, she buys cheaper processed food rather than fresh food from the supermarket and can only afford to take her kids out to McDonalds for a family meal. Sometimes, the family is forced to use food banks. She cannot afford childcare, so the kids are often left home alone while she is out working, and she does not have the time to make sure that they are doing their homework and going to school regularly. Because she does not earn very much from her job, she does receive some benefits, but even this is not enough some weeks. The stressful and meagre lifestyle takes its toll, and she falls ill. She finds she has type II diabetes. Whilst in hospital, the doctor tells her she needs to change her diet and exercise, but she says she has no time or money to afford a healthy diet or to exercise. As a result of her sickness, she is not able to work and therefore earn a living for her family.

In this scenario, you can see how the woman's **agency** – or the individual **power** she holds to shape her situation – is curtailed. Under neoliberal **governance**, she is made solely responsible for her own economic and health conditions and the raising of her children, their education, health and wellbeing, and few rights are granted to her by her employer or the State. She is isolated. Her children are also likely to suffer due to her situation.

The spread of neoliberalism and economic policies associated with it has been secured through **globalisation**, a process of trade liberalisation at the global level underpinned by neoliberal political economic principles. Although globalisation was facilitated by various converging factors, including technological development and its effects on the mobility and flow of both people and ideas (Castells, 1999), it should primarily be regarded as a process of creation of exploitative global markets dominated by the West, where colonial relations were refashioned into a north/south split of consumption/production (Wallerstein, 2005).

In what ways, if at all, is any of this relevant to sex and crime? The pursuit of sexual freedom as one expression of individual freedom has certainly intensified during the time liberalism has been dominant. However, such sexual freedom is curtailed in such instances as when it is perceived as harmful.

In those instances, the government is called upon to intervene. For instance, Craig Rich and colleagues (2012) talk about a neoliberal sexual politics in the context of the American military where LGBT+ servicemembers feel pressure to keep their sexual identities private, in the 'home' or in the 'bedroom'. We will return to the heteronormative culture of the military in Chapter 8. Ideas about what is harmful to society have changed over time, particularly in relation to sex. Yet, given that liberal societies continue to be hierarchical, patriarchal, capitalist and individualistic, the manner in which **harm** is understood and regulated will reflect these structural facts.

Risk

Though significant within criminological study, it is the discipline of anthropology which has long been concerned with cultural constructions of risk as a matter of social organisation, power distribution and related distinctions between acceptable and unacceptable behaviours. The work of Mary Douglas (1992, 2002[1966]) and Douglas and Aaron Wildavsky (1983), explored, among other things, how risks are by their nature uncertain, and how social and cultural responses to risk are value-laden, varied and multiple. They advocated for a cultural approach to the study of risk, which 'can make us see how community consensus relates some natural dangers to moral defects' (Douglas and Wildavsky, 1983: 7). Out of all existing risks and dangers, it is only some, not all, that receive attention and warrant social and political interventions. The choice will largely depend on the shared values and beliefs of a given social body or community. For instance, the risks associated with drug taking or unprotected sex are identified and intervened in through moral, criminal justice and **public health** efforts, whereas the risks associated with extreme sports receive no such treatment. Start to think about why this might be.

A shared understanding of risk and danger allows for certain moral attitudes and behaviours to be formed and maintained. The aim of such shared understandings is partly functional; it is about maintaining a certain social, cultural and political order. In general, any challenges to such order are reacted to through blame, repression or exclusion. Even in societies where formal criminal law and criminal justice systems, as we understand them, do not exist, we can still observe the exercise of social control through such mechanisms (see, for instance, Douglas's (2002[1966]: 162–3) account of the way that incest and adultery are punished by the Nuer people of South Sudan).

Contemporary classic sociology identifies risk as a central category of study for understanding **modernity**. Despite some differences, the works of Ulrich Beck (1992), Zygmunt Bauman (2013) and Anthony Giddens (1998) all suggest that, to understand contemporary social organisation, we must conceptualise the role of risk within it. Through the concept of 'the risk society', Beck and Giddens highlighted how the nature and understanding of risk has changed following modernisation processes, the ensuing scientific developments and technological change. While such changes are observable, the basic aims and functioning of risk management remain unaltered in their quest to promote a certain kind of social order that reflects power distribution. As such, certain peoples will be considered to be at greater risk than others. Young, white women, for instance, are often figured as the 'ideal' victim of crime in public space, and imagined to be at greater risk than other groups. Conversely, figures who are considered to be risky are also constructed along stereotyped images. The influence of intersectionality is important to consider here.

One relevant aspect of these sociological analyses of risk concerns the role of scientific knowledge in its understanding. Whereas in non-modern societies, social understandings of risk were not grounded in science but in lay knowledge, today some institutions in society develop and apply scientific knowledge to the understanding of risk. This produces interesting dynamics in relation to the cases we examine throughout this textbook. We can observe the application of both lay and scientific knowledge, and the associated attitudes and control mechanisms, in relation to the risks of chemsex, for example, which we encounter more of in Chapter 9.

Criminal law deals with the attribution of harm, risk and blame to maintain 'the public good' (Douglas, 1992) by enforcing lay knowledge to distinguish acceptable, moral behaviour (for instance, heterosexual, monogamous, sober sex) from unacceptable, immoral behaviour (for instance, homosexual, group sex under the influence of illicit substances). Contemporaneously, public health institutions apply largely scientific knowledge to understand the risks associated with such behaviours and produce interventions to at the least minimise, and at the most control, such risks.

Calculating risk can also be thought of as working to avoid harm. The study of harm is known as 'zemiology'. Ultra-realist approaches to leisure and to criminology more broadly, are avowedly anti-capitalist and critical of the capitalist realist apologia that they witness within contemporary discourses about risk, security and politics (Hall and Winlow, 2018: 50). In a sense, ultra-realism is reacting against the transformation of parts of the left realism that preceded it into cultural criminology. They critique the neoliberal figure of 'special liberty' – the notion that some individuals consider themselves to be uniquely permitted to behave badly, to cause harm, as a manifestation of their individual liberty in the pursuit, as they put it, of 'the libidinal energy of obscene enjoyment' (Hall and Winlow, 2018: 49). They critique the political left for, as they see it, falling down the rabbit hole of 'identity politics', where minority rights must be protected and censorship of free speech prevails; where subjective universalisms are formed, and progress stagnates around individual sensitivities (Hall and Winlow, 2018: 44–5). Instead, they argue, **objective** harms must be taken seriously; environmental harms, sexual exploitation, slavery and arms dealing cause objective harms which ought to be more of a cause for concern to criminologists than they currently are. 'Standpoint interest groups', they argue, dilute this possibility and reproduce 'complacent' attitudes to social life (Hall and Winlow, 2018: 55).

Certainly, one of the main points of studying criminology, and of studying deviant sexual practice in relation to crime, is to become (more) furious about the status quo and to rail against the way that people, groups, ideas, humans and non-humans are exploited, perhaps, by those who think that they enjoy 'special liberty' to do harm. We see this, for instance, in the exercise of contemporary **rape culture**. However, where these ultra-realist approaches could be said to go somewhat awry, it might be in their conceptualisation of minority rights.

Steve Hall and Simon Winlow (2018: 44) argue that 'what were once suppressed knowledges have ... been brought to light to occupy newly "privileged" positions ... which have subsequently become closed and protected from critiques'. And later: 'radical feminist analyses are too restricted to female victimhood' and pursue a 'very specific agenda focussed on violence against women' (2018: 46, 50).

If the book that is currently in your hand, and other books like it, tell you anything, they tell you that this is an idealistic misreading of feminist and, we might add, queer approaches to crime. Studies of masculinity, male victims of rape and domestic violence and abuse, trans rights, AIDS activism, LGBT+ politics, which do not centre the heterosexual cisgender woman's experience, exist in no small part only because feminist and queer scholars have taken gender and sexuality seriously as a locus of analysis; something that white male scholarship like that of Hall and Winlow (2018) has worked to dismiss again and again. And, as the conversations in these fields and this book demonstrate, dissent, debate and critique are rife in these fields. Rather than the 'echo chamber' silos that Hall and Winlow rightly decry, feminist politics (which receive specific mention by these scholars as opposed to any other politics of the marginalised: you can draw your own conclusions about that!) tend to be dialogic spaces. These spaces have made room for structural, political, environmental, capitalistic harms to be identified and urgently responded to. These outcomes rather resonate with, rather than counter, the ethos that appears to underpin ultra-realism.

Resistance

Though not a body of theory in itself, the concept of resistance is nonetheless helpful for us to understand how dissident movements have helped to bring about social change, and the analytical methods that they have used to do so. We talk more about the practice of resistance in Chapter 15, because resistance is obviously something that you *do*. But you also *do* theory, as we have seen from the discussions above.

To resist is to refuse to go with the flow. To resist is to make a stand. Something which is resistant is awkward, insistent: it sticks. In the context of **social justice**, it is no exaggeration that most movements and changes in social attitudes towards questions of justice have been brought about by resistance movements.

In his 1849 tract calling for the end of slavery in the USA, Henry Thoreau explains that governments and democracy are not inherently benevolent, that laws are not always right, that governments do not always act in their citizens' best interests, and that given this, there ought to be no obligation on citizens to obey unjust laws (Thoreau, 1993[1849]). Thoreau argues that voting for politics you believe in is not enough to bring about change. Instead, mass action and mass disobedience are what he says are necessary. A refusal to pay taxes, for instance, a refusal to sit in a different part of the bus, a refusal to leave the lunch counter at Woolworths, a refusal to sit down on a plane, a refusal to go to school, a refusal to register with the State, all become ways of pushing back against unfair laws. Other active practices, such as punching Nazis, speaking out against unjust law, gathering in public spaces to protest, and using drones to interfere with the air space at airports, also work to resist the politics of the States.

Thoreau's theories have influenced resisters and activists including Martin Luther King and Mahatma Ghandi. The act of putting resistance into practice is achieved, according to Paulo Freire (2017[1970]: 25), by developing a praxis: a 'reflection and action upon the world in order to transform it'. Theory is nothing without practice, for Freire. It is not simply enough to say that minority sexual rights should be protected, or that the homeless should not be persecuted; it is also important to live in a way that helps your politics come to life.

Freire was inspired by an anti-colonialist politics. Fanon (2001[1963]), too, whose ideas we encountered in the context of CRT, was committed to anti-colonial causes. He espoused the importance of rejecting colonial structures. Around education and around politics, this looks like rejecting the hierarchical structures which have characterised colonial rule. For Fanon, colonialism is a dehumanising violence that has only been able to thrive because of the violence of colonisers in all areas of life: language, religion, policing, sexuality, work, health and the family. It should be met with violence in all these realms. Calls for violence like this are unsettling and are not commonly encountered as legitimate in protesting movements, and yet condoning violence can, itself, become a powerful tool for resistance.

Another unsettling call for resistance might be that which is articulated through hopefulness and desire. For Freire (2017[1970]: 64–5), hope moves movements.

It is easy to give up hope, to think that the world is a dreadful place and that we have a bleak future, but this, Rebecca Solnit 2016[2004] suggests, is what people invested in an unjust status quo *want you to think*; that there is no point in trying, so that you will not do anything at all to resist. Hope might appear vapid or naïve as a tool of resistance, but it is 'rooted in men's incompletion' (Freire, 2017[1970]: 65); the sense that there might be something more or something else that we might not yet have tried. As Freire (2017[1970]: 65) put it, 'as long as I fight, I am moved by hope; and if I fight with hope then I can wait'.

The same sort of provisional optimism can be found in bell hooks' centring of passion and pleasure as tools to upturn the status quo. Political action starts from a place of pain, or of struggle (hooks, 1994: 74), but freedom can be found by following desire paths, recognising moments of ecstasy, and, importantly, recuperating intimate love – or the erotic – into political practice. Indeed, for Lorde, the fact that erotic power has, in capitalist societies, become relegated to all that is sexualised – and private – is an attempt to curtail the potentiality of this power (recall the example of Rhianna in Chapter 1); 'recognising the power of the erotic within our lives can give us energy to pursue genuine change within our world' (Lorde, 1978: 59). Indeed, centring the pleasurable, the ecstatic, the hopeful and the erotic in this way can seem counter-intuitive to political action. And this counter-intuitiveness becomes part of what makes it so useful for resistant politics.

The politics of power, domination and marginality, which all these scholar-activists explore, also helps us to mount a resistant praxis by calling into question the structure of what dominates the centre. So, whiteness, wealth, able-bodied-ness, heterosexuality, being English language-speaking, passport-holding and well-educated are all loci of power. People outside of these positions are at the margins. Yet, as hooks and Lorde help us to see, being at the margin can enable activists to scrutinise the way that the centre is held in place. And to resist it. And to cause it trouble (Fanghanel, 2019).

BOX 2.1

We are going to look at the facts of this case and then offer different analyses through different theoretical lenses in order to outline how different theoretical perspectives can help us to understand the case; how to put theory to good use.

Amy Kaler (2003, 2004) conducted research on how men in Malawi talk about HIV. As part of her research, she encountered some interesting narratives shared by the men that she spoke to.

(Continued)

In Southern Malawi, where Kaler's research takes place, 19 per cent of the population are thought to be HIV positive (HIV+). HIV/AIDS is known to be prolific in East African countries and, as such, public health messaging and AIDS education have successfully raised awareness about the potential consequences of risky sexual behaviour. Education is centred around using condoms or other barrier methods of contraception and avoiding promiscuity. Education programmes have been so successful at getting the message of the dangers of AIDS across, that, among young men who are perhaps sexually promiscuous and do not always use condoms, there is the sense that contracting AIDS is inevitable, and that if a man has ever had risky sex he probably is HIV+. This fatalism is compounded by the fact that, especially in rural parts of Malawi, there is not enough funding for the widespread testing of HIV status, therefore many people do not actually know their HIV status, and, believing that they are probably already HIV+, decide there is probably no point in continuing to be 'careful' and use condoms, because it is too late (Kaler, 2003: 352–3).

Men who therefore believe themselves to be HIV+ articulated narratives and discourses around the virus which reconfigure what it means to be infected. Given that men who are HIV+ are assumed to be promiscuous, the HIV+ status becomes a sign of virility; that one is a 'real man' (Kaler, 2003: 359). Promiscuity is also associated with mobility, of being a man of the world, thus knowing the world and being HIV+ can be thought to go together. Having the virus, having sex with women and infecting them with the virus, for the women to then go and infect other men with the same virus is also figured within these discourses as an expression of successful masculinity (Kaler, 2003: 363). The men who do the infecting position themselves as being more virile – more masculine – than the man who is infected; who is, in fact, humiliated. Men, in these stories, who *do* use condoms and who *are* 'careful' are conceptualised as being less fully masculine than those who claim their 'right to a high-grade sexual experience'; the sort that can only be achieved without a condom (Kaler, 2003: 362).

How might the different theories that we have encountered in this chapter – and that we use in this book – illuminate our understanding of Kaler's (2003, 2004) analysis? In Table 2.1, we sketch out some suggestions.

Table 2.1 Putting theory into practice

Feminism	A gendered analysis of this case demonstrates how these narratives around HIV+ status reinforce a hetero-patriarchal construction of gender relations. Idealised masculinity is active in the sexual encounter, women are mere vessels who may become infected, or may not be, but become the conduit through which men assert their dominance over other men. The emphasis on mobility, on desirability and on masculinity which is virile because it is infected with HIV, reinforces patriarchal power relations and normative constructions of hetero-masculinity.

Queer theory	There is the potential here to bring a queer analysis to bear on the way that men who have sex with women who then go on to infect other men are figured. These expressions of hyper-sexualised masculinity are figured as queer because, through the erasure of the woman in the way that the story is recounted, the heterosexually virile men become figured as heterosexually virile through practices which would typically be associated with queer sexual practice. Glorifying these encounters can be read as an expression of queerness, and certainly a non-normative way of doing heterosexual masculinity.
CRT	The men (and women, though they are not the subject of the research here) live in a poverty (compared to the Global North) that is a consequence, in part, of a history of European colonialism (see Sibongile Ndashe, 2013). The power imbalance that this implies becomes a normative backdrop in which the men's responses to HIV prevention discourse happen. The men refuse the West-centric imaginary of HIV+ status as being inherently negative. They reformulate a specific Malawian-centred AIDS culture beyond the dominant medical-centred Westernised discourses.
Neoliberalism	Pharmaceutical companies here have not made medical testing affordable for the men in this study. The power of wealthy companies operating in poorer countries with less free medical care is evident here. The risk discourses around HIV prevention seek to create a responsible neoliberal subject who cares for himself and his wellbeing. The legacy of colonialism and the dominance of capitalism create, in part, a situation where men believe they are HIV+ but are unable to find out whether they are HIV+.
Risk	Medical and education programmes set up by the government and NGOs offer a risk-averse approach to safeguarding the self against AIDS. Risks have to be calculated and harm has to be accounted for. Here, the men deem that they have already taken the risk and that any further safeguarding is futile, thus potentially putting themselves and future partners at risk of becoming HIV+. This apparent medical nihilism might be thought to be produced by these risk-averse discourses.
Resistance	The men in this study are never happy to be HIV+, but their discourse resists dominant narratives around HIV+ status. They transform this into a mark of their own masculine power, in what might be otherwise fairly disempowering circumstances. The apparent valorisation of HIV+ status that they espouse might seem counter-intuitive to outsiders from the Global North, but mark a resistance to the negative framing HIV receives in dominant discourses. This is also a resistance to the public health messages about safe sex and a usurping of those discourses; the men have already failed to follow the advice, so now they no longer need to try.

Summary

Different perspectives help us to understand this story in different ways. And it is not just this story about HIV in Malawi; in this book, many topics can be understood from different perspectives. This is why the subheading to this chapter is about 'how to think'. We encourage you, in your reading of the chapters that follow, to try to see how the same issue can be interpreted by looking at it in different ways – ways that do not contradict each other but which often illuminate different aspects of the same problem.

Review questions

1.   Which of the theories that we have outlined in this chapter resonate most with you?
2.   Can you think of any other theoretical approaches you have encountered already in your studies which may add to these different perspectives?
3.   The next time you read a news story, think about how different theoretical positions help you to understand different elements of how the world is. What are the differences you note?
4.   Remember: theory is next to useless if it is not put into practice, so keep experimenting!

Other chapters that this links to

All of them ...

3

Sex and crime in time and space

CHAPTER OUTLINE

The purpose of this chapter is to provide a background to the rest of our study of sex and crime. We do this by situating contemporary debates about sex in their temporal and geographic contexts. This is partly to show you that what we 'know' today about crime, **deviance**, and how sex comes into it is not a natural given. Rather, everything has a history and (at least one) point of origin. For this chapter, we want you to adopt the position of critical outsider. We will explore ideas that are often taken for granted – such as the legality of heterosexuality, or the fact that rape is a violent crime – your role is to join us in observing how and why these things came to be. In doing this, bear in mind that nothing is neutral; all ideas and knowledge come from somewhere. By focusing on the 'when' and 'where' of sex and crime, we will be able to better see how we come to know what we think we know.

By the end of this chapter, you will understand more about:

- the importance of history, **colonialism**, politics and **power** in terms of how sexual activity and knowledge are sculpted by the tools of justice
- how issues, which at first may appear to have nothing to do with sex, become sexualised
- how these debates will feed into the specific topics we examine in the rest of the book.

Why is sex such a big deal?

One of the reasons why there is such an explicit link between sex and crime is that the juridical and quasi-juridical regulation of **sexuality** has been variously employed as a tool through which to control and manage a population.

Over the centuries, even in pre-modern times, there developed the understanding that in order to create a community with an identity – today we would see this as a **nation-state** – what was needed was a healthy, productive, law-abiding population. This heralded a raft of measures, regulations and incentives to make sure that the population is in good shape, and the **state** is strong. The control of **sexual practice** through law and criminal justice is just one of the ways in which this control and regulation unfolded (another way is health care discourse – see Chapters 9 on disability and 10 on risk; the family and the education system are others; you can probably think of more). In this chapter, we are going to examine how ideologies of **nation**, and good citizenship, have been put to work to regulate sex across time and space. We will look at this in more depth in the context of the regulation of heterosexuality and homosexuality, and in the creation of the crime of rape. In our discussion, we draw on examples and illustrate how these different nation-building projects function in various national contexts.

Building the nation (why is the State in my bedroom?)

Arguably a foundational philosopher of the relationship between state, sex and history was Michel Foucault (1998[1976]), whose specific interests lie in the way that knowledge is created, and how we know what we know. He also examined the different ways that power works, and observed, in the context of sex, that appropriate and inappropriate conduct is incited, regulated and controlled by a myriad of exercises of power, which he called **discourses**. Power, in this context, is not necessarily uniform, hierarchical or top-down, but operates in relation to people and things:

> It had long been asserted that a country needed to be populated if it hoped to be rich and powerful ... its future and its fortune were tied not only to the number and uprightness of its citizens, to their marriage rules and family organisation, but to the manner in which each individual made use of his [sic] sex. (Foucault, 1998[1976]: 26)

In order to produce an obedient, healthy and 'good' population, Foucault identified four exercises of power mobilised as techniques of sexual control (pp. 104–5). The first strategy, the 'hysterization of women's bodies', a rendering of the female body as inherently sexual, and necessarily tied to medical discourses, expressed a concern about reproductive rates, the wellbeing of children and the sustenance of family life (we see more of this in Chapter 6). The 'pedagogisation of children's sex' (which we see more of in Chapter 12) concerns the fact that children's expression of sexual desire posed 'physical and moral' dangers and that this should be controlled by families, doctors or educators. The 'socialisation of procreative behaviour' addresses fertility, and the desire that some members of the population reproduce and contribute to a healthy citizenry, but that those who are considered to be too old, too disabled, too young, too poor, too non-white, too deviant or too immigrant desist from reproducing. The 'psychiatrisation of perverse pleasure' moves sexual paraphilia, or what is seen as sexual deviance (for instance, homosexuality or fetishes), from the legal realm to the medical one, making sexual deviance a medical problem (see also Hacking, 1986).

Of course, Foucault's theorisations can only apply in the **post-industrialist**, modernist context that Foucault had in mind when he was writing, but we can see its influence in laws, policies, educational approaches, the development of 'norms' and social taboos that govern how we think about sexual practice across time and space.

The influence of such thinking is evidenced by Jeffrey Weeks' (1981) discussion of the production of a healthy population, which saw the creation of the Factory Acts of 1802, 1819 and 1847 which limited child labour in Britain, and the Poor Law 1834 which would consign the poor to workhouses and discourage them from 'reckless overbreeding' (Weeks, 1981: 123). Later, the construction of the mother as the key to the nation gave rise to policies and campaigns that sought to keep women out of public life and to centre them in the role of child-bearing and rearing (pp. 126–7). Eugenicist discourses naturally run through all of these incentives, because, of course, not all women were invited to people the nation; in an African-American context, Patricia Hill Collins (2005) outlines exactly how this sense of nationhood is racialised.

Even advances in sexual rights and the decriminalisation of, for instance, homosexuality or abortion in certain states are marked as the advancement, or progress, of the health of the nation. In Britain, calls for private acts of homo-sexual sex to be decriminalised started as early as 1921. The 1957 Report of the Departmental Committee on Homosexual Offences and Prostitution, known as the Wolfenden report, called both for the decriminalisation of private consen-sual homosexual sex between adult men and a crackdown on street **prostitution**. Can you guess which of these recommendations was implemented first? We talk more about Wolfenden in the next section of this chapter. It is interesting to note here that tolerance of homosexuality has now become framed as the liberal act of a civilised nation (Weeks, 1981: 242–3). This is only something that became possible in the conditions available to Britain as, for instance, a late-twentieth century, post-war, politically and economically liberal state.

One hundred years before this, the opposite was true. Britain, along with other European countries like France, Spain and Portugal, were in the fullest throws of colonialism – the policy of occupying and exploiting other countries for political and economic advantage – and the education that Foucault notes, about appropriate sexuality, was one of the tools of colonialism. Homophobia and the criminalisation of same-sex relations became a tool of empire building, notably in Malawi, Uganda and Nigeria, which Britain began to colonise at the end of the nineteenth century (Ekine and Abbas, 2013: 78). Meanwhile, in the twentieth century, the notion that homosexuality was 'un-African' and a colo-nial import also emerged as a mainstream discourse (Ekine and Abbas, 2013). To date, Uganda has some of the most punitive anti-homosexuality laws in the world. Yet there is also some vociferous and effective **LGBT+** activism in Uganda (Kitsule, 2013; Mwikya, 2013), whose contributions to these debates are often obliterated by mainstream press and politics (Ndashe, 2013). But, from a **Western/Global North** perspective, the slow advances that these countries have made in terms of recognising LGBT+ rights are not good enough. Indeed, in some cases they are actively discriminatory; in 2005, same-sex marriage was prohibited in Uganda, as opposed to simply being ignored. In 2011, Nigeria followed suit. The crime of LGBT+ marriage carries the penalty of life imprisonment.

In 2011, David Cameron (Prime Minister of the UK, 2010–16) and Barack Obama (President of the USA, 2009–17) joined forces to tie conditions to aid donations in countries where LGBT+ rights are not protected. Threatening to cut aid to countries where homosexuality is illegal, they called for equality for

LGBT+ peoples as a **human right**. What might appear to be a laudable political effort on their part reveals a more problematic and **neo-colonialist** power play which, as Sokari Ekine and Hakima Abbas (2013) demonstrate, does more **harm** than good to LGBT+ people living in these places; LGBT+ people become scapegoats within their communities, the loss of aid impacts directly on the provision of education and health services for LGBT+ people, and creates further local divisions (Nana et al., 27 October 2011). This policy was called out by Ugandan advisors as bullying behaviour which was akin to treating the Ugandan state 'like children'; 'Uganda is, if you remember, a sovereign state and we are tired of being given these lectures by people' (Nagenda; cited in BBC, 31 October 2011). Indeed, given that homophobia is arguably a colonial British construct, and until recently the British – and specifically the Conservative party's – treatment of homosexuality has been appalling, it could be considered hypocritical to impose these sanctions, even as it is also offered as a marker of how 'progressive' the British state has become. However, hypocrisy lies in British responses to states who persecute the LGBT+ community. In Saudi Arabia, homosexuals can be sentenced to death because of their sexual orientation. In 2014, a Saudi Arabian man was sentenced to be whipped 450 times and to spend three years in prison for using Twitter to try to meet other men for dates (Simpson, 25 July 2014). Yet, in 2019 the British government entered into a £650 million arms trade deal with Saudi Arabia (Cowburn, 22 July 2019); so, it seems the UK government remains selective about just how important it considers LGBT+ rights abroad to be.

Jasbir Puar argues that this can be understood as an expression of **homonationalism**, or 'how "acceptance" and "tolerance" for gay and lesbian subjects have become a barometer by which the right to, and capacity for, national sovereignty is evaluated' (Puar, 2013: 336). In her analysis, Puar has in mind the justifications made for the USA and UK invasion of Iraq and Afghanistan: saving queer brown men and women from the barbarism of their own space and time (Puar, 2007: 9) – an act which, Puar argues, is an expression of empire. This so-called 'pinkwashing' is used to obfuscate the violences that a state might enact on its own non-conforming people, including the deportation of undocumented migrants and asylum seekers, or to stoke sentiments of racialised hatred of the 'other' in the name of protecting vulnerable LGBT+ communities 'over there'. This too is an act of **Orientalist** nation-building; of creating a sense of national, tolerant exceptionalism, of the figure of the backward and undemocratic 'other', and of claiming liberal and progressive credentials which are meant to distract from the abuses a state allows to be enacted in its name.

A similar practice has been identified as **femonationalism** by Sara Farris (2012). Femonationalism 'brings together anti-Islam and anti-(male)-immigrant concerns or nationalist parties, some feminists, and neoliberal governments under the idea **of gender** equality' (2012: 187). That is, nations – especially in Europe, but also in North America and Australia – figure the Muslim 'other' as some sort of backward **misogynist** who oppresses women, hates sexual freedoms and stones gays to death. Here, feminist ideas about the oppression of veiled women are co-opted by right-wing politics to justify either invading 'their' countries to save 'their' women (white men saving brown women from brown men; Spivak, 1988), or excluding them entirely from 'our' culture and space though aggressive anti-immigration policies (see also debates about trafficking in Chapter 7).

In sum, in the service of creating a dominant and effective nation, the control and regulation of sexuality has a long, complex and often violent history. Rooted to colonialism, to health care discourses, to anxiety about degeneracy and poverty, to international relations and war, the sexed and sexual body has been intrinsic to the creation of the modern nation, of international relations and war (for more discussion of war, see Chapter 8).

The next two sections explore how homosexuality and heterosexuality in particular have been regulated in order to serve the project of nationhood, and how such regulations have developed and changed over time and space, leading to and resulting in the perceptions we hold today.

Regulating (homo)sexuality

In this section, we explore the evolution of the regulation of homosexuality. While sexual behaviour is not simply controlled by law – for instance, a bisexual woman may not feel like she can come 'out of the closet' because of the expectations or prejudices of her family, even though in the UK there has never been any law against the bisexuality, or homosexuality, of women – legal regulation does interact with the social and cultural regulation of people's behaviour. While sexual desires are very difficult to legally regulate, sexual acts can be. This is how legal controls have been exerted over gay men. The criminalisation of the act of sodomy – anal penetration with a penis – has a long history across the world (in Britain, the term buggery was used, which is synonymous with sodomy). Yet, while criminalisation of the act of penile penetration of the anus does not specifically relate to gay men, as, for example, heterosexual couples can and do enjoy anal sex, criminalisation and prosecution have focused on gay men.

The moral landscape of anal sex

The perceived dangers of homosexuality that are expressed in media discourses are mere echoes of the way that homosexuality was figured in the legal imaginary. For example, in France – which we might note was one of the first countries in the world to decriminalise homosexuality and is often seen as a country deemed to be sexually liberal – we find examples of how sexual behaviour between people of the same sex has nonetheless been designated as 'immoral' and has been regulated through law. While sodomy was decriminalised in France from 1791, this was because the new penal code created during the French Revolution made no reference to the criminality of anal sex. Other offences relating to sexuality continued to be illegal – gross public indecency, sexual relations with an underage partner, and 'corruption of young people' – and Michael Sibalis (2002) shows us that the French courts, at least in principle, treated heterosexuals and homosexuals in the same way as each other. However, such equitable treatment ended during the Second World War when the Vichy government (the government responsible for the civil administration of France during Nazi occupation) set the age of consent for homosexual sexual acts between men at 21, compared to 13 for heterosexual acts. The difference in age of consent remained in place until 1982, when the disparity was corrected.

Meanwhile, in England and Wales sexual acts between men have been criminally regulated, initially by the church and then through criminalisation by the state. The 1533 Buggery Act constructed the crime of buggery as penile penetration of the anus of a man or woman, or the anal or vaginal penetration of an animal by a man or woman. Other sexual acts between men (oral sex, for instance) were not criminalised until 1885, with the enactment of the Criminal Law Amendment Act, often referred to as the Labouchere Amendment. The statute identified homosexual sexual acts as 'gross indecency' and so allowed for the prosecution of men who engaged in sexual acts with other men beyond anal penetration. Gross indecency was far easier to prosecute than buggery, which required proof that penetration had occurred – a challenge if the sexual act was consensual and wanted, as both partners would be committing the offence and would self-incriminate if reporting the other. Note, as we will see below, that before 1994, non-consensual anal penetration was not deemed to be rape under the law, as the act of anal penetration was already illegal whether there was consent or not. It therefore could never be legally consented to, and so it could never be rape under this legal iteration.

In Britain, in 1957, Sir Wolfenden was asked by the Conservative government to consider the legal status of both homosexuality and prostitution in the wake of a number of high-profile convictions of well-known men for offences related to homosexuality. Weeks (1981: 239–42) notes that, in the post-war era, homosexuality was increasingly seen as evidence of a decline in moral standards and was thus accompanied by an increased police 'zeal', which peaked in 1953, for prosecuting homosexual men. Wolfenden's committee considered the merits of continuing to prosecute homosexuality, which was – rightly or wrongly – increasingly being seen as a medical condition rather than a crime. Indeed, the report notes that 'the purpose of the criminal law was to preserve public order ... and to protect the weak from exploitation. It was not to impose a particular moral behaviour on individuals' (Weeks, 1981: 242–3), thus private acts of consensual homosexual sex ought to, according to Wolfenden, be decriminalised.

Yet, it was not until 10 years later, with the passing of the Sexual Offences Act 1967, that consensual homosexual acts between two men aged 21 or over, conducted in private, stopped being illegal. While consensual *homosexual* anal sex was decriminalised by the 1967 Act, consensual *heterosexual* anal sex was not, and remained a criminal offence, punishable by up-to-life imprisonment, until 1994. Paul Johnson (2019) argues that this occurred in part because buggery was thought of as being a purely homosexual act, but also due to belief in Parliament that anal sex was so immoral that men should be prohibited from performing it upon their wives. It seems that there was a general disbelief that a woman may want to be anally penetrated.

A key element of the 1967 Act was that sexual activity between men was only legal if done in private, which did not include:

(a) when more than two persons take part or are present; or

(b) in a lavatory to which the public have or are permitted to have access, wither on payment or otherwise. (Sexual Offences Act 1967 s1(2))

The privacy requirement was strictly interpreted: men who had sex in hotel rooms were deemed to be having sex in a 'public' space, and the presence of other people in a private space, such as someone's home, meant the space was no longer considered 'private', even if the two men were having sex in a separate room from the other(s). As such, while the passing of the 1967 Act was progressive, it did not hold same-sex sexual activity to be equal to heterosexual or lesbian sex.

Given the continued involvement of the law in matters relating to sexual relationships between men, it is obvious that the British state continued to police and regulate male sexuality that was deemed to be immoral and dangerous. Peter Tatchell (1992), a UK-based LGBT+ and human rights campaigner, argues that the prosecution of gay men intensified after 1967. Such conclusions are supported by police recorded data, which shows that prior to 1967 the average number of offences for buggery and gross indecency recorded each year were 248 and 567; after 1967 the average each year was 723 and 1,010 (Home Office, 2016). The continued focus on the perceived immorality of homosexuality is further apparent in the decision to include homosexual sexual acts as part of the 1997 Sexual Offences Act, which introduced the sexual offenders register. As Nick Dearden (1999) argues, by conflating homosexuality with paedophilia, the law responded to the unjustified and anecdotal belief held by wider society that gay men are predatory and pose a risk to 'proselytise vulnerable youngsters (specifically impressionable 16–17-year-olds) ... to seduce them into a gay lifestyle from which they may later find it difficult to escape' (1999: 321). As we shall see in Chapter 12, this conflation also enabled paedophiles to hijack debates about LGBT+ justice to further their own agenda (see Tom O'Carroll, 1980).

Being queer in the classroom

As we have already outlined, the regulation of sexuality is completed not only though the law, but also through the social and cultural dynamics of life. The construction of homosexuality as something immoral and dangerous which therefore should not be 'taught' or otherwise 'encouraged' found its pedagogic manifestation in Section 28 of the innocuously named Local Government Act of 1988, which applied in Great Britain. The section stipulated that:

1. A local authority shall not—

    (a) intentionally promote homosexuality or publish material with the intention of promoting homosexuality;
    (b) promote the teaching in any maintained school of the acceptability of homosexuality as a pretended family relationship.

2. Nothing in subsection (1) above shall be taken to prohibit the doing of anything for the purpose of treating or preventing the spread of disease.

As you can see, this section prohibits schools from teaching pupils about homosexual relationships, except when doing so might help to prevent disease. It is probably not difficult to guess that legislators had HIV in mind here. Even though no local authority was ever prosecuted for 'promoting homosexuality' in its schools, it is easy to see how the creation of such a law demonstrates the status that LGBT+ issues had in 1980s and 1990s Britain. The Act was only repealed – after considerable struggle – in 2003. A consequence of this is up until the early years of this century young people received no school education about LGBT+ sex, no information about LGBT+ relationships, were forced to adopt **heteronormative** models, had few LGBT+ role models, and few ways in which to understand non-heteronormative sexualities as legitimate and acceptable; figuring them instead as 'pretended' family relationships.

   Carl Stychin (1995: 42–3) notes how anxiety about positive representations of homosexuality ('promotion') was rooted in a fear of people 'choosing' to become gay or lesbian or bisexual or **trans** once they had more knowledge of the culture. This panic constructs homosexuality or queerness as a contagious threat to 'traditional, deep-rooted family values', which will be the cornerstone of the strength of the nation.

Regulating (hetero)sexuality

Beyond administering the legal status of sex between men, criminal justice systems around the world have an established history of regulating appropriate and inappropriate heterosexual encounters. One prominent way in which this can be seen is in the changing understandings and interpretation of the crime of rape.

Do we know what rape is? Or, what 'counts' as rape? Perhaps today we can answer 'yes' to these questions, as rape is often characterised as a crime that is clear in its definition. In English and Welsh law, it is currently defined as the intentional penetration of the vagina, anus or mouth of another person with a penis, without consent or without reasonable belief of consent (Sexual Offences Act 2003, s1) – we discuss the challenges of understanding consent in Chapter 4.

However, as Joanna Bourke (2007) argues, rape is a social performance: a ritualised and socialised attack which is acted out and interpreted differently depending upon time, location and context. The same act (for instance, penetration of the vagina with a penis) will be understood as rape in some contexts and not as rape in others. As such, it has social, cultural and legal meanings that are rooted in historical perspectives and are different in each society. While the following analysis is predominantly based on English and Welsh law, similar focuses can be seen in other legal jurisdictions, particularly those former colonies that have inherited English legal traditions, such as Australia, Canada and the USA.

Rape: from theft to consent

While today we see rape as a violent crime which is about exerting power, this has not always been the case. Historically, rape was closely connected in law to crimes of property and stealing something of value, rather than violence. The origin of the word 'rape' is the Latin verb *rapere*, which, in classic Latin, meant 'to seize'. As Caroline Dunn (2017) argues, during the thirteenth and fourteenth centuries 'rape' was used to describe both sexual assault against women and also to describe the abduction or consensual elopement of a woman and her lover from her husband or parent's/guardian's family.

As such, the laws were concerned not with the emotional and bodily impact of sexual violence on the woman who experienced it, but with the impact on the man who had control and ownership over her body and sexuality.

The control of women by their male kin (relations and wider family circle) is perhaps apparent in the fact that in 1382 the law was amended so that the right to prosecute a man suspected of rape was extended to the woman's male kin or guardians (Saunders, 2001); this change facilitated criminalisation in cases where the woman consented to the elopement and therefore did not want to bring a charge against her lover (Dunn, 2017). The wronged party was often identified as the woman's family, rather than the woman herself.

Virginity is important in this legal context of rape. The crime of *raptus* was seen to be more heinous if committed against a virgin (Dunn, 2017). It was also considered to be easier to 'prove' due to the physical impact of the damage to the hymen. Virginity was highly prized, so there was greater motive for prosecuting these attacks and there was more to gain from the prosecution as the woman's value would have been reduced by the 'loss' of her virginity and thus damage to her marriage prospects. Rape prosecutions were much less likely to be brought by women who were not unmarried virgins, or by women of lower social status and wealth. This once again indicates the wider social perception that the true crime in these cases was one of social and financial loss to the men who controlled the woman (the victim/survivor).

We use the term 'victim/survivor' to refer to people who have experienced non-consensual and/or unwanted sexual activity and sexual violence. We have chosen this terminology specifically to recognise the differing experiences of individuals in relation to rape and sexual assault. For some, it is important that their victimisation is recognised. For others, the focus is their survival and moving on from that experience. It is no one's place to tell a person how they should feel about their own experience, and so we use this language to acknowledge and legitimise the differing responses of people who experience and live through sexual violence.

Virginity and the law

Virginity is a social concept that holds substantial weight in society, both historically and today; think, for example, of the significance of the Virgin Mary. Yet what is virginity? What does it mean to be a 'virgin'? How do we define it? And why is it seen to hold such importance?

In her history of the phenomenon of virginity, Hanne Blank (2007: 3) argues that virginity has no tangible existence, and can only be determined to exist due to the presence of its effects or side-effects within society. The term 'virgin' comes from the Latin *virgo*, meaning a girl or a never-married woman (Blank, 2007: 10). Historically and across multiple languages, as Blank outlines, the term is used to describe girls and women, rather than boys.

And virginity as a concept continues to be associated much more closely with women and girls than with boys and men. Similarly, it is most often associated with a specific expression of heterosexuality; of a woman having vaginal penetrative sex for the first time. Images of virginity are also racialised, as in the Western world virginity is traditionally symbolised as **Whiteness** and connected to virtue, purity and goodness (such as is depicted in Christian images of the Virgin Mary). In contrast, sin, corruption and evil are associated with dark colours and **Blackness** (Blank, 2007). Women and girls of colour are much more likely to be sexualised and perceived as 'immoral' or 'promiscuous' than their white peers, as we explore in Chapter 7.

The connection of virginity to a first sexual encounter is dubious, as it relies on a fixed definition of 'sex'. For example, if a man and woman intimately touch each other and/or have oral sex, are they virgins? What if they have anal sex? Are you a virgin if you have masturbated? Would a woman be a virgin if she or someone else inserts a finger or sex toys into her vagina? Would people who have only ever engaged in same-sex sex, rather than heterosexual sex, be virgins? If a man's penis is only slightly inserted into a woman's vagina, or just rests at the entrance, are they still virgins? If contraception is used during penal-vaginal penetration, or the man pulls out before he ejaculates, would virginity 'remain' in these circumstances? Interpretations of what constitutes virginity 'loss' and what can cause it are varied and multiple. For example, in her study interviewing young adults in the USA, Laura M. Carpenter (2001) found that numerous forms of genital sex were seen to result in virginity loss, and many participants argued that virginity could not be lost through rape; the phenomenon was conceptualised as a gift, a stigma or part of a process.

The unbreached hymen – a membrane, located inside the opening of the vagina – is often considered to be evidence of virginity. It is thought that a hymen remains in place until it is penetrated by a penis through sexual intercourse; thus 'removed', it becomes a physical demarcation of the 'loss' of virginity in women. However, as Blank (2007: 23) states, 'the hymen is nothing more or less than a functionless leftover, a tiny idle remnant of flesh that remains when the opening of the vagina forms' – unfunctional because, unlike, for example, the hymens of whales, which keep out water, or of guinea pigs, that dissolve when fertile – the human hymen does very little of anything (Blank, 2007). The human hymen can wear away due to activity other than vaginal-penal intercourse – through finger penetration by someone else or yourself, physical activities such as horse riding, gymnastics and hockey, the use of menstrual cups or tampons. Furthermore, some women are born without the flap of skin and some women's hymens will tear or rub away with limited physical engagement with the genital area, so that they have not noticed it has 'gone'. The cultural myth that the 'breaking' of the hymen will cause substantial bleeding and pain is most certainly not a universal experience.

Therefore, if virginity is a construction that is neither agreed upon as a phenomenon nor physically identifiable, then why does it hold such significance, both historically and today? The clearest answer to this lies in the structure of heterosexuality and society around the principles of **patriarchy** and private property. Ownership of possessions, land and titles, for example, and the organisation of society into groups based on 'kin', centralising the man as the head of the household, with control over his wife and children, gave rise to a need to protect men's lineage and patrimony: the inheritance from father to son down the male line of the family. Within this socio-cultural-economic organisation of society, virginity becomes a functional requirement so that a man may 'know' that the children *his* woman births are, in fact, *his* children, and not the off-spring of some other man. Prior to the very recent invention of paternity tests, it was impossible to tell who had impregnated a woman, unless you were certain she had never had penal-vaginal sexual intercourse with another man, and were assured of monogamy. To secure this, it was thus necessary for a woman be a 'virgin' upon marriage, so as to not bring another man's child into her husband's family, and also that she remained 'chaste' following marriage, only engaging in sexual activity with her husband.

One of the consequences of this construction of virginity is that women who are perceived to not be 'chaste' were considered to be sexually immoral and impure. Such focus on women's sexuality as a mark of their inherent 'quality' became even more important to a woman's character in the nineteenth century, with ideologies of the 'fallen' woman. These perceptions of sexuality which denote a woman's worth and quality have impacted perceptions of rape and resonate into the present day, as we will see in Chapter 7 on trafficking and exploitation, children's sexuality, as outlined in Chapter 12, and motherhood and reproduction, as outlined in Chapter 6. This is not to say that women never engaged in consensual sexual relationships outside of marriage, but, within most social circles, such sexual engagements were kept discreet and secret so as to avoid the 'scandal' and 'ruin' of a woman's reputation and, with hers, potentially also her husband's and/or father's. For working women such as servants, a ruined reputation could mean an inability to find employment, at a time when there was little to no social support for the impoverished.

Modern-day perceptions about 'loose' women, 'sluts' and 'whores' continue to be a feature of women's **sexuality** in ways that they are not for men, and are expressions of **rape culture**. Therefore, social and cultural regulations of the acceptability of women having sex outside of a monogamous relationship are an example of historical thinking about sex that has failed to develop and modernise.

BOX 3.1

Task: Reflect on what you have read about the concept of virginity and consider:

- What is the significance of virginity in regards to the crime of *raptus* in fourteenth-century England, as outlined above?
- How important is 'virginity' for men and women today?
- How would you define virginity? Has your definition changed in reading this section of the book?
- If society was structured around matrilines (tracing the family through the female line), would we be so concerned with the virginity of girls and women? Would we have other worries?
- Is the concept of virginity or chastity still connected to perceptions we have of sexual violence? If so, how?

'Against her will'

While the term rape came to be defined as sexual violence alone, statutory definition of the offence only appeared in the late twentieth century; prior to this, the offences continued to exist in England and Wales only as a **common law** offence. It was defined as 'the carnal knowledge of a woman forcibly and against her will' (Blackstone, 1791: 210). This common law definition was exported widely to countries outside of England, as British rule and influence spread during the period of colonialism. Thus, it has shaped and influenced the legal understanding of this form of sexual violence in many jurisdictions.

There are a number of important points to note about the common law definition of rape, the first being that the offence operated only on the basis of a female victim and a male perpetrator, and the offence required the insertion of a penis into a vagina (carnal knowledge). As such, other forms of sexual assault fell under the category of buggery (as outlined above) or indecent assault, an offence that historically focused on sexual engagement with girls; defining the age of consent (see Chapter 12). Thus, under this legal definition, non-consensual penetration of the anus or mouth was not defined as rape. Consequently, legally, a man could not be raped by anyone (man or woman) and a woman could not be raped by a woman, even if sexual acts were committed without consent or were unwanted.

Married-to-your-rapist laws

One category of men who were immune from prosecution were men who raped their wives. As this law worked on the basis that within marriage a man had the right to sexual relations with his wife, it was a legal impossibility for the 'carnal knowledge' to be 'against her will' and for the man to commit rape against her, as 'by their mutual consent and contract the wife hath given up herself in this kind unto her husband, which she cannot retract' (Hale, 1736: 629). It was not until 1991 that this common law legal principle was overturned. In the case of *R v. R*, the House of Lords (the highest court in the UK at the time, as the Supreme Court of the United Kingdom assumed jurisdiction in 2009) upheld the conviction of a man who raped his estranged wife, stating:

> It seems to us that where the common law rule no longer even remotely represents what is the true position of a wife in present day society, the duty of the court is to take steps to alter the rule if it can legitimately do so in the light of any relevant Parliamentary enactment. (*R v. R* [1991] UKHL 12; [1992] 1 A.C. 599 at 610)

According to the United Nations Statistics Division (2015), only 52 countries to date have passed laws against marital rape: that is, only one in four countries across the globe.

In some instances, women who are raped are forced to marry their attacker in order to assuage the shame or burden to the family of having a woman so 'despoiled' by rape. We may see the marriage between a rapist and the victim/survivor of the sexual assault as something that only happened in the past; however, in numerous legal jurisdictions laws exist allowing men who would be prosecuted for rape to be exonerated if they marry the woman/girl they have raped. Overturning such laws is a focus of UN Women (2019b) activism, which has seen some success over recent years with Tunisia, Palestine, Jordan and Lebanon recently changing their laws to prevent perpetrators from escaping prosecution in this manner. However, many more countries still permit men to marry the woman they have raped, and campaigning against this form of gender-based violence continues.

BOX 3.2

Consider the following:

- What factors do you think might have influenced countries to make it illegal for a man to rape his wife? You might want to look back to Chapter 2 for ideas.
- What factors might explain why three-quarters of countries have not yet implemented laws to criminalise marital rape?
- Why might communities be happy for victims/survivors of rape to be married to the man who attacked her?
- What do such social pressures and decisions tell us about how women are regarded and about women's rights in these countries?

Ejaculation and rape

A further way in which heteronormativity is inscribed in cases of sexual violence lies in how courts decided that the 'carnal knowledge' was 'forcible and against her will'. A determining factor of rape which characterised prosecutions from the late eighteenth century was the need to prove that the accused had ejaculated inside the vagina of the victim/survivor (or anus in cases of buggery). This legal development occurred following the trial of Samuel Hill in 1781, where the jury determined that he should not be executed for the rape of Mary Portas as she could only confirm that Hill had penetrated her vagina with his penis, but not that he had ejaculated. Following this case, the crime of rape was determined to have occurred (the *actus reus* of the offence) only if the complainant could swear that both penetration *and ejaculation* had occurred; it would then be left to the jury to determine if her witness testimony was convincing on both points (Block, 2016[2013]: 32). The importance of ejaculation in the legal definition of rape remained a feature of the law, hampering convictions until 1828 when the government legislated that 'the carnal knowledge shall be deemed complete upon proof of penetration only' (Offences Against the Person Act 1828).

The significance of the carnal knowledge being 'against her will' has impacted and shaped understandings of rape for centuries and continues to be a feature of rape trials today. In her ground-breaking text of 1975, *Against Our Will*, Susan Brownmiller advocates that, for women, the crime of rape occurs when a woman chooses to not have intercourse with a man and a man chooses to have that intercourse with her *against her will*; so, for women it is a crime based on their right to consent to what happens to their body. However, historically the legal understanding of rape has been predicated on the principles and evidence of force. Proof of rape has often relied on physical evidence of an extreme struggle. Joan McGregor (2012) argues that this emphasis on force expresses a direct connection to the concept of virginity again, and the belief that a woman of moral virtue would do all she could to prevent her virginity from being 'stolen' by an unknown man. The law, criminal justice and society assumed that women valued their chastity highly (indeed, their intrinsic value as humans was often defined by it) and so would protect it with their lives. Failure to demonstrate such a level of resistance was deemed to suggest that a woman had consented to the sexual activity; women who were seen not to have put up enough of a fight were considered not to have been raped. For example, in a case from the USA, *Brown v. State* 106 N.W. 536 (Wis. 1906), it was ruled that a 16-year-old girl had not been raped as she did not adequately demonstrate she had not consented, even though she had tried to scream, was physically knocked to the ground and her attacker physically forced himself upon her (McGregor, 2012). It also meant that women who were threatened with violence, deceived, pressured, manipulated or coerced into sexual intercourse through means other than physical force or restraint, were not considered to have been raped. In England, it was not until 1885, under section 3 of the Criminal Law Amendment Act, that it became illegal to have 'carnal connexion' with a woman or girl through threat or intimidation, false pretences or representation.

The emphasis on force shaped much feminist analysis of the law and campaigning for a change in the latter half of the twentieth century. Sexual violence became a key focus for feminist activism during second-wave feminism of the 1960s, 1970s and 1980s. Feminist voices rose to tell stories of women's experiences of sexual violence, aiming to illustrate that these are everyday experiences for many women, not infrequent occurrences for the unfortunate few.

Academic writing and political campaigns led to the opening of rape crisis centres, protests against men's violence towards women, as well as criminal justice responses to such violence, particularly in the use of women's sexual history to discredit her testimony when giving evidence in court, and drew attention to the law's inability to recognise martial rape (see Edwards, 1981; Kelly, 1988; Russell, 1975; Smart, 1977, 1989; Stanko, 1985; Temkin, 1987). Ultimately, many feminists identified that rape was an expression of the dominance of men over women, rather than being about sex, and that it formed part of a wide spectrum of violence and control exerted over women by men they encounter: partners, friends and family, as well as acquaintances and strangers.

BOX 3.3

In the UK, we now have more specific and explicitly worded criminal offences relating to non-consensual sex. However, the current law still leaves us with a number of challenges as to how we legally define and understand sexual violence. Take a look at the following questions and see what you think might have impacted on our legal understandings of rape, considering the historic and social influences outlined in this chapter:

- Across the UK, rape is defined as penile penetration, and yet it is based on the concept of consent. If a person uses another person's penis to penetrate their own anus, mouth or vagina without the consent of the person whose penis it is (for example, a woman performs oral sex on a man without his consent), do you think this fits a legal definition or rape? Do you think it should fit a legal definition of rape? Why do you think the law of rape has not captured this form of non-consensual sex?

(Continued)

- Alongside the crime of rape is the crime of 'assault by penetration', which is the insertion of an object or a body part other than a penis into the anus or vagina of another person without their consent. Across the UK, laws have specifically considered this to be a crime distinct from rape (although the punishment is the same). This is different from other legal jurisdictions, for example in Canada the word rape is not used and the law criminalises 'sexual assault'. What is the significance of the term 'rape' in law? Do we still need it to distinguish from other sexual acts that occur without consent? Why are we still concerned with the penetration of the body with a penis? Penetration with other implements may potentially be more traumatic or damaging than a penis, for example penetration with a knife or broken bottle.

- The law is based on a defendant's belief that the victim/survivor consented, rather than on the simple fact that the victim/survivor says they did not consent – for example, if the victim/survivor did not want to have sex but did not say anything due to a fear of the repercussions for showing a lack of consent, and so there were no outward signs of non-consent (except perhaps lack of enthusiasm), then the crime of rape has not been committed. Do you think this is right? Could the law operate in any other way? If so, how? What might the legal repercussions be for the accused?

Summary

The regulation of sexuality and sexual practice through law and criminal justice has an established history that echoed around the world. Of course, the criminal justice system is not the only way that sexuality is policed. It acts in dialogue with government policy, medical discourses, religion, education and the family, to name a few. We have seen how this plays out to control, guide and manage a population and to build a strong nation. The way in which sexual activity is understood and regulated also depends very much on the spatio-temporal context of the activity: who the actors are, their ages, the country, the era that we are living in, and what they are doing. Contemporary understandings of sex and sexuality are laced with historical legacies, as we have explored in the examples of the decriminalisation of homosexuality and the changing nature of rape law.

One thing that is apparent from this chapter is that whether it is to do with LGBT+ rights or the right of a man to rape his wife, legal reform often follows in the footsteps of social change. We have also seen how these changing laws become an expression of nationhood: with progressive feminist policies or legalising gay marriage becoming a stick with which to beat other, supposedly less 'progressive' countries, and a mask behind which to hide racist and otherwise problematic policies and practices.

As you move through this book, hold on to this critical analysis of the context of crime, sex, law and justice. Ask yourself where the knowledge about what you are encountering comes from, in terms of time (when it is happening), space (in which national, global or local context it occurs) and what it seeks to achieve. What does it actually achieve? (This last one is a hard one to answer.)

Review questions

- How do ideas of nationalism impact on understandings of normative sex?
- How have ideas of acceptable/non-acceptable sex been shaped by patriarchy?
- What will normative sex look like in the future? In the UK? In other countries?
- What socio-cultural factors will impact the development of ideas of sex and sexuality?

Other chapters that this links to

Chapter 4 (Consent and its discontents)
Chapter 5 (Sex and institutional cultures of abuse)
Chapter 6 (Reproduction, sex and crime)
Chapter 7 (Sexual exploitation and the State)
Chapter 12 (Children, sexualisation and the law)
Chapter 15 (How to change your life)

Part 2

State, Sex and Crime

4

Consent and its discontents

CHAPTER OUTLINE

The concept of consent is one of the key areas of focus in the regulation of sex. In sexual activity, consent is often perceived to be the line that is drawn between sex that is OK (wanted, morally right, legal) and sex that is not OK (not wanted, morally wrong, illegal). As the concept of consent holds an important focus in understanding sex and crime, we need to spend some time unpacking what is meant by the term and some of the challenges that are faced in interpreting and applying principles of consent in sexual activity. The chapter is mostly based on English and Welsh laws around consent and sexual violence. However, the theoretical ideas explored are relevant to other legal jurisdictions and ideas around sexual violence that fall outside of the law.

By the end of this chapter, you will understand more about:

- the concept of consent and factors that are needed to determine whether or not consent exists
- the legal limits that have been placed on the concept of consent
- social and cultural factors that can impact understandings and interpretations of consent
- why it can be so difficult to determine whether consent has truly been given, and, in connection to this, why it is sometimes so difficult to refuse 'consent'.

Note that lots of the discussion in this chapter refers to consent and consent violation in the context of rape and sexual violence. These can be difficult topics to read about, so give yourself time, take breaks and discuss any difficult feelings or thoughts that you have with someone you trust.

Consent in sexual interactions is a tricky concept, as it relates not just to desire, but also to willingness, which can vary in degrees (Malm, 1996). For example, you can be willing to do something because you know it is expected of you, with expectations being socially and culturally conditioned, without actually wanting to do it: most of us pay income tax because we know we have to and therefore are willing to do it; it does not necessarily mean we are happy about it. The same can be true of having sex. What consent actually is – in other words, what mental processes and physical actions occur in order for consent to exist – continues to be subject to debate. For example, Heidi M. Hurd (1996) argues that consent is an attitude that is formed in the mind of the consenter: only if the consenter intends to consent, to allow or enable another's actions, will that amount to valid consent. In contrast, Nathan Brett (1998) argues that consent is a performative action: consent is speaking or doing, during which process other parties are given permission to act. Both perspectives pose challenges, as Sharon Cowan (2008) argues, because to see consent as simply a mental attitude negates the question of ambivalent mental states and how consent is determined. But to see consent as purely performative 'could minimize the contextual importance of substantive conditions that drive consent, and could therefore be over-inclusive' (2008: 903). Within this chapter, we will take a look at some of the challenges that occur when attempting to conceptualise consent and whether or not consent has been given.

A note on terminology

In this chapter, the term rape is used as a shorthand when referring to non-consensual sex. However, it is important to note that consent is also a factor in behaviours such as touching, saying things of a sexual nature, texting or sending images. While these aspects of sexual activity will not be discussed directly, the theory and ideas about consent explored here are relevant to those sexual encounters. Similarly, at times, the terms rape, sexual violence or sexual assault are used in relation to non-consensual sexual activity. However, that does not mean the behaviour would meet a legal definition of a sexual offence – this, as we will see below, is one of the challenges of understanding consent and sexual violence. Connected to this, we use the term 'victim/survivor' to refer to people who have experienced unwanted or non-consensual sexual activity and sexual violence; see Chapter 3 for our rationale for using this terminology.

Much of the discussion and literature in the chapter focuses on consent within heterosexual relationships, where the woman is the party who may not have consented. This focus is not to suggest that non-consensual sex does not take place outside of heterosexual relationships, nor that it is always the male partner who may violate consent, or the woman whose consent will be violated. However, as will be outlined below, much of the research has focused on heterosexual encounters to assess concepts of consent because the statistics demonstrate, and accounts from women illustrate, that consent violations occur between men and women at an alarmingly high rate. Nevertheless, most issues discussed here have relevance to any sexual situation, regardless of the **gender** or **sexuality** of those involved.

Reasonableness of the belief of consent

Consent has not always been a feature of the law of rape, as we examined in Chapter 3. The legal definition of rape was first written into statute only in the latter half of the twentieth century. In section 1(1) of the Sexual Offences (Amendment) Act 1976, rape is defined as a man having:

a.   ...unlawful sexual intercourse with a woman who at the time of the intercourse does not consent to it; and
b.   at that time he knows that she does not consent to the intercourse or he is reckless as to whether she consents to it.

Notice how this legal definition was predicated on the concept of consent, not force, as it had been defined historically. However, controversy lay at the heart of the new definition due to section 1(2) of the Act, which read:

It is hereby declared that if at a trial for a rape offence the jury has to consider whether a man believed that a woman was consenting to sexual intercourse, the presence or absence of reasonable grounds for such a belief is a matter to which the jury is to have regard, in conjunction with any other relevant matters, in considering whether he so believed.

The focus on 'reasonableness' became a central aspect of the debate of consent and defining rape under the law. The change in law occurred following the appeal of three men against their rape conviction. Here are the details:

In 1973 a man (Morgan) was drinking alcohol with three other men whereupon he invited them to his house to have sex with his wife, Daphne. The four men proceeded to gang rape Daphne, dragging her from her bed and holding her down while each of the other men forced themselves upon her. Upon conviction for rape (Morgan was tried for aiding and abetting rape as a man could not legally rape his own wife until 1991) the three men appealed their conviction on the basis that they believed that Daphne had consented as her husband had told them to not be surprised if she struggled as she was 'kinky' and it was the only way she could get 'turned on' (DPP v. Morgan (1975) UKHL 3 at 7). The House of Lords ruled that honest but mistaken belief of the woman's consent would provide a complete defence to the accusation of rape as, 'if the defendant believed (even on unreasonable grounds) that the woman was consenting to intercourse then he cannot have been carrying out an intention to have intercourse without her consent'. (DPP v. Morgan at 31)

The consequence of the judgement was that a man's belief in the consent of the victim/survivor to sexual intercourse did not need to be a reasonable one; any other person may feel that it is unreasonable to believe that a woman has not consented on the basis of her behaviour, but if the jury are convinced that *this* accused man *did* in fact believe it, even if it turned out to not be the case, then he has not committed the crime of rape.

It was not until the twenty-first century that the principle of unreasonable but mistaken belief in consent was removed from the crime of rape in England and Wales. The Sexual Offences Act 2003 marked a significant change in the legal definition of rape and other sexual offences, introducing oral penetration with a penis as an act of rape (anal penetration without consent was defined as an act of rape in 1994 through section 142 of the Criminal Justice and Public Order Act, the first time it was acknowledging in English and Welsh law that men can also be raped). The 2003 Act also clearly stated that the belief in consent must be 'reasonable', which is determined as 'having regard to all the circumstances, including any steps A has taken to ascertain whether B consents'. The Act also specifically defined consent as something to which a party 'agrees by choice, and has the freedom and capacity to make that choice' (s74). Corresponding legislation was enacted in Northern Ireland in 2008 (Sexual Offences (Northern Ireland) Order) and for Scotland in 2009 (Sexual Offences (Scotland) Act).

So, consent is now firmly written into the criminal law relating to sexual activity, but what does 'consenting' actually mean? This is what we discuss in the rest of the chapter.

Consent – what, when, where, how

Academic understanding of the concept of consent in connection with sexual activity has been slow in developing, with the focus often based on popular beliefs about consent 'without critically engaging with the concept or providing an explicit definition' (Beres, 2014: 374). Definitions of consent have been driven by medical understanding in the context of conducting medical procedures and research. The Nuremberg Code of 1949 emphasises the importance of participants having free **power** to choose to participate in any medical procedure. Consent is widely determined to be valid if three criteria can be met – the capability to consent, freedom to refuse, and evidence that the consequences of consenting are understood and accepted. While on the face of it the criteria may seem self-explanatory and easy to determine, the discussion we outline below will illustrate that this is not always the case. Much of the difficulty that occurs in terms of criminal justice involvement in sexual activity, including in proving that sexual activity was non-consensual and therefore was sexual violence, stems from how consent is conceptualised and interpreted.

Capacity

Perhaps the most straightforward of the three criteria, capacity denotes the ability to consent – the extent to which it is deemed you are able to agree to something. In order to be able to consent (to sex, to the terms within a contract, to a medical procedure), it is required that you hold sufficient capacity. It is generally assumed that everyone holds capacity, with some widely accepted exceptions.

Age

For the early period of our lives, it is deemed that we do not have the capacity to make decisions about a range of aspects of life, such as voting, having an operation and having sex. The age of consent for sexual activity is set by the **State**. The lowest age of consent worldwide is in Nigeria, where it is set at 11 years old. However, the concept of age as a means of determining capacity is not straightforward; as we will see in Chapter 12, the age at which a person can legally have sex with someone can change, depending on the context of that sexual engagement. Similarly, a number of countries also have what are known as 'Romeo and Juliet' laws, whereby if the people having sex are under the age of consent but close in age then the laws of consent do not apply. For example, in Canada, a 14- or 15-year-old is able to consent to sexual activity as long as the sexual partner is less than five years older and there is no relationship of trust, authority or dependency, or any other exploitation of the young person. A further dynamic of age of consent lies in the distinction drawn by some states between heterosexual and homosexual relationships, with the age of consent being higher for same-sex sexual relations in some jurisdictions.

Non-human animals

Animals that are not human are widely deemed to be unable to consent to sex, and in many countries, laws have been enacted to prohibit sexual activity between human and non-human animals. As we saw in Chapter 3, in England and Wales it has been a statutory offence since 1533 to have intercourse with an animal, under the offence of buggery. Today, intercourse with a non-human animal is widely known as 'bestiality'.

Mental capacity

There are situations whereby a person will not be deemed capable of giving consent due to their mental incapacity. Such situations may be time-limited, for example following an operation where you have been under general aesthetic and you are advised not to sign any contracts. A person may not be deemed to have mental capacity for the entirety of their lives, if, for example, they have a learning disability or condition that impairs their brain function. Mental incapacity may also be something that develops, for example following an accident or the onset of an illness or disease such as dementia – in Chapter 10, we further consider mental disability, capacity and sexual activity.

Being asleep or unconscious

In many legal jurisdictions, being asleep or unconscious is determined as a state in which a person is unable to consent, and so laws prohibit sexual activity at this time. While this may seem like an obvious example of lack of capacity, numerous criminal cases of sexual assault and rape have hinged on whether the victim/survivor consented prior to passing out or falling asleep (either verbally or non-verbally through gestures and actions), and therefore whether or not the accused had secured consent (see, for example, the case of Ched Evans which we discuss below).

Intoxication

Drugs and alcohol and sexual activity create a tricky situation in regard to determining consent, particularly if the substances are willingly and consentingly consumed. If substances that intoxicate are given without that person's permission or knowledge, such as in the situation of a 'date-rape' drug like rohypnol being administered, allowing the victim/survivor to be more easily overpowered for the purpose of sexual activity, then this will constitute an offence as, quite clearly, consent to sexual activity has not been given. However, if the consumption of a mind-altering substance was voluntary, then the question of consent is far murkier.

In *R v. Bree* [2007] EWCA 256, the Court of Appeal in England and Wales ruled that if, through alcohol or for any other reason, a person had temporarily lost their capacity to choose whether to have sexual intercourse, then they were not consenting. However, where a person had voluntarily consumed substantial quantities of alcohol, but remained capable of choosing whether to have intercourse, and agreed to do so, then that would not be rape. Further, the Court identified that the capacity to consent may evaporate well before a complainant becomes unconscious, but that measuring when this point of the removal of capacity occurs would be different in each case. This ruling does not provide us with a clear idea of where the line between intoxicated and *able* to consent, and intoxicated and *unable* to consent lies, or how it is determined by a sexual partner and, possibly, later by professionals within the criminal justice system and a jury.

Furthermore, as Amanda Clough (2019) argues, there is also a difference between legal definitions of rape if someone is taking advantage of someone else's intoxication in order to have sex with them when they would be likely to say no if sober, and the moral wrong of such behaviour. Clough has deemed this 'inauthentic, yet legally valid consent, unless a person is almost at the point of unconsciousness' (2019: 62). Consider for yourself how and why it might be difficult to determine whether consent exists in the following situations:

- Mark is involuntarily intoxicated by David; Will does not know this and so has sex with Mark; Mark instigated the sexual activity.
- Herminder agrees to drink alcohol but does not know that Phil is buying her large shots with her mixer, so gets far drunker than she intended. While at this higher level of drunkenness than she intended, Herminder agrees to have sex with Phil, later believing she would not have had sex if she had been sober.
- Seema voluntarily took ecstasy; while high, she made sexual advances to Carlo, who invited her to his home. Seema agreed and then said yes when he asked her to come to bed with him. The next day, Seema regrets sleeping with Carlo, believing that she did not mean to say yes to going back to his house or to having sex with him, and only did so due to the drugs impacting her thought process.
- Jay is voluntarily drunk, and the consequence of his drunkenness is that he cannot stand and has vomited several times. Yuuko goes home with Jay and they have sex. The next morning, Jay cannot remember the journey home, nor having sex with Yuuko.
- Meera has sex with Claudine, who is unconscious after drinking alcohol. Prior to falling unconscious, Claudine said she wanted to have sex.

Freedom

One of the key aspects of consent is having the freedom to choose whether or not you want to take part in the proposed activity; this is sometimes referred to as 'voluntariness'. On the face of it, freedom to choose may seem like a simple and straightforward concept, as within neo-liberal society we are advised that we are all individual subjects who have the liberty to decide what we do with our lives. There are some obvious examples of when sexual encounters take place against a person's free choice – the perpetrator holding the victim/survivor down and physically forcing participation in the sexual activity. As we saw in Chapter 3, the law of rape has historically been based upon the principle of forced participation in sexual activity 'against her will', but such definitions of sexual violence were challenged specifically due to the fact that sexual assault and rape occur more commonly without physical force being used. Therefore, we need to think more critically about what we mean by 'freedom to choose' in the context of sexual violence.

As we explored in our discussion of neoliberalism in Chapter 2, choice to shape a situation is often curtailed by **agency**, or the individual power a person holds. The curtailing of individual freedom needs to be understood within the framework of **intersectionality** (also discussed in Chapters 1 and 2) as we can often see a direct correlation between the advantages in society a person holds and their belief that they have the ability to say no to sexual activity or interaction. Let us consider some examples:

- A personal assistant, Dev, is asked by his boss if he wants to stay late in the office to have a drink. As conversation progresses, his boss puts their hand on Dev's knee. Dev is not sure whether or not to rebut the sexual advances as he is very conscious of the fact that he may lose his job if he says no.
- In bed each evening, Mike starts removing his wife's clothes. Yasmin never really wants to have sex, but she knows that Mike expects it and so she goes along with it.
- While auditioning for a part in a play, Rose is asked to meet with the producer in his hotel suite. When Rose arrives at the meeting, the producer is dressed only in a bathrobe and suggests that it would be nice if Rose joined him in the jacuzzi and not to worry that she doesn't have a bathing suit. Rose is nervous about saying no to the producer as he will have a big say in whether or not she gets the part.
- Sam knows that if they don't agree to have sex with their partner, Alex, then Alex will be uncooperative, unpleasant, and will brood for days. Deciding it's not worth it, Sam agrees to have sex even though they don't want to.
- Chiagozie is homeless and has been sleeping rough. She is approached by a man she does not know and told she can sleep in his spare room rent free. In return, the man wants Chiagozie to agree to have sex with him at least four nights a week.

David Archard (1997) makes a distinction between consent and assent – consent is to agree *to* something, whereas assent is agreement *with* something; in other words, consenting to something does not necessarily mean that you want it to happen, that you will it to occur. However, we need to unpack this idea of agreeing *to* something and consider the circumstances in which a person would say 'yes' to sexual activity if they are aware that they do not really want to do it and/or do not believe they will enjoy it. In legal jurisdictions across the UK, consenting to sex you do not want would not be rape or sexual assault as the law is not based on whether or not you *want* to have sex, but on whether consent *has been given* and if the accused has a *reasonable belief of consent being given*.

Furthermore, as Melanie Ann Beres (2014) argues, in some jurisdictions consent is constructed as an agreement to participate in sex regardless of the context of that agreement. In such instances, rape has not occurred in law if people acquiesce to sex, even if the agreement is as a product of pressure or coercion, including feeling like you are not in a position to say 'no', as outlined in the scenarios above.

A follow-up question exists in terms of how that choice to consent is communicated and understood. For example, Beres (2014: 374–5) discusses a case from Texas in the USA in the mid-1990s where a woman begged her 'knife-wielding attacker' to use a condom, believing she was going to be raped and hoping to avoid the contraction of a sexually transmitted disease; this was later used in court as evidence of her consent to have sex with him. In contrast, other jurisdictions define consent as only being granted with the absence of *any* coercion or force. However, feminist theorists have criticised this conception of 'coercion' because of the already unequal power dynamics that exist between men and women in society and because of the **patriarchal** structures that life operates within. We discuss this below.

Information and consequences

The final criterion required for consent to be valid is an appreciation of what you are consenting to and what it entails; this includes understanding the consequences of agreeing to what is being proposed. As with the other factors of consent, this may perhaps seem quite a straightforward idea, but the complexity lies in relation to how much information a person needs and the possible consequences that may occur if they are unaware of information due to an omission, or if they are misinformed, or circumstances change following consent, so that the situation no longer reflects what was initially consented to.

Consider the following situations and think about whether or not sufficient information is present to warrant consent:

- Emma agrees to have sex with James, anticipating that he will wear a condom. James puts his penis inside Emma with no condom on.
- Tom consents to have oral sex with Olga. While Olga is giving Tom a blowjob, she puts her finger into his anus. Tom was not expecting this and feels uncomfortable about this sexual interaction.
- Craig slips off the condom before penetrating Gary; Gary is unaware of this and believes Craig is wearing the condom.
- Carlotta agrees to have sex with Dan without a condom after Dan agrees he will withdraw his penis from her vagina before he ejaculates. Dan does not withdraw before ejaculation.
- Pete agrees to have unprotected sex with Meike as she has told him she has recently been checked for STIs and the results came back negative. Meike has not been checked for over a year and has gonorrhoea.
- Michelle agrees to have sex with Gabby as she is under the impression that they are only having a relationship with each other and no one else; Gabby does not correct Michelle's incorrect belief.
- Alex tells Kit that they are on the pill and so cannot get pregnant; Alex is lying.

So how much is *enough* information? David Archard (1998: 46) argues that a person does not need to know everything about someone they plan to have sex with; 'only everything that would make a real difference to whether or not [they] consented'. Without this information, the consent would be invalid. Such information would include what is being consented to, prior or background information bearing on what is being consented to, and what may transpire as a consequence of giving consent.

Consent to sexual activity may be obtained fraudulently, which is recognised in criminal law in many jurisdictions. Fraud can occur in two ways: first, in misrepresentation of the act itself or the identity of the person involved in the act (for example, a doctor falsely states that sexual intercourse with a patient is a form of vaginal examination or surgery); second, in terms of the information about consenting, which impacts on the person's decision to consent (for example, a doctor falsely states that sexual intercourse is a necessary part of a patient's treatment). In the first instance, the person does not know what they are agreeing to; in the second, they are misled as to the reason for doing what has been agreed to (Archard, 1998). We see more of these types of fraud in Chapter 11 in the context of the digital realm.

The concept of legitimate consent based on sufficient information is an element that continues to feature in criminal cases of sexual violence. For example, in England and Wales, Jason Lawrance was convicted of raping two women after he falsely told them he had had a vasectomy; he was given leave to appeal his conviction in March 2020 (Lowbridge, 11 March 2020). In a similar case, a man agreed to withdraw from vaginal intercourse before ejaculating; here, the High Court ordered the Crown Prosecution Service to review the decision to not prosecute the man for rape (*R (on the application of F) v. The Director of Public Prosecutions and 'A'* [2013] EWHC 945 (Admin)). It is unknown whether or not the man was in fact prosecuted (Lowbridge, 26 September 2019). Misinformation about gender identity has also resulted in convictions for sexual offences, as we will see in Chapter 11.

Other examples of invalid consent have included instances where partners have refused to use a condom, which was one of the issues under consideration in the extradition case against *WikiLeaks* founder Julian Assange. The ruling stated that sex without a condom would be a sexual offence in England and Wales if the partner had only agreed to sex with a condom (*Assange v. Swedish Prosecution Authority* [2011] EWHC 2849). Such a ruling raises questions about the consequences of the sexual behaviour known as 'stealthing', which involves a man agreeing to use a condom and then non-consensually removing the condom without the knowledge of their partner. We discuss 'stealthing' in more detail in Chapter 14. Similarly, men who have infected sexual partners with HIV after not using a condom, despite being aware of their HIV status, have been convicted of causing grievous bodily harm (BBC, 18 April 2018; 30 October 2018). In these instances, the men were not convicted of sexual offences based on lack of consent, but rather of a non-fatal offence against the person because of the physical **harm** caused to the people infected.

However, not all forms of misinformation or fraud are deemed to invalidate consent. In *R (oao 'Monica') v. DPP (Admin)* [2018] EWHC 3508, the judicial review of the decision by the Director of Publice Prosecution not to prosecute a former police officer for rape, R believed that she was having a sexual relationship with a fellow environmental activist, when the man was actually an undercover police officer spying on the protest group she was a member of. R contended that her lack of knowledge as to the officer's true identity vitiated her consent to sexual relations. The review found against her, ruling that fraud in consent related to sexual intercourse itself rather than the broad circumstances surrounding it. As such, under English law being deceitful in identity is not sufficient to invalidate consent. We discuss the ethics of police officers having sex while undercover in detail in Chapter 5.

BOX 4.1

Consider the case of R *(oao 'Monica') v. DPP (Admin)*, reflect on and discuss the following:

- Do you think the ruling was correct and that consent to sexual activity is not invalidated by fraud in the wider circumstances?
- What forms of fraud would make consent invalid in your opinion?
- At what point in miscommunication, and what actions, would invalidate sexual consent?

The limits of consent

In 1987 in Manchester, England, the police intercepted a video tape which appeared to show the sadomasochistic torture of a group of men (we discuss bondage, domination, submission and sadomasochism (BDSM) further in Chapter 9). The video, the police feared, was a film that actually showed the murder of some of the men. Beatings, penile lacerations and what appeared to be other genital injuries featured on the tapes. An investigation called Operation Spanner was launched to try to find the men, to identify the victims and to prosecute the perpetrators. Once identified, the 16 men who participated in the BDSM acts all readily confirmed that they consented to the sex and the acts of violence inflicted on each other, that they did not need medical attention, and therefore, they argued, that no crime had been committed. Nevertheless, the police prosecuted, and the men were convicted of the offences of assault occasioning actual bodily harm and wounding with intent. The men appealed their convictions to the

Court of Appeal, then the House of Lords, and then to the European Court of Human Rights, on the basis that the acts were committed in private and that all participants, including the 'victims', consented to the violence. The Lords dismissed the appeal and upheld the men's convictions, ruling that the consent of the participants was irrelevant as 'deliberate infliction of actual bodily harm during the course of homosexual sadomasochistic activities should be held unlawful' and consent is not a defence to unlawful acts that result in bodily harm (*R v. Brown* [1993] 97 Cr App R 44 at 45). The dismissal of the appeal raises questions about the limits of consent to violence and to sexually gratifying acts. In exploring the issue, the Lords named a number of situations in which consent of the victim would be a defence to acts causing bodily harm: surgery, ritual circumcision, tattooing, ear-piercing, violent sports including boxing and parental chastisement.

What is interesting about the ruling is that the court confirmed that certain behaviour that could result in serious bodily harm, notably boxing, could be lawful if the wounded party consented to the violence, while BDSM sexual activity resulting in bodily harm could not be. To contextualise this judgement, let us take a look at some of the consequences of the bodily harm inflicted through boxing: a sport that is premised on the ability to hit one's opponent as hard and as often as possible so that you are the last (wo)man standing. One of the forms of bodily harm that has received considerable attention in recent years is chronic traumatic brain injury (CTBI), also known as chronic traumatic encephalopathy, which shares many characteristics with Alzheimer's disease. Symptoms of CTBI present years after the brain injury was sustained following the act of violence, but at a far younger age than most people develop Alzheimer's. Barry D. Jordan (2000) argues that CTBI associated with boxing occurs in approximately 20 per cent of professional boxers, while Lundberg (1985) puts the figure closer to 70–87 per cent of boxers who participate in many fights.

Considering the severity and long-lasting bodily harm that is known to be inflicted through boxing, it is appropriate for us to question the basis of the judgement in *Brown*, where the men involved in the BDSM sexual activities stated there was no long-term injury to any participant. To assist us, let us look at some of the comments made by the judges in the ruling. Lord Templeman stated:

> The violence of sadomasochistic encounters involves the indulgence of cruelty by sadists and the degradation of victims. Such violence is injurious to the participants and unpredictably dangerous. I am not prepared to invent a defence of consent for sadomasochistic encounters which breed and glorify cruelty … Society is entitled and bound to protect itself against a cult of violence. Pleasure derived from the infliction of pain is an evil thing. Cruelty is uncivilized. (*R v. Brown*, at 52)

And Lord Lowry argued:

> Sadomasochistic homosexual activity cannot be regarded as conducive to the enhancement or enjoyment of family life or conducive to the welfare of society. A relaxation of the prohibitions ... can only encourage the practice of homosexual sadomasochism, with the physical cruelty that it must involve (which can scarcely be regarded as a 'manly diversion'). (*R v. Brown*, at 67)

Thus, by rejecting the possibility that people engaging in BDSM can use the defence that they consented to acts of violence, the Lords transformed intimate sex acts where adult men are consenting to, apparently, risky sex on their own terms into one that is a social problem that menaces civilisation – the family, society – itself. This view of BDSM is in contrast to contact sports, in which the violence perpetuated is deemed to be legal and the activity socially acceptable and in the public interest, despite the high levels of long-term injury (Farrugia, 1997).

BOX 4.2

Reflect on *R v. Brown* and consider why the courts may have come down so forcefully on these acts of consensual BDSM sex:

- Is violence within sexual activity acceptable if consented to by all parties? If so, is there a line where acceptability ends? Should it be criminalised? If so, which behaviours should be legal and which illegal?
- Should we have the ability to consent to violence when conducted in the context of **sexual practice**?
- What assumptions did the House of Lords make about what sorts of sex, and violence within that, are acceptable?
- What sort of consensual sex do you think merits criminal justice intervention?
- What do you think the House of Lords may have been influenced by?
- How far do you think that the outcome of the case was influenced by the fact that it was a case of homosexual sexual practice?

What does consent even mean?

So far in this chapter, we have examined the three factors required for consent to sex to be valid: capacity, freedom to decide, and a clear understanding of the consequences. We have also seen that each of the factors that lead to and make up consent are not without grey areas nor challenges in comprehension. Such difficulties in defining and then delivering consent in sexual relationships go a long way towards explaining why sexual violence continues to be so prominent. Current figures from England and Wales indicate that one in five women will experience some form of sexual violence at least once in their lifetime (CSEW, 2018). In the USA, it is estimated that one in six American women will be the victim of an attempted or completed rape at least once in their lifetime (RAINN, 2019). However, it should be noted that these statistics are likely to be low compared to the number of actual instances (Home Office and Ministry of Justice, 2013). Furthermore, contrary to popular belief, the vast majority of rapes do not occur between strangers, in a dark alley, with the perpetrator holding down the victim/survivor who is struggling and screaming for help. Instead, approximately 90 per cent of victims/survivors of rape know the person who raped them prior to the attack (Home Office and Ministry of Justice, 2013), and much sexual violence occurs within established relationships and between people who have had previous sexual encounters with each other.

It is the interpersonal nature of rape that has been the focus of much of the feminist research from the 1970s to date. Many second-wave feminists see rape as the logical conclusion of relationships between men and women within patriarchal society. Within this scholarship, male sexuality is located as the foundation of sexual violence. As such, these feminists reject the argument that rapists are crazy, sadist psychopaths, arguing instead that they are normal everyday men (our brothers, friends, colleagues) who use sexual violence to dominate women. The domination of women is a product of cultural ideas around masculinity and the idea that a 'real' man will be strong, domineering and superior to women (see Russell, 1975). This perception of masculinity is often referred as **'hegemonic' masculinity** – the normative standard of heterosexual masculinity, which endorses an ideology of male domination. First theorised by R.W. Connell (1995), the principle is that masculinity is not a fixed entity but is negotiated and practised in varying ways within different contexts; as such, there is not one masculinity, but many. Within this understanding of men and masculinity, sexual violence is understood to be part of what it means to be a 'real' man in **Western** society: given the 'social privilege of masculinity', sexual abusers feel that it is their right to exercise power over women, because they are 'authorised by an ideology of supremacy' (Connell, 1995: 83).

If we accept these feminists' arguments that rape is a product of masculinity and male domination over women, then our understanding of consent as a means of defining whether sex was legal or illegal, or 'good' or 'bad', becomes even more complex. As Susan Brownmiller (1975) argues, popular belief holds that it is in the nature of men who fulfil the ideal masculine role (hegemonic masculinity) to penetrate and dominate women in acts of sex, while it is the woman's role to either 'resist' or 'submit'. Therefore, it is not the actions of the man that society and criminal justice use to determine if sex was actually rape, but the woman's as to whether or not she consented to the domination and penetration. Using such arguments, some feminists have concluded that the concept of consent is in effect redundant for women when engaging in sexual activity with men.

Catharine MacKinnon (1989) is one of the leading radical feminist scholars to make this point, arguing that the concept of consent is futile as women are socially denied the right to refuse sex as they lack an entitlement to bodily integrity and protection from sexual violence. Furthermore, society considers that women often routinely consent to violent or forceful sex and this belief frames societal perceptions of women's responses to sexual advances. MacKinnon argues that violence underscores all heterosexuality and that the threat of violence is everywhere for women within patriarchal society; as such, women's submission to men's desires is interpreted as an act of consent, which makes consent meaningless. For example, the woman who goes on a date and then agrees to have sex due to concerns over the man's response and actions which may ensue if she says 'no' is *technically* consenting, but she does not actually *want* to have sex and is being forced to through fear of saying no and wider social pressures and assumptions of heterosexuality. As Robin Morgan (1980) argues:

> Rape exists any time sexual intercourse occurs when it has not been initiated by the woman out of her own genuine affection and desire ... Anything short of that is, in a radical feminist definition, rape. Because the pressure is there, and it need not be a knife blade against the throat; it's in his body language, his threat of sulking, his clenched or trembling hands, his self-deprecating humor or angry put-down or silent self-pity at being rejected. How many millions of times have women had sex 'willingly' with men they didn't want to have sex with? Even men they loved? How many times have women wished just to sleep instead or read or watch 'The Late Show'? It must be clear that, under this definition, most of the decently married bedrooms across America are settings for nightly rape. (1980: 134–5)

Such arguments by radical feminists have been challenged on numerous grounds, partly due to the lack of intersectional analysis. Nevertheless, the ideas have remained prominent in research around rape, consent and willingness to have sex. It is also important to note that arguments that consent is either not possible or is not a useful conceptualisation for thinking about positive sexual experiences, are rarely accompanied by calls for the law to be broadened in order to encompass further instances of 'bad' and therefore illegal sex. Even MacKinnon (1989) believes that it is culture that needs to change, not increased criminal justice involvement. Similarly, Robin West (1996) has highlighted concerns about possible changes to the legal definition of rape in the USA (at the time she was writing, most states in the USA required sex to be both forceful *and* non-consensual in order to be legally defined as rape). Changing the legal definition would potentially result in wide examples of 'immoral' sex being classified as criminal.

BOX 4.3

To explore West's (1996) argument about the distinction between non-consensual and non-forceful sex, consider whether you think the following situations should be captured under criminal law as illegal forms of sex:

- Dario would rather not have sex, but Soraya really wants to and uses her hand to arouse him. He agrees because it is easier to say yes than say no.
- Pablo agrees to have sex with Milo because he believes Milo is clearly expecting it after buying dinner.
- Chris knows her boyfriend, Rob, gets really 'unpleasant' when she does not want to have sex – aggressively throwing things around the room, giving her the silent treatment and starting arguments – it's easier just to say yes.
- Precious told Daniel that she was single, and they started a sexual relationship on that basis. Later, Daniel finds out Precious is in fact married and so she has both lied to him and put him in a position whereby he is now facilitating her affair.
- Helen believes sex should only occur in committed relationships and so waits to have sex with Ayesha until they are both committed enough to say they love each other. After they have sex, Ayesha tells Helen that she does not really love her, and the relationship is over.
- Wallace tells Rita that he is a pilot and that he spends his days flying around the world. Several weeks after they have had sex, Rita finds out he is actually a postal worker; she believes she would not have slept with him if she knew the truth about his career.
- Shuab tells Jolene that he is a virgin and she has sex with him without a condom for that reason. Later, she finds out he was lying.

In questioning whether such examples of immoral sexual practice should be criminal, West (1996) concludes that widening legal definitions and therefore bringing more of this problematic sexual practice under the control of criminal justice does not necessarily mean sex will get any better, for women in particular. There are still many harms created through consensual sex, which may be legal while nevertheless being incredibly problematic and distressing for those involved (Gavey, 2019; West, 1996).

The idea that consent may not be a helpful concept in determining good experiences of sexual relationships is one that in recent years has taken hold in research, particularly feminist research, around rape and sexual violence. For example, Zoe D. Peterson and Charlene L. Muehlenhard (2007) argue that the principle that sex is either consensual and wanted or non-consensual and unwanted leaves no room for ambivalence between the two. As such, they propose a quadrant approach in which consenting and wanting are understood as distinct, albeit interacting dimensions. While this model provides us with a more complex framework by which to understand how and why people engage in sexual activity, it does, as Emily J. Thomas and colleagues (2017) argue, present a problematic view of positive sexual relationships. In their research, Thomas et al. (2017) refer to 'problematic' sex, defined as women who agree to take part in sex that they do not want. However, the researchers outline that the term 'problematic' cannot clearly capture the experiences of women. Without adequate language to enable women to speak about and describe these sexual experiences, either for themselves or when attempting to articulate to their male partner, unwanted yet consensual sex will continue. The research conducted by Thomas et al. originated as an exploration of women's accounts of feigning sexual pleasure (faking orgasms) when having sex with men. However, very quickly the research team determined that, despite participants being recruited to discuss consensual sex, all women in the sample spoke about unwanted/unpleasurable sex and connected the practice of faking an orgasm to problematic sex in order to end the sex and to 'get it over with'. A key conclusion of the research is that women often find it easier to consent to and partake in sex that they do not want than to say 'no' to their male partner. Refusing to have sex is not culturally normative and expectations that intercourse *should* happen and a belief that consenting to intercourse is *necessary* to maintain the relationship, are key considerations in women's decisions to consent to sex against their desires (against their will?). In such situations, faking an orgasm is seen as a reasonable solution to problematic sexual encounters. These findings highlight the extent to which heterosex follows a script which prioritises male pleasure, and where the male ejaculatory orgasm signifies the 'end' of sex, in which women are unable to finish sex outside of this culturally normative 'ending'. Indeed, how many films have you seen, or books have you read, where the grunt of the male orgasm signifies the end of sexual intercourse for everyone? Moreover, within this script, a woman's orgasm is asked only to denote a man's sexual expertise and abilities (Thomas et al., 2017).

While the practice of faking an orgasm for sex to end may offer an in-the-moment solution for women, as Thomas et al. (2017) argue, there are negative psychological and physiological effects of consensual but unwanted sex, including that it exacerbates women's difficulties in articulating and making sense of these problematic sexual experiences. Furthermore, as participants in the study used the same discursive structures to describe a wide range of sexual experiences, from wanted-yet-unsatisfying sex, to unwanted, unpleasant and often painful sex, all characterised it as 'problematic' sex, there is a blurring within these understandings of negative experiences of sex:

> When wanted and consensual yet disappointing/unsatisfying, sex is talked about in the same manner as experiences of unwanted and/or coercive sex and sexual assault, unwanted experiences may be at risk of being passed off as simply not pleasurable. Within dominant constructions of sexual assault, which dichotomize sex as either consensual and wanted or non-consensual and unwanted (rape), all other experiences that do not meet either definition may be dismissed as 'just (bad) sex'. (Thomas et al., 2017: 296)

It is for this reason that scholars such as Beres (2018) have concluded that we need to move beyond the concept of consent, as it is too low an operating standard. However, these scholars do not suggest that we should broaden the definition of rape in criminal law to capture such sexual practices, but rather that we should develop sexual education about sexuality and sexual violence prevention in order to prevent harm through sex. Beres argues that we need to address the normative constructions of heterosex itself and the ways that it provides a scaffolding that supports rape (see Gavey, 2019).

One attempt that has been made to address the challenges of the problematic nature of consent and how this is understood and communicated is through the concept of 'affirmative consent'. This mechanism seeks to work to rewrite the scripts of consent, so that consent violations are not simply put down to a misunderstanding of signals or because there was no outright 'no' delivered during the encounter. Rather, affirmative consent requires clear and explicit consent communication – a clear yes – and it is the responsibility of all individuals to ensure that those participating in the sexual activity have actively communicated consent and continue to do so throughout the sexual activity. Furthermore, campaigns promoting affirmative consent have operated on the basis that consent is positive, good and sexy (compared to non-consent, which is bad and non-sexy), thus eroticising the consent negotiation process. The key message of affirmative consent is a move away from 'no means no' to 'only yes means yes' through words and actions (Gotell, 2008). Such campaigns to address sexual violence have been prominent on college campuses in the USA. However, as Kristen N. Jozkowski (2016) argues, before an affirmative consent policy can be effective, an affirmative approach to sexuality is necessary, as consent communication remains largely embedded in gender roles that lead to imbalances and inequalities in consent communication; this is a similar conclusion to that drawn by Beres (2018), Gavey (2019) and Thomas et al. (2017).

BOX 4.4

Considering the discussion of consent that we have explored in this chapter, analyse the following case of Welsh footballer Ched Evans who successfully overturned his conviction for rape on appeal. Think about the case not in terms of whether Evans raped X, but in terms of how consent is being defined and expressed as a concept and what this case can tell us about consent.

R v. Evans [2016] EWCA Crim 452

Evans and his friend McDonald had intercourse with a woman (known in the case as 'X') in a hotel room after a night of drinking. X woke up the next morning naked, alone and confused, with no memory of the night before. After discussing the experience with friends, X spoke with the police. At no point did X say she had been raped; she has always maintained that she does not remember having sex and asserted in an interview with police that she would not have had sex with a stranger. Evans was convicted of rape, while McDonald was acquitted by the jury.

In appealing his case on the basis that his conviction was unsafe, Evans wished to introduce evidence of X's previous sexual history. Inclusion of such evidence is generally prohibited under law, only admissible in specific circumstances under section 41 of the Youth Justice and Criminal Evidence Act 1999 (YJCEA), in order to guard against the twin rape myths that 'unchaste women are more likely to consent to intercourse and in any event are less worthy of belief' (R v. Evans at 44). Evans requested permission from the court to introduce evidence from Mr Owen about his previous sexual activity on a number of occasions with X, where she appeared to be sober enough to consent the night before but in the morning would report that she did not remember what happened and would ask if they had had sex. On one of these occasions, Owen and X had intercourse and during sex X requested they move into the doggy-style position (with the woman on all fours and the man penetrating her from an upright kneeling position behind her) and shouted the phrase 'fuck me harder!' repeatedly while Owen penetrated her. This sexual activity happened two weeks after X reported her sexual encounter with Evans to the police. A further witness, Mr Hughes, was also called by Evans, reporting that he had had sex with X on numerous occasions, including when they first met, and that on several of those occasions they had had sex in the doggy-style position and she had used the phrase 'go harder, go harder'. The appeal focused on the addition of new evidence as support for Evans's claim that X was capable of consenting and did consent. During the appeal, Evans's barrister relied upon what he described as:

> the 'striking detail' of the accounts from Mr Owens and Mr Hughes as compared with the appellant's description. They all describe a woman who in May and June 2011, having been out drinking, engaged in sexual intercourse in a particular way; she was not only an enthusiastic participant, she directed her sexual partners to have sexual intercourse with her

in particular positions including the 'doggie position' and used a distinctive expression demanding intercourse with her harder. Their accounts bear sufficiently close resemblance to the appellant's account as to make the evidence 'so similar' that it cannot be reasonably explained as a coincidence. (*R v. Evans* at 39)

The Court of Appeal found for Evans and overturned his conviction, ordering a retrial. The Court allowed evidence of X's sexual history on the basis of section 41(3)(c)(i) of the YJCEA, as the previous sexual experience of X was deemed by the court to be so similar to the sexual behaviour in the complaint as to be a relevant issue in the case.

At retrial, Evans was found not guilty.

Consider the following questions in line with the details of the case provided here:

- What evidence is there that X had the capacity to consent to sex?
- What evidence is there that X had the freedom to consent to sex?
- What evidence is there that X had an understanding of the consequences of consenting to sex?
- English and Welsh law works under the principle that Evans was required to have a reasonable belief that X had consented to sex: what evidence is there that he had this belief? What evidence is there that Evans should not have reasonable belief of X's consent?
- How helpful is the concept of consent in assessing the nature of this example of sexual activity?
- To what extent does this case reflect 'problematic' heterosex and the challenges of the concept of consent, as outlined by Beres (2018) and Thomas et al. (2017)?

Summary

Within this chapter, we have explored the challenges that come from understanding the concept of consent and applying that concept. Three core elements are required for consent to be present: the capacity to consent; the freedom to say no; and information about what you are consenting to and the consequences of that decision. However, these three elements are not always easy to establish and in certain circumstances may never be established, hence some of the difficulties in determining, interpreting and communicating consent.

As we have seen with the *Brown* case, the law limits our ability to consent, and we, as legal subjects, do not have complete autonomy to consent to whatever we choose, thereby removing criminal sanctions. However, as feminists have argued, the law and criminal justice have been ambiguous in their interpretation of consent, including in instances where women feel uncomfortable about sexual situations but feel compelled or expected to give their consent. This creates a complex situation in which certain forms and interpretations of consent, in certain situations, are considered to be far more relevant and important to the law than others. As we will see in the remaining chapters in this book, interpretations of sexual activity as 'good' and therefore 'legal', or 'bad' and therefore 'illegal', is not an uncommon feature of law and criminal justice.

Review questions

- Think about the shifting ways in which consent has been articulated in law and in academic writing: which do you find most convincing?
- Think about affirmative consent: are you convinced that 'yes' always means 'yes'? Are there any limitations to this?
- Think about the sex education you have received in your life (if any): what were you told about consent? What information should effective sex education about consent include?

Other chapters that this links to

Chapter 3 (Sex and crime in time and space)
Chapter 5 (Sex and institutional cultures of abuse)
Chapter 9 (Pleasurable risk)
Chapter 11 (Digital sex)
Chapter 14 (The future)

5

Sex and institutional cultures of abuse

This chapter will examine different institutional settings in which sex crimes occur. Drawing from case examples of the media, the church and the police, the chapter examines the relationship between sex, crimes and **institutions** as sites of **power** with intrinsic cultures shaped by masculinity and control. As we have seen in Chapter 3 and throughout this book, power and sex are intimately connected. While we established that power is not always necessarily uniform, hierarchical or top-down, we need to recognise that institutions hold significant power as part of the **State** apparatus. These institutions are organised as tight hierarchies; they also display specific institutional cultures that encourage certain modes of behaviour, and, like most institutions, they are male-dominated, or, in the case of the Catholic church, exclusively male.

By the end of this chapter, you will understand more about:

- the way sex crimes occur within certain institutions
- how institutions can avoid accountability by evading criminal justice
- how certain standards of masculinity encouraged within institutions may be conducive to abuse.

In this chapter, we have chosen to focus primarily on cases from the anglophone world, though we do not believe that institutional sex crimes are limited to this world alone. We have also chosen not to focus extensively on the perspectives of victim/survivors. This is not because we do not believe in their centrality. Given that our task is to understand institutions, our focus lies primarily on them and those who operate within them. However, we do recognise that, too often in the context of institutional sex crimes, victim/survivors' perspectives are silenced, and we take this as a point of departure, considering the work of many who have spoken about victim/survivors' narratives and perspectives (see, for example, Chibnall et al., 1998; Frawley-O'Dea, 2004; Hunter, 2010; Swain, 2015; Van Wormer and Berns, 2004). Despite institutional sex abuse attracting more public attention than other forms of power abuse, justice in this domain remains hard to come by.

Power, the State, institutions and control

Power is often expressed through asymmetrical relationships. Non-consensual and unwanted sexual relations involving a range of actions, from unwanted touch all the way to sexual violence and rape, exhibit power asymmetries. In other words, people who enact non-consensual sexual acts towards others hold power over them. This power can be understood as both temporary and long-lasting. Temporary meaning in the moment, during the act, while making a physical imposition; long-lasting because the physical, and especially the psychological, consequences of abuse usually last over time.

In 1959, anthropologist Robert LeVine discussed how the Gusii of Kenya used rape as a tool of social control. In this context, rape was institutionalised, in the sense that patriarchal social structures were maintained via the use of rape, and in that society, at that time, rape was not considered a criminal offence in the way that it is at other times and in other contexts. Hence, rape here can be regarded as an instance of institutional control aimed at maintaining given patriarchal social structures. In Chapter 3, we have seen how marital rape was only legally recognised as a criminal offence in relatively recent times. As such, marital rape was also institutionalised by not being recognised as rape at all. There is a clear relationship between institutions, power, sex and control. As you will see in Chapter 8, rape is used as a weapon of war to subjugate and control, both literally and symbolically. However, this relationship between institutions, power, sex and control is not necessarily straightforward. Different institutional cultures may generate different dynamics of sex crimes and the relations therein.

What do religious institutions, the media, the military and the police have in common? They are all state-sanctioned institutions that are male dominated. Whereas the latter two institutions express the State's laws through legitimate use of force in the name of protection of a given territory and its citizens, the former two institutions are sites where popular beliefs are shaped. Sociologist Max Weber (1919: 1) defined the State as a 'human community that (successfully) claims the monopoly of the legitimate use of physical force within a given territory'. This definition clearly displays the connection between the State, violence (physical force) and control (of a given territory and its citizens). But how does the State attain this monopoly? In part, it does so by social contract, guaranteeing certain rights, services and protection to its citizens in exchange for taxation.

However, the State also obtains and maintains this monopoly via sanctioned institutions. The media informs citizens, but it also shapes culture within the State via the flow of information; it therefore has significant power over how and what information enters the public domain, and what information does not. Religious institutions and the State are, perhaps, not as united and overlapping as they once were. In many Western countries, religious institutions are formally independent from states. Yet, historically, church and State were intimately connected, and the remnants of this connection are still evident today. Religious institutions hold significant power over shaping cultural beliefs. They are also, in many ways, above the law. They have their own internal rules, norms and cultures. What happens within them often escapes the public eye and the exercise of lay justice. The police are an arm of the State; this institution formally exists to protect the public and enforce the State's laws. However, as students of criminology and social science may already be aware, the police have been called a gendered institution, a racist institution and a corrupt institution rife with power abuses.

In this chapter, we ask: what happens when institutional cultures promote and normalise unrealistic expectations of the people they involve? For instance, absolute celibacy by priests, or the normalisation of the use of deception in the police, encouraging police officers to lead double lives when they go undercover?

It seems that the State and its criminal justice system struggle to deal with institutional abuse, in part because these institutions are tied to the very state that delivers criminal justice. If they are not direct agencies of the State, like the police, they have an intimate connection to the State by being part of its broader apparatus. One way of approaching the problem is to understand these institutions' central function as the exertion of control. Sex is a primary way to establish control. An alternative reading is that sex and sexuality pose challenges to people's ability to control themselves. As discussed in Chapter 3, in Michel Foucault's view, 'the political significance of the problem of sex is due to the fact that sex is located at the point of intersection of the discipline of the body and the control of the population' (Foucault, 2000[1976]: 125). In other words, sex is a problematic realm because it is at the centre of states' efforts to control individuals, but also to control entire populations.

To understand the issue of institutional sex crimes, we need to move beyond a simple notion of institutional abuse that places blame on individuals and think instead about what it is about these institutions that makes them sites prone to abuse. For this purpose, we need to ask how power distribution and institutional culture play a role in the normalising and silencing of abuse. As criminologists Chris Greer and Eugene McLaughlin note in their commentary on institutional sexual abuse in the context of corruption:

> It is important to realise that in these institutions ... we find concentrations of status hierarchies and networks, privilege, power relations, vested interests and ideological agendas. They are also places where secrets and lies are monitored and policed, and because of the nature of the crime, where various forms of blackmail take place. (Greer and McLaughlin, 2015: 113)

Thus, we must begin to address the workings of hierarchies, networks, privilege, power relations and cultures in institutional contexts to understand the sex crimes therein.

The silent silencing of institutional abuse

The themes of silence and silencing run across a variety of cases of institutional abuse. It is enough to look at some of the titles of articles in the field to recognise the importance of silence in this domain. Examples include: 'suppressed voices' (Antosik-Parsons, 2014); 'silencing the lambs' (Dixon, 2004); 'silencing violations' (Stanley, 2016); 'the culture of silencing' (Caprioli and Crenshaw, 2017); 'it's not the abuse that kills you, it's the silence' (Downes, 2017); 'first, do not speak' (Warren, 1996); and 'institutional abuse and societal silence' (Middleton et al., 2014). Sociologist Thomas Mathiesen (2005) put forth the concept of 'silent silencing' to explain processes of silencing that are invisible, rather than overtly coercive. Mathiesen conceptualises the process of silent silencing as structural, normalised and geared towards exempting the State and its agencies from responsibility.

Silent silencing is noiseless; it goes unnoticed, so what is silenced is also easily legitimated (Mathiesen, 2005: 14). While reviewing the whole conceptual framework and process of silent silencing is beyond the scope of this book, it is useful to borrow a few ideas from Mathiesen's framework to understand that the process of silencing institutional sex crimes is not necessarily a coercive process. In fact, coercion is seldom adopted by institutions to silence abuse. Often, people who are abused silence themselves by not speaking out; or, they are silenced by the disbelief they encounter from those around them.

When institutions discover that abuse has been perpetrated by people in their ranks, not only are they likely to cover it up, they may also use euphemisms and innuendos to refer to it; they may use the term 'indiscretion', rather than abuse, for example (Fedje, 1990). Not calling something by its proper name is a powerful tool to diminish the gravity of the act. This is part and parcel of the process of professionalisation within institutions. Through this process, 'conceptualisations are gradually simply taken for granted, they become something which is not questioned or doubted, and they become, to the professional, a part of ... "common sense knowledge"' (Mathiesen, 2005: 16). After professionalisation comes legalisation: Mathiesen discusses this process in a juridical context, but this can be easily transposed to an institutional context where matters become sanctioned, or legalised, by the institution. Institutions like the church and the police are, in many ways, above traditional justice and the criminal law; they have their own internal systems and mechanisms of accountability.

Michael White and Karen Terry (2008) argue that institutional responses and accountability structures of the church and the police are too much alike to ignore. They discuss the tendency of both the police and the Catholic church to rely on the 'rotten apple' explanation (first used in the context of police corruption in the 1970s; Sherman, 1978), when matters of abuse and corruption by individuals within institutions come to the surface. Accordingly:

[T]he Catholic Church response to the sexual abuse crisis and how the problem should be addressed parallels the 'rotten apple' assertions often made by police chiefs in the wake of a corruption or brutality scandal. That is, the deviance is a result of a single, rogue officer (or, in this case, priest) who operated alone without organizational knowledge or support. (White and Terry, 2008: 659)

By calling out the rotten apples, the process of individualisation of blame allows institutions not to take responsibility and to continue with business as usual. However, this is not simply a question of bad apples, but rather one of 'bad barrel' (Death, 2015). Historically, within the Catholic church, when a priest was found to have abused members of his flock, the institutional response was to simply move him along to a different parish (White and Terry, 2008) to ensure that this 'indiscretion' did not hurt the reputation of the institution (Dunne, 2004). In this way, countless cases of abuse never saw the light of day, while perpetrators could continue engaging in the same behaviour, only in a different geographic location. Generally, when a police officer is accused of abusing his power, the institution uses its own internal accountability mechanisms to investigate the issue. Police officers can face criminal prosecution. A freedom of information request revealed that several police officers have been prosecuted in England and Wales (BBC, 24 July 2015). Yet, many undercover police officers who established sexual and romantic relationships with the people they were gathering intelligence on have not been prosecuted (BBC, 14 December 2018), and the few prosecutions that were brought forward have been unsuccessful (see also Chapter 4). This is not limited to the church or the police, but happens in other powerful institutions like the military. Stacy Banwell (2020) discusses how the USA government used the 'rotten apples' explanation to distance itself from the crimes committed by soldiers at Abu Ghraib, thus evading responsibility. While media institutions are subject to the criminal law, to which the most recent conviction of Harvey Weinstein can attest (Aratani and Pilkington, 11 March 2020), cover-ups and silence remain rife, as we will see in discussions about the BBC in the wake of the Jimmy Savile scandal (see Chapter 12; Greer and McLaughlin, 2013).

The media: sexual abuse 'scandals' revealed

Sexual scandals involving public institutions are rather common. In the style of the 'rotten apples' explanation, they are often depicted by the mainstream media as isolated incidents involving deviant, predatory or even sick individuals. Rather than seeing scandals as isolated incidents, we should consider the notion that such scandals are *systemic* issues, whereby power concentration opens up the possibility for power exploitation within specific institutional *cultures*.

The uncovering of sexual abuse scandals within institutions has increased over time, in tandem with their lessening social acceptability. In other words, we have moved from a society where sex abuse involving less powerful people was *silently silenced*, to one where abuse is increasingly called out and investigated. According to Kathleen McPhillips (2016: 35), 'cultural shifts around discourses of sexuality and childhood in late modernity [have] engendered a "culture of disclosure"'. As we will also see in Chapter 12, such shifts are underpinned by developing social awareness of the rights of children and feminist activism, which have contributed to the creation of specific language that allows us to recognise and explain abuse, as well as identify the (patriarchal, capitalist) framework(s) within which abuse takes place.

BOX 5.1

There are many historical sex scandals. Let's think about a story many of us are familiar with: that of Henry VIII and his six wives. This story has resonance and important consequences, for example in instigating the separation between the State and the Catholic church in England and Wales. Let's leave that to one side and instead reimagine the story for a more contemporary reading:

- How would we explain and understand the story today?
- Would it be a sex scandal plastered all over tabloid newspapers?
- What if we read Henry VIII's story through a twenty-first century feminist lens?
- Would we talk about femicide?
- Would we talk about institutional power abuse?
- Would we talk about sex crimes?

In Anglo-American culture throughout the nineteenth and twentieth centuries, the liberal media turned sex scandals into a popular news genre (Gamson, 2001). The professionalisation of journalism in the liberal age has helped to reveal institutional sex scandals and to read them in a new light. The rise and establishment of the liberal press and the tradition of investigative journalism and 'speaking truth to power' has been a key mechanism for uncovering abuse; however, there are severe limitations to this, because the uncovering of abuse does not translate into a seismic shift in institutional cultures. Western criminal justice systems generally struggle to deal with structural issues, focusing instead on individual blame (Douglas, 1992). Individual freedom as a value is inscribed in Western criminal justice, so much so that one of the ways in which we punish people is to deny them their individual liberty: to imprison them (see Chapter 2). Western criminal justice systems are therefore not very well equipped to deal with structural or systemic issues that underpin crime, particularly if the crime takes place within powerful institutions that are supported by the State and reflect dominant cultural discourses, including patriarchy.

Feminists the world over might be celebrating the conviction of Harvey Weinstein (sentenced to 23 years' imprisonment by a New York judge in March 2020), but whether this exemplary sentence will shift the culture of abuse within powerful media conglomerates remains to be seen. Examples of sexual abuse scandals have littered the media for decades. Donald Trump, Jimmy Savile, John Profumo, Silvio Berlusconi, Harvey Weinstein and Jeffrey Epstein are but some of the men involved in the most high-profile scandals of our times. What do these 'scandals' have in common? For one thing, they have all been perpetrated by powerful men within institutions. In each of these cases, these men tried to use their power – in the form of money, status and privilege – to silence accusations of abuse, and often they succeeded. The supposed benevolence of institutions is used to disguise systematic abuse (Greer and McLaughlin, 2017). It is difficult to accept that institutions that are meant to protect, guide and inform us actually fail us, or put us in danger, or abuse us.

In institutional settings, power is primarily deployed through silencing, denial (Cohen, 2001), and by discrediting and delegitimising victim/survivors and their allegations. Institutions can use covert means of silencing, such as offering money in exchange for silence. This may be done through legal means such as non-disclosure agreements, or by controlling what information enters the public domain. The media occupies a paradoxical position here. It is an institution where sex crimes occur, but also the main institution tasked with informing the general public about all things, including sex crimes. Thus, this institution possesses the power to liberate us, by keeping us informed and by 'speaking truth to power', but also the power to suppress and hide the truth by being selective about what it discloses to the public.

While we tend to think about the media as a unified corpus, the media is no monolith. In fact, it contains an array of diverse cultures and traditions within it, ranging from serious investigative journalism, all the way to tabloid news, soundbites and clickbait. Although these different traditions give rise to a diverse media environment, the latter remains 'ruthlessly competitive' (Greer and McLaughlin, 2013: 244). In this environment, scandals function as important income generators for media organisations. The bigger the scandal, the more profile the media organisation may build through it, and the more profit it may generate. While some media sources are regarded as more reputable than others, even supposedly reputable sources such as the BBC can fail to be forthcoming, particularly when the investigative lens is turned on it. For example, in the context of the Jimmy Savile scandal, 'the BBC stood accused by the UK press of being in denial not only about what it knew, but also about its role in enabling and covering up Sir Jimmy Savile's sex crimes' (Greer and McLaughlin, 2013: 244).

Greer and McLaughlin (2015) identify the year 2012 as a watershed moment for the acknowledgement of institutional abuse in the UK public domain – this despite attempts of feminist campaigners, investigative journalists and survivors to bring the issue of institutional sex abuses into the public eye since the 1980s. 2012 was the year the Savile scandal unfolded. Jimmy Savile was a well-known media personality who worked for the BBC in the UK and used his status and privilege to engage in charitable work, or at least this is how most people knew him before 2012. In the space of a few months, and only after his death, his reputation went from much-loved celebrity to predatory paedophile (Greer and McLaughlin, 2013). Crucially, his sexual assaults largely took place on institutional premises, either at the BBC or in care homes that he funded through his charitable work. Interestingly, the accusations ruptured into the public domain via a documentary made by ITV, a competitor of the BBC. The BBC initially denied the allegations.

In their anatomy of institutional scandals, Greer and McLaughlin (2013) distinguish what they call a latent phase, characterised by open secrets, hearsay, gossip and non-legitimised complaints and accusations, from an activated phase, when media organisations start publicly reporting the abuse: the proverbial naming and shaming. While also applied in other contexts (see Eilenberg, 2018), this model was developed specifically in relation to child sexual abuse crimes because they activate scandals more successfully due to their triggering of moral outrage, exploiting the figure of the child as being innocent and in need of protection (see Chapter 12). Institutional denial, which tends to be the initial response, pushes the issue into a 'trial by media' where it is impossible to establish facts: there are only claims and counterclaims (Greer and McLaughlin, 2015). Stanley Cohen's (2001) tripartite denial framework is useful to understand how institutions behave in response to scandals. He distinguishes between *literal, interpretive* and *implicatory denial*, the latter being the most pernicious in the context of institutions. While accepting the facts of the crime itself, *implicatory denial* entails rejecting the significance and implications of the crime and/or its consequences for victim/survivors.

The process of individualising blame – the 'rotten apples' explanation – is one that is repeatedly used by institutions in order to avoid dealing with systemic modes that make abuses proliferate in institutional contexts. For example, Shurlee Swain (2015) has discussed how historical abuse cases in the care sector between the 1940s and the 1980s in Australia were, more often than not, dealt with internally in order to prevent the tarnishing of the organisation's or institution's reputation. Yet, the pattern that was uncovered by subsequent public inquiries is one of systematic and widespread abuse across the care sector (Swain, 2015: 292); a pattern also exhibited by the Catholic church. This pattern is diffuse and can be observed in response to accusations across all the institutions in question and beyond. While in the context of media sex crimes, there have been successful prosecutions in the UK, including those towards famous entertainer Rolf Harris (BBC, 4 July 2014) and celebrity publicist Max Clifford (Halliday, 2 May 2014), these appear harder to come by in other institutional contexts. The abuse perpetrated by the Catholic church, or undercover police officers, has seldom been recognised as a crime by a court of law.

The Catholic church and clerical masculinity

In general, Judaeo-Christian religions shun sex as sin and operate by imposing precise rules about sex, often prohibiting the very expression of people's sexuality, desire and sexual practices. In these religions, and within their institutions, celibacy is generally highly regarded or aspired to, and sex is only considered acceptable for the purpose of procreation (see Figure 1.1 in Chapter 1; Rubin's (1984) The Sex Hierarchy). Sex is completely forbidden to those who preach within institutions such as the Catholic church.

What is it about the Catholic church that makes it a site prone to sexual abuse? While 'most child abuse is committed by lay people, including some parents, close relatives, teachers and sports coaches, and not all is committed by Catholics' (Kenny, 2009: 63): most sex abuse is perpetrated by men in positions of authority within institutional settings (in which we could also include families). Estimates suggest that between 4 and 9 per cent of Catholic priests in Ireland and the USA have perpetrated sexual abuses; though numbers are patchy and studies in other regions are limited, cases have surfaced in Latin America, Africa and Asia (Bingemer, 2019; Conway, 2014; Keenan, 2015; Robertson, 2005; Terry, 2015). A review of the literature on child sexual abuse in the Catholic church worldwide establishes two main strands of research in this field, which can be characterised as individual psychopathological explanations on the one hand, and institutional explanations on the other (Böhm et al., 2014). For the purposes of this chapter, we focus mostly on the latter.

In the aftermath of the 2004 *Boston Globe* 'Spotlight' investigation, where investigative journalists uncovered a sustained pattern of sexual abuse by Catholic priests in the city of Boston, USA, increased international and scholarly attention was paid to the issue of sexual abuse in the Catholic church (Terry, 2015). While social scientists had attempted to investigate abuse prior to this scandal, they had found it difficult to access and gather data (Terry, 2008). A USA survey-based study carried out by scholars at John Jay College of Criminal Justice established the large-scale nature of sexual abuse within the USA Catholic church, finding over 4,392 priests allegedly abusing 10,667 people (Terry, 2008: 549). While getting precise empirical data on the numbers on a global scale has not been feasible, there is sufficient evidence to suggest that this is a global phenomenon (Keenan, 2013; Terry, 2015), and that there is a high 'dark' figure (Böhm et al., 2014), meaning that much crime of this nature is neither reported to nor recorded by the police.

In a review of the psychological and psychoanalytic literature on child sexual abuse in the Catholic church, Kathryn Dale and Judith Alpert (2007) find that among the most common motives underpinning the abuse are institutional power, celibacy, hierarchy and cover-ups. While Dale and Alpert (2007) stress that the 'predator priest' exists, and that he exhibits the characteristics of a 'typical' sex predator, Marie Keenan (2013) reminds us that using labels such as sex predator or even 'perpetrator' is reductive, in this context and beyond. Totalising identities, such as those of 'victim' and 'perpetrator', flatten and simplify the lived experiences of individuals, and homogenise otherwise diverse groups; 'by casting "victims" and "perpetrators" as homogenized groups, each with identifiable symptoms and absolute and unchangeable identities, further social injustices are likely to occur, this time couched in the language of social justice' (Keenan, 2013: xxiv).

Keenan's (2013) psychosocial account of institutional abuse in the Catholic church from the perspectives of perpetrators offers a very insightful take on the issue from a loving, rather than arrogant, perspective (see Chapter 1 for our discussion of this method of analysis). She tells us that there is no evidence that people join the Catholic church to gain access to children for the purpose of sexually abusing them. As such, simplistic, individualising explanations that concentrate on understanding abusers solely as sexual predators miss the point. As we will discuss in detail in Chapter 12, paedophiles and certain kinds of sex offenders are regarded as among the most heinous of criminals in our society; they tend to be labelled and shunned, and little effort is made to understand their motivations or their struggles.

In Joshua Gamson's analysis of sexual scandals, he notes that, in the context of institutions, 'the individual nonconformity to sexual norms may actually reveal a sort of conformity to institutional norms' (2001: 198). Gamson's original intention was different, but this quote is striking nonetheless if taken literally, because it suggests that certain institutional norms may encourage sexual behaviour that is non-normative in wider society. This is particularly relevant in the context of the Catholic church as a closed institution which operates by its own rules and norms. Within these rules and norms, two intrinsically problematic aspects are worth noting: the institutional culture of handling abuse by the church, and the expectations imposed by clerical masculinity. According to Keenan (2013), the Catholic church is a unique cultural case, as it involves only the male gender, while professing the values of chastity, protection, guidance and charity to its flock. These are all values which stand directly in opposition to acts of sexual abuse. Keenan tries to expose a form of organisational pathology whereby centralised leadership, hierarchical structures, lack of public accountability, and expectations of clerical masculinity make for a site where abuse can proliferate. Following Robert Merton's (1968; cited in Keenan, 2013: xxvi) theory of organisational deviance, the suggestion is that routine nonconformity is in fact conforming fully to institutional norms. Here, we return to Gamson's quote above, and Keenan's reasoning, to ask: is abuse inbuilt into this 'pathological' institution that first suppresses sexuality, then hides and condemns all forms of sexual expression?

BOX 5.2

Extracts from 'Gay priests and the lives they no longer want to hide' by the *New York Magazine* journalist Andrew Sullivan:

> Like many solitary gay Catholic boys, I saw in Jesus a model – single, sensitive, outside a family, marginalized and persecuted but ultimately vindicated and forever alive.

> In many ways, the old, elaborate High Mass, with its incense and processions, color-coded vestments, liturgical complexity, musical precision, choirs, organs, and sheer drama, is *obviously*, in part, a creation of the gay priesthood. Their sexuality was sublimated in a way that became integral and essential to Catholic worship.

> The scale of [sexual abuse] in the late twentieth century was extraordinary – but, in retrospect, predictable. If you do not deal honestly with your sexuality, it will deal with you. If you construct an institution staffed by repressed and self-hating men and build it on secrecy and complete obedience to superiors, you have practically created a machine for dysfunction and predation.

> Externalized homophobia: What you hate in yourself but cannot face, you police and punish in others. It remains a fact that many of the most homophobic bishops and cardinals have been – and are – gay. Take the most powerful American cardinal of the twentieth century, Cardinal Francis Spellman of New York, who died in 1967. He had an active gay sex life for years while being one of the most rigid upholders of orthodoxy.

(Sullivan, 21 January 2019)

From reading these quotes:

• What do you think about the suggestion that the Catholic church is, in many ways, a 'gay' institution?

- What do you think the consequences of denying people the ability to express their sexuality might be?
- What further points of reflection can you extrapolate from these quotes?

In his article, Sullivan asks uncomfortable questions about the role of homosexuality in the construction of the Catholic church as an institution. He imagines the church as a place of solace for struggling homosexual youth; those youth who do not fit in by nature of their sexuality may find a safe place that allows them to express themselves, at least in part, despite denying them sexual expression. Repression of people's sexuality in general, and the criminalisation of homosexuality in particular, may have pushed many men to look to the church as a haven for homosexuals and even paedophiles who could not express their deviant sexuality in public and in their social environment. Many might have entered looking for salvation and a cure for their deviant desires, finding instead a culture of abuse and secrecy given by people's inability to fundamentally change or shift their desires.

Going back to Keenan's observations about her interviews with priests, she notes:

I was not in the presence of 'monsters', nor was I in the presence of individuals who had an 'illness'. I began to think there must be more to the abuse problem than 'simply' individual psychopathology, and I began to inquire into the situational and institutional dimensions of the abuse problem. (2015: 65)

While Keenan (2013) tells us that prospective priests do not choose the church because it is perceived as a haven for sexual predators, a finding supported by consecutive studies conducted by John Jay College in the USA (Terry, 2008; John Jay College Research Team, 2004, 2006), it may be that some choose it as a haven for healing their deviant sexual orientation or sexuality. But when the pressures and unrealistic expectations of clerical masculinity are experienced, 'the problem develops systemically and that seminary experience and the ways in which clerical masculinity is fostered and adopted is significant in how this problem comes to be' (Keenan, 2015: 65). The problem is compounded by the institutional leadership's responses to abuse, which, by way of at most denial, at least a degree of secrecy and relocation, are unlikely to put a stop to abusive behaviour by priests. Keenan and McPhillips agree that 'the sociology of gender is largely missing from the research literature on clerical sexual abuse, without which such abuse becomes concerned with risk factors or is relegated to theories of moral deprivation and "evil"' (McPhillips, 2016: 34).

Moving away from an individual psychopathological perspective, Keenan argues that 'clerical men who adopted a way of "doing" clerical masculinity that was built on an idea of celibate perfection were more likely to become the child abuse perpetrators' (2015: 65). To situate the problem in its social and cultural setting, and not in psychopathology, Keenan relies on the power/powerlessness conundrum. She notes that while priests appear to have a dominant position of power in the public domain, they reveal significant experiences of powerlessness and lack of autonomy in their personal lives and in their relationships with their superiors. Interestingly, not all priests responded to these structural issues by way of exploiting their pastoral power to enact abuse. Many priests in Keenan's sample reported to have found healthy and adaptive ways to cope with expectations of clerical masculinity, including having sex with consenting adults, and managing their feelings of guilt and shame by accepting their human frailty. Conversely, those priests who had unrealistic expectations of themselves to fulfil a perfect standard of clerical masculinity were also those more likely to engage in abusive behaviour.

The Perfect Celibate Clerical Masculinity construct put forth by Keenan is useful to understand attempts by clerical men to deny both their 'maleness' and their sexuality. In this construct, intimacy and the female gender are both seen as a threat, and sex is regarded as sin. Men who aspire to this ideal try to become detached and asexual. Following this perspective, 'human perfection is the aim in serving God, and failing to achieve perfection is interpreted as personal failure and must be covered up' (Keenan, 2015: 67). This view of masculinity underpins the institutional culture of the Catholic church; it could be argued that this is what **hegemonic masculinity** looks like in the institutional culture of the church. Despite differences among the group that subscribed to this ideal of masculinity in terms of the extent of abuse perpetrated, all men in this group assumed they would be protected by secrecy, a secrecy assured by both the children and the institution.

Relying on Irving Goffman's (1968; cited in Keenan, 2015) concept of the total institution, Keenan notes how clerics' strategies to manage institutionalisation produce different forms of clerical masculinity. These in turn produce different responses to the problem of sexuality and the emotional realm of the men:

> That some clerics turned to children and young people, that others turn to vulnerable women, religious women, 'consenting' adults, Internet technologies, or indeed to spirituality and God, to meet their emotional and sexual needs, speaks to the variants of clerical masculinity that underpinned each man's embodiment of clerical life and his way of performing priesthood or religious brotherhood. (Keenan, 2015: 71)

In sum, the combination of pastoral power in public and powerlessness in the private realm, coupled with strict institutional hierarchy, secrecy and unrealistic expectations imposed by perfect clerical masculinity, underpin a culture of abuse in the Catholic church. Institutional hierarchy, secrecy and unrealistic expectations also matter in the context of the police, as does masculinity. We could look at the incidence of domestic violence and abuse by police officers as one expression of masculinity, as we do in the context of the military (Chapter 8), and as others have done in other contexts (Goodmark, 2015). Our intention is not to be deterministic about the role of masculinity (Silvestri, 2017); rather, we want to reflect on the interplay of institutional power, secrecy and deceit with unrealistic expectations placed on individuals within an institution. We do this by turning to the case of undercover police officers.

The police and undercover love

Imagine you are an undercover police officer – maybe one day you will be – and as part of your brief, you have been asked to infiltrate and observe an animal liberation activist group. You need to learn about their plans and their tactics. You need to find out when they are going to strike and what weapons they have available to them. Are they planning to get more weapons? You need to get them to trust you. Your superiors have told you to use 'any means necessary' to blend into the group. What do you think this means? What do you think the limits are? Should you get high with them? Should you go vandalising with them? Should you have a baby with some of them?

In 1968, the London Metropolitan Police (colloquially known as 'the Met') created the Special Demonstration Squad (SDS). This squad was tasked with leading undercover operations against animal rights and environmentalist groups. Its unofficial motto was 'By Any Means Necessary' (Cadwalladr, 2013; cited in Spalek and O'Rawe, 2014: 155). More recently, another unit of the Met, a reincarnation of the SDS named the National Public Order Intelligence Unit, came under fire after revelations of the workings of undercover police officer Mark Kennedy. In 2010, Kennedy was unmasked by the environmental activists he was gathering intelligence on during a seven-year long operation which resulted in failed prosecution, 'leaving a trail of collateral damage – up to £1 million lost on the trial, hundreds of thousands wasted on his surveillance work, a community torn apart, lives shattered' (Hattenstone, 26 March 2011). This case received significant media attention, in part due to the length of time Kennedy spent undercover and his romantic and sexual involvements during that time. Box 5.3 contains an extract from an interview with Mark Kennedy, published by *The Guardian* newspaper and conducted by Simon Hattenstone.

BOX 5.3

Did he have to be an incredibly good liar to do this job? 'Yes'. Was he always a good liar? 'Not in that sense. I was lying because it was my job to lie. I'm not a dishonest person. I had to tell lies about who Mark Stone was and where he was from for it to be real'. He pauses. 'To be fair, a lot of the things you do, say and talk about are very much based upon who you are as a person and the places you've been to and the things you've done, because five years later somebody will go, "Ah, Mark, didn't you say you went here?" and you have to remember that. So, a lot of the things I would talk about were pretty true'.

Such deceit was on a different level from what he'd practised on the streets, buying drugs and guns. 'If I'm going to buy a kilo of coke, the dealer doesn't really want to know me that well; it's all about the commodity. But this is different. People don't actually want anything from you – all they want is to know you and be your friend'.

Can you do the job without it mentally unbalancing you? 'I don't know'. Where does Kennedy end and Stone begin? 'Well ... there is no line. You just can't say'. He finally reaches a conclusion of sorts: 'I always have understood and had a concern for the issues I was infiltrating. I don't think you could do this work if you didn't care about the climate'.

Perhaps that is what ultimately made life impossible for Kennedy: he wanted to honour both sides – be the honest cop and the genuine activist. But, in the end, he was caught in the middle, despised as a Judas by both sides.

Consider the following in relation to the extract:

- How would you analyse and interpret what Kennedy is describing?
- What considerations does Kennedy share about his identity during his time undercover?
- Do you think he was confused about who he was?
- Do you think he suffered negative psychological consequences as a result of being undercover?
- Do you think Kennedy is to blame for his actions in this context? Should he be prosecuted?

How should we interpret this case?
  We could argue that undercover policing of this sort represents a raw abuse of power and trust by an agency that is meant to serve and protect the public through policing by consent. If we were to observe this purely from an arrogant perception, we would likely miss the complexity and nuances of individual struggles within institutional settings. At an individual level, the issues

are complex and subtle. How is an individual like Mark Kennedy to balance their commitment to an institution and its predicaments, when the institution is demanding that he behave immorally? How are undercover police officers meant to maintain the boundaries between the personal and the professional? Surely, conducting a life undercover makes such boundaries impossible to sustain. As such, the prosecution of individual undercover officers, even if successful, would do little to change the institutional culture that premised and supported their actions in the first place.

When anthropologists and social scientists conduct ethnographies, they talk of 'going native', which is the tendency for researchers who spend a lot of time fully immersed within a group to become 'like them', developing a strong sense of belonging and allegiance to the group. This leads to feelings of confusion about one's identity. Michael Loadenthal (2014) discusses the issue of 'going native' directly in relation to an undercover police officer's use of sexual infiltration. He first notes how counterterrorism, particularly post 9/11, has been used as a justification by police to infiltrate leftist groups. While these were traditional police targets long before 9/11, as the case of British police infiltrating animal rights groups since the 1970s demonstrates, these groups do not usually display violent or terrorist-like behaviour, which makes their targeting somewhat contentious. Loadenthal (2014) notes how, while groups on the political right are also targeted, the specific activity of sexual infiltration tends to occur more often in the context of left activist target groups than their right-wing counterparts.

Most undercover policing is relatively short-lived, meaning people may go undercover for weeks or maybe months at a time. Conversely, sexual infiltration of environmentalist groups has been characterised by very extensive periods undercover. Establishing sexual relations to gain the group's trust is regarded as a winning strategy for undercover police. To explain the rationale beneath this strategy, Loadenthal (2014: 26) uses Foucault's concept of 'docile bodies', arguing that 'the deployment of undercover police, informants, provocateurs and other clandestine, activist-appearing agents constitute a disciplinary power encouraging a placid populace of self-regulating, inactive individuals'. Traditional, public displays of power have often been used by the police to target activist groups, including heavy-handed physical tactics during protests (Markham and Punch, 2004). Yet, this clandestine use of power represents a more insidious technique of control. Sexual infiltration represents a way for state power to enter a private domain, through an 'invasion of spaces presumed to be beyond state surveillance': the activists' bedrooms (Loadenthal, 2014: 28).

In their exposé of undercover policing in the UK, journalists Paul Lewis and Rob Evans (2013) highlight the significant scale and scope of the issue in Britain. After interviewing several undercover officers, they found that the use of sex to gain trust was part and parcel of the institutional culture of under-cover policing. Anecdotally, as long as no love was involved on either side, sex was seen as a good way for undercovers to gain trust. The assumption here is that feelings can be managed and controlled, in a true 'manly' style. In Britain, nine police officers (including one female) are alleged to have engaged in sexual relationships with activists, with two having fathered children, many cohabiting, and one having married a woman from his target group (Lewis and Evans, 2013). Should we be surprised by these revelations? Basia Spalek and Mary O'Rawe think not. After all, 'in the sexist militarised cultures which inform our dominant world view, it is even a no brainer. Undercover policing is all about gaining the upper hand, developing methods of control of situa-tions and of people. Sex is the ultimate weapon of power' (2014: 158).

According to testimonies by both the officers and the women involved, superiors were aware of sexual relations between undercovers and their tar-gets. Mark Townsend and Tony Thompson (22 January 2011) report that undercover police officers claimed that a culture of undercover love was at least tacitly supported by superiors within the police. Conversely, the Association of Chief Police Officers denied this vehemently, stating that sexual relations between undercover officers and targets is not permitted and consid-ered to be 'grossly unprofessional'. This is an example of institutional trial by media, where there are only claims and counterclaims. One officer in particu-lar discussed how the lack of explicit guidelines and instruction provided to him by the police and his superiors was motivated by a tacit understanding that officers should do 'whatever it takes' to gain the trust of their targets, including engaging in sexual relations, drinking and taking illicit drugs.

Robert Lambert (2014) offers a perspective informed by his experience as an undercover officer with the SDS, which is directly critical of Lewis's and Evans's account. In this reflection, Lambert openly admits to using trust instrumentally while undercover. He also discusses the issue of scapegoating of 'individual front-line public servants' as a classic institutional tactic of deflection. Lambert notes that 'social scientists and criminologists in particular should be well placed to unpack issues of agency, police culture, and organi-sational versus individual responsibility' (2014: 167). He then, somewhat controversially, goes on to suggest that 'the violence carried out by animal rights extremists should be categorised as terrorism', directly justifying decep-tion as a legitimate tool and asking what alternative means the State has to combat violent terrorism (2014: 174–5).

While asking a series of insightful questions about some sections of socie-ty's lack of comfort in accepting undercover operations targeting leftist groups compared to far-right groups, he does not, anywhere in his article, openly engage in discussion about sexual relations by undercover cops. Elsewhere, Lambert was alleged to have had four sexual relationships while undercover. He also fathered a child who in 2019, at age 26, sued the Metropolitan Police, citing psychiatric damages upon discovery that his father was a spy (Evans, 14 May 2019). It is worth noting how, in this instance, a case was brought against the police as an institution, rather than Lambert as an individual. However, in classic institutional scapegoating style, the police have in turn taken legal action against Lambert (Evans, 14 May 2019).

During his time undercover, and despite being married with children, Mark Kennedy had a number of sexual relationships with women in his target group, the longest of which was with Lisa Jones over the course of six years. Officer Jim Boyling spent five years undercover targeting yet another group of environmental activists. Boyling had sexual relations with three women while undercover, without disclosing his real identity. The anonymous campaigner 'Monica' took Boyling to court for rape, indecent assault, procurement of sexual intercourse and misconduct in public office (Evans, 14 November 2018). Monica's case was premised on the issue of consent; her defence argued that, had she known Boyling's real identity, she would not have consented to sex with him. This legal argument, based on consent, was not entirely dismissed, but the judges felt that such a legal reinterpretation of consent was beyond their remit and should be done by legislative, and not juridical, authorities (Evans, 14 November 2018; for a discussion about consent in the context of this case, see Chapter 4). Evans notes that 'undercover officers who infiltrated political groups often had intimate relationships with women without disclosing their real identities. The Crown Prosecution Service (CPS) has prosecuted none of them. The legal challenge by Monica was the first to try to overturn the CPS's stance, and it was unsuccessful' (14 November 2018).

In the case of Lambert, one female activist who had become sexually involved with him, 'Jacqui', characterised her experience as one of 'being raped by the State' (Lewis et al., 24 June 2013). Other women have spoken about a conspiracy to rape or coordinated rape by the police (BBC, 4 March 2019). These are interesting labels because they recognise the roles and responsibilities of the State and its agency, the police, in creating the conditions for and perpetuating the abuse.

- Do you think these women are justified in saying that the State is complicit?
- Have the women been subjected to institutional abuse?
- Have they been 'raped by the State'?

An undercover policing inquiry was set up in 2015 with the aim to investigate undercover police activities in England and Wales since the 1960s (Ellison, 2014). Despite being the subject of harsh criticism from activists and some media sources, undercover policing practices have largely remained outside the realm of public and judicial scrutiny. The inquiry has been slow to progress and, five years later, the first evidence hearings that were due to begin in June 2020 have been postponed in response to the global COVID-19 pandemic (Undercover Policing Inquiry, 17 March 2020). Somewhat ironically, while scrolling the inquiry's official website (www.ucpi.org.uk), you may notice that the documents available for download on the first few pages are in fact penal notices protecting female participants' anonymity. They are Lisa, Naomi, Andrea, Alison, Rosa, Mary, Lindsay, Jane, Jacqui, Monica, Maya, Sara, Bea, Wendy, Lizzie and Jessica.

While we wait for the outcome of this inquiry, it is important to think about what justice might mean in this context. We have seen that prosecutions against individual officers have been largely unsuccessful, and few prosecutions have attempted to implicate the police itself. To reflect on this further, we turn to the question of justice.

What does justice for institutional sex crimes look like?

Earlier in this chapter, we mentioned how, in general, Western criminal justice systems are individualistic in their apportioning of blame, guilt and punishment. As such, they struggle to deal with the systemic and structural issues that are at the core of institutional sex crimes (Gleeson, 2016). This is further exacerbated as institutions can use their power and connection to the State to effectively escape responsibility by dealing with matters internally, often in ways that are not geared towards stopping the abuse, but simply to relieving institutions from responsibility and accountability to the public. How can we seek *institutional* justice when our justice tools are geared to blame *individuals*?

The most common manner of doing justice is the punishment of individuals, following the 'rotten apples' logic. In this way, individuals may face punishment and scorn, but institutions themselves are not addressed as sites of abuse. Then, there are public inquiries and commissions, which are perhaps a little more equipped to at least place individual deviance within institutional contexts. The more novel, and perhaps more interesting, justice initiatives are those that depart from an individualised conception of justice, attempting to address and involve institutions as well as communities. These are informed by the practice of **restorative justice** (RJ), inspired by indigenous and tribal cultures and later incorporated into anglophone criminal justice, and the practice of **transitional justice**, transposed from its more traditional place of conflict resolution contexts. We will briefly discuss these different approaches with examples of their applications, to encourage you to reflect about what you think justice looks like in this context.

The undercover policing inquiry in the UK is but one example of a growing number of commissions and public inquiries investigating institutional sex crimes and abuse in the anglophone world. There are other examples of such undertakings, most notably in Australia (McPhillips, 2016; Swain, 2014; Wright and Swain, 2018) and Ireland (Gleeson, 2016; Keenan, 2015), but also Canada, Norway, Iceland, Sweden, Denmark, Germany and the UK (Gilligan, 2012; Sköld, 2013). Swain (2014) notes that at least 83 public inquiries investigating abuse of children, including child sexual abuse, have occurred in Australia between 1853 and 2013. One issue worth highlighting is this: if public inquiries were an effective justice and accountability tool, then we would have expected to see significant shifts in institutional cultures in the aftermath of inquiries. However, this is not the case. On an optimistic note, Wright and Swain (2018) discuss the recent Australian Royal Commission into Institutional Responses to Child Sexual Abuse as being unprecedented in its depth and scope, and as different from previous inquiries in its attempt to engender institutional change. However, they also note that it is too soon to ascertain its wider effects. A more negative reading about this Royal Commission is offered by Jodi Death (2018), who argues that inquiries and commissions should be configured more critically as governing tools. While assuaging the public's desire for justice on the surface, public inquiries do little to address underlying power asymmetries and continue to marginalise victims/survivors' voices. Anne Marie McAlinden and Bronwyn Naylor (2016) also discuss the limits of public inquiries in delivering justice to victims/survivors of child sexual abuse; they advocate instead for a hybrid system that includes the principles and practices of RJ as a way forward.

Still in the Australian context, Kate Gleeson (2015) discusses *Towards Healing* – a RJ programme led by the Catholic church. Similar programmes have been delivered in-house by the church in a number of countries, partially in response to accusations that the church's approach to justice was legalistic and out of touch with the needs of victims/survivors, and partly also due to the increasing popularity of RJ approaches in criminal justice. While these schemes were heralded as innovative, community-based and inclusive, which stood in stark opposition to previous initiatives lacking victim/survivors' focus, Gleeson (2015) remains critical, questioning whether RJ principles and practices are compatible with the church's modus operandi, including its use of reparations. Is the use of reparations in the form of money compatible with restorative principles? In general, RJ has primarily been implemented in cases that involve individuals. The question remains as to whether RJ can work between individuals and institutions, particularly as institutions hold significantly more power than individuals.

Gleeson argues that 'the Church's use of reparations to resolve liability is incompatible with restorative justice ideals and best practice' (2015: 318). Restorative practices should be underpinned by the principle of voluntariness, while their processes should be geared towards minimising power imbalances. In the case of *Towards Healing*, the church used the language and principles of RJ to its advantage in two ways: by limiting victims/survivors' options and by using reparations. There is a linguistic difference between reparation and compensation, but the actual difference is negligible in the context of the scheme. According to Gleeson, 'the use of "reparations" in Towards Healing to describe payments functions perversely to resolve liability, rather than to compensate for acknowledged harm, while invoking RJ ideals to set the program apart from the civil law as providing better outcomes for victims and, indeed, the community' (2015: 326).

Citing mediator Greg Rooney, Gleeson says that 'some experience reparations as "like being paid for sex"' (2015: 326). From this account, it appears that, while incompatible with the principles of RJ, adopting the language of RJ was compatible with the interests of the church, which exploited RJ principles and practices to resolve liability problems.

A different, potentially promising, approach to justice is transitional justice. Transitional justice has historically been deployed in post-conflict contexts, such as those discussed in Chapter 8, where a given society must reckon with a legacy of conflict, war, human rights violation and even genocide. James Gallen (2016) proposes that this justice framework be applied to sexual abuse by the Catholic church. He notes that this is the only justice framework that does not focus primarily on individuals. Transitional justice has four parts or phases: truth, prosecutions, reparations and institutional reform. As such, it incorporates elements of traditional and restorative justice (prosecutions and reparations respectively) but goes further in its collective involvement and in seeking institutional change. Accordingly, the search for truth is not done by investigators or law enforcement, as it would be in traditional justice, but collectively, by actively involving different groups that have been affected and providing a platform to voice their truth. In some way, it resembles a public inquiry. As such, a transitional justice framework borrows elements from more established justice models to fashion a broader justice process which, crucially, also involves institutional reform as the endpoint. While Gallen (2016) believes in the promising nature of this justice framework, there have been no attempts to implement it in the context of institutional sex crimes to date. Whether advocacy for transitional justice in this context will increase remains to be seen.

Inspired by Margaret Urban Walker's (2006, cited in Gleeson) idea of moral repair for systemic crime, Gleeson (2016) proposes a different notion of justice grounded in feminist institutionalism, offering a way to understand the continued lack of integrity by institutions that perpetrate abuse, and the continued maintenance of the integrity of such institutions by the state. She notes the 'unusually privileged status of the Church ... that is associated with a *de facto* immunity from civil justice in a majority of historical child abuse claims'

(Gleeson, 2016: 780). However, it is also important to acknowledge institutional dynamism in this context, as 'there have been formidable changes to the ways in which formal institutions including police services, the government, the Church and the criminal law' address sex crimes (Gleeson, 2016: 806), slowly incorporating feminist knowledge and praxis, rights-based discourses, and scientific and medical knowledge. This political change is significant, but has not, as of yet, resulted in deep reform that provoked a fundamental shift of the burden of responsibility, and an ensuing justice process, from the individual to the institution.

BOX 5.4

Reflect on these different formulations of justice.
  What are the strengths and weaknesses of:

- Traditional juridical justice systems?
- Restorative justice?
- Transitional justice?

Which do you find most convincing? Which do you like the least? Can you think of other ways of dealing with institutional sex crime?

The tendency for institutions to cover up, deny and silence abuse, and their dealing with matters internally, means that deviant individuals seldom face prosecution. More importantly perhaps, while models of justice that can target and address institutional failings, and not simply the individuals within, do exist at least in theory, they are yet to become established. Ultimately, our individualistic models of justice may be unfit for purpose, and real change in this domain may require transformations beyond criminal justice. For these transformations to begin, we must question the foundations of institutional cultures, including hierarchies, privilege, masculinity, silence and the denial of sexuality. We must also address the frameworks that support such foundations, including the patriarchy.

Summary

In this chapter, we have seen that institutions like the police, the Catholic church and the media hold considerable power through privilege, networks, hierarchies and institutionalised masculine cultures, but also via their authoritative status and their intimate connection to the State. They often use their power to diminish or deny their role in perpetuating sex crimes. They rely on silent silencing and denial to escape responsibility and are in many ways above the law and criminal accountability. Meanwhile, our criminal justice systems are not fit for dealing with institutional crimes, primarily because their instruments are shaped to intervene in the lives of individuals, and not institutions.

However, these institutions are responsible for sex crimes in more ways than one. They are responsible by creating inhumane environments for individuals that operate within them, including by forcing impossible and toxic standards of masculinity and sexuality, allowing individuals to accrue power and privilege that take them above public and criminal accountability, and normalising deception and deceit between people as a professional aspiration. Ultimately, it is these very features of (masculine) institutional cultures that support the proliferation of sex crimes, making institutions into sites prone to abuse.

In recent times, we have seen the engendering of a new culture, underpinned by feminist knowledge, of speaking truth to power and institutional sexual abuse by creating a new language to address and understand it. This new culture is slowly insinuating itself into politics, the media and criminal justice, attempting to use its existing instruments, and seeking to establish new ones, to create new models of justice and bring institutions to account.

Review questions

- Should we class the cases of abuse discussed in the chapter as sex crimes, despite the lack of widespread prosecutions? What would we gain from such a classification?
- What do you think we should do about institutional sex abuse?
- What does justice look like in this context, in your view?
- How do we move forward?

Other chapters that this links to

Chapter 4 (Consent and its discontents)
Chapter 7 (Sexual exploitation and the State)
Chapter 8 (Sex and war)
Chapter 12 (Children, sexualisation and the law)
Chapter 15 (How to change your life)

6

Reproduction, sex and crime

As reproduction can be a consequence of sexual interaction, how the **State** controls and regulates human reproduction is of great importance to our study of sex and crime. Throughout history and across geographical space, we see that societies give considerable focus to controlling and regulating who can reproduce and the impact of that reproduction (see our discussion in Chapter 3). The possibility of becoming pregnant, stopping a pregnancy, trying to become pregnant, ending a pregnancy, carrying a pregnancy, and birth, labour and delivery are all activities that involve state intervention in one way or another. Within this chapter, we are focused specifically on the impact ofstate intervention in pregnancy and reproduction from the perspectives of women who are pregnant and those who may become pregnant.

By the end of this chapter, you will understand more about:

- how ideas of control and choice over reproduction have changed, and are con-ceptualised today
- the ways that the State regulates reproduction through law and criminal justice and how that impacts people differently
- the connection between control and regulation of reproduction and women's rights.

A key theme, when exploring involvement of the State in reproduction and pregnancy, is the concept of personal rights. Reproductive rights are **human rights** (see our discussion of human rights in Chapter 7). As the United Nations (2014: 13) outlines in its publication, *Reproductive Rights are Human Rights: A handbook for national human rights institutions*:

> Reproductive rights embrace certain human rights that are already recognised in national laws, international laws and international human rights documents and other consensus documents. These rights rest on the recognition of the basic rights of all couples and individuals to decide freely and responsibly the number, spacing, and timing of their children and to have the information and means to do so, and the right to attain the highest standard of sexual and repro-ductive health. It also includes the right to make decisions concerning reproduction free of discrimination, coercion and violence, as expressed in human rights documents.

The nature of pregnancy and reproduction means that it is women, rather than men, who are most likely to experience situations whereby state criminal laws and the application of criminal laws through criminal justice clash with their individual rights. As such, the focus of this chapter is on women's experiences of pregnancy and how the law and criminal justice can and do come into con-flict with women's human rights in relation to reproduction. This is one of many areas of state intervention in reproduction that we could focus on. Due to space limitations, we do not have the capacity to explore wider issues; but, at the end of the chapter, we list other areas of study that are of relevance to the topic of state control and reproduction.

Before we begin, it is important we outline relevant terminology. Throughout the chapter, the term foetus is used to refer to a human developing in the womb from the point of conception until birth. The term foetus is used for ease and readability (in American English, it is spelt 'fetus'), but please note that this is not the technically correct term for all periods of gestational development, with different terms associated with different periods of development: zygote (at fertilisation), blastocyst (up to implantation, six to ten days after ovulation), embryo (following implantation) and foetus (from eight weeks until birth). In contrast, we only use the term 'baby' to refer to a child that has been born (either alive or stillborn). We are making this distinction between 'foetus' and 'baby' for a very specific reason – in most legal jurisdictions, the law differentiates between human beings before they are born (and so are *in utero*, meaning inside the uterus of the pregnant woman), and human beings when they are born. As we will see in this chapter, this distinction has a significant impact on how the law works, is applied through criminal justice, and the impact on reproductive rights of all involved.

One further note of caution: within this chapter, we discuss women's inability to access abortion services. This can be a distressing topic, and so we advise caution to our readers, remembering to deploy the self-care techniques we discussed in Chapter 1.

Why is the State in my womb?

There has been a massive shift in how pregnancy is conceptualised, understood and approached over the last 300 years. Today, specifically in what we might call the **Western** world, pregnancy is a highly medicalised and managed state, regulated and monitored by medical professionals with the support of the law and criminal justice. However, this has not always been the case. Prior to the twentieth century and the rise of the medicalisation of reproduction, pregnancy, labour and delivery were generally conducted in the community, and operated as a female-dominated sphere of life (Gowing, 1997). This included advice around how to avoid pregnancy, how to bring on menstruation if a woman's period was late and she therefore might be pregnant when she did not want to be, and support in labour and delivery. During this time, knowledge and understanding of pregnancy was limited. Awareness of pregnancy might be indicated by nausea, increased breast size or signs of 'quickening' (the point at which a woman first feels the foetus move inside her, typically at 15–17 weeks of gestation), but otherwise a pregnancy was unable to be confirmed until a woman's labour was in its final stages. In her study of the history of the medical care of pregnant women, Ann Oakley (1984) argues that the mechanics of pregnancy were unknown, and no body of knowledge or set of techniques to manage pregnancy existed; consequently, there was no rationale for medical supervision.

During the twentieth century, the conceptualisation of pregnancy changed. Medical knowledge developed and pregnancy was pathologised, offering an opportunity for medical surveillance and treatment (Oakley, 1993). Tests to diagnose pregnancy were developed, and the hormonal pregnancy test became available for use by doctors in the 1930s (Oakley, 1984). Pregnancy and childbirth moved from being a female-led, community-based experience, to an **institution**-based, medical experience, managed predominantly by male professionals.

The drive towards the medicalisation of reproduction has been attributed to the professionalisation of medicine, with (almost exclusively male) doctors in Europe and the USA seeing the newly developed areas of obstetrics and gynaecology as key areas where they could demonstrate their professional practice. This solidification of their control on the field of childbirth occurred through presenting (usually female) community midwives as unsafe because they completed tasks that fell outside of 'proper' roles for women; in contrast to medical men who were now presented as being trained, licenced and a legitimate source of medical knowledge (Ehrenreich and English, 2010; Wertz and Wertz, 1989).

The second driver for the medicalisation of pregnancy was a greater focus and concern with infant mortality, and consequently the health of the foetus *in utero* and in labour, and the pregnant woman (Reagan, 2010; Wertz and Wertz, 1989). As part of this, wealthy women sought 'treatments' for labour and delivery that would make the experience both safer and less painful. It was within this climate of women seeking treatment for the symptoms and pains of labour that pregnancy and childbirth became pathologised and considered a 'potentially diseased condition that *routinely* requires the art of medicine to overcome the processes of nature' (Wertz and Wertz, 1989: xvi). As a consequence, labour and delivery were regularly supervised by medics and under medical control. However, as the dominant medical view was that birth would generally progress without intervention and often doctors could not do anything to assist with the birthing, most births continued to occur with limited assistance. Nevertheless, the desire for women to be 'treated' by their doctors led to the development of techniques to 'assist' women to birth a child: for example, the creation of forceps to pull the foetus from the birth canal (an instrument that has developed little since first used in labour and delivery). Use of such techniques in this early period of medical development often did little to increase the safety of childbirth. In fact, it is argued that, while there have been dramatic increases in the number of babies and women surviving childbirth, this may be more due to improvements in general **public health** – child-spacing, housing, hygiene and nutrition – rather than obstetric medicine (Strong, 2000). Furthermore, it is argued that the focus on specialisation in obstetrics has actually made pregnancy more dangerous due to the adverse effects of these interventions in the process of labour and birth (Wagner, 2006). However, what medical interventions did do was to construct pregnancy as a period of danger in which much can go wrong, and so women and society anticipate problems and therefore expect further medical intervention, thus normalising the involvement of the medical community in reproduction (Wertz and Wertz, 1989).

The birth of criminal abortion

Opening up reproduction to the scrutiny and control of medical doctors changed the dynamics not only of how pregnancy is understood, but also of what behaviours are deemed acceptable and appropriate in relation to reproduction, as opposed to unacceptable and inappropriate (if not criminal). One clear example of this is the changing nature of the control and regulation of pregnancy termination. Prior to the 1800s in both the UK and the USA, abortion was either legal or, while technically illegal, was not prosecuted or a focus of criminal justice, particularly in cases of women ending their own pregnancies. Furthermore, the practice of taking herbs and medicines if a pregnancy was suspected was an accepted sexual and contraception practice, particularly prior to quickening (see Luker, 1984 who discusses the USA; and McLaren, 1984 who researches reproductive rituals in the UK).

Doctors (who were overwhelmingly men) played a significant role in the regulation of women's bodies and the process of abortions by lobbying politicians as a further means of obtaining official recognition for their trade. Medical men presented themselves as the only people who had the knowledge, skills and training to determine if the termination of a pregnancy should be allowed and performed for 'legitimate' reasons, as opposed to women in the community who had traditionally offered this form of support in pregnancy and were presented instead as unnecessarily killing unborn children (Keown, 1988; Luker, 1984). The consequence was that abortion became a crime in many jurisdictions around the world, and the conceptualisation of what an abortion is and what it means began to change. No longer was abortion seen as an everyday part of women's sexual and reproductive life. Instead, the ending of a pregnancy was much more closely associated with the killing of a child.

A clear example in the connections made between abortion and a form of killing can be seen in the language of section 58 of the Offences Against the Person Act (OAPA) 1861, which is still in force in England and Wales today:

> Every woman, being with child, who, with intent to procure her own miscarriage, shall unlawfully administer to herself any poison or other noxious thing, or shall unlawfully use any instrument or other means whatsoever with the like intent … shall be guilty of felony, and being convicted thereof shall be liable to be kept in penal servitude for life.

1861 was the first time that the law specifically stated that a woman could be criminalised for ending her own pregnancy. The OAPA 1861 passed with very limited Parliamentary debate, so we have very little understanding as to why self-abortion became a focus at this time. While John Keown (1988) argues that women could have been held criminally liable prior to this point due to self-abortion being a **common law** offence, the very limited number of convictions means it is incredibly difficult to determine if women were ever prosecuted (Dickens, 1966). Other historians have argued that statutes regulating abortion enacted before 1861 were more concerned with abortion providers who caused the death of a woman due to the performance of the abortion, rather than criminalising the ending of a pregnancy. As Angus McLaren (1984) argues, the wording of a previous version of the law was, 'thereby to murder, or thereby to cause and procure the miscarriage of any woman', suggests that abortion was seen as another form of murder in which the woman, not the foetus, was the victim.

BOX 6.1

The idea of when abortion is acceptable is one that is shaped by individual choice and personal perspective. To help explore your thinking, consider the following scenarios and make a note of whether, in your opinion, an abortion would be acceptable in these cases.

Here's a quick reminder of the different gestational stages of a foetus:

- zygote – the union of the human egg and sperm
- blastocyst – the period up to implantation in the uterine wall, 6-10 days after ovulation
- embryo – following adherence to the uterine wall
- first-trimester foetus – from 8 weeks until 12 weeks gestation
- pre-viable foetus – up-to 24 weeks gestational development – the foetus cannot survive outside the uterus
- post-viable foetus – following 24 weeks gestational development – the foetus can survive outside the womb, but may need specialist medical care to breathe, etc
- full-term foetus – after 37 weeks gestational development – the foetus is considered ready to be born.

		Gestational development of the foetus						
		zygote	blastocyst	embryo	first-trimester foetus	pre-viable foetus	post-viable foetus	full-term foetus
Age of the woman	Under 13 years of age							
	Under 16 years of age							
	16-24 years of age							
	25-40 years of age							
	40-45 years of age							
	45+ years of age							

		Gestational development of the foetus						
		zygote	blastocyst	embryo	first-trimester foetus	pre-viable foetus	post-viable foetus	full-term foetus
Nature of relationship	Married/ civil partnership / committed relationship							
	Single							
	Divorced/ Separated							
	In a casual/ non-committed relationship							

		Gestational development of the foetus						
		zygote	blastocyst	embryo	first-trimester foetus	pre-viable foetus	post-viable foetus	full-term foetus
Nature of sex	Consensual and wanted sex in casual relationship/ one-night-stand							
	Consensual and wanted sex within committed relationship							
	Consensual and wanted sex with someone who is not your partner (e.g.as part of an affair)							
	Rape							

(Continued)

		Gestational development of the foetus						
		zygote	blastocyst	embryo	first-trimester foetus	pre-viable foetus	post-viable foetus	full-term foetus
Contraception	No contraception used							
	Condom broke							
	Forgot to take oral contraception							
	Uses abortion as a form of contraception							
	Used long active reversable contraction (such as a coil or IUD) that failed							
	Morning after pill (plan B) failed							

		Gestational development of the foetus						
		zygote	blastocyst	embryo	first-trimester foetus	pre-viable foetus	post-viable foetus	full-term foetus
Health of the foetus	No apparent foetal abnormalities							
	Foetal abnormality resulting in post-birth death							
	Foetal abnormality resulting in severe life-limiting post-birth disability							
	Foetal abnormality resulting in minor post-birth disability (e.g. a cleft palate)							
	When born, the child will have a high likelihood of developing a debilitating health condition (e.g. such as Huntington's disease)							
	Foetus has died in utero							

		Gestational development of the foetus						
		zygote	blastocyst	embryo	first-trimester foetus	pre-viable foetus	post-viable foetus	full-term foetus
Desire to continue the pregnancy	Woman wants to continue the pregnancy but the man does not							
	Woman does not want to continue the pregnancy but the man does							
	Neither the man nor the woman want to continue the pregnancy							
The pregnant woman does not …	want a baby ever							
	want to attend her own wedding while she is pregnant							
	want to attend her sister's wedding while she is pregnant							
	want to be tied to the man who got her pregnant through a child							
	want a foetus of this sex							
	want to be pregnant right now							
	feel they can afford a(nother) child							
	want to disrupt her new job and risk her boss and colleague's negative of her opinion by being pregnant so soon after starting her employment							
	does not want to be pregnant while on her dream holiday							
	feel she has stable enough mental health to look after a child							
	feel she needs to explain her reasons for seeking an abortion to anyone							
	want to be pregnant while at university							

Consider your answers in relation to the following observations:

• Arguments are often made about the morality of abortion becoming more problematic as the foetus develops. Why might we consider the woman's

(Continued)

personal situations or personal factors to be a less valid reason for an abortion as the foetus grows? If life is life, then why is a foetus' life not the same throughout the period of gestation?

- Arguments are often made that young women and girls should be given greater access to abortion than older women. To what extent are such ideas of 'valid' age to have an abortion/ to not have an abortion dictated by ideas we hold of women as 'natural' mothers? And, connected to this, the idea that young women and girls should not be mothers?

- In many legal jurisdictions, abortion is allowed in instances where women can prove they became pregnant after rape, incest, or child abuse, whereas they would not be allowed an abortion if the pregnancy occurred after consensual sex. Why would the woman being a victim of male violence mean she has more right to bodily autonomy and to decide whether or not she continues a pregnancy?

- To what extent do we consider the validity of women wanting an abortion to be connected to her sexual behaviour? Why might we be more critical of a woman who has had unprotected sex with a man she does not know and therefore be considered less 'worthy' of an abortion than a woman who had sex with a long-term partner and used protection that failed to work?

Look back at the table and consider:

- In what instances should a woman be punished if she chooses to end her own pregnancy? What should her punishment be?
- What do you think the consequence of criminalising and punishing women for abortion might be? Think about:
  o   the number of abortions that occur;
  o   the health of women who have abortions;
  o   women's rights.

Abortion and punishment

As a consequence of the OAPA 1861, today it is still illegal for women in Great Britain to self-abort a pregnancy, facing one of the most stringent punishments across Europe: life imprisonment. Yet, in spite of the law, abortion is relatively easy and free to access for most people living in Great Britain. This is due to the passing of the Abortion Act in 1967, which removes criminal sanctions for abortion if it is:

- conducted by a registered medical practitioner, AND
- two registered medical practitioners are of the opinion that the abortion is being conducted for one of the following reasons:

  a. that the pregnancy has not exceeded its 24th week and that the continuance of the pregnancy would involve risk, greater than if the pregnancy were terminated, of injury to the physical or mental health of the pregnant woman or any existing children of her family; or

b.   that the termination is necessary to prevent grave permanent injury to the physical or mental health of the pregnant woman; or

c.   that the continuance of the pregnancy would involve risk to the life of the pregnant woman, greater than if the pregnancy were terminated; or

d.   that there is a substantial risk that if the child were born it would suffer from such physical or mental abnormalities as to be seriously handicapped. (Abortion Act 1967, s1)

The consequence of the law is that, while women are able to access abortion, they do not have a legal right to an abortion – instead, they only have the right to ask two doctors to consider if they will grant an abortion. The law does not decriminalise abortion – instead, it provides legal protection for doctors who perform them within the rules.

Sally Sheldon (2016) argues that the current legal position of abortion in Great Britain illustrates medical **paternalism**, as the law constructs women as being incapable of making a morally significant decision about pregnancy. This legal regulation is out of step with the widely held understanding that women are autonomous people with the capacity and rights to make decisions about their own bodies. Sheldon concludes that criminal controls on abortion are outdated and out of step with modern medical science, serving to hinder clinical best practices. Furthermore, Sheldon argues that the law stigmatises women who need abortions, imposing clinically unwarranted and bureaucratic restrictions on medical practice with no evidence that such restrictions reduce the number of abortions that take place each year. The law would also prohibit the use of new forms of contraception that are being developed. For example, new drug-based regimes are being explored whereby women could take a monthly hormonal pill on a planned schedule close to their expected period of menstruation. Other drugs are being developed that women would take if their period was late, without the need for a pregnancy test. As both drugs would operate around the time of implantation of the embryo in the wall of the uterus (six to ten days post-ovulation), both drugs would be illegal under section 58 of the OAPA (Sheldon, 2015). A national campaign to decriminalise abortion across the UK is now being fought – *We Trust Women* (n.d.).

BOX 6.2

Abortion in the period of crisis

Evidence that current laws prohibit clinical best practice and prevent women from seeking the medical procedure of abortion became apparent during the

(Continued)

coronavirus crisis of 2020. Due to the criminal sanctions on abortion, women requiring early medical terminations need to visit clinics for a consultation and to obtain two pills (the first – mifepristone – ends the pregnancy; the second medication is misoprostol, which causes the uterus to expel the pregnancy). There is no clinical reason why a physical appointment for a medical consultation to determine treatment to end a pregnancy needs to take place in person. Both medications can be taken safely at home by women who have no underlying medical conditions, and a telephone consultation with a woman will determine if home-use of medication is not appropriate for her on health grounds. The only barrier to this safe form of health care delivery is the fact that women (and the clinic staff prescribing the medication) would be breaking the law, and be liable to a life sentence.

At the beginning of the period of national lockdown (March 2020), the British Pregnancy Advisory Service (BPAS) warned that at least 44,000 women would be forced to unnecessarily leave their homes to access abortion services over the next 13 weeks. Furthermore, women with underlying health conditions or living with vulnerable people susceptible to the virus were effectively denied access to abortion due to the need to self-isolate (Oppenheim, 25 March 2020). After initially announcing that telemedical abortion services would be made available, the UK government U-turned on the decision, announcing that the change was 'published in error' (Hern, 24 March 2020). One week later, the government approved home-use of both pills, to be dispatched to women by post after a telephone or e-consultation with a doctor (Mohdin, 30 March 2020).

The period of COVID-19 highlights the extent to which women's abilities to control their own bodies and make reproductive decisions are constantly on a knife-edge. This is not only the case in the UK, but in other countries too, for example the USA (Davis et al., 31 March 2020). Furthermore, the change in government policy to home-use raises questions as to why clinic visits for the medication would be necessary at any other time.

Attempts have been made to repeal section 58 of the OAPA, and thus remove abortion from the criminal law. Two Private Members Bills (bills introduced by Members of Parliament and Peers who are not government ministers) were introduced into the House of Commons in Parliamentary sessions 2017–19. However, both Bills failed to progress due to the calling of general elections in 2017 and 2019 (UK Parliament, n.d.a). At the time of writing, a Private Members Bill (starting in the House of Lords) has passed the first reading (January 2020), with a date for the second reading yet to be announced (UK Parliament, n.d.b). Meanwhile, progress has been made in Northern Ireland, with decriminalisation coming into force in October 2019. The legislation was passed by the UK Parliament because the Northern Ireland Executive and Assembly had not restored itself after it collapsed in 2017 (Northern Ireland Office, 2020).

Northern Ireland had the most restrictive abortion laws in the UK, resulting in over 1,000 women each year travelling to Great Britain to access a termination due to there being no legal provision of services in Northern Ireland unless the life of the mother was at risk (BBC, 13 June 2019). As such, the following story was not an uncommon experience for women in Northern Ireland:

> When it was over, I got dressed, had my biscuits – Crawford's Shorties as I recall – and the car arrived to take me to the airport at about 3pm. All so normal ... I remember chatting to the driver this time, wanting to think about anything else than what had just happened. He asked where I was travelling to. When I told him Belfast he said in a very kindly voice 'we get a lot of passengers from there, it's not right is it?'. I shook my head, tears forming in my eyes, you know the way they do when you are trying to hold something back and just one kind word has you crying. He must have noticed this as he quickly changed the subject to annual holidays. He was a kind man and as we pulled up at the airport he wished me good luck. [It's] funny how small kindnesses make such a difference to you. Once in the airport I had to wait to check in as my flight wasn't till 7pm. I was sore, bleeding, exhausted and all I wanted to do was lie down, instead I had to wait 3 and a half hours till my flight. (Alliance for Choice, cited in Now for NI, n.d.)

Now, no woman in Northern Ireland who ends a pregnancy up to 24 weeks of gestation will be at risk of prosecution. As of 31 March 2020, a new regulatory framework is in place which allows lawful access to abortion services without conditionality for the first 12 weeks of pregnancy. Abortions beyond 12 weeks of gestation are lawful in cases where:

- The continuance of the pregnancy would involve risk of injury to the physical or mental health of the pregnant woman or girl, greater than the risk of terminating the pregnancy up to 24 weeks gestation.
- Severe foetal impairment and fatal foetal abnormalities without any gestational time limit.
- There is a risk to the life of the woman or girl, greater than if the pregnancy were terminated, or where necessary to prevent grave permanent injury to the physical or mental health of the pregnant woman or girl, including in cases of immediate necessity without any gestational time limit. (The Abortion (Northern Ireland) Regulations 2020, regs 3–4)

While this is good news for the women of Northern Ireland, at the time of writing, women in Great Britain continue to face imprisonment for ending their own pregnancies at any stage of gestation, and thus are denied the right to control their own bodies.

In terms of the application of the law, prosecutions under section 58 of the OAPA most often comprise men who attack pregnant women, causing the foetus to die (Sheldon, 2016). Very few women are ever prosecuted for the offence. The lack of criminal justice use of this law occurs despite evidence that numerous

women are obtaining illegal abortions each year. In 2017 it was widely reported
that 645 abortion pills were seized in 2015 and 2016 on their way to addresses in
England, Wales and Scotland (Kirby, 15 February 2017). The small number of
women who have been prosecuted for procuring their own miscarriage (two in
the last 20 years) have terminated a foetus in the very late stages of pregnancy
after buying drugs via the Internet and giving birth to a foetus that may have
been born alive (Sheldon, 2016). However, as Emma Milne (2020a) has argued,
we should see these cases not as an abortion, but as a form of foetal homicide.

Foetal homicide is a term used to describe the intentional killing of the foetus; most often this is conceptualised as a foetus that is viable and therefore
able to survive outside of the uterus. As Milne argues, foetal homicide is conceptually different from the ending of a pregnancy. The ending of a pregnancy –
an abortion – is a common medical procedure that one in three women in the
UK will experience at least once in her lifetime (NHS, 2016). The vast majority
of terminations – nine out of ten – are carried out at 12 weeks of gestation or
less, and 80 per cent are conducted before the 10th week of pregnancy.
Abortions that occurred at or after the 24th week of pregnancy (the point of
viability, when the foetus can survive outside of the womb) totalled 289 in
2018: 0.1 per cent of the legal abortions that occurred (Department of Health
and Social Care, 2020). Abortion is a widely accepted medical procedure;
76 per cent of Britons believe that abortion should be legal in most or all
circumstances and 2 per cent believe abortion should always be legal (Wells
and Thompson, 2011). As Sheldon (2016) argues, the law does not prohibit
abortion, rather it prohibits abortions that are not conducted in line with
the Abortion Act 1967. While the few women who have been prosecuted
for procuring their own miscarriage have, technically, committed the act
of illegally ending their own pregnancy (due to being conducted outside of
the Abortion Act), their behaviour should be seen as different to the vast
majority of abortions that take place every year (Milne, 2020a). It is on this
basis that Milne argues that women who act to end their pregnancies in
the late stages of gestation should be deemed to be committing foetal homicide, rather than an illegal abortion. It is not unlikely that, in these situations,
the foetus would be born alive and then killed or allowed to die after birth,
so, conceptually, is a very different situation to an abortion. However, even
with this conceptual difference between an abortion and foetal homicide,
Milne (forthcoming) is critical of the use of laws to punish women who kill
foetuses, even in the late stages of pregnancy. In her analysis of contemporary
cases of women convicted for illegal abortions in England and Wales, she
concludes that women who take such steps to end a pregnancy are incredibly
vulnerable and are experiencing a pregnancy that causes them a fundamental
life crisis: a crisis pregnancy. In such circumstances, Milne questions what
purpose conviction and punishment serve, as women only end up in the situation of illegally ending their pregnancy, and therefore killing a viable foetus,

due to lack of support from the State to assist them with their reproductive choices and wider social problems (such as mental health issues and experiences of abuse; Milne, 2019).

Milne (2020a) further criticises criminal justice use of the offence of procuring a miscarriage in these cases due to the structure of English and Welsh law. In this legal jurisdiction, the killing of a foetus is not considered an act of homicide (murder, manslaughter or infanticide) as foetuses are not protected under law as people who are born. The differing legal protection for foetuses is due to them not being a 'reasonable creature *in rerum natura* [in existence]' (Coke, 1644[1681]: 50–1). The protection of law is only granted to a person once they have been fully born (completely expelled from the birth canal) and are alive (see Milne, 2020a). The only crime that can be committed against the foetus is child destruction – the killing of a child capable of being born alive, only applicable after the woman has been pregnant for 28 weeks. As with procuring a miscarriage, this offence is mostly used to prosecute men who attack pregnant women, causing a miscarriage or stillbirth (Sheldon, 2016). As we will see in the next section, in other legal jurisdictions foetuses have been granted legal personality, which has significantly changed the experience of being a woman of reproductive age.

Pregnancy, bodily autonomy and legal personality

Compared to 50 years ago, the United States of America is now a very different legal landscape for pregnant women and for women who could become pregnant. Two key and interrelated developments have occurred. First, the legality and accessibility of abortion services has changed. Second, in most states, foetuses have been provided with legal personality, meaning they can be victims of crimes before they are born alive. In this section, we will explore both developments and consider the implications for women's rights and for wider society.

Abortion in America: from 'choice' to 'justice'

As outlined above, abortion was only criminalised in states in the USA during the 1800s. The campaign to decriminalise was hard-won and long-fought, and it was not until 1973 that the Supreme Court ruled in the landmark case *Roe v. Wade* 410 U.S. 113 (1973) that outright abortion bans by state legislatures were unconstitutional. Prior to *Roe*, abortion was legal in certain circumstances, as outlined by doctors (as was and still is the case in the UK). Abortions that occurred outside of doctors' approval remained illegal. According to Rosalind Pollack Petchesky (1990), the re-legalisation of abortion in 1973 occurred because it was not feasible for it to remain illegal any longer. Abortion bans could no longer be enforced, even symbolically, as they had lost credibility due to the number of women prepared to flout the law and have an illegal abortion.

The Great Depression of the 1930s resulted in many women facing situations where they could not afford to have children, and so a greater number of appeals were made to doctors for both legal and illegal abortions. Social and economic factors, as a driver for abortion, assisted in expanded physicians' acceptance of social conditions as a legitimate reason to perform a *legal* abortion under the technical reasoning of 'saving a woman's life' (Flavin, 2009; Luker, 1984; Reagan, 1997). However, legal abortions provided by hospitals were far more accessible to white, middle-class women who resided in urban spaces, than to poor and ethnic minority women, or those who lived outside of large metropolitan areas. As such, women who lacked the informal networks to access illegal abortions from trained professionals were often required to give birth or attempt to self-abort: often with life-threatening or fatal consequences. Fear of being reported to police by medical staff discouraged women from seeking help when self-abortions went wrong, making illegal abortions even riskier. The wider social context of *Roe* was women's greater access to education and employment, the decentring of marriage and childbearing, which led to calls from women to be able to control their fertility. The increase in birth control practices, and the ideology of population control, which certainly had origins in racism, and capitalist concerns over the availability of resources in an over-populated world, are key aspects of the *Roe* ruling (Petchesky, 1990).

The basis under which *Roe* struck down state and federal abortion bans was on the principle that the Fourteenth Amendment to the US Constitution provides a fundamental 'right to privacy' and so protects a pregnant woman's liberty to choose to have an abortion without excessive government restriction. However, the court held that this right is not absolute and must be balanced against the government's interests in protecting women's health and protecting prenatal life, connecting state regulation to the trimester of pregnancy:

- first trimester (1–12 weeks of pregnancy) – no prohibition on abortion
- second trimester (13–27 weeks of pregnancy) – states could require reasonable health regulations for abortions
- third trimester (28+ weeks of pregnancy) – abortions could be prohibited entirely, except where necessary to save the life or health of the mother.

As such, *Roe* established the legal principles of foetal personhood, the idea that foetuses should have a legal personality and be protected under law as born people are. Furthermore, *Roe* established the idea that states have a legitimate interest in protecting the foetus. *Roe* operated on the premise that, while abortion is a 'choice', it is neither a good one, nor one that any woman wants to make, but instead is done out of necessity. Petchesky (1990) argues that feminist arguments that legal abortion is a positive for all women for sexual, social and health freedoms have been lost in the rhetoric around abortion. The idea that restricting abortions results in forced motherhood was not embraced as part of the ruling, nor within the minds of the general public. This construction of abortion continues to have an impact on women's reproductive rights and on state regulation of pregnancy today.

Almost immediately after the *Roe* judgement was announced, backlash began at both state and federal level. For example, eight days after the *Roe* decision was announced, Lawrence Hogan, the representative from Maryland, introduced a draft amendment to the constitution to make a foetus a 'person' under the Fourteenth Amendment of the Constitution. If passed, it would have defined life as beginning at conception. Within three years, over 50 differently worded amendments seeking to restrict or ban abortion had been introduced to the USA Congress (Hull et al., 2004). Rickie Solinger (2005) argues that attempts to overturn *Roe* were symbolic of the backlash against women's reproductive rights. As abortion and contraception allow a woman to decide if she will accept the outcome of her sexual liaisons (pregnancy), both challenge traditional ideas of men's authority and women's 'natural' role as a mother. Susan Faludi (1992) similarly argues that 'pro-life' campaigns (which focus on the life of the foetus, rather than the life of the pregnant woman) reflect wider social anxieties, particularly those held by men, surrounding women's reproductive autonomy, the removal of male control over the family and their wives, and the extent to which abortion and contraception in general facilitate women's sexual independence: deciding when to have a baby, who to have it with, and how many to have.

However, when we think about women's reproductive autonomy, we need to think beyond women's ability to access abortion. This position has been argued strongly by American First Nation women and women of colour, as a critique of the concept of 'choice' within the debates about abortion. As we explored in Chapter 2, one of the key ideas promoted is that all individuals have the ability to make choices about their lives. However, as the story of Marion, the low-paid worker in that chapter, illustrates, this is not always the case. The same principle is true in relation to women's ability to choose the outcome of their pregnancy and other aspects of their reproduction. For First Nation women and women of colour fighting for women's reproductive rights in the lead up to *Roe*, abortion was not necessarily the biggest issue that needed to be tackled. A key violation of reproductive rights that was at the centre of campaigning by women of colour was the forcible sterilisation of women in the process of other obstetric procedures: an unwanted pregnancy that ended with an illegal abortion, a hospital consented abortion or a caesarean section (Gordon and Gordon, 2002; Nelson, 2003; Reagan, 1997). The sterilisation of women of colour was often completed without their knowledge and consent, who would only find out about the procedure afterwards. As this state violence was committed against women of colour, it was not an active aspect of the reproductive rights campaigns organised by White, middle-class, liberal feminists fighting for 'choice'.

Feminists from poorer backgrounds and of colour also argued that for a 'choice' of abortion to be meaningful, women must have reasonable means to raise a child if she so wanted. Lack of available resources – health care, childcare, housing, for example – that allow a woman to raise a child, limits her **power** to 'choose' to continue a pregnancy and keep a baby after birth (Nelson, 2003; Petchesky and Judd, 1998; Roberts, 1997). Thus, during the 1980s and 1990s the concept of reproductive justice was developed, defined by SisterSong (n.d.) as 'the human right to maintain personal bodily autonomy, have children, not have children, and parent the children we have in safe and sustainable communities'.

By using a frame of reproductive justice, we are able to understand and conceptualise all aspects of reproduction – having sex, being able to prevent a pregnancy, becoming pregnant, ending a pregnancy, continuing a pregnancy, raising a child – as core features of human rights. As such, reproduction is something the State should work to protect, and also an area of life that requires support to assist those who do not have the means to support themselves. Sadly, as the Guttmacher Institute (2019) outlines, within the realm of abortions many states are not only not supporting women's rights, they are actively violating them, with an unprecedented wave of bans on all, most or some abortion across many states in the USA in 2019. Such bans are often justified as being necessary to protect foetal life. Furthermore, American politics around abortion have impacted the ability of women outside of the USA to access the medical procedure. Stacy Banwell (2019) has reviewed USA foreign policy on abortion under the Trump administration. Her research unpacks how the revised global gag order draws implicitly on conservative ideas about **gender, sexuality** and maternity, which deny female survivors of wartime rape access to safe abortion (see Chapter 8 for discussions of wartime rape and sexual violence).

As outlined above, the USA Supreme Court confirmed that the government has a legitimate interest in the life of the foetus. In many states this has resulted in foetuses being granted legal personhood. Which, as we will explore in the next section, has had substantial impact on the lives of pregnant women and, in some states in the USA, women who *could* become pregnant.

Pregnancy, risk and criminal law

Sexually active women who stop using birth control should stop drinking alcohol, but most keep drinking ... Alcohol can permanently harm a developing baby before a woman knows she is pregnant ... The risk is real. Why take the chance? (CDC, 2016)

The Centers for Disease Control and Prevention (CDC) released this press statement in 2016 as part of its new campaign to limit the exposure of foetuses to alcohol. The significance of the message lies in the fact that it is directed not only towards women who are pregnant or are trying to become pregnant, but also at women who have the *potential* to become pregnant. This would include any woman of reproductive age who is not proven to be infertile (bearing in mind that even long-acting reversible contraception like the IUD/coil or the implant is not infallible), as well as women who are not engaging in wanted sex, due to the high rates of rape (see Chapter 4 for discussions of consent and sexual violence). The perception that women should put the needs and wellbeing of their foetus before their own (even if they are not yet pregnant or intending to be pregnant) has been defined by Milne (2020a) as the 'foetus-first mentality'. The belief that putting the foetus first is appropriate and responsible behaviour for pregnant women is closely connected with ideals of motherhood, and a belief that 'good' mothers always put their child first, including their foetus. The influence of the foetus-first mentality is very noticeable within the medical 'treatment' of pregnancy, with a general expectation that women will adhere to medical advice and will alter their lives to protect their unborn child, such as changing their diet and avoiding exposure to diseases, substances and stressful situations.

Modern conceptions about risk and how risk is managed play out in the experience of pregnancy (see Chapter 2 for our discussion of theories of risk). As outlined above, developments in obstetric medicine has resulted in doctors focusing on the wellbeing and health of the foetus. New medical developments have dramatically changed the way pregnancy and risk are conceptualised, and, as a consequence, the behaviour of pregnant women. As part of this changing understanding of foetal health and risk, the foetus has been conceptualised as a patient distinct from the pregnant woman, while the pregnant woman is perceived as a foetal carrier, incubator or container (Bordo, 2003; Lupton, 1999; Martin, 1987). Furthermore, the role of risk management of the foetus now lies with doctors (rather than pregnant women) who protect the foetus from **harm**, including harm that might come from the pregnant woman (Ruhl, 1999).

Milne (2020a) argues that criminal law and criminal justice now play a key role in risk management on behalf of the foetus, as well as in the punishment of women who are deemed to have behaved in a way that has, or could have, harmed the foetus. This developing role of criminal justice is most apparent in the USA where at least 38 states now have laws protecting foetuses, and at least 29 of these states apply their laws to the early stages of pregnancy, such as the point of conception or implantation. Women in the USA who are pregnant, or who have been pregnant, have been arrested for everyday activities such as taking prescription drugs; painting a fence (due to substance exposure to the foetus); falling down the stairs (due to a belief that it was intentional to bring on a miscarriage); and refusing a caesarean section (due to the foetus dying and the woman's behaviour being interpreted as an act of homicide). As with many examples of law enforcement, the women most impacted by criminal justice intervention have been women of colour and poor women, particularly Black women. A review of newspaper reporting between 1973 and 2005 of pregnant women arrested, detained and forced to have medical treatment found 413 cases – 59 per cent of those detained were women of colour, with Black women making up 52 per cent; regardless of 'race', the women were overwhelmingly economically disadvantaged (Paltrow and Flavin, 2013). The overrepresentation of women of colour in criminal justice interventions is due first to racial stereotypes of women of colour being bad mothers or drug-users, despite there being similar levels of drug use among white women. Second, it is due to public hospitals being more likely to report pregnant women's drug use than private hospitals; women from poorer communities do not usually have access to private facilities (Roberts, 1997; Siegel, 1992).

The collaboration between medical staff and law enforcement has had significant consequences for the health of pregnant women and their unborn children. Women have avoided seeking medical treatment while pregnant due to fears of criminalisation, and there are also reports that women have terminated wanted pregnancies after threats of prosecution (Murphy, 2014). The irony of the situation is that it is widely reported that lack of access to adequate prenatal health care, along with poor socioeconomic background of pregnant women, are the leading causes of poor pregnancy outcomes, rather than the behaviour of the woman (Kampschmidt, 2015). Therefore, the criminal justice policing of pregnancy is likely to be causing harm rather than relieving it. Furthermore, there is stark evidence that imprisoning pregnant women often results in poor outcomes for both the woman and her foetus (Bard et al., 2016).

If there is limited evidence that criminalising pregnant women helps foetuses, then why have most states in the USA created laws that protect the foetus, with many states using them to punish women? It is important we remember that many foetal protection laws came from a place of good intent. One of the key reasons why states introduced these laws was to facilitate the prosecution of men who attack pregnant women (mostly partners or ex-partners), causing the foetus to die from the injuries sustained. California was the first state to enact a foetal homicide law in 1970 after it was ruled that Robert Keeler could not be convicted of homicide after he attacked Teresa, his ex-wife, causing the stillbirth of her baby. However, as Jeanne Flavin (2009: 102) has argued, 'Fetus-centred homicide laws are, at root, *fetal* protection laws. They are not designed to protect and support the woman who carries the fetus'. Flavin and other scholars have argued that, with the enactment of foetal protection laws, it is often forgotten that it is a woman who is attacked by a man and so who is the primary victim of that violence. Pregnancy is a time when intimate partner violence is more likely to begin or escalate, with women at increased risk of harm from their male partners (Tuerkheimer, 2006). Adding the foetus as a victim is unlikely to prevent violence against women. Instead, it obscures the woman and injuries inflicted upon her and so removes her from consideration altogether, 'effectively preclude[ing] an account of the nature of her suffering, or even recognition of her existence as a person who has been harmed' (Tuerkheimer, 2006: 697).

For many women's rights activists, the exclusion of women is the key reason behind the creation of foetal protection laws. While declaring the foetus a legal person may not directly prohibit or limit women's access to abortion, it does contribute to a 'pro-life' cultural message that portrays abortion as immoral (Ramsey, 2006). The natural consequence of foetal protection laws is that if the law declares that a foetus can be murdered by a man who attacks a pregnant woman, then is it not logical to conclude that a pregnant woman who has an abortion is also committing murder? And so, for many feminists, the role and purpose of foetal protection laws are to attempt to limit women's rights to abortion, reproductive autonomy, and so freedom and bodily integrity (see MacKinnon, 1991; Paltrow, 1999). The impact of these laws on women's rights is exemplified by a case in Alabama in 2019 where a man was given leave by the courts to sue an abortion clinic and the manufacturer of abortion medication on behalf of himself and the estate of an aborted foetus (Filipovic, 8 March 2019). Ryan Magers impregnanted his teenage girlfriend (which she did not want to be) after they had sex (which she reportedly did not want to have; see Chapter 4 for discussions of consent). This case indicates a worrying development for women's rights; compelling a woman to stay pregnant because it is the wish of a man who deposited sperm within her is a form of coercive control of women by men, and should be understood as a form of gender-based violence (Rowlands and Walker, 2019).

Beyond access to abortion, other implications of foetal protection laws exist – notably that the laws are discriminatory against women and interfere with women's rights to liberty and privacy (Johnsen, 1989). By holding women criminally liable for behaviour that is only illegal because of a positive pregnancy status (such as painting your fence or taking controlled substances – remembering that consumption is often not illegal, unlike possession and dealing), then the State is specifically discriminating against women *because* they are pregnant. Consequently, sanctioning women for conduct while pregnant reinforces traditional sex-based discrimination by disadvantaging women based on their reproductive capacity; in spite of the fact that having a child involves a woman taking on an important function necessary for the survival of the human species.

The creation and application of such laws require women to live in line with the ideals of motherhood and to put the needs of their foetus before their own, or to fear punishment by the State. Such a notion of putting other people's wellbeing first is not expected in any other situation, including parental duty to children following birth. As such, the state is promoting a State-sanctioned motherhood: prescribing behaviour and threatening women who do not comply with arrest and conviction (Cherry, 2007). The consequence of this State coercion is potentially to put all women in fear of becoming pregnant and so of having sex, because a positive pregnancy test will require her to transform her behaviour or to risk being sanctioned by the State for failing to put the foetus first, and so being a good-enough mother (Milne, 2020a). And so, once again, we see State intervention in the lives of women, justified through messages of protection.

As we have seen, under English and Welsh law, which is outlined above, the foetus does not have legal personality. Because of this, you might believe that the punishment of women for harm to the foetus does not occur. However, as Milne (2020a) has argued, despite the 'born alive' rule, prosecutors still appear to be influenced by the foetus-first mentality. Evidence from Milne's research into criminal justice responses to women suspected of harming foetuses or killing newborn children suggests that prosecutors are using alternative offences to punish the same behaviour, as seen in cases in the USA. Therefore, even where the law does not support criminalisation, we see examples of women being criminally punished for failing to be 'good-enough' mothers.

BOX 6.3

Should we give foetuses legal personhood or citizenship? Reflect on the information above and consider the pros and cons of seeing the foetus as a legal person with equivalent legal protection and standing as a person who is born. To inform your debate, consider the following:

- The foetus is situated inside the body of another person – what impact will giving the foetus rights have on the restrictions of the person who is pregnant? Consider this in relation to reproductive rights as human rights.

- As women who are of reproductive age – on average between the ages of 13 and 50 years – could become pregnant, if they are not planning a pregnancy then they may not know they are pregnant for at least the first six weeks of the pregnancy. What possible impact would foetal citizenship have on women's freedoms during the window of fertility (35+ years) to, for example, have sex, work in a profession that exposes them to substances harmful to a foetus (such as working on a nuclear submarine) or consume substances that may be harmful to a foetus (this includes food such as rare steak and mould-ripened soft cheese such as brie and camembert, as well as alcohol, cigarettes and narcotics)?

- If we would legally compel a pregnant woman to act in the best interests of her 'child' (her foetus), should we also compel other parents to act in the best interests of their born children? For example, should we legally compel fathers to undergo surgery to donate organs to save their children (such as a kidney or part of a liver) against their will?

- If we see the foetus as a legal person, does that mean we would not be able to deport a pregnant woman or send her to jail, as this would also involve imprisoning or deporting a foetus who may have legal rights to remain in their birth country, and who has not broken the law?

- How far would we expect the pregnant woman to go to protect the legal person within her (the foetus)?

  o   Limiting her choices and desires (which may include giving up her career and substantially changing her lifestyle)?
  o   Compromising her right to control her body and what she does with it (such as taking medication she would otherwise avoid)?
  o   Suffering grave injury (such as surgery) to protect the foetus?
  o   Risking death (if the foetus' right to life is prioritised over hers and so doctors work to save the 'child' over the pregnant woman in an emergency situation)?

- Is there a limit to the amount we would expect a pregnant woman to sacrifice for a foetus? Where would that line sit? If the foetus is a legal person, with equal rights to the pregnant woman, how do we draw that line?

- If regulation of pregnant women may actually result in negative outcomes for foetuses, then is foetal personhood ever going to be a good idea?

Summary

Throughout this chapter, we have seen how State involvement with, and regulation of, reproduction has a significant impact on the rights of women. This chapter potentially has limited satisfaction in terms of outcome as there is no clear or straightforward answer to the issues that we have raised. We do not need to look very far to see the negative consequences of criminal law and justice involvement in women's ability to become pregnant and in decisions about pregnancy. At the same time, if we deem the foetus to be a legal person, should we, and how can we, balance the rights of this 'person' with the rights of the pregnant woman?

Review questions

In concluding this chapter, we wish to draw your attention to other issues that are important to focus on and consider beyond legality and access to abortion, and women's rights in relation to foetal protection:

- Reproductive technologies – in vitro fertilisation (IVF) and surrogacy:

  o Are 'test-tube' 'babies' ethical?
  o Who should pay for the significant financial costs of IVF?
  o Should we pay/compensate people who 'donate' reproductive matter (sperm, ovum, fertilised eggs), or who carry a pregnancy for other people? What might the consequences of this be?
  o Who counts as the 'parent(s)' in cases of IVF and surrogacy?

- Obstetric violence:

  o Should non-consensual vaginal examinations by medical professionals in the process of labour and delivery be considered acts of violence or sexual violence?
  o Should we force pregnant women to have medical procedures that they do not want (such as foetal heart surgery) if it will save the life of the foetus?
  o Should we force women to have a caesarean section against their will if it will save the life of the foetus?

- Infanticide:

  o In certain countries (India and China, for example), baby girls are more likely to be killed than baby boys), how should we respond to this form of femicide?
  o In some legal jurisdictions (England and Wales, Ireland, Canada and New Zealand), the homicide offence of 'infanticide' exists to allow women lenient treatment if they kill their infant and their behaviour is deemed to be due to giving birth to or caring for the child. Should such lenient treatment be allowed? What about men who kill their infants?

- Artificial wombs:

  o In the future, will we be able to eliminate the gestational role of women and grow foetuses in human-made wombs?
  o What ethical considerations would this medical development bring?
  o What impact will artificial wombs have on reproductive rights?
  o Will society let everyone grow a baby? Or will we limit some people's ability to access children in this way? If so, who are we likely to limit and what does that say about who we think *should* be parents?
  o Consider the role of **capitalism** in this scenario.

Other chapters that this links to

Chapter 3 (Sex and crime in time and space)
Chapter 4 (Consent and its discontents)
Chapter 7 (Sexual exploitation and the State)
Chapter 8 (Sex and war)

7

Sexual exploitation and the State

This chapter examines how sexual exploitation is configured both within states and across borders. While grooming, trafficking and **prostitution** are distinct phenomena, each deserving specific attention, it is also important to draw connections between these phenomena as they fall under the umbrella of sexual exploitation. A quick search on Google Scholar highlights that the term 'sexual exploitation' gained currency in the 1980s. At this time, scholarship began to broaden the scope of research about rape (Brownmiller, 1975) and abuse (a label used particularly in relation to children; Finkelhor, 1984), using sexual exploitation as a more encompassing label. Primarily associated with women and children, sexual exploitation evokes different forms of exploitative behaviours, ranging from sexual abuse and rape through to prostitution, which is often associated with grooming and trafficking persons (Farley et al., 2004; Outshoorn, 2005). Put simply, grooming entails the building of a bond with a child, or anyone under the legal age of consent, for the purposes of sexual exploitation. Sex trafficking entails the transportation of bodies from one place to another for the purposes of sexual exploitation. Prostitution entails the exchange of sex for money and is considered a form of sexual exploitation by some (see, for example, Bindel, 2017).

By the end of this chapter, you will understand more about:

- the effects of social, political and economic inequalities within the state and between the *Global North* and *South* on sexual exploitation
- how to explore the phenomenon of online and localised grooming with reference to technology, 'race', class, gender and institutional failure
- the process whereby states use fear of sexual exploitation to justify the tightening of border control and the deportation of migrants
- the lack of widespread criminalisation of demand in prostitution and sex tourism, and what this implies.

The word 'prostitution' has negative connotations. The fact that we use it to denote the activity does not mean we endorse the idea that the act of selling sex is always necessarily exploitative. We acknowledge that many prefer the term **sex work** and its overall more positive connotations. There are disagreements in the literature, and indeed between the authors of this book, about the nature of this activity. We want to allow some space for debate without providing a single unified view, or final argument on this, as we hope students are enabled to approach these debates with an open and critical mindset. To strike a compromise between the two positions, we will refer to the activity as prostitution, while we refer to those involved in it as sex workers.

In this chapter, we will think about whether and how grooming, trafficking and prostitution intersect, not just in terms of the similarities or overlaps between them, but also in terms of governmental responses towards them. In this way, we will also address them as discursive constructs.

Scholarly debates on these issues are not without controversy. However, there seems to be some agreement that grooming, trafficking and prostitution should be understood in the context of widespread economic inequalities, institutionalised **patriarchy** and **neoliberal globalisation**. Hence, this chapter reflects on the forces that shape the conditions for sexually exploitative relations. The trajectory towards a more interconnected world, punctuated by neoliberal globalisation (see Chapter 2 for a discussion of neoliberalism), has consequences that are of relevance for the way in which sexual exploitation may occur, but also for the way in which different societies understand it and intervene in it. In this market-driven, technology-enhanced context, bodies are increasingly made into disposable, surplus subjects.

The chapter recognises the push-and-pull factors of **migration** and inequality for exploited groups within a neoliberal globalisation context. We trace the beginning of both the **human rights** and the trafficking **discourses** on the global arena (Milivojevic and Pickering, 2013). More specifically, we will see how the human rights discourse represents deep contradictions between theory – that all human beings have equal rights – and practice – that some humans are privileged by nature of the position they occupy geographically, economically, socially and culturally. We then explore the intersections of migration, sexual exploitation and labour, trafficking and control. Spearheaded by international governmental and non-governmental organisations (NGOs), and embraced by states in an era of tightening borders, the trafficking discourse often conflates economic migration with human trafficking, simplifying a complex issue while relying on the criminal law as a tool of the state to intervene in and control immigration. We will explore, for example, how the trafficking discourse colludes with **abolitionism** in the context of prostitution.

Another theme we recognise in this chapter is the widespread use of the victim narrative across trafficking, prostitution and grooming discourses and how this impacts our understanding of **agency**, specifically its denial. We also deal with another form of denial: that of states' responsibility for **colonialism** and their supporting of postcolonial configurations. This is expressed through a renewed commitment to nationalism by states, a nationalism tied to ethnic groups, known as **ethnonationalism**. This is visible in nation-states' increasing efforts to curb and control migration through criminalisation. This process is evident across all issues under scrutiny: in prostitution, primarily through its conflation with sex trafficking, we find persistent attempts by states and other agencies to shift our attention away from inequality as being the root cause of prostitution, towards blaming the immorality and criminality of the other, be it the sex buyer, the human trafficker, or in some cases still, the sex worker, who has now largely been relegated to the status of victim. In the case of grooming, ethnonationalism and **femonationalism** (see Chapter 3) are encapsulated by public discourses that point the finger towards British Asian men grooming white young girls, in the media and in the public domain.

The human rights turn

The human rights discourse represents one key development in the construction of a global shared cultural understanding, providing an instrument to define people's rights in the twentieth and twenty-first centuries. The creation of a system of cooperation supported by international governmental institutions such as the United Nations (UN) has consequences because of its ability to form binding agreements among **nations**, but also, and perhaps more crucially, its ability to construct and shape new ideas and principles which states should, in theory, abide by, and which people come to consider *sacred*.

Human rights, in the contemporary sense of the term, are a twentieth-century **Western** invention. Indeed, many of the principles stemming from religious morals do ascribe versions of what we would now understand as universal human rights, but our current description of human rights comes from the Universal Declaration of Human Rights, ratified by the UN in 1948. This universal declaration marked the beginning of conceptualising all human beings as having equal rights regardless of 'race, colour, sex, language, religion, political or other opinion, national or social origin, property, birth or other status' (Article 2, Universal Declaration of Human Rights). Human rights have become an important, if not dominant, frame of reference, providing impetus for collective action, particularly for advocacy around the recognition of marginalised, stigmatised (as we see in Chapter 10, in the context of disability) and even criminalised groups. There are many examples of organisations using human rights as a principle on which to construct their advocacy, ranging from people who use drugs (International Network of People Who Use Drugs; Ezard, 2001), to sex workers (Global Network of Sex Work Projects; Jackson, 2016; Kempadoo and Doezema, 2018), to refugees and other disenfranchised groups (Goodhart, 2016).

BOX 7.1

Consider the following:

- When you hear the words 'human rights', what comes to mind?
- Are human rights sacred?
- Are human rights universal?

The repurposing of the human rights idea as a tool of liberation, as a beacon of hope for the disenfranchised, does not come without its problems. Poverty, inequality and the variety of extant moral standpoints, cultural norms and legal systems prevent such rights from becoming realised (Cornwall and Molyneux, 2006). A universalising discourse always hides a sinister side: namely that human rights is a Western philosophical and juridical conception that is criticised for having little applicability or resonance beyond the West (Pollis et al., 2006). Even in a Western context, it has thus far proven impossible to build universal equality on the foundation of continued patriarchy, economic inequalities and lasting colonial relations. Susan Dewey and colleagues (2018) have noted that efforts to regulate sex stem from dominant (read Western) values and concerns that shape our understandings of and interventions in sexual behaviour, work, public health and even human rights.

More concerning still, Elizabeth Bernstein (2012) argues that the human rights discourse is being exploited by apparently benevolent forces – principally made up of White feminist moral reformers – to justify simple narratives that reduce the problem of trafficking to sexual exploitation alone, rather than acknowledging its deeper political and economic drivers. These benevolent actors often advocate for the criminalisation of deviant individuals as the solution to the sexual exploitation problem, thus individualising blame (see Chapter 5 for a detailed discussion of this process). While it is important to acknowledge that sexual exploitation by deviant individuals does take place, it is even more important to interrogate the structural drivers, the socio-political and cultural mechanisms, that underpin such **deviance**. Too often, as will become apparent in the following sections, states and institutions rely on a reductive understanding of sexual exploitation to escape responsibility and to justify repressive measures against vulnerable, rightless groups, including sex workers, migrants and young girls.

The political economy of sexual exploitation

In general terms, the political economy of neoliberal globalisation (that we encountered in Chapter 2) entails greater transnational mobility for people and goods, extensive use of mobile and Internet technology, and high levels of migration through both legal and illicit channels. It also features deep levels of inequality and lack of opportunities, particularly for people from the Global South (Aas, 2013; Hickel, 2017). However, it is worth remembering that such high levels of inequality do not just characterise Global North–South relations; they are also at the heart of the political economic system within states in the Global North (Alvaredo et al., 2018; Kuhn et al., 2016).

In this context, immigrant populations are disproportionately affected, partly as a result of rising nationalism.

Countries that were once regarded as lands of opportunity are increasingly experienced as hostile environments by immigrant populations old and new (Webber, 2019). It is enough to think about some recent events in the anglophone world to see this in action. In the UK in 2018, we saw the unfolding of the Windrush scandal, which involved the threat of deportation – because they were undocumented – of some Black Britons who arrived as children on their parents' passports in the UK between the 1940s and the 1970s; a time when the British state needed cheap labour from former British colonies (Monrose, 2019). We can also observe the proliferation of detention centres that incarcerate undocumented migrants, refugees and asylum seekers in Australia, Canada, the USA and the UK; these places are characterised by the brutal treatment of migrants, including the separation of families and indefinite periods of incarceration (Mainwaring and Cook, 2019). Finally, the Brexit referendum and subsequent exit of the UK from the EU was premised on rising anti-immigration sentiment, as was the political success of Donald Trump in America.

Political scientists have found a link between increasing levels of inequality and rising nationalism. Diversionary nationalism is the process whereby states re-invest in the nationalist project to distract citizens from the harsh realities of economic inequality (Solt, 2011). Other researchers have found a link between rising inequality and Euroscepticism in the EU (Kuhn et al., 2014). Nationalism and Euroscepticism have implications for issues of security, crime control and border politics. We have been witnessing the shaping of a paradox: on the one hand, the universalist ideas and institutions of Western liberal societies are being forcefully spread through Western economic and political dominance via globalisation, the governance of international governmental institutions, and the spread of ideas like universal human rights; on the other hand, Western liberal states are becoming further obsessed with sovereignty and security (Aas, 2013), while waves of **populism** and ethnonationalism are sweeping through Western states, creating increasingly hostile environments (Heinisch et al., 2019). The contrast between global mobility and the tightening of border controls defines our current condition.

But what does all this have to do with sexual exploitation? In a sense, the way we experience and intervene in sexual exploitation is shaped by this very contrast between freedom and mobility as the liberal values underpinning the globalisation project, and the controls and regulations that states exert upon this freedom. In the words of Piyasiri Wickramasekara (2008: 1249), 'while there has been greater integration of global markets for goods, services and capital across borders, its impact on the cross-border movement of people and labour remains much more restricted, regulated by a complex web of immigration laws and policies that uphold the principle of state sovereignty'.

This contrast between greater mobility and harsher restrictions manifests itself vividly in the context of human trafficking and trafficking for sexual exploitation. It also has relevance for understanding recent changes in some states' shifting approaches to address prostitution. Inequality, and lack of opportunity, remain core drivers for people's decision to migrate and/or sell sex. Yet, rather than tackling these root causes, states continue to invest their efforts in the criminalisation of undocumented migrants and people involved in the sex industry, or in the targeting of individual deviance.

Multiple vulnerabilities create prime opportunities for certain groups to become subjected to exploitation. These vulnerabilities include, but are not limited to: being undocumented, coming from a poor background, being young, being female, being alone or isolated, having no access or recourse to justice or protection from law enforcement, and having no status or credibility. We will examine how these vulnerabilities, as shaped by the current political economic context, play out as the state interacts with grooming, trafficking and prostitution.

Grooming

In this section, we discuss online and localised grooming as being relevant and distinct phenomena tied to sexual exploitation in the context of globalisation and the state. The issue of grooming presents us with unique dilemmas, in part because grooming involves children and young people who are always regarded as victims, unable to consent to sex (something which we explore at length in Chapter 12). However, grooming remains underpinned by political, economic and cultural processes, and should not be regarded simply as a phenomenon caused by deviant individuals. The spread of mobile and Internet technology opens up new opportunities for online grooming, but also legislative, criminal justice and vigilantes' responses. Unlike online grooming, localised grooming is not a new phenomenon. We focus on grooming cases involving **BAME** perpetrators and young white victims. Here, gender, 'race' and class have a role to play, while multiple levels of vulnerability make for more successful targets in the grooming process.

Taking (online) grooming seriously

In 2017, the Serious Crimes Act in England and Wales was amended to create the offence of grooming: 'for anyone aged 18 or over to intentionally communicate with a child under 16, where the person acts for a sexual purpose and the communication is sexual or intended to elicit a sexual response' (Ministry of Justice, 3 April 2017). Similar legislation exists in Australia, Norway, Singapore and the USA. Much of this legislation targets grooming which happens online, using mobile phones, social networking sites, email, and so on.

Different techniques are used to try to identify grooming before sexual abuse occurs (Penna et al., 2005). The placing of investigative officers in chat rooms to record and possibly entrap would-be offenders is a time-consuming and precarious technique that has been used to detect adults who are attempting to groom children (Pendar, 2007: 235; Penna et al., 2005: 1). Several software-based interventions are being developed in an attempt to detect people who may be grooming children online. Network-monitoring software that identifies the Internet Protocol (IP) address of computers can be used when a suspected offender has been identified. Algorithms designed to detect suspected adults who are posing as children, or to detect conversations – especially hidden or secret conversations – can also be used to detect grooming. Lyta Penna and colleagues (2005) suggest that analysing the discourses between different speakers can help to identify potential sex offenders: by analysing the length of the message, the complexity of the sentences and the length of time it has taken to compose the response, potential groomers can also be identified. However, there is a risk that these 'sting' operations inadvertently cajole people into trying to meet children for sex when they otherwise might not have gone that far. There is also a risk that by posing as a child online, officers risk jeopardising the conviction of child abusers.

Other examples of using software to detect adults who groom children online include the interactive avatar known as 'Sweetie', a computer-animated child created by children's rights organisations to obtain the personally identifiable data of predators that could then be reported to law enforcement agencies. Posing as a 10-year-old Filipino girl, over a ten-week period, 20,000 men contacted Sweetie, with 1,000 offering to pay money for her to perform sex acts. However, as with investigative officers posing as children in chat rooms, there are concerns that the use of Sweetie may prevent prosecutions due to concerns over perpetrators being entrapped. Sweetie is also designed and operated by a private Dutch organisation affiliated to *Terre des Hommes*. Though, by their own account, *Terre des Hommes* has been able to use Sweetie successfully to identify the location of groomers and report these to the police, it is worth reflecting on the fact that this is an extra-judicial organisation and not a formal law-enforcement agency. How far do you think it matters that *Terre des Homme* is an extra-judicial organisation? Should we be wary of extra-judicial initiatives, or should we embrace them as filling a gap left by law enforcement?

Creating software which can stop the sexual abuse of children before it happens is obviously desirable, however there are a number of challenges that prevent this from being an easy task. Private conversations, for instance, which happen via messenger systems, cannot be monitored in the same way that chat rooms or forums might be. This is even more problematic when one considers that adults who successfully groom children do so by befriending them, making the use of private chats even more likely (see Gámez-Guadix et al., 2017). Potential offenders who use virtual private networks (VPNs) to hide their location, or who benefit from the anonymity that the Internet affords by holding several email addresses with unverified identity information, can also evade detection. Researchers suggest that developing more complex algorithms capable of conducting more complex cryptoanalyses, including the enhanced ability to detect pornographic stories or images featuring children, will help in detecting suspected child abuse before it happens.

All of this happens online of course, and the online realm is a good place for offenders who seek to molest children to search for them while successfully hiding their identity. As part of their analysis of the process of grooming, Samantha Craven and colleagues (2007) note that potential sex offenders seek out ideal opportunities to engage with children in order to identify vulnerable ones who might be easier to contact for abuse. They also help us to bust the myth of the paedophile groomer by emphasising that grooming is not something that is committed by paedophiles alone. Child abusers are not necessarily paedophiles and, moreover, limiting a definition of grooming to a practice undertaken by paedophiles obscures the mundane ways that children can be groomed by people known to them: neighbours, family friends, the parents of friends, and club leaders, for instance. Grooming occurs as a precursor to sexual abuse, or attempts at sexual abuse, and sex trafficking.

Does the legislation against grooming actually work? In the Norwegian context, Elizabeth Staksrud (2013) is doubtful. She argues that anti-grooming laws target an imagined groomer–victim relationship that is 'highly inaccurate'. Very young children are not usually online, though more recent reports show an upward curve of children as young as four having their own devices, enabling them to get online (Turner, 4 October 2018). Staksrud (2013: 154) suggests that 'Internet-related sex crimes involving adults and juveniles mostly fit the standard model of statutory rape' because adults usually seek to contact and seduce children who are aged between 13 and 15. These facts do not reflect the popular imaginary of naïve children being preyed on by adults. Indeed, as we see in Chapter 12 in the context of teen sexting, children have agency over their sexual practices, which they exercise. The notion of the stranger lurking online does not reflect the way that children who interact with these adults experience them. Manuel Gámez-Guadix and colleagues (2018: 16) note that, as part of the process of being groomed, children can become emotionally invested in their relationship with the groomer; they might be 'highly motivated to connect with the aggressor ... and even report being in love with them'. This kind of intimacy is hard to underestimate. Staksrud (2013: 158) suggests that, for some children, a stranger (or 'a new person', as Staksrud puts it) whom they meet online might become a 'friend' in as little as 15 minutes. After that, children report that, from time to time, they do meet people in the offline world whom they first met online. Of these, 59 per cent reported that they 'had a good time' at the meeting, with only 2 per cent reporting that they had been attacked or verbally abused at the meeting (Staksrud, 2013: 161).

One of the reasons for this is that the online tendency among children is not to pretend to be someone they are not or to create a false profile. People 'know' who they are speaking to and, as a result, sexual violence against children happens 'through the establishment of trust and intimacy, rather than deceit and violence' (Staksrud, 2013: 162). In the context of grooming, most children have 'online coping strategies' to help them to avoid risky situations (2013: 162). Building resilience, knowing when to ignore a potential abuser's request, or knowing when to ask for help prevent potential abuse in a way that anti-grooming legislation cannot. The blurring of categories between child molester, abuser and paedophile means that these acts of child abuse become hard to discern, especially when the abuser takes the guise of a boyfriend or girlfriend. Acknowledging children's agency may increase resilience and enhance children's ability to discern abuse.

BOX 7.2

Consider the following questions:

- Is anti-grooming legislation too heavy-handed?
- Does it target the wrong sort of abuser?
- Is there a better way to target the online and offline grooming of children? Or is the sexual abuse of children so abhorrent that notwithstanding the imperfect application of the legislation, it still serves a social good?
- Do you think other approaches focusing on education for children about how to use the Internet, including a risk-reduction approach that accepts some risk is acceptable, might work best? Or is all risk to be avoided when it comes to children?

Localised grooming in the UK: 'race' and place

Grooming can also take place offline, as part of a localised effort. In 2011, the Child Exploitation and Online Protection (CEOP) Command recognised 'localised grooming' as a tactic used to sexually exploit children. Localised grooming is defined as occurring:

where children have been groomed and sexually exploited by an offender, having initially met in a location outside their home. This location is usually in public,
such as a park, cinema, on the street or at a friend's house. Offenders often act
together, establishing a relationship with a child or children before sexually
exploiting them. Some victims of 'street grooming' may believe that the offender
is in fact an older 'boyfriend'; these victims introduce their peers to the offender
group who might then go on to be sexually exploited as well. Abuse may occur
at a number of locations within a region and on several occasions. (CEOP
Command, 2011: 7)

Indeed, in his account of paedophilia discussed in Chapter 12, Tom O'Carroll
(1980) confirms that paedophiles seeking to meet children in order to groom
them (though he does not use this terminology), might well take up a position
as a scout or youth group leader, or volunteer as a sports coach, in order to
increase their chances. In his own words, 'a paedophile working as a voluntary
helper has the opportunity gradually to win the confidence and affection, and
perhaps, ultimately, the erotic interest, of youngsters, over a period of months
or even years' (O'Carroll, 1980: 119).

O'Carroll justifies this behaviour as a form of befriending a child. Intimacy
is formed as a way of separating the child from their peers or family to better
foster between the adult and child the notion that they are in a relationship
with each other. The keeping of secrets is part of this intimacy. Keeping
secrets helps to obscure the abuse. If a child believes their abuser to be their
girlfriend or boyfriend, or if they believe that they are friends, they are more
likely to keep those secrets. If children – who might often be kept in the dark
about sexual practices, anyway – do not recognise forms of touching or hug-
ging as being sexualised, they may not themselves realise that they are being
abused. It is worth highlighting that children who are groomed and abused
are often those who are likely to be already vulnerable in other areas of their
lives. Children with poor relationships with their parents, children in care or
children living in other precarious situations are likely to be especially vulnerable as they are flattered and given attention and gifts as part of the
grooming process.

There have been several cases of localised grooming in the UK which have
received significant media attention, particularly in the aftermath of the
Rochdale, Bradford and Rotherham scandals in the north of the UK in the
2000s. Nine men were jailed in Bradford for grooming and sexually abusing
two 14-year-old girls who were classed as 'vulnerable' (BBC, 27 February
2019). Another nine men were jailed for the grooming and sexual abuse of girls
as young as 13 in Rochdale, and seven men were jailed in Rotherham for
similar crimes (Halliday, 29 October 2018). These male abusers have often
been portrayed as belonging to an organised group or 'gang' in media coverage.
Most of these men are British Asian, while many of the girls are white. These
cases triggered a specific brand of moral outrage with racist undertones,

evident in the political and media commentary at the time that awareness of the abuse ruptured into the public domain.

BOX 7.3

In 2011, Jack Straw, Member of Parliament for Blackburn, UK, at the time, noted 'a specific problem which involves Pakistani heritage men ... who target vulnerable young white girls' (BBC, 8 January 2011). In an interview, Straw continues:

> These young men are in a Western society, in any event, they act like any other young men, they're fizzing and popping with testosterone, they want some outlet for that, but Pakistani heritage girls are off-limits and they are expected to marry a Pakistani girl from Pakistan, typically ... So, they then seek other avenues and they see these young women, white girls who are vulnerable, some of them in care ... who they think are easy meat. (BBC, 8 January 2011)

Now, let us pause and reflect on this opinion:

- What was your initial reaction to this?
- Do you feel outraged in any way?
- Do you feel like this sort of commentary is justified?

On the one hand, one thing that Jack Straw unquestionably got right was in identifying the vulnerability of victims of grooming. Successful grooming is often underpinned by the multiple vulnerabilities of victim targets. On the other hand, we could argue that Straw's opinion is steeped in **Orientalism,** which shapes our representation and understanding of British Asian men's 'dangerous masculinities' (Tufail, 2015). Ella Cockbain (2013) discusses the creation of the 'Asian sex gang predator' figure in the aftermath of the Bradford, Rochdale and Rotherham cases. The racialised nature of the label starts with the word *gang*, a word normally reserved for BAME deviant groups. The ensuing media portrait is that of Asian men as being both *natural* and *organised* predators of young white girls (Gill and Harrison, 2015). Interestingly, the media attention given to these men tends to be far greater than that given to their white groomer counterparts. In this way, the problem is identified as one of 'race', rather than one of gender, masculinity and power. White groomers, such as Jimmy Savile (see Chapters 5 and 12), statistically make up the majority of sexual predators, yet they are seldom, if ever, identified as being part of a gang (even though their abuse may be facilitated by being part of a group, in which case it would be called a 'ring'). They are even less likely to be identified as white. Their ethnic group belonging is not considered relevant: call it the power of privilege (Miah, 2015).

A review of the child sexual abuse case in Rotherham (Jay, 2014) found that 1,400 children and young people were abused over the course of 16 years. 'Race' and class, along with institutional failure by the police and social services, played a significant role in the unfolding and continuation of the abuse. Accordingly, senior figures both in the police and child protective services were aware of the abuse but believed reports to be grossly exaggerated due to the status of victims, many of whom were young, 'troublesome' girls in the care system. The ethnic background of perpetrators was not made explicit by authorities out of fear of accusations of racism. It was reported that 'council and other officials sometimes thought youth workers were exaggerating the exploitation problem. Sometimes they were afraid of being accused of racism if they talked openly about the perpetrators in the town mostly being Pakistani taxi drivers' (Pidd, 27 August 2014).

Many victims were rendered invisible by their working-class, underprivileged background, but also by gendered assumptions. A trend we see in state intervention in children's sexuality is the impact that perceptions of deviant sexuality has had on the policing of the behaviour of girls and young women. In Rotherham, the police directly targeted girls who were being abused through arrests for drunken behaviour, ignoring the underlying abuse these girls were being subjected to. The police also stopped monitoring some of these girls because they were either pregnant or had given birth, despite many being under the age of consent (Jay, 2014; see Chapters 4 and 12 for discussions of age of consent).

The regulation, control and punishment of girls' sexualities has historically informed welfare policy and social support from the state. As Pamela Cox (2003) outlines in her study of the gender development of the British juvenile justice system in the first half of the twentieth century, the difference in juvenile justice responses to girls deemed to be 'troublesome' could depend on whether the girl was deemed to be sexually innocent or sexually precocious. Most often, state sanctions were targeted towards working-class girls, and the courts were used to 'protect' girls who had, or were believed to be at risk of losing, their virginity. We have already discussed the significance of virginity in Chapter 3. The loss of virginity may have been as a consequence of child sexual exploitation (historically, and too often today, referred to as 'child prostitution'), as part of an emotional relationship, or due to sexual abuse. Regardless of the nature of the sexual encounter:

> girls leading 'wayward' lives and who 'chose' to be sexually active were thought to bear much, if not all, of the responsibility for their choice. But even in abuse cases, the very fact that a girl was able to articulate her experience often worked against her. A child possessing the vocabulary to describe a sexual act was no 'innocent' child. (Cox, 2003: 41)

Such state responses to sexually active girls (including those who had been abused or were being sexually exploited) is deeply troubling when we consider that the girls had not committed an actual criminal offence. They were being brought into the juvenile justice system purely because of their sexual activity. Responses by state officials were a blend of protection of and punishment for the girl, but, as Cox argues, were also designed to protect other children as 'she could "contaminate" the other children with this "knowledge of evil"' (2003: 41). Thus, as we can see here, the 'good' girl, the one who does not need to be punished, is the sexually innocent one.

The sexualisation of girls' delinquency has not been confined to the history books. These processes are visible in the Rotherham case, and have been high-lighted in numerous studies by feminist criminologists completing work on girls' involvement in criminal justice (see, for example, Chesney-Lind and Shelden, 2013; Mallicoat, 2007). Furthermore, such controls and regulations are saturated with the wider discrimination of 'race' and class, as working-class girls and girls of colour are much more readily sexualised, and have their sexual activities policed to a greater extent (Gaarder et al., 2004; Rosenbaum and Chesney-Lind, 1994).

In Rotherham, some of the abused girls were internally trafficked between towns and cities in the north of England. Here, we can reflect on how our ideas of trafficking may themselves be influenced by Orientalist assumptions. Trafficking does not necessarily involve an exotic victim, who is Black or Eastern European being groomed and exploited. It can happen closer to home, and to girls who are white and Western. Being female, young, isolated and poor make up the multiple vulnerabilities that create the conditions for suc-cessful grooming and trafficking. These vulnerabilities may make one invisible, or only visible as a troublesome youngster, to state authorities. However, successful grooming and trafficking also require the presence of a set of configurations shaped by both discourse and state responses, to which we now turn.

The 'invention' of trafficking

Anne Gallagher (2001) argues that international efforts to tackle trafficking were mainly driven by concerns over state sovereignty and security at a time of the expansion of illicit global markets. The Palermo Protocols, a series of agreements ratified by UN member states between 2000 and 2003, represented the first coordinated action by states to address the issue of trafficking as a form of lucrative transnational organised crime. The Palermo Protocols were con-cerned with all manner of trafficking, not just the sexually exploitative kind.

And yet our shared social imagery tends to be more concerned with trafficking for sexual exploitation than it is with other forms of trafficking for labour exploitation (Alvarez and Alessi, 2012). The Protocols define human trafficking specifically as:

> the recruitment, transportation, transfer, harbouring or receipt of persons by means of the threat or use of force or other forms of coercion, of abduction, of fraud, of deception, of the abuse of power or of position of vulnerability or of the giving or receiving of payments or benefits to achieve the consent of a person having control over another person, for the purpose of exploitation. Exploitation shall include, at a minimum, the exploitation of prostitution of others or other forms of sexual exploitation, forced labour or services, slavery or practices similar to slavery, servitude or the removal of organs. (UN, 2004: 42)

In the above list of types of exploitation, prostitution and sexual exploitation appear first, even though most human trafficking seems to occur for purposes other than sexual exploitation (ILO, 2017). Still, trafficking for sexual exploitation does occur. In a 2017 report, the International Labour Organisation (ILO) estimated that, globally, 24.9 million people are in forced labour, and 4.8 million people in forced sexual exploitation, with women and girls being disproportionately affected (ILO, 2017). In its Global Report on Trafficking in Persons (2018), the United Nations Office on Drugs and Crime (UNODC) made a contrasting claim that most trafficking occurs for the purposes of sexual exploitation, albeit there are regional variations. This claim is based on the numbers detected by law enforcement. Here, it may be the case that more resources are being directed at the investigation and detection of trafficking for sexual exploitation than other forms of human trafficking. Official statistics show an upward trajectory from 2003 to 2016, with the numbers of detected victims increasing over this time period (UNODC, 2018: 7). Note the start date: 2003 is when the Palermo Protocols came into force, and efforts to record international trafficking began. If global trafficking was happening to the same extent prior to 2003, we would not know about it, because records are patchy at best. Other numbers worth highlighting are countries of destination – with the wealthy countries of the Global North more likely to be destination countries – and the gender split of victims: 'the vast majority of the detected victims of trafficking for sexual exploitation are females, and 35 per cent of the victims trafficked for forced labour are also females, both women and girls. At the same time, more than half of the victims of trafficking for forced labour are men' (UNODC, 2018: 10).

It appears that, over the past two decades, we have become more concerned with trafficking for the purposes of sexual exploitation than ever before. We could argue that this is a positive development; why should we not be content that sexual exploitation has risen on the international agenda, becoming a global concern punctuated by intervention efforts? It is tempting to reach such a conclusion. However, there are issues we need to consider before becoming blinded by optimism. First, despite such efforts, the numbers of sexually exploited people worldwide do not seem to be dwindling. Indeed, we must be careful of making assumptions based on numbers, as, with any 'slippery statistics' that characterise illicit markets, there is a dark figure (Gozdziak and Collett, 2005). Furthermore, a constructivist view of statistics would highlight that these numbers tell us more about the institutions that control and record, than the actual reality of trafficking. This means that when resources are invested into tackling trafficking for sexual exploitation, as they have been since 2003, the numbers of detected victims may increase simply because trafficking, and its recording, has become a priority for law enforcement.

There are other, more sinister sides to this issue. The expansion of global markets under neoliberal globalisation does not stop at licit goods and services; illicit markets are also expanding. Johan Lindquist (2010) notes that, along with illicit drug markets and terrorism, human trafficking is the fastest growing global market. He is not interested in proving whether this is the case, as he recognises that statistics in this field are, at best, misleading (something that others have agreed with; see Weitzer, 2014). He does, however, point to the manner in which trafficking is established as being a problem through cultural artefacts, such as counter-trafficking films. The early 2000s were characterised by the shaping of what Laura Augustin (2005) calls 'the rescue industry' – organisations that came into existence for the purpose of establishing trafficking as a problem, and intervening in it by creating a simple victim narrative that separates the issue of trafficking from the broader political economic conditions in which it occurs. This is what Lindquist (2010: 226) calls 'a depoliticizing function through the concern with – and intervention on behalf of – a particular type of migrant, namely, the "victim," rather than broader issues such as labour rights and the freedom of mobility'. Separating the issue of trafficking for sexual exploitation from other forms of economic exploitation and vulnerability is a useful tactic to blame organised crime and the deviant individuals therein, rather than the system that supports them. Then, the problem is not of a political or an economic nature, and the solution is not political economic reform. Rather, the problem is the deviance and opportunism of individual offenders, the traffickers of the world, and the solution is targeted intervention through law enforcement and rescue organisations.

Here, we need to return to the contrast outlined above: on the one hand, freedom and global mobility characterise the neoliberal globalisation narrative, engendering the hopes and aspirations of people around the world; on the other hand, it is only a minority of people who are afforded such freedoms and rights, making the rest more vulnerable to all forms of exploitation through widespread poverty, inequality, lack of labour protection, and tight border controls. In this context, economic migrants can more easily become, and be portrayed as, sexually exploited victims (Augustin, 2005). Interestingly, law enforcement interventions are principally aimed at victims or perpetrators, with no comparable regulations, interventions or programmes that target sex buying and sex tourism. We will return to this issue later in the chapter. For now, let us focus on the case of a USA celebrity-sponsored anti-trafficking campaign targeted at men who buy sex.

#RealMenDontBuyGirls

In 2011, Hollywood actors Ashton Kutcher and Demi Moore launched the *Real Men Don't Buy Girls* campaign, enlisting a series of Hollywood celebrities to carry this message through an advertising campaign after learning about the extent of trafficking worldwide and in the USA. According to Kamala Kempadoo (2015: 12), initiatives such as *Real Men Don't Buy Girls* appear genuine on the surface: 'the main thrust behind such celebrity campaigns and attention is the rescue of women, particularly young women and underage girls from what they deem to be "modern-day slavery" and "sex trafficking"'.

So far so good. But what do they imply? Kempadoo explains that this campaign is made up of 'videos that make fun of things that "real men" don't do (such as driving while blindfolded, making a grilled cheese sandwich with an iron, shaving with a chainsaw, etc.)' (2015: 12). The jokes are in the exaggerated tools men use in the ads, carrying a connotation of lack of responsibility and cluelessness which supposedly shows a 'woke' attitude towards gender. Aside from the disconnection between the rather trivial jokes in the ads and the sombre realities of trafficking and sexual exploitation, there is an interesting role reversal whereby some gendered activities are recast as manly. Yet, the 'real men' of the campaign rely on their status as masculine celebrities to call upon an ideal of 'moral masculinity' within a postcolonial configuration; 'so rather than producing a self-reflexive white subject, we are presented with the image of a daring knight whose moral obligation is to save the world – especially Asia and Africa – from itself and an affirmation of white masculinity as, amongst other things, powerful, heroic, and morally superior' (Kempadoo, 2015: 16).

As Sarah Steele and Tyler Shores (2014) have compellingly argued, celebrities' role as engaged activists and stakeholders has increased through extensive use of social media, to the point that they have come to be considered 'expert-advocates' by a general public who places trust in them. Of particular concern is the ability for these celebrities to reach expert status and large audiences without understanding the complexities of any given issue, giving way to inaccurate representations (Steele and Shores, 2014). As the celebrity reaches 'expert-advocate' status, they can reinforce the state's sovereign mandate to intervene in trafficking, tightening border controls and further criminalising migrants. These celebrities become agents of the sovereign state, creating a straightforward connection between real men and moral masculinity, and state intervention and control. An alternative reading is that of Samantha Majic (2018), who argues that the Kutcher and Moore campaign promotes an 'individual responsibility norm' which masks structural solutions to human trafficking. Whichever reading you find more convincing, there is a commonality between the two: ignoring structural determinants and advocating for interventions focused on *individual behaviour*, whether it is stopping individuals from buying sex, or stopping individuals crossing borders. Thus, the system that produces and reproduces inequalities across 'race', class and gender is not called into question. Rather, individual deviants are singled out and criminalised, while business continues as usual.

Kempadoo sees any attempt to intervene in aiding the trafficking victim as being embedded in a system of patriarchy, postcolonial convictions and White supremacy, where:

> the rescue fantasy is a means through which the endeavors are legitimized as altruistic and humanitarian, obscuring the reliance on and reproduction of the racial knowledge of the Other in the historical tropes of, on the one hand – the hopeless victim, impoverished and incapable of attending to one's own needs – and, on the other, the benevolent civilizing white subject who must bear the burden of intervening in poor areas of the world. (2015: 14)

This resonates with Elizabeth Bernstein's (2012) account of anti-trafficking organisations and benevolent White feminism. White supremacy is intertwined with the power of Western states and their colonial legacy. As such, this moral crusade:

> locates its moral obligation and civic responsibility in great part in the rescue of 'prostituted' women and children (victims) from the clutches of male privilege, power, and lust (sex trafficking) and celebrates its success in extending its international reach (especially in Asia), reproducing the colonial maternalist position in relation to the non-Western world while reconfirming white Western feminine subjectivity as benevolent. Contemporary antislavery advocates share a similar dimension of the modern 'white man's burden' in that they see themselves as leading a moral crusade against an 'unconscionable evil' that proudly claims to be following in the footsteps of the British and American nineteenth-century evangelical-inspired movements to abolish the enslavement and trade of Africans. (Kempadoo, 2015: 14–5)

On this reading, abolitionism is the new anti-slavery movement that obsesses over trafficking for sexual exploitation over other forms of labour exploitation. When an abolitionist logic is uncritically applied to the context of sexual exploitation, it results in multiple erasure effects. It erases the distinction between sexual exploitation and sex work, rendering agency meaningless and championing instead the idea of a powerless victim in need of rescue. It also erases the difference between undocumented migrant and trafficked victim. Lastly, it contributes to individualising blame for sexually exploitative relations. This abolitionist shift is very visible in the context of changing approaches towards prostitution and its regulation.

State responses to prostitution

In this next section, we discuss how state responses towards prostitution have developed, noting the recent trend towards shifting the burden of responsibility away from those who sell sex and towards those who buy it. We reflect on some of the limitations of this approach in an increasingly globalised context, where even those who cannot legally buy sex in their native country are still able to travel and buy sex elsewhere by engaging in sex tourism. Meanwhile, those who sell sex outside their country of birth, migrant sex workers, can face prosecution, detention and even deportation, while having limited access to licit labour market opportunities and limited recourse to justice.

'Get off in Thailand': Why don't we regulate sex tourism?

In February 2019, AirAsia introduced an advertising campaign in Australia, affixed on public transport, using the tagline 'Get Off in Thailand'.

This advert presumably targeted Australians, and particularly Australian men, as a 'double entendre'. In theory (and often in practice), Global North passport holders can travel to any country and do what they like with their powerful passports and money in their pockets, including buying sex. However, the 'Get off in Thailand' advert received harsh criticism from members of the organisation Collective Shout: a campaigning platform against the sexualisation of women and children in the media. Collective Shout took this opportunity to expose the scale of sex tourism from Australia into Thailand. Such criticism then triggered negative reactions from public officials. After only a few weeks, AirAsia removed the advert and released a public apology (France24, 27 March 2019).

How would you interpret this chain of events? Since the advert was removed, one could argue that this was a victory for rights-based advocacy against sexual exploitation. However, despite the successful targeting of advertising campaigns by advocacy groups, there are no easily enforceable regulations preventing men from travelling to Thailand to buy sex, nor are there regulations preventing men from earning disproportionately to their needs and having large disposable incomes. Indeed, Thailand's economy relies on leisure and sex tourism in a significant way (McDowall and Wang, 2009). Havocscope (2015) estimated that up to 10 per cent of Thailand's Gross Domestic Product (GDP) originates from the sex industry. This is an estimate, but it remains an indication of the size and importance of the sex industry in the Thai economy.

Should states be doing more to regulate sex buying? Should they criminalise it? In general, relatively few states worldwide have attempted the regulation of the purchase of sex, and not without controversy. To date, legislation that criminalises the purchase of sex was implemented in Sweden first in 1999, later followed by Norway, Finland and Iceland, and more recently by Belize, Canada, France, Ireland, Israel, Martinique and Northern Ireland. One issue with this approach has to do with scope. Any such legislation can only target incidents within a given country's territory, and not across borders. There is no easily enforceable regulation criminalising sex tourism, and no simple way of establishing whether people engage in sex tourism or not when they travel. Criminalising the buying of sex in Sweden does not prevent Swedish people from travelling to Thailand to buy sex.

A further dimension of this debate is that the criminalisation of the purchase of sex has come under fire by some academics and sex workers' rights groups (Scarlet Alliance; the Rose Alliance; the English Collective of Prostitutes; the Global Network of Sex Work Projects are some examples). Scholars and activists have been critical about using the criminal law as an instrument of liberation (Bernstein, 2010; Scoular and Carline, 2014), about the mistaken assumption that criminalising demand will not drive supply further underground (Scoular and O'Neill, 2008), and about the negative effects criminalisation has on the most vulnerable among sex workers. There are profound inequalities in the treatment and regulation of tourists versus other travellers, such as migrants. Migrant sex workers (those who sell sex in a country different from their country of birth) and survival sex workers (those who exchange sex as a means of survival) are particularly vulnerable. Scholars also point to the process of individualising blame, echoing the femonationalistic debates we encountered in Chapter 3 whereby gender inequality is seen exclusively in the actions of a few 'bad men' towards women who are victims, rather than as a structural problem (Harrington, 2018).

Whether you think criminalising the purchase of sex is a positive, progressive practice or not, there are some things worth considering. This approach generally does little to tackle gender and economic inequalities, unless it is part of a much broader package of welfare reforms targeting such inequalities, as was the case in Sweden:

the Swedish woman-friendly welfare state's reliance on gender equality through women's participation in the labour market and men's entry to the home as care takers, the gender-equal tax system designed to facilitate such practices, and the sexual politics where 'free and equal sex' was promoted, all suggested that men and women were essentially alike and in need of the same rights and social benefits to make a good life. In this context, the gendered and violent reality of prostitution did not make prostitution seem like a job, rather a vehicle perpetuating gender inequality. (Yttergren and Westerstrand, 2016: 48)

While Sweden is often pictured as one of the most gender-equal countries in the world, this presumed equality is tarnished by ethnonationalism and heteronormativity (Schierup and Ålund, 2011). Welfare reforms were implemented primarily for the benefit of Swedish nationals, and not immigrant groups. Meanwhile, this approach denies people any choice to engage in sex work as a legitimate occupation, meaning that sex workers are denied any agency in the matter (Levy and Jakobsson, 2013). Niina Vuolajärvi's (2019) ethnography across Sweden, Norway and Finland has highlighted that migrants make up the majority of sex workers in the region, and that, instead of prosecuting clients, Nordic states are busy prosecuting migrant sex workers through immigration laws. Nationals are being afforded the welfare of the generous Nordic states through support, counselling and exit programmes. Meanwhile, foreigners increasingly become targets of punishment and deportation: a trend not unique to Nordic states (Pickering and Ham, 2014).

In sum, efforts to regulate prostitution are inherently limited by hegemonic norms which transfer into law (Scoular, 2010), and by a system of nationalist allegiances and borders which is antithetical to the globalisation of markets. In this context, while states are busy fortifying and deporting, moral campaigners are focusing our attention on the immorality of buying sex. Meanwhile, they want to convince us that sex workers are victims of sexual exploitation; but what if the realities of prostitution were more complex than that?

Sex workers, austerity and survival

So far, we have identified some trends that are shaping the prostitution landscape, including the framing of the problem in terms of trafficking and sexual exploitation, the rise of abolitionism and the criminalisation of buyers in some countries, and the targeting and deportation of migrant sex workers. We will conclude the chapter by reflecting on the effects of criminalisation and the political economy of austerity on sex workers in England.

While the act of selling sex from person A to B is not illegal in many jurisdictions, and indeed the same goes for the act of B buying sex from A (minus the countries outlined in the earlier section), many of the activities *associated* with prostitution are criminalised. In England and Wales, the Sexual Offences Act 2003 and the Policing and Crime Act 2009 are the central pieces of legislation regulating prostitution. Under these Acts, activities including soliciting, causing or inciting prostitution for gain, controlling prostitution for gain, paying for the sexual services of a prostitute subjected to force, and loitering (as covered by the Street Offences Act 1959) are criminalised. It is also illegal for two or more people to sell sex from the same premises.

There are significant variations in the law and application of the law across the UK, at both jurisdictional and local level. Northern Ireland notably adopted the criminalisation of buyers' model in 2014 (Huschke, 2017). Meanwhile, different police forces across the country have adopted distinct and often contradictory approaches to prostitution, varying from the innovative Merseyside model, which treats violence against sex workers as a form of hate crime (Campbell, 2016), to waves of eviction and 'cleansing' of specific areas as being tied to gentrification, particularly evident in the country's city centres (Neville and Sanders-McDonagh, 2017). Lastly, there has been increasing investment in anti-trafficking operations, leading to detention and deportation. For example, a report by the organisation After Exploitation found that, in 2018, hundreds of trafficking victims were placed in detention centres awaiting deportation (Taylor, 9 July 2019).

The English Collective of Prostitutes (ECP) is a sex worker-led advocacy organisation. Box 7.4 contains an excerpt from its website. We would like you to read it carefully.

BOX 7.4

The English Collective of Prostitutes (ECP) is a network of sex workers working both on the streets and indoors, campaigning for decriminalisation and safety.

We fight against being treated like criminals. We've helped sex workers win against charges of soliciting, brothel-keeping and controlling – the last two most often used against women who are working together for safety.

Most sex workers are mothers trying to do the best for their children. We campaign against austerity cuts and for housing and other survival resources so that any of us can leave prostitution if and when we want.

We have an international network including sister organisations in Thailand (Empower) and the US (US PROStitutes Collective).

WHAT WE STAND FOR:

- Decriminalisation of sex work – on the street and in premises – as in New Zealand. The laws land us in prison, divide us from families and friends, make us vulnerable to violence, isolate us. Criminal records trap us in prostitution.
- Protection from rape and other violence.
- An end to police brutality, corruption, racism and other illegality. Prosecute police who break the law.

- No zones, no licensing, no legalised brothels – they are ghettos and state pimping.
- Self-determination. Sex workers must decide how we want to work – not the police, local authorities, pimps, madams/managers who profit from our work.
- An end to racism and other discrimination within the sex industry.
- Rights for sex workers like other workers: the right to organise collectively to improve our working conditions, a pension and to join trade unions.
- No criminalisation of clients, which would force sex workers underground and into more danger. Consenting sex between adults is not a crime.
- Free and accessible health services for all: no mandatory health checks.
- Cis and trans women's right to organise independently of men, including of male sex workers.
- Economic alternatives: no one should be forced into sex by poverty. People who want to leave the sex industry (or any industry) should have access to resources.
- Shelters and benefits for children/young people so they don't have to beg or go into prostitution to survive.
- No 'rehabilitation' schemes which punish us or force us into low-paid jobs.
- The right to freedom of movement within and between countries. Stop using anti-trafficking laws to deport sex workers.

Source: Adapted from the English Collective of Prostitutes website (ECP, n.d.)

Take some time to summarise the issues identified in this position statement, then reflect on the following:

- What does this organisation stand for?
- What are its demands?
- What problems does it identify as affecting sex workers?
- What solutions does it propose?
- Who is the organisation speaking on behalf of?
- How do you feel about the above positions? Do you agree or disagree with them and why?

Recently, the ECP collected a series of articles on its website coming from disparate news sources, all pointing to the same issue. The headlines read:

Selling sex for £5 is the only way I can survive after universal credit chaos. (Sky News, 25 October 2019)

Universal credit: MPs call for action on women driven to 'survival sex'. (BBC, 25 October 2019)

Universal credit: Women say they are forced into 'survival sex' by DWP's five-week wait, MPs warn. (Sandhu, 25 October 2019)

Why is it only when universal credit forces women into sex work the government actually listens? (Aspinall, 25 October 2019)

These headlines point to 'the violence of austerity' (Cooper and Whyte, 2017). They are interesting because they identify the state as being responsible for pushing women into prostitution as a direct result of austerity and welfare reform. Austerity has been the dominant political economic approach in the UK in response to the 2008 economic crisis. As discussed in Chapter 2, this approach entailed extensive cuts to public services and a substantial review of the structure of welfare benefits, which culminated in the creation of Universal Credit. Hailed as a one-stop shop to replace a more antiquated and fragmented welfare benefits system, Universal Credit has received widespread criticism and been deemed a policy failure (Norris and Rutter, 2016).

While survival sex work in the context of austerity appears far removed from conceptualising prostitution as a free choice for women, it is also a far cry from the idea that prostitution should be understood solely as a form of sexual exploitation, or even as an expression of gender inequality. Inequality is a core driver, but inequality should always be understood as intersectional. In the context of austerity, the state enables entry into prostitution because of its failure to provide alternatives for the most vulnerable in society, including migrants and people in poverty. It is unsurprising then that sex workers' advocacy groups, along with many academics, see attempts by the state to criminalise any aspect of prostitution as a bogus solution to the problem.

Summary

In this chapter, we have observed the somewhat disparate yet interconnected issues of grooming, trafficking and prostitution, with the aid of key concepts and structural categories, including the usual suspects: gender, 'race' and class. We insist on observing the way these categories intersect to support our understanding of these phenomena and state responses to them under the umbrella of sexual exploitation. The recognition that sexual exploitation takes place in the context of grooming, trafficking and prostitution does little to address their causes. What is more, such recognition can be used by states in perverse ways. States use the fear of sexual exploitation and trafficking to justify the tightening of borders and their policing. They use this fear to justify punitive responses towards individual deviants such as British Asian groomers and sex buyers, but also migrant sex workers. These state interventions do not halt these phenomena in any significant way, and often do more harm than good; for example, by fostering cultural stereotypes about groomers, by driving prostitution further underground, by rendering sex workers more vulnerable and by detaining and deporting migrant sex workers.

If we are to give validity and meaning to the rhetoric of universal human rights, we must start by actively addressing the rights of people who are marginalised and made vulnerable in these contexts. Conversely, and by relying on dominant discourses about trafficking and sexual exploitation shaped by undercurrents of ethnonationalism, femonationalism, colonialism and abolitionism, states continue to support criminal justice interventions targeted at individual deviants, rather than investing in systemic change. Such change would require addressing the root causes of economic and social inequalities and redesigning political economy away from neoliberal globalisation, something that cannot be done through criminal justice reform alone.

Review questions

- In what ways does nationalism play a role in state responses to grooming, trafficking and prostitution?
- What are the limitations of current understandings of, and state interventions in, sexual exploitation?
- What should states do differently to address the causes of sexual exploitation?

Other chapters that this links to

Chapter 3 (Sex and crime in time and space)
Chapter 5 (Sex and institutional cultures of abuse)
Chapter 8 (Sex and war)
Chapter 12 (Children, sexualisation and the law)
Chapter 14 (The future)
Chapter 15 (How to change your life)

8

Sex and war

CHAPTER OUTLINE

The purpose of this chapter is to demonstrate how rape (specifically genocidal rape) and sexual(ised) violence are used as weapons of war. The chapter also considers the relationship between militarised masculinity and sexual violence within and by military **institutions**. Below, we set up our discussion of these topics with two examples, one from popular culture and one from 'national security' political discourse. Please note that some readers might find the content of this chapter upsetting and so you should take your time with the material, take breaks and discuss anything that comes up for you with people you trust.

By the end of this chapter, you will understand more about:

- the use of rape (specifically genocidal rape) and sexual(ised) violence as weapons of war and the legacy and unresolved trauma associated with these war crimes
- how militarised masculinity serves as a proxy for **hegemonic masculinity** in the context of war/armed conflict, and the implications of this
- how military sexual assault is a 'practice' that takes place within a heteronormative institution
- how the themes you have addressed so far in this book play out in the context of war/armed conflict.

BOX 8.1

In 2019, HBO aired the TV show *Watchmen*: Damon Lindelof's version of the 1986 graphic novel created by Alan Moore. The legacy of racism, racial violence, and the unresolved trauma caused by those phenomena are the key themes of this series. The theme of transgenerational or inherited trauma (trauma passed down from one generation to the next) is viscerally depicted in episode six of *Watchmen*, entitled 'This Extraordinary Being'. In this episode, Angela, our main character, overdoses on Nostalgia, a pill that allows you access to past memories/experiences. Not only does she take too much of the drug, she consumes someone else's Nostalgia: that of her grandfather's, Will Reeve. Under the influence of the drug, Angela relives and bears witness to Will's experiences of institutional and violent racism during the 1930s in New York City. As both subject and onlooker, Angela is forced to confront the legacy of the 1920s Tulsa massacre[†] and the impact it has had on her grandfather. By reliving Will's experiences, the (unresolved) trauma of this pivotal event is passed down to Angela.

Ahead of the repeal of the American military's 'Don't ask, don't tell'[‡] (DADT) policy in 2010, the then Republican senator John McCain voiced his opposition

---

[†]During this event, White supremacists destroyed the homes and businesses of Black residents in the Greenwood neighbourhood of Tulsa.

[‡]DADT was a policy introduced by President Clinton in 1993. Replacing the ban on gay men and women serving in the military, this measure would allow individuals to serve as long as they did not reveal their sexual orientation. It was repealed under President Obama in 2011.

(Continued)

to the repeal of this policy, using 'national security' and 'unit cohesion' to justify his position (Rich et al., 2012). Here, it is worth quoting him at length:

> Mistakes and ... distractions cost Marines' lives ... Marines come back after serving in combat and they say ... anything that's going to break or potentially break that focus and cause any kind of distraction may have an effect on cohesion ... If you go up to Bethesda, Marines are up there with no legs, none. We've got Marines at Walter Reed with no limbs ... I hope that when we pass this legislation [repealing DATD], that we will understand that we are doing great damage, and we could possibly and probably ... harm the battle effectiveness which is so vital to the ... survival of our young men and women in the military. (cited by Rich et al., 2012: 270–1)

In their analysis of this speech, Craig Rich et al. (2012: 271) argue that the references to torn and limbless bodies – bodies that have been physically impaired – also suggest bodies that have been 'materially mutilated and symbolically castrated'. Furthermore, implicit in this statement is the suggestion that allowing gay men to serve in the military results in 'torn, mutilated, and disabled (presumably heterosexual) male bodies'. Simply put, 'the overt presence of homosexuality leads to violence against (straight, male) soldier[s]' (Rich et al., 2012: 271).

Think about these two examples as you read through the chapter. We will return to them in due course.

We start this chapter with a review of the rape as a weapon-of-war thesis. This is followed by two case studies. Our first case study is children born from genocidal rape. Genocidal rape is when rape is used to commit the act of genocide (a more detailed definition is provided below). Drawing on the concept of transgenerational trauma (Rinker and Lawler, 2018), as depicted in the episode of *Watchmen* discussed above, we unpack the lived experiences of children born of wartime rape during the genocides in Bosnia and Herzegovina (BiH) and Rwanda in the early 1990s. The key themes we address are **ethnicity**, nationality, legacy and trauma. In our second case study, we trace the relationship between heterosexual militarised masculinity and rape and sexual violence within and by the military. **Heteronormativity, hetero/hypermasculinity** – as reflected in the statement made by John McCain that you read about above – informs our review of these violence(s) within and by the military.

A note on terminology: here, in order to acknowledge the secondary victimisation of children born of genocidal rape, we use the term 'victims' rather than 'survivors' when referring to this group. This is also in keeping with the victims interviewed by Myriam Denov and her team who did not see themselves as 'survivors' of the Rwandan genocide, but rather felt they were 'victims' of the crimes committed against their mothers. For all other groups, where appropriate, we use the term victim/survivor (see Chapter 3 for our discussion of this choice of language).

Rape as a weapon of war: is this always the case?

It might be surprising to think of rape as something that can be used as a weapon of war. And yet, at the macro-level, rape is used as an official strategy of war. It is used as a political device to achieve genocide and ethnic cleansing (Waller, 2012: 85). It can also be used to attack a nation, which, as we saw in Chapter 3, is a key motivator for controlling sexuality and sexual practice in the first place. In the context of war, the female body becomes the vessel through which national, ethnic, racial and religious identities are reproduced (Cohn, 2013: 14). Rape against the individual female is thus rape against the **nation**. It is also, according to Laura Sjoberg (2013), an attack against 'enemy' men who have failed to protect the women belonging to 'their' group. This strategic/tactical use of wartime rape falls within the weapon-of-war paradigm (Buss, 2009; Card, 1996; Farwell, 2004).

At the meso-level, the military institution (within patriarchal and **phallocentric societies**) socialises men to embody a violent and aggressive heterosexual masculinity. Not only is rape normalised within this setting, it is also used to perform this type of masculinity. 'Recreational rape' (Enloe, 2000), which views wartime rape as an opportunistic crime, can be placed at the micro-level. It is related to the 'pressure-cooker' theory which views rape as the result of men's biological/innate sexual urges (Fogelman, 2012; Mullins, 2009). Within this line of thinking, and in contrast to the weapon-of-war paradigm, rape is conceived as a by-product of the chaos of war.

Wartime rape and sexual violence against males have received far less attention compared with the vast amount of research and information on female victims. Despite the dearth of literature on this topic, the phenomenon has taken place in over 25 conflicts over the last 30 years (Vojdik, 2014). Described as 'unrecognised and/or invisible victims' (Gorris, 2015; Lewis, 2009), underreporting (due to shame, fear, stigma and the criminalisation of homosexuality) is common among men. This, hitherto, impedes our ability to access complete data on the number of victims/survivors (see Christian et al., 2011; Lewis, 2009; Vojdik, 2014).

Male-to-male conflict-related sexual violence (in the form of rape, castration,[§] sexual mutilation and/or torture) subordinates the male victim, depriving

---

[§]Typically, this involves the removal or destruction of the male testicles, thus rendering the male impotent.

him of his manhood and masculinity (Baaz and Stern, 2009; Christian et al., 2011; Clark, 2017; Ferrales et al., 2016; Lewis, 2009; Vojdik, 2014). Here, we are reminded of our earlier discussion (in relation to DADT) about materially and symbolically mutilated and castrated bodies.

This disempowerment takes place at the individual and communal levels. As Sandesh Sivakumaran (2007: 274) explains, 'sexual violence against men symbolises the disempowerment of the national, racial, religious or ethnic group. Specifically, [t]he castration of a man is considered to emasculate him, to deprive him of his power. The castration of a man may also represent the symbolic emasculation of the entire community'. It is worth noting that these messages of subordination, humiliation, emasculation and feminisation are heightened when perpetrated by females.

For Janine Clark (2017: 3), these examples of male sexual victimisation speak to the vulnerability of the penis. She states:

> This 'side' of the penis is rarely seen. Within contemporary discourses on sexual violence ... the penis is typically framed as a weapon. It is a hard, aggressive object that penetrates and tears, causing pain and suffering ... the exposure of [the vulnerability of the penis] strips the phallus of its power and strength ... hence its dominance. (Clark, 2012: 3)

Clark (2017: 5) argues that when men are raped and sexually assaulted through genital mutilation and castration, the weakness of the phallus is revealed. This is destabilising because war, she argues, 'is the ultimate expression of **phallocentric masculinity**, and the penis is required to perform in a way that upholds and defends the phallocentric – and heteronormative – status quo'. How useful is this notion of the vulnerability of the penis? How do we reconcile this seemingly para-doxical notion of the vulnerable penis when, in cases of male-to-male rape, the penis is used as a weapon against other men? Here, we offer a more useful illustra-tion of this thesis. During the conflict in Darfur (2003–5), in addition to rape, soldiers and the Janjaweed would cut off the penises of their victims and insert them into their mouths (Ferrales et al., 2016). For us, this act of sexualised violence, rather than rape, is a more accurate portrayal of the vulnerability of the penis.

Are these acts about sex or power?

Many have argued that rape is not about sex, sexual desire or, indeed, sexual pleasure. Rather, it is about power and control over the victim. As Maria Baaz and Maria Stern (2018) note, the removal of the sexual has its roots in early radical feminist work. Susan Brownmiller, for example, in her seminal text, *Against Our Will: Men, Women and Rape* (that we have already encountered in Chapters 3 and 4), argued that rape was not the product of desire but, rather, an act of aggression. She states: rape 'is the quintessential act by which a male demonstrates to a female that she is conquered – vanquished – by his superior strength and power' (Brownmiller, 1975: 49). Following on from this, 'rape was cast as a collective violent and political act ... [used] ... as a tool of power and **patriarchy**' (Baaz and Stern, 2018: 299).

Let us apply this to the context of war. As noted above, in some instances rape is an official strategy of the war. This was the case in Bangladesh, the former Yugoslavia, Rwanda, Darfur and the DRC (Banwell, 2020). However, unlike these examples of systematic and genocidal rape, the use of rape against Jewish women during the Holocaust was not an official element of the Nazi genocide (Banwell, 2015; Goldenberg, 2013). Given the aim of the Final Solution – the elimination of all European Jews – rape, in this case, became a redundant weapon of terror (Goldenberg, 2013).

During the Holocaust, women's quintessentially feminine attributes were diminished. Entry into the camps meant their heads were shaven, they were forced to wear formless clothing and a lack of food meant loss of body weight, especially from their breasts and hips (Banwell, 2015, 2020). Yet German men did not refrain from raping them. Prior to this, before they were subjected to the physical degradations listed above, the motivation to rape these women may have been rooted in sexual desire and sexual gratification (Banwell, 2015, 2020). However, in the latter states of their confinement – when their feminine attributes and conventional attractiveness had been undermined – aggression, male power and dominance may have been the motivation behind these assaults (Fogelman, 2012; see also Banwell, 2015, 2020).

Exceptions to this 'desexing' of wartime rape include Cynthia Enloe's notion of recreational violence, the 'pressure cooker' theory and opportunistic rape (discussed above). However, as Baaz and Stern (2018) point out, these approaches present wartime rape as being inevitable and run the risk of reviving biological determinism. All deny agency to the actors and reduce the culpability of perpetrators. We will return to this later.

Having outlined the relevant themes within the literature on wartime rape, we now move on to our first case study, in Box 8.2.

Children born as a result of genocidal rape in Bosnia and Herzegovina (BiH) and Rwanda

This section is set out in three sections. First, we outline the concept of genocidal rape, reviewing three historical examples of this phenomenon. We then review the literature on transgenerational trauma before, in the final section, applying this to children born of genocidal rape in BiH and Rwanda. Here, we explore the individual narratives of these young adults, placing them within the broader cultural and collective memory of their post-genocide societies.

The concepts of 'hybridity', 'stickiness' (Takševa and Schwartz, 2018) and 'de-ethnicization' (Kuradusenge, 2016) are used to explore the haunting of these unresolved traumatic events, specifically the exclusion and marginalisation of the **abject** 'ethnic other'.

The definition of genocide is based on committing certain acts 'with [the] intent to destroy, in whole or in part, a national, ethnical, racial or religious group'. The most obvious example is 'killing members of the group'. Relevant to our discussion below are elements d and e of the genocide convention: 'imposing measures intended to prevent births within the group [and] forcibly transferring children of the group to another group' (Convention on the Prevention and Punishment of the Crime of Genocide; UNGA, 2014).

When rape is used intentionally and systematically (the weapon-of-war paradigm), it can be classed as genocidal. Examples include the 1971 Liberation War in Bangladesh, the conflict in BiH and in Rwanda. Given our focus on forced pregnancy and children born of genocidal rape, we will limit our discussion to the latter two.

Genocidal rape in the form of enforced impregnation of Muslim and Croatian women by Serbian men was a feature of the genocide in BiH (Sharlach, 2000; Takševa, 2015). Forced pregnancy, as defined by The International Criminal Court (ICC), is the 'unlawful confinement of a woman forcibly made pregnant, with the intent of affecting the ethnic composition of any population' (Rome Statute of the Criminal Court, 2011: 4). Figures suggest that between 25,000 and 40,000 Bosnian women were victims of this crime (Takševa, 2015). And it is estimated that between 500–600 children were born as a result of genocidal rape in 1993 (see Carpenter, 2000).

During the genocide, women were detained in 'rape camps' where they were repeatedly raped until they became pregnant. They were confined until access to safe abortion was no longer possible (Sharlach, 2000; Takševa, 2015). As outlined in the definition of genocide, this prevents births within the group as women's wombs are occupied with babies from a different ethnic group. It also means the birth of ethnically mixed children. Furthermore, as noted by Christopher Mullins (2009: 18) and Alexandra Takai (2011), these children – in family structures where patrilineal parentage decides lineage membership – become members of the father's ethnic group rather than the mother's. This results in 'transferring children of the group to another group'.

Genocidal rape was also a feature of the Rwandan genocide. During the 12 weeks of this genocide, between 250,000 and 500,000 Rwandan Tutsi women were raped. The assailants were primarily Hutu men (Buss, 2009; Mullins, 2009; Sharlach, 1999, 2000). Sexual mutilation and torture were a feature of these rapes. According to Paula Donovan, a UN advisor on Africa, 'between 2,000 and 5,000 children were born to women who were raped from April to July 1994' (cited by Kamuzinzi, 2016: 170; see also Denov et al., 2017; Hogwood et al., 2018). There is also evidence to suggest that the deliberate transmission of HIV was a further feature of genocidal rape in Rwanda. Survivors reported that HIV + Hutu men raped Tutsi women in order to transmit the disease to them (see Sharlach, 1999, 2000).

The fate of children born from genocidal rape has, until fairly recently, remained largely obscured from view compared with the copious amount of literature on the female victims of genocidal rape (Brownmiller, 1975; Mullins, 2009; Sharlach, 1999, 2000; Takai, 2011; Takševa, 2015). This, to paraphrase Carpenter (2000), is surprising given that children born as a result of these rapes were a key element of the genocidal equation.

Following Carpenter's (2000) early work on the marginalisation of children born of genocidal rape, numerous scholars have drawn attention to the plight of these children (Denov, 2015; Denov and Kahn, 2019; Denov et al., 2017; Eramian and Denov, 2018; Erjavec and Volčič 2010a, 2010b; Kahn and Denov, 2019; Woolner et al., 2019; see also Hogwood et al., 2018). Historically, however, within legal discourse, forced impregnation was regarded as a crime against the woman only. When they *were* considered, children born as a result of genocidal rape – who, as outlined above, would take on the ethnic identity of their fathers – were 'seen not just as non-victims but somehow as perpetrators' (Carpenter, 2000: 445; see also Erjavec and Volčič, 2010a, 2010b; Hogwood et al., 2018). In the words of Laura Eramian and Denov (2018: 374), these children 'possess the ethnic "heritage" of two groups, but do not fully belong to either'. In cases where the identity of the father is unknown, children face further marginalisation and stigma. This can lead to 'physical, psychological and structural violence' from family members and the wider community (Eramian and Denov, 2018: 374; see also Denov et al., 2017). In Rwanda, they are often referred to as 'enfants de mauvais souvenirs' (children of bad memories) or 'enfants de la haine' (children of hate) (Denov et al., 2017: 5). And, in BiH, they are described as 'children of the enemy', 'bastard children', 'Chetnik's whore child' and 'children of hate' (cited in Erjavec and Volčič, 2010b: 362, 368). In the next section, drawing on the experiences of young adults, we unpack the legacy and unresolved trauma of the genocides in BiH and Rwanda.

What is transgenerational trauma?

Teresa Evans-Campbell (2008: 320; cited in Denov, 2015: 64) defines intergenerational trauma as:

> [a] collective complex trauma inflicted on a group of people who share a specific group identity or affiliation – ethnicity, nationality, and religious affiliation. It is the legacy of numerous traumatic events a community experiences over generations and encompasses the psychological and social responses to such events.

Transgenerational trauma is experienced by individuals who were not directly exposed to the trauma/violence in question but who, nevertheless, '"catch" some effects of that experience by virtue of being in contact with individuals who have experienced it, or by being in a society that has experienced chronic violent conflict or trauma' (Rinker and Lawler, 2018: 153). It is also referred to as 'collective trauma' (Rinker and Lawler, 2018) or 'cultural trauma' (Lehrner and Yehuda, 2018). Currently, there are over 500 published scholarly works on the intergenerational transmission of trauma (Lehrner and Yehuda, 2018). This phenomenon can be traced back to the 1960s when children of survivors of the Holocaust began seeking psychiatric treatment for trauma-related disorders in Canada (Denov, 2015; Rinker and Lawler, 2018). As Amy Lehrner and Rachel Yehuda explain (2018: 25), these children 'learned of the Holocaust, saw the direct effects in their parents, and for many, felt its complex legacy within themselves'.

Below, based on empirical research with victims, we apply this concept to children born of genocidal rape in BiH and Rwanda.

'I am a cancer': the narratives of victims from BiH

Erjavec and Volčič (2010a) interviewed 19 Bosniak females aged 14–16. All were born as a result of genocidal rape. They were either living in institutions or with their mothers. They found that metaphors – employed by all of their participants – played a significant role in how the girls thought of themselves and made sense of their experiences. The metaphors used can be demarcated along the following three themes: I am a shooting target; I am a cancer; and I am a fighter. We will deal with each of these in turn (see also their article 'Living with the sins of their fathers', Erjavec and Volčič, 2010b; this is based on the narratives of 11 adolescent girls born of genocidal rape in BiH).

In relation to the first theme – I am a shooting target – through the use of vehicle metaphors, the girls conveyed how they felt excluded and isolated from their wider communities. As articulated by Aida: 'In my school I am a *shooting target*. Anyone can attack me. And this happens every day ... I am a target ... I am their *shooting target* ... a *target* into which everyone *shoots* ... Everyone is allowed to *shoot* ... The war here still goes on, it is not over yet' (Erjavec and Volčič, 2010a: 530).

Others, who referred to themselves 'as a cancer', employed biological metaphors to compare themselves to a type of malignant disease. As Marina explains: 'I see myself *as a cancer* ... as a cancer that divides weak and sick cells in the blood, and destroys all the strong, the good cells. Yes, the malignant cells destroy the good ones' (Erjavec and Volčič, 2010a: 534). Interestingly, the identity and origins of this second category of girls were not known to the wider community and yet, they had adopted, pre-emptively, a particularly negative self-image, fearing the responses they believed they would receive if/ once their identities were revealed.

The final category offers a more positive outlook for children born of genocidal rape. This group, in contradistinction to the first group, used vehicle metaphors to describe themselves as fighters rather than those who are shot at. In the words of Amda: 'I perceive myself as a fighter for peace ... I think I need to be that ... because as a child who has blood from two different groups, I am able to negotiate more, and act as a peacekeeper ... between both nations in order to overcome divisions and conflicts' (Erjavec and Volčič, 2010a: 536).

'Hybridity' and 'stickiness'

In their article 'Hybridity, ethnicity and nationhood', Tatjana Takševa and Agatha Schwartz (2018) apply the concepts of 'hybridity' and 'stickiness' to the narratives of the girls interviewed by Erjavec and Volčič (2010a, b). With regards to the former, individuals who have lived in multiple cultures or come from a mixed cultural background are believed to exist in cultural hybrids. These cultural hybrids subvert monolithic ethnic, national and community identities. As a result, they are excluded and treated as 'Other' (Takševa and Schwartz, 2018). Allied to this, 'stickiness' uses repetitive language to consolidate who is considered abject, repulsive and in need of expulsion (Sarah Ahmed; cited in Takševa and Schwartz, 2018).

To illustrate how these concepts are at work in survivor accounts, Takševa and Schwartz (2018: 468) also draw upon the biography *Leila, ein bosnisches Mädchen* (Leila, a girl from Bosnia) by Alexandra Cavelius. This will be our focus here. The book is based on the story of a 24-year-old Bosniak survivor, Leila. Before Leila is rescued by a Bosnian Serb, she is brutally raped by Serbs and Muslim militia. Following her escape, Leila embarks upon a personal relationship with her liberator with whom she subsequently has a child. Leila and her child are subject to harassment in post-conflict Bosnian society: 'Leila because she is seen as a "Serbian whore" and her child because he is the product of a "mixed" union deemed undesirable and "contaminated"' (Takševa and Schwartz, 2018: 468).

For Takševa and Schwartz (2018: 467), 'stickiness' and hybridity are present within Leila's story. Both mother and child carry with them the trauma of the war 'but also the "stickiness" of the rapes committed by the enemy and/or of sexual relations with the "enemy"'. The child has a 'mixed' ethnic identity, reflecting a hybridity that challenges 'national division lines' in post-conflict BiH. As a result of her post-conflict relationship with a Serb, Leila is marked as a 'betrayer of her ethnic group', while her child is regarded as the 'embodiment of that betrayal and a symbolic repository of ethnic hatred' that sparked the genocide (Takševa and Schwartz, 2018: 467).

Let us unpack this in more detail. Genocidal rape is used to attack a nation. It divides and tears and leads to the physical and social death of the ethnic group targeted for destruction. We agree with Takševa and Schwartz (2018) who suggest that Leila's story represents a subversion of this process. Despite being raped by a Serb during the genocide, Leila chooses to engage in a relationship with a member of this group. This demonstrates, Takševa and Schwartz (2018: 468) argue, that 'ethnic labels are meaningless beyond the ideological contexts that construct them, and that it is individual choices that matter'. They believe that Leila's individual choice 'undermines dominant ethno-nationalist discourses of identity that operate on the basis of ethnic purity and exclusion'. Her actions loosen 'the grip of ethnic identifications that predominate in Bosnian society'. This is reminiscent of Amda's belief (presented above) that she might overcome the divisions and conflict between the two nations.

'We are children like others'**: the stories of children from Rwanda

The qualitative research project, led by Myriam Denov, which included 60 participants, provides the most comprehensive data on the experiences of children born of genocidal rape in Rwanda (see Denov and Kahn, 2019; Denov et al., 2017; Eramian and Denov, 2018; Kahn and Denov, 2019; Woolner et al., 2019; see also Hogwood et al., 2018, who conducted interviews with ten young people born of genocidal rape in Rwanda).

In-depth interviews and focus group discussions were carried out by Denov and her team of young adults in their earlier twenties (31 males and 29 females) in 2016. All were born as a result of the rapes that occurred during the 1994 Rwandan genocide. The majority of the participants lived with their maternal family, often including extended family members such as aunts, uncles and/or grandparents. Some lived only with their mother, or with their mother and their 'new reconstituted family' after their mothers had remarried (Denov et al., 2017: 9). The key themes identified from the qualitative data included 'identity and belonging', 'ambivalence in the mother–child relationship' and 'truth-telling' (Denov et al., 2017; see also Kahn and Denov, 2019; Woolner et al., 2019). In terms of feeling accepted by their families and the wider community, all participants felt that the origins of their birth hindered their ability to fit in and feel a sense of belonging. All described being

---

**This is the title of the article by Kahn and Denov (2019).

ostracised and marginalised by both their families and their communities. This led to internalised feelings of shame and stigma. As Sarilee Kahn and Myriam Denov (2019: 518) explain, this was compounded by 'the knowledge that their mothers were deeply traumatised by the genocide and sexual violence that they had endured and that, somehow, participants themselves were ultimately to blame for their mothers' suffering'. As articulated by one survivor:

> When I was 7 years old, I noticed the way she [mother] was treating me differently from my brothers ... The relationship is now almost good, though me and her know that she used to be traumatised by the fact that I was born from an unwanted pregnancy. Due to that trauma she was not open to me. Even now we have never talked about how she was treating me in such a manner ... What I don't like the most is that she did not provide maternal care as other children normally get from their mothers. (cited by Denov et al., 2017: 11–12)

De-ethnicisation in post-conflict Rwanda

In terms of moving forward, on both an individual and societal level, participants acknowledged that self-acceptance was key to the former, while truth-telling, self-revelation and formal recognition by Rwandan society, were vital for achieving the latter (Eramian and Denov, 2018; Kahn and Denov, 2019; see also Hogwood et al., 2018). While such attempts to move forward are encouraging, the ability to achieve this is obstructed by the ethno-political context of post-conflict Rwanda (Eramian and Denov, 2018). Below we unpack this in more detail.

Since the genocide, ethnic labelling has been prohibited in Rwanda and ethnicity has been removed from government identity cards (Denov and Kahn, 2019). Indeed, the use of ethnic labels – defined as a crime of 'divisionism' – is regarded as a criminal offence that can carry jail time (Denov and Kahn, 2019). This law is called the Prevention, Suppression and Punishment of the Crime of Discrimination and Sectarianism (Kuradusenge, 2016). Added to this, the Punishment of the Crime of Genocide Ideology was put into law in 2008 (Kuradusenge, 2016). Genocide ideology is defined in article 2 as 'an aggregate of thoughts characterised by conduct, speeches, documents and other acts aiming at exterminating or inciting others to exterminate people basing on ethnic group, origin, nationality, religion, colour, physical appearance, sex, language, religious or political opinion' (Reyntjens, 2013: 75; cited in Denov and Kahn, 2019: 155).

Despite these attempts to eradicate ethnic divisions or, rather, because of these measures, the expression of ethnic identity has become a key concern for Rwandans. As Claudine Kuradusenge (2016: 61) explains: '[t]he state policy of attempting to eliminate ethnicity as a dividing line between Rwandans – either

by accident or by design – has ... resulted in reifying ethnic identity and con-
cretising social and political lines between Hutus and Tutsis'. These attempts
to de-ethnicise post-conflict Rwandan society resonates with the aspirations of
the young adults discussed above. Reconciliation was a key objective for these
victims. Yet, their experiences of abuse, marginalisation and alienation – in
sum, their treatment as the 'enemy other' – hinder their attempts to fully integrate into post-conflict Rwandan society.

Legacy and unresolved trauma

At this point, we return to where we began this chapter: *Watchmen* and the
legacy and trauma associated with racism and racist violence. In the examples
reviewed above, the children born of genocidal rape, like Angela, experience
transgenerational or inherited trauma. The trauma of the rape and forced
impregnation continues to haunt their mothers. This unresolved trauma is
inscribed – both materially and symbolically – upon the bodies of their children. Here, things become complicated. On the one hand, by virtue of being
born as a result of genocidal rape, these children inherit the trauma visited
upon their mothers. They are the embodiment of the violence she endured.
However, on the other hand, the stigma and trauma they experience are
related to their genetically mixed ethnic identities (specifically their align-
ment with the 'enemy' group) and the rejection they face from their society.
Indeed, because of their hybrid identities – which serve as both literal and
symbolic reminders of the genocide – these children are excluded and marginalised. They experience transgenerational trauma and their own/separate
trauma (related to these events) simultaneously. As we saw in both cases,
despite their attempts to move past these hybrid identities (and broader, state-
wide attempts at de-ethnicisation in Rwanda), as well as Leila's efforts to
move past divisive ethno-nationalist labels, the trauma and 'stickiness' of
these events remain unresolved for their wider, post-conflict societies. The
latter compounds the experience of victims and curtails their attempt to move
forward towards reconciliation.

BOX 8.2

Questions and reflection

Before you begin, we suggest that you refamiliarise yourself with the definition of
genocide. For this exercise, you may want to read the definition in full. Do also

look up the definition of forced pregnancy provided by the International Criminal Court.

Now consider the following:

- How useful is the concept of genocidal rape? Does this create a hierarchy of wartime rape where genocidal rape is considered more severe than recreational or opportunistic rape?
- Can wartime rape be genocidal if it does not involve elements d and e of the genocide convention – in other words, if it does not lead to forced impregnation and the birth of an ethnically mixed cohort of children?
- In what other ways might wartime rape destroy the group? The work of Sharlach (1999, 2000) and Takai (2011) will assist you in thinking about these questions.
- How useful is the concept of transgenerational trauma? Do you think it reflects the experiences of children born of genocidal rape? What limitations do you identify with this concept?
- Can you think of other examples of unresolved trauma that have been passed down from one generation to the next?

Rape and sexual violence within and by the military

Our second case study is divided into two sections. We begin by addressing militarised masculinity and the use of rape and sexual violence in combat zones, specifically the Democratic Republic of Congo (DRC), before moving on to consider rape and sexual assault within the American armed forces. While the DRC forms the basis of our analysis in our first example, we also acknowledge the use of rape and sexual violence by (USA) military personnel against civilians in occupied territories. For example, personnel from the USA have abducted, raped and sexually assaulted women and girls at their bases in Okinawa, South Korea and the Philippines (Mesok, 2016; see Park, 2016 for a detailed review of militarised masculinity in South Korea). There are also reports of American soldiers abducting and assaulting Kosovar women during the Kosovo war (Cerretti, 2016). Added to this, the American military has committed acts of sexualised violence and torture against Iraqi male prisoners at Abu Ghraib following the invasion and occupation of Iraq (for a detailed review of this work, as well as some new insights, see Stacy Banwell's (2020) analysis of this case in Chapter 5 of her open-access monograph, *Gender and the violence(s) of war and armed conflict: More dangerous to be a woman?*).

Rather than simply focus on war/armed conflict which, as Nancy Farwell (2004) points out, 'is a time-limited process', we unpack the broader issue of militarisation. This is because the 'military, largely a masculine institution in terms of its members and policies, determines and reinforces hierarchies of power ... thereby reinforcing and re-creating gender relations and patriarchy' (Farwell, 2004: 394). To this end, our second example examines rape and sexual assault within the US military. This phenomenon is not limited to the USA: other (Western) examples of sexual harassment and assault within the military include both the UK and Canadian armed forces. However, for our purposes here, we focus on the US armed forces which consist of the Army, Marine Corps, Navy, Air Force, and Coast Guard (US Department of Defense).

We will start our analysis by unpacking the term militarised masculinity.

Militarised masculinity

Hegemonic masculinity – the most dominant type of masculinity, positioned above all other masculinities (and femininities) – is constructed as heterosexual. As noted earlier, hegemonic masculinity is linked to **phallocentrism**. The military institution – where men learn to fight and kill on behalf of the nation/ their women – is where aggressive hegemonic heterosexual masculinity is enacted. This is referred to as militarised masculinity (see Meger, 2010; Rich et al., 2012; Trenholm et al., 2013; Zurbriggen, 2010). In this context, militarised masculinity serves as a proxy for hegemonic masculinity.

A key element of militarised masculinity is 'anti-femininity' and 'No Sissy Stuff' (Branon, 1985; cited in Zurbriggen, 2010: 539). This requirement to 'avoid being seen as feminine leads men to purge the self of anything feminine'. It also involves 'devaluing women and believing that women are different from, and inferior to, men. Such devaluing is correlated with sexual aggression perpetration' (Zurbriggen, 2010: 540; see also Rich et al., 2012). Added to this purging of all things feminine, the heterocentric culture of the military also requires its members to renounce 'queer' identities (Rich et al., 2012). Stereotypes of gay men as threatening and predatory are reproduced within military discourse, leading to fears of penetration reflected in the infamous adage 'don't drop the soap'. This tongue-in-cheek advice relates to the fear that if a man bends down to pick up the soap in the shower, he will expose himself to penetration (by gay men) (Britton and Williams, 1995; cited in Rich et al., 2012: 278).

This reminds us of the statement (included above) by John McCain. The ostensible argument about 'unit cohesion' and 'national security' is, in reality, about the fear gay men pose to the heterosexual male soldier. Reminiscent of

Clark's (2017) thesis regarding the vulnerability of the penis discussed above, Rich et al. (2012: 271, 276) note: '[t]he soldier is predator, not prey; invulnerable, not vulnerable; the penetrator, not the penetrated.' Indeed, as they argue, homophobia and transphobia are so entrenched within the military institution that, even in a post-DADT context, **LGBT +** soldiers continue to conceal their sexual and gender identities. This 'self-policing ... leaves uncontested the heteronormative and patriarchal image of the soldier that remains at the military's core' (Rich et al., 2012: 283). Rich et al. wrote their article in 2012; since then, President Trump (in 2019) has banned trans men and women from serving in the military.

Rape and sexual violence by soldiers in the DRC

Now that we have outlined militarised masculinity and the heteronormative culture of the military more broadly, our discussion moves on to consider the use of military rape and sexual violence within combat zones. Militaries across the world use rape as a weapon of war. In this context, rape is used systematically to target women who belong to the enemy group (see Farwell, 2004 for a historical review). The DRC is no exception. Rape is used by soldiers to terrorise the civilian population (Banwell, 2014, 2020). According to Sara Meger (2010: 128), understanding why individual soldiers actively choose to engage in rape and sexual violence 'requires an understanding of the social constructions of masculinity both within Congolese society and, most importantly, within the military institution'. We review both below.

According to localised discourses of hegemonic masculinity, Congolese men are expected to have financial stability, a high sex drive and multiple wives (Mechanic, 2004: 15; cited in Meger, 2010: 129). In addition, they are required to have 'the physical, economic, and social power to protect their wives from other men' (Mechanic, 2004: 15; cited in Meger, 2010: 129). Their ability to fulfil these requirements is obstructed by a number of ethnic, cultural and socio-economic constraints (Banwell, 2014, 2020). The military, as Marie Ohambe et al. (2005: 46) point out, offers these young, impoverished men – who lack other employment options – a stable income and the opportunity to acquire 'social promotion and power'.

These marginalised soldiers take advantage of the chaos of war and perform militarised masculinity (which involves the use of rape and sexual violence) to subvert their marginal positions within the gender hierarchy (Banwell, 2014, 2020). Baaz and Stern (2009), in their interviews with one of the main perpetrators of rape and sexual violence in the DRC, the FARDC, discovered that, for these soldiers, it was their failure to live up to the expectations of 'the provider' (the equation of manhood with money and material wealth) and 'the sexually potent fighter' (Baaz and Stern, 2009: 511), alongside 'negative and sexualised images of women', that led them to rape (Baaz and Stern, 2009: 507; see also Trenholm et al., 2013). The narratives of these soldiers drew upon constructions of heterosexual masculinity (and femininity). These are formed and reproduced within the military institution. Within this context, soldiers' sexual needs were treated as a 'natural driving force which required "satisfaction" from women whose role it is to satisfy these needs' (Baaz and Stern, 2009: 505).

In this example, rape is both a political and sexual act. At the macro-level, it is used as an official weapon of war (reinforced, at the meso-level, within the military institution). At the micro-level, it is used by individual soldiers seeking to perform militarised masculinity and satisfy sexual urges. In this instance, it is both sexual (recreational rape/pressure cooker theory) and non-sexual (about power, dominance and control).

Sexual violence within the USA military

The inherent sexism and misogyny within the USA military facilitate the persistence of rape and sexual assault (Maxwell, 2010). Sexual assault is defined by the US military as 'intentional sexual contact characterized by use of force, threats, intimidation, or abuse of authority or when the victim does not or cannot consent' (Department of Defense, 2017: 3; cited in Wood and Toppelberg, 2017: 622).

The 1991 Tailhook scandal is a telling illustration of this environment (Cerretti, 2016; Maxwell, 2010; Wood and Toppelberg, 2017). During the 1991 annual conference for active and retired members of the US Navy and Marine Corps, a number of male officers wore T-shirts which read: WOMEN ARE PROPERTY (on the back) and HE-MAN WOMEN HATERS CLUB (on the front) (see Department of Defense; cited in Maxwell, 2010: 112). These T-shirts are illustrative of the reservations that were circulating at the time about whether women should serve in the military. They were worn by men who took part in the annual 'Gauntlet'. This is a scheduled evening event that takes place during the convention. Drawing on the Department of Defense's (DoD) inquiry into the incident, Caitlin Maxwell (2010: 112) runs us through what happened:

> At an agreed time, male Navy and Marine Corps personnel lined the hallway of the hotel's third floor and pretended to 'mill about'... until a female approached. Once a woman entered the hallway – and was deemed sufficiently attractive for the group's purposes ... the men closed themselves around her on both sides so that she could not escape, and proceeded to pass her amongst the group so

that those present could touch, grab, and otherwise violate her breasts, but-tocks, and genitals. In many cases, men groped beneath the undergarments of women or went so far as to rip or remove their clothing.

Following the incident, 140 junior officers were referred for investigation. Only six of these faced court martial (a court martial is a court used for mili-tary cases when members of the armed forces have broken military law). Charges against all six were subsequently dropped. While 29 admirals were implicated in the 'incident', they did not face any charges (Warner and Armstrong, 2020). The following July (1992), American soldiers were accused of committing 31 acts of sexual assault against female soldiers in the Persian Gulf (Cerretti, 2016). And five years later, reports of rape, inappropriate sexual behaviour and sexual assault were revealed at the USA Army's Aberdeen Proving Ground (Cerretti, 2016). This was followed by the USA Air Force Academy sexual assault scandal in 2003 and the USA Air Force Training scan-dal in 2009–12. Based on these examples, we suggest that sexual assault within the military, and the way it is dealt with, is both a symptom and a reflection of **rape culture**.

A number of academics and reporters have written about the prevalence and scale of military rape and sexual assault (see, for example, Cerretti, 2016; Maxwell, 2010; Mesok, 2016). In her 2011 article for *The Guardian*, about rape within the USA military, Lucy Broadbent included the following sub-heading, 'A female soldier in Iraq is more likely to be attacked by a fellow soldier than killed by enemy fire' (Broadbent, 9 December 2011). Let us take a minute to let that sink in.

In 2010, the USA military reported 3,158 cases of sexual crimes; only 529 received a court martial, while only 104 resulted in a conviction. This is only the tip of the iceberg. For the same year, at least 19,000 cases of sexual assault went unreported (Broadbent, 2011). More recently, the DoD's annual Report on Sexual Assault in the Military, reported 20,500 cases of 'unwanted sexual contact' for the year 2018. These numbers are higher than in previous years (Philipps, 2 May 2019). The same report noted that 63 per cent of these assaults were perpetrated against women, despite the fact that they only make up 20 per cent of the military (Philipps, 2 May 2019). To put it another way, 'one out of every 16 military women reported being groped, raped or otherwise sexually assaulted within the last year' (Philipps, 2 May 2019). In fact, as Elizabeth Mesok (2016) points out, the 'crisis' of sexual assault within the military has been linked to women's increased presence within the insti-tution and the failure of the military to fully integrate its female members. In this retelling, sexual assault is framed as simply another example of the 'growing pains' the military has faced over the years. Servicemen are also victims of sexual harassment, sexual assault and rape. According to a 2012 DoD report, of the 26,000 victims of 'unwanted sexual contact', 14,000 of these were male (Scarborough, 20 May 2013). We will discuss their experiences shortly.

Stories of victims being blackmailed by their units are common (Broadbent, 9 December 2011). The culture of silence that surrounds rape and sexual assault within the military compounds the trauma experienced by victims, who are forced, in many cases, to work alongside the perpetrator. Suicide, homelessness and various mental health problems are common among survivors (Broadbent, 9 December 2011). The testimonies of these survivors are included on 'mydutytospeak.com' (Broadbent, 9 December 2011; see also Service Women's Action Network (SWAN), which addresses sexual violence within the military). Our use of the term survivors here is in keeping with the terminology used by Broadbent and mydutytospeak.com.

This situation is exacerbated by the fact that the USA military investigates cases of sexual assault, unlike in Britain, for example, where cases are dealt with by the civilian criminal justice system (see Broadbent, 9 December 2011). In their review of 585 cases of sexual assault within US military bases in Japan, Carolyn Warner and Mia Armstrong (2020) found that, despite the military's attempts to address and punish these crimes, a lack of evidence meant that many cases were not 'prosecutable' or could not be tried as sex crimes. The results by Warner and Armstrong (2020) found that when individuals were found guilty, the punishment/penalty ranged from mandatory counselling, to short periods of confinement, to dishonourable discharge. Based on their analysis of these cases, they come to the conclusion that 'the military ... does not take sexual assault seriously, and so protects, rather than prosecutes, the perpetrator' (2020: 287).

What about the experiences of LGBT+ servicemembers?

Those who identify as gay, bisexual or transgender are particularly vulnerable to sexual assault (Matthews et al., 2018). Indeed, in their 2016 Sexual Assault Report, the DoD included sexual orientation as a demographic factor for the first time. Their review supports findings that LGBT+ servicemembers are at a higher risk of sexual assault (see Gurung et al., 2017). Sitaji Gurung and colleagues (2017) conducted empirical research with LGBT+ servicemembers based on their experiences of military sexual trauma (MST). MST ranges from overt acts, such as unwanted sexual contact (for example, sexual assault), to covert acts like stalking and the use of sexually charged language (sexual harassment). It can also manifest in sexual orientation discrimination (Gurung et al., 2017). Research on MST among the LGBT+ population is in its infancy. Most studies are based on descriptive statistical analysis with limited theoretical engagement. As a starting point, we suggest drawing on research that addresses sexual gender-based violence (SGBV) against LGBT+ individuals within the wider population. This SGBV includes hate crime or transphobic violence (where victims are targeted on the basis of their gender identity) and heterosexist abuse/homophobic violence (where victims are targeted on the basis of their sexuality). Caterina Peroni (2015) has written about this and draws on **neoliberalism** and (hetero)**patriarchy** to explain SGBV against the LGBT+ population. (Some of these theories are also discussed in Chapter 2; and see Chapter 3 in which we discuss the regulation of homosexuality.)

Research on 'corrective rape' in South Africa might also offer some insights into understanding rape committed against LGBT+ servicemembers. Commonly, corrective rape contains two elements: (1) the punishment of Black African lesbians for violating traditional gender norms by persons of the opposite sex; and (2) the belief that rape will 'cure' them of their 'deviant' sexual orientation by 'turning them straight' (Brown, 2012). Increasingly, the term is being used to describe rape against all sexual minorities in order to 'correct' their sexualities (Brown, 2012). Mirroring the context in which military rape takes place, corrective rape takes place within a male-dominated society that normalises and privileges heteronormativity and heterosexuality.

Military rape and sexual assault against men

As noted earlier, sexual assault is perpetrated against male servicemen. According to the Pentagon, an estimated 10,000 men are sexually assaulted ever year by the US military (Philipps, 10 September 2019). Victims are young, low-ranking members of the military (Matthews et al., 2018; Philipps, 10 September 2019). Sexual assault is either used as part of a hazing or initiation ritual or to humiliate male victims (Jaycox et al., 2015; cited in Matthews et al., 2018).

Echoing the experiences of male victims/survivors discussed above, shame and stigma prevent many men from coming forward to report these crimes. As one victim/survivor articulated: 'if you came forward and said you were raped, people would have thought you were a queer or a child molester – you were treated like it was your fault' (Philipps, 10 September 2019). In order to address the underreporting of male victim/survivors, the Army introduced the Male Survivor Tribute and Portrait Tour. The tour presents the narratives of servicemen who have been victims of sexual assault in the hope that it will incentivise other victims to come forward (Vergun, 2016). In addition, in 2016 the DoD started working on the Plan to Prevent and Respond to Sexual Assault of Military Men (DoD, 2016).

How do we explain military male-to-male rape and sexual assault?

Military sexual assault is about 'dominance and power, not about sexual desire or the sex of the victim' (Mesok, 2016: 58). Given the heteronormative environment of the military, how do we interpret the use of male-to-male rape and sexual violence? Furthermore, if militarised masculinity relies on the performance of heterosexual masculinity, how does male-to-male rape assist soldiers in accomplishing this?

In the context of war, as discussed above, the logic of rape and sexual violence is clear: it marginalises the male 'enemy' while simultaneously demonstrating their failure to protect their women/nation. However, outside of the ethno-politics of war – where, in cases of genocide and ethnic cleansing, rape is used to destroy the 'enemy' group and/or the nation – why do men rape and sexually assault other men who are fighting on the same 'side'? What purpose does rape serve in this instance?

In their article on the persistence of sexual assault within the USA military, Elisabeth Wood and Nathaniel Toppelberg (2017: 625) distinguish between 'rape as practice' and 'rape as a strategy of war'. In the case of the latter, rape can be used as a tool to target civilians, but it may not always be 'ordered, authorised or institutionalised'. For the authors, military rape and sexual assault are 'pattern[s] of violence that [are] ... tolerated by officers, and ... driven by social dynamics among soldiers' (Wood and Toppelberg, 2017: 621). This 'practice' persists, they argue, due to a combination of informal socialisation (processes among peers such as a sexualised hazing or initiation ceremony) and formal socialisation (top-down processes that take place during recruitment).

Conversely, can these acts be explained by the pressure cooker theory? Do men, in these closed institutions, use rape to satisfy sexual urges? Is military rape recreational rape? Baaz and Stern (2018) have voiced their concerns about the erasure of the sexual from explanations of wartime rape and, concomitantly, the view that this type of violence is always and already about power and a tool of patriarchy. However, within the (heterocentric) context of the military (and the militarised masculinity it fosters), how else do we understand military rape other than as an act designed to humiliate, feminise and emasculate the male victims? Arguably, for men who are concealing homosexual or queer identities, rape may be rooted in sexual desire. Indeed, victim/survivor testimonies talk of broken bodies and of feeling they are no longer real men. This, they explain, is because '[r]eal men don't get raped' (see Philipps, 10 September 2019). The following words, from a male victim/survivor of military rape, brings together our earlier discussion about DADT, Clark's (2017) vulnerability of the penis and broader explanations of male-to-male (wartime) rape. He says: 'Our society treats men differently when they have been raped ... In society's eyes I am somehow less of a man because I have been raped, or I must be a latent homosexual. Rape is a very emasculating thing' (see Broadbent, 9 December 2011).

BOX 8.3

Consider the following:

- Can you find other examples where rape by soldiers is both sexual (recreational rape/pressure cooker theory) and non-sexual (about power, dominance and control)?
- What are your thoughts on our suggestion that sexual assault within the military is both a symptom and a reflection of rape culture?

Before you engage with this thought exercise, we suggest revisiting our definition of militarised masculinity outlined above.

Militarised masculinity, like all masculinities, is performed: 'What would this performance look like without the penis?' (Clark, 2017: 13), which, as noted earlier, is often framed as a weapon. In other words, what happens if we decouple masculinity from phallocentric masculinity? Is this even possible? As a thought exercise, start thinking about the ways in which we might challenge the power of the phallus and de-centralise the penis from the construction of militarised masculinity. We will return to this in Chapter 14, where we outline our thoughts on the future relationship between sex and crime.

Summary

In this chapter on sex and war, we have examined how rape (specifically genocidal rape) and sexual(ised) violence are used as weapons of war against both sexes.

We have considered how wartime rape is sometimes used as an official strategy of war (in cases of genocide and ethnic cleansing), while, in other instances, it is treated as a by-product of war, a crime of opportunity. We also asked whether or not these crimes are always and already about power and control.

In order to unpack the legacy and unresolved trauma associated with genocidal rapes that took place in BiH and Rwanda, we explored the experiences of children who were born as a result of these war crimes. We argued that the trauma experienced by these victims was both separate from, and directly connected to/as a result of, the trauma experienced by their mothers (i.e. transgenerational trauma).

As you learned, military rape and sexual assault take place within a heteronormative and hypermasculine institution. In the two examples that we reviewed – rape by soldiers in combat zones and rape and sexual assault within the military – militarised masculinity is at work. In the case of the former, rape is used both as a political and a sexual act. In the latter, military rape and sexual assault against women can be connected to the wider rape culture in which we live. In the case of men, given the heteronormative context of the military, we argued that humiliation, feminisation and emasculation best explained these crimes. Research on MST against LGBT+ servicemembers is limited. More qualitative research on their experiences is needed. For now, we suggest drawing insights from the broader literature on SGBV against LGBT+ populations as well as research on corrective rape.

Review questions

- How and why is rape used as a weapon of war? What does this type of violence achieve?
- What is the material, symbolic and cultural legacy of genocidal rape? Think about this in relation to both the direct and indirect victims of this crime.
- What is the relationship between militarised masculinity and the use of rape and sexual violence both within and by the military?
- In terms of rape and sexual assault within the military, how do the experiences of servicewomen, servicemen and members of the LGBTQ+ community differ? Do we require different explanations/understandings of their victimisation?

Other chapters that this links to

Chapter 3 (Sex and crime in time and space)
Chapter 5 (Sex and institutional cultures of abuse)
Chapter 6 (Reproduction, sex and crime)
Chapter 13 (Illegal representations)
Chapter 14 (The future)

Part 3

Sex, Cultures and Crime

9

Pleasurable risk

CHAPTER OUTLINE

In this chapter, we explore sexualised risk and its intersection with **harm** and pleasure. We do this by analysing three case studies against a contemporary background of anxiety about **public health,** the role that pleasurable violence should have in society, homophobia, racism and **misogyny**. Drawing on examples principally taken from the UK and the USA, we explore how these instances of pleasurable sexualised risk-taking have evolved, and how, as criminologists, we might think about them. To do this, we revisit the themes of consent, resistance and harm that we have already seen in Chapters 2 and 4. We add to this a more explicit discussion of risk, and how risky leisure may be conceptualised.

By the end of this chapter, you will understand more about:

- how pleasure and risk interact with contemporary **deviance studies**
- how the criminal justice system and **public health** institutions respond to sexualised risky pleasure
- how homophobia, racism and misogyny have inflected these criminological debates.

In this chapter, we will be looking at the different ways in which we might explore the question of risk. We do so by analysing three cases – BDSM, bug-chasing and chemsex – and consider what sort of criminal justice responses exist towards them, against what might be appropriate. BDSM is an umbrella term that stands for 'bondage, domination, submission, sadomasochism', and is a form of sexualised **power** play between consenting practitioners; bug-chasing is the practice of deliberately having unprotected sex in order to contract a sexually transmitted infection: usually HIV; chemsex is the practice of having sex while taking different sorts of drugs. We have chosen these cases because they all offer examples of risky sexualised practice that is also usually undertaken consensually by the party who risks the harm (the person taking drugs, the person experiencing bondage and the person chasing an HIV + status, for instance). We ask: what are the criminological implications when people want to do things that are considered to be dangerous, even deadly? How do we think about risk? What are the social, cultural and political implications of actively seeking to harm the self as a form of sexual pleasure? What perspective should a criminologist adopt when it comes to thinking about, and reacting to, deviant sexual behaviours that seem to actively harm the self?

Sex on drugs, sadomasochism and actively chasing HIV infection (seroconversion) are controversial activities. It can be difficult to understand what their appeal might be. When encountering the discussions in this chapter, it might be helpful to think about them from the perspective that Maria Lugones (1987) describes as 'loving perception' or 'world travelling', that we encountered in Chapter 1. That is to say, we recognise that some of these practices may seem unusual – maybe even shocking – and the justification for them hard to fathom, but we suggest that, in order to do the work of sound criminology, we must encounter them with an intellectual curiosity that 'travels' to the perspective of the people who engage in these risky practices. We must, as far as is possible, suspend what we already think we know in order to try, with loving perception, to put ourselves in the shoes of people for whom these risks are thrilling sexual choices. Remember that there may be people that you know, in your class, or out of it, who may engage in these sorts of practices. It might even be helpful to think about any risks that you willingly take, or have taken in the past, to approach these questions. Extreme sports are a good example of pleasurable, thrill-seeking, risky behaviour that people engage in that is culturally accepted, and in some cases even glorified, despite the inherent risks they entail.

BOX 9.1

By yourself, reflect on the following questions:

- What drives *you* to take risks?
- What does it feel like?
- How much harm is too much to caution you against risk?
- How do we measure this harm?
- What are the implications of deliberately exposing yourself or other people to harm?
- What about harm that people have consented to?
- What do criminal justice systems do about this?
- Does it work?

We will see that deliberate sexual risk-taking has implications beyond the field of criminology or criminal justice, and that this is part of what makes it such a complex and important issue for our understanding of sex and crime. We will also highlight that sexual risk-taking is not so intrinsically different from other forms of risk-taking, and yet it is treated differently due to its ties with non-normative sexualities, which we have also encountered in other chapters.

How to think about risk, pleasure, harm and criminology

Before we unpack the socio-cultural, criminal and political implications of BDSM, bug-chasing and chemsex, it is worth revisiting some of the ideas we explored in Chapter 2 about how we understand the concepts of risk and harm, and how the construction of these has evolved in contemporary criminological thought over the past few decades.

Risk and danger

As organised, social communities, we define danger in terms of what threatens the public good, and then we use blame to persuade people to contribute to its maintenance by abstaining from dangerous practices (Douglas, 1992). However, this process does not happen outside existing social and cultural hierarchies. As such, definitions of risk and danger and exertions of blame will be dependent upon power distribution in a given society. In our **capitalist**, hierarchical, **patriarchal** and **heteronormative** social organisation, certain risks, dangers and blames will be recognised and labelled more than others, regardless of the **objective** degree of harm they may incur. Hence, extreme sports, such as mountain climbing, sky diving or caving, which are associated with being performed by heterosexual, able-bodied, masculine males, are usually glorified, in accordance with standards of **gender** performance connected to **hegemonic masculinity**, regardless of the risks and harms associated with them (e.g. **morbidity** and mortality rates). At the same time, practices such as BDSM, chemsex and bug-chasing might be cast as risky, dangerous, polluting and immoral, and intervened in through institutions of social control. It is worth noting that social control is not an exclusively criminal-legal realm. Practices such as chemsex are targeted through a combination of penal and medical interventions. They are understood and intervened in through a medico-penal framework that establishes the boundaries of acceptable behaviour while trying to manage their risks and consequences.

Pleasure and edgework

Pleasure is key when it comes to understanding why some risk-taking is so popular. It takes its etymology from the Old French *plesir* and the Latin *placer*, meaning 'to please, give pleasure, be approved'. Thus, like risk, pleasure can be thought to emerge within an intersubjective dynamic, meaning it is something which might be thought to occur between different human and non-human subjects, or by a person's interaction with objects, events or ideas that are pleasing. There is not a vast amount of discussion of pleasure in criminological accounts of crime. And yet, arguably, pleasure is intrinsic to idealised notions of **sexual practice**. We need to take pleasure seriously if we are to understand how it interacts with sexualised risk-taking.

A theory which addresses the relationship between pleasure and the pleasurable taking of risks developed by anthropologist Stephen Lyng in 1990 is edgework. The term, taken from Hunter S. Thompson's (2005[1971]) semi-autobiographical account of travelling around Las Vegas while high on drugs and alcohol, describes wilfully putting the body into dangerous – risky – situations to explore how much the body can take and how far it can go. The reason why people take these risks is in order to lead a full, authentic and rewarding life. Rather than be stifled by the moribund, hum drum everyday by seeking to avoid risks, for edgeworkers, it is the taking of risks themselves that enables them to develop fully as humans (Lupton, 1999: 155). For Lyng (1990: 857), edgework describes encountering 'a clearly observable threat to one's physical or mental wellbeing or one's sense of an ordered existence'. Lyng developed this theory in the context of his work with skydivers. Other risky leisure pursuits, including mountain climbing, motorcycle racing and bungee jumping might all count as edgework. But, as Lyng and Rick A. Matthews (2007: 78) explain: 'in the purest expression of edgework, one negotiates the edge by striving to get as close to it as possible without actually crossing it ... [and] the edge can assume different forms.' Hence, edgework can also describe taking risks such as consuming vast amounts of drugs or alcohol, as in the novel *Fear and Loathing in Las Vegas*, or participating in high-stakes gambling. Stockbrokers, elite surgeons and cycle couriers (Kidder, 2006) might all be said to be edgeworkers; taking high risks in the course of their work, which, if they succeed, they are rewarded for, but if they do not – if they fail – they know that they risk reputational disgrace, dismissal, even death.

Edgework describes the thrill of putting the body into a risky situation in order to cheat death or serious injury or serious reputational damage. It could be said to emerge as a neo-liberal response to the imperative in modernist life to avoid risk as far as possible and to prioritise security at all costs. How do we interpret this in the context of sexual practices? The thrill of taking, and surviving, a risky sexual experience describes some of the allure of sadomasochistic sexual encounters (see Newmahr, 2011) that we will discuss more of in this chapter. It could also be used to account for sexual practices that are risky because of the context (deliberately risking unwanted pregnancy, or infection with an STI (sexually transmitted infection), or seroconversion (which we also see more of in this chapter), or because of the place it occurs in (for instance, in outdoor space (Bell, 2006), in a toilet (Hollister, 1999) or online (Van Doorn, 2010), or because of the people involved (think, for instance, of swinging or partner-swapping). Valli Rajah (2007) has suggested that the theory of edgework can also be used to account for the decision that some women make to stay in a violent relationship, in order for them to gain a level of mastery over an otherwise chaotic life.

Accompanying this conceptualisation of risk as a form of leisure activity, is the notion of 'deep play' developed by anthropologist Clifford Geertz (1973).

Building on philosopher Jeremy Bentham's (1887) observations about leisure practices (such as gambling), where the loss can never beat the reward, Geertz argues that deep play – where the risks are impossibly high and it cannot make sense to take them – is a form of culture-building where anxieties about status and society are played out via hugely dangerous – reckless even – leisure practices. When thinking about the examples in this chapter, consider whether they might be examples of edgework, or deep play, or something else.

Research on edgework has rightly been criticised for its white, male-centric focus. Though women certainly participate in extreme sports and subcultural practices, these are communities dominated by **cisgender** men (Laurendeau, 2008). The focus on mastery of the body, on developing the skills, strength and capacity to climb higher, to dive deeper, to drive faster, is accompanied by an ableist **discourse** about the sorts of bodies that might be valorised as risk-takers. They are also accompanied by neo-liberal responsibilisation discourses, or the imperative to be responsible for yourself. In edgework, the idea is to go as far/ as fast/and as much as you can – to meet your edge – and then to come back. To go too far is to do poor edgework: it is to have failed. Deep play, on the other hand, does not have the same sense of responsibility not to destroy yourself. But this sort of leisure, like edgework, could be considered nihilist and selfish. If it is these things, should criminologists intervene? And, if so, how?

Anthropological concepts and understandings, such as Lyng's concept of edgework, become central to cultural criminological analyses (see Ferrell, 1997; Hayward, 2002; Hayward and Young, 2004). Yet, the enthusiasm of cultural criminology for the edgy and transgressive has more recently been challenged by accounts that sought to re-establish the centrality of harm as an objective category.

Harm

The type of edgework which has received attention from sociologists, social anthropologists and criminologists has also been figured under an ultra-realist analytical perspective as a form of 'deviant leisure'. We encountered ultra-realism in Chapter 2. Scholars of deviant leisure, including Oliver Smith and Thomas Raymen (2018), seek to attenuate the early enthusiasm for pleasurable risk-taking evidenced in the cultural criminological accounts of things like edgework. For them, deviant leisure – like chemsex, BDSM or bug-chasing, perhaps – describes behaviour which 'if not always illegal, appears close enough to the boundary between deviance and illegality to invoke discussion around police response' (Smith and Raymen, 2018: 64). Deviant practices, including graffiti, joyriding and BASE jumping (Laurendeau, 2011; Presdee, 2003), have been optimistically figured by cultural criminologists as practices that seek to resist the mainstream, to push back against authority, to become a form of counterculture that enables practitioners to establish their individual **agency** free of the tyranny of intervention of **the State**, authority or rules (see, for example, Garrett, 2014; Williams, 2009).

Such apparent hedonism happens without attending to the **neoliberalism** that underscores this notion of individualism, or the capitalistic devices that are used to recuperate apparently subversive practices into the mainstream. Instead, Smith and Rayman (2018), Steve Hall (2012), and Hall and Simon Winlow (2018), among others, ask that leisure studies attend to the type of harm that specific practices might inflict, and from this decide whether a practice is troublesome or not for criminologists.

Recall from our discussion in Chapter 2, that ultra-realists critique the 'special exceptionalism' that they argue some actors – here, risk-takers – hide behind in order to justify actions that are generally harmful, to society, to the environment or to other people. Deviant leisure studies provide us with a lens through which to see the harms that are taken for granted as part of normalised leisure activities. This helps us to see how the norms that underpin leisure are themselves composed of and constrained by the capitalist imperative of individualisation, which causes social and cultural harm.

Given these diverse approaches to risk and pleasure, how can we understand sexualised risks that people take for fun? Will the constructivist approach to risk better account for why people take risks – sometimes with fatal consequences – in pursuit of their own sexual satisfaction? Or, rather, is it the case that these sexualised risks are taken as a sign of resistance to authority and the rule of law? Is it mastery of the self and an expression of powerful skill that motivate some of these practices? Or is it an ignorance of harm and a sense of exceptionalism borne out of a selfish notion of 'special liberty' that motivates sexual risk-takers?

BDSM, consent and criminal justice

Consider scenario 1 in Box 9.2.

BOX 9.2

Scenario 1: Consensual violent sexual play leads to death

On your account, after beating her, Natalie's requests became more extreme. She asked you to insert a bottle of spray carpet cleaner into her vagina, as a

(Continued)

sexual stimulant. This was a large object with a trigger. It became lodged in her vagina and you could not get it out. You went to get a bottle of lubricant to try and remove it. The pathological evidence was that the bottle caused lacerations to her vagina, resulting in arterial and venous haemorrhage ... It seems to me [that this] was something which came about on your account because once you had beaten Natalie, she wanted something more extreme done to her. As I have said, I am prepared to accept in your favour that she instigated this. It seems to me that this act was not unlawful, notwithstanding that it did in fact injure her. The insertion of the bottle came at the end of your sexual activity with Natalie when it must have been plain to you that she was now very drunk indeed, becoming falling down drunk and, in your own words, talking 'gobbledy gook'. Just because she wanted that item inserted into her vagina did not mean that you had to do it. Your own account to the police was that you would draw the line when her sexual demands were too extreme for you, and that you did so that night (e.g. by hitting her with your boot rather than a belt) ... That bottle of carpet cleaner should never have been anywhere near her vagina no matter what she demanded of you. You chose to do something which, even if not unlawful, carried a high degree of risk.

Source: *R v. John Broadhurst* (Birmingham Crown Court, 17 December 2018), sentencing remarks.

The case of *Broadhurst* is a recent controversial instance of involuntary manslaughter in England. The facts of the case are outlined in the sentencing remarks above, as is the legal problem at issue. This case concerned the death of a young woman following considerable alcohol consumption and consensual violent sexual play at the house of the defendant in 2016. The defendant was asked by the woman to penetrate her vagina with an object that caused her a serious internal injury. He did not help her to seek medical attention for her injuries, and this led to her death. The defence suggested that, because his partner had asked him for something 'more extreme' than the other BDSM play that they had participated in, namely spanking her breasts and buttocks, she had *given her consent* for the act to happen (see Chapter 4 for our discussion of consent).

When is consensual BDSM a crime?

BDSM, sometimes known as 'kink' or as 'SM' in different contexts, tends to describe the consensual pushing of boundaries in the context of sexual practice (Newmahr, 2011). To participate in BDSM is known in the vernacular as 'to play', which indicates that it is supposed to be a leisure activity, it is supposed to be exploratory and it is supposed to be fun. It can look like many things:

the consensual spanking, caning or whipping of parts of the body that feature in the Broadhurst case, and that you may have encountered in the *Fifty Shades of Grey* novels (although see Bonomi et al., 2014 for critiques of this); the orgasm and diet control that we encounter in the 2002 film *Secretary* (although see Weiss, 2006 and Wilkinson, 2009 for critiques of this); the PVC, restraints and rope play that we find in Rihanna's *S&M* music video; and the pet play (when people pretend to be domestic animals such as cats and dogs) that you may have seen on the streets of London (see Fanghanel, 2019). Practices which perhaps have not hit the mainstream in the way that some BDSM has, include electricity play, asphyxiation and play with needles, with blades or with fire. These carry higher levels of risk than other sorts of kinky practice, but they can be considered to be part of BDSM practice. People who practise BDSM might consensually agree for someone to electrocute them or tape a plastic bag over their head so that they cannot breathe.

These latter practices bring with them increased risk of injury. Certainly, if they were undertaken without consent, they would clearly be criminal acts. And, as we have seen in Chapter 4, consent of the 'victim' is not necessarily a valid legal defence to committing the criminal offence. So, what is the draw of this sort of BDSM practice, and what does the law say about it?

BDSM or kinky sexual behaviour as a subculture has received an increase in academic attention in recent years. Much of this attention is given over to explaining first what BDSM is, from an almost ethnographic or anthropological perspective (Newmahr, 2011; Weiss, 2011); second, attention is devoted to understanding BDSM sexual practice from a sympathetic public health perspective (Lee et al., 2015); third, attention is given to the dynamics of consent within sexual encounters (Barker, 2013; Pitagora, 2013); and, finally, academics have considered the political implications of BDSM for transformative **social justice** (Califia, 1994; Downing, 2013; Fanghanel, 2019; Rubin, 1997; Weiss, 2006, 2011).

Staci Newmahr (2011) suggests that people who participate in BDSM are doing so as a form of edgework. As we have seen, edgework describes the deliberate taking of risks in order to gain and demonstrate mastery over particularly perilous situations. Edgeworkers report that they enjoy taking risks and find a difficult or painful encounter satisfying. Developing skill at taking risks, being able to do things that other people are unable to do, and developing a reputation as a successful risk-taker, enables an edgeworker to develop their sense of self. In the context of BDSM, becoming recognised as having this prowess is an important way in which to develop status in a BDSM community and to ascend the hierarchy (Fanghanel, 2019). But BDSM is not simply motivated by the competitive element of edgework. The desire to push the body further, to explore more and more intense or extreme experiences, to delve further into a passion than ever before, could be understood as an expression of an erotic drive through which the edgeworker also gets a sense of fulfilment – which is why people who practise more extreme BDSM might also emphasise the consensual element of it (Lee et al., 2015).

In the context of consent, in Chapter 4 we encountered the famous case of *R v. Brown* [1993] 97 Cr App R 44, in which a collective of men was found guilty of, among other things, grievous bodily harm for their consensual BDSM activities with other men. In *Brown*, it was ruled that it was not legally permissible to consent to have violence that causes more than transient injury exacted upon you for sexual gratification. Compare this judgement to later cases of consensual BDSM that have come before the court:

R v. Slingsby [1995] Crim LR 570

In the case of *Slingsby*, a woman whose vagina and rectum had been consensually penetrated by her partner with his fist was injured by a ring that he was wearing on his finger. As a result of the internal injury she sustained, she contracted scpticaemia and died. The court held that because the injury and ultimate death of the victim was as a result of an unforeseen injury that neither party expected or intended, this was not a case of manslaughter. The act that gave rise to the injury was consensual and not usually especially risky, so the defence that she did consent to the injury (the defence raised in *Brown*) had not arisen as there had been no intent to injure the complainant.

R v. Wilson [1996] Crim LR 573

The case of *Wilson* concerns a husband who branded his initials onto the buttocks of his wife with a hot knife at his wife's behest. The burns needed medical attention and the medical practitioner to whom Mrs Wilson showed her burns reported the injury to the police, who subsequently charged Mr Wilson with actual bodily harm. At first, following the judgement in *Brown*, the judge held – reluctantly – that the wife could not consent to activity that caused her this more than transient injury. On appeal, however, it was ruled that this case was not comparable to *Brown* because *Brown* concerns 'sadomasochism of the grossest kind, involving, inter alia, physical torture' (*R v. Wilson* at 749), whereas this consensual activity was no more dangerous than tattooing, which people can freely consent to. Moreover, they said, 'consensual activity between husband and wife, in the privacy of the matrimonial home, is not a proper matter for criminal investigation, let alone criminal prosecution' (*R v. Wilson* at 750). Thus, evoking Gayle Rubin's (1984) notion of the 'charmed circle of **sexuality**' that we met in Chapter 1, this judgement returns private sex acts from an issue of public police and public health concern into a private matter that ought to be beyond the reach of the criminal court.

Here, it might be helpful to look carefully at the differences between the injuries sustained by the so-called 'victims' in each case. In *Slingsby*, the female participant in the sex act died. In the case of *Wilson*, the wife needed medical attention, whereas, in *Brown*, the appellants did not need any medical attention and suffered no permanent injuries. In all cases, the acts were committed by consenting adults in private. Yes, in *Brown*, the participants videotaped themselves and shared those videos, effectively making extreme pornography (see Chapter 13 for our discussion of illegal images), but this element was not salient in the debates around whether or not their consent was valid.

BOX 9.3

Think about this idea that sex in the matrimonial home should simply not be a matter for the courts. What assumptions is that based on? What norms is this judgement perpetrating? *Brown* has been criticised as a display of '**paternalism** of an unelected, unrepresentative group who use but fail to openly acknowledge th[eir] power' (Giles, 1994: 111). What does this mean, and do you agree?

R v. Emmett [1999] EWCA Crim 1710

Perhaps it helps to see the *Brown* case in dialogue with that of *Emmett*. Here, once more, a male and female couple engaged in consensual BDSM activity, including, on one occasion, asphyxiating the woman with a plastic bag to the point where she might have lost consciousness and needed medical attention. On another occasion, the defendant poured lighter fluid over the breasts of his partner, which he then set alight, and which caused a 6 cm burn on her skin. Again, he encouraged her to seek medical attention for this injury. The second visit to the doctor caused the doctor to report the incidents to the police. The defendant was charged with actual bodily harm and was found guilty based on the *Brown* judgement that there is no defence of consent for 'sadomasochistic encounters which breed and glorify cruelty' (*R v. Emmett*, citing *Brown* at 4). Unlike in *Wilson*, in the case of *Emmett* the court decided that:

the degree of actual and potential harm was such, and also the degree of unpredictability as to injury was such, as to make it a proper cause from the criminal law to intervene. This was not tattooing, it was not something which absented pain or dangerousness and the agreed medical evidence is in each case, certainly on the first occasion, there was a very considerable degree of danger to life; on the second, there was a degree of injury to the body. *(R v. Emmett*, citing *Brown* at 6)

These four cases bring us to some sort of understanding of the interaction between risk, harm and pleasure in the context of consensual kinky sexual activity. We see, in English courts at least, a reluctance to intervene in the domestic arrangements of consenting adult couples. We see the limits of this turn on the severity of the injuries and the risk of lasting or serious injury that they might entail. We see this emerge from a case in which the BDSM acts that occur between consenting groups of men were described as cruel, evil and uncivilised, even where the acts themselves were not serious enough to merit medical attention, as in the case of branding. We also see the latent homophobia of judges who occupy dominant positions – economically, socially and politically – in society fuse 'homosexual sadomasochism' with the 'physical cruelty *that it must* involve' (*R v. Brown*, at 67, our italics; see also Ashford, 2010; White, 2006).

BOX 9.4

Think back to the case of *Broadhurst* with which we started this section. Feminist commentators have criticised the judgement as a form of victim-blaming; the idea that she 'asked for it' by asking for what might be considered extreme sexual practices to take place (see Harman and Garnier, 19 July 2019 and the campaign We Can't Consent to This). How might we understand this?

- Do you agree that the approach of the judge was too permissive by finding that Broadhurst had consensually used the carpet cleaner bottle to penetrate his partner?
- Is this victim-blaming? And, if it is not, what is it?
- If it is victim-blaming, what does this interpretation mean for the role of the criminal justice system in the matrimonial bedroom?
- Was this case an example of deep play?
- Was this case an example of edgework gone too far?
- What would an ultra-realist reading of this case have to say about it?
- Is it tied to shame?
- Is it tied to a sense of 'special liberty'?

Bug-chasing and the law

Bug chasing is defined by David A. Moskowitz and Michael E. Roloff (2007a: 347) as an 'active desire to voluntarily contract the human immunodeficiency virus (HIV)'. It is supposed to describe a subculture of men who have sex with men without using barrier methods of contraception (known as bare-backing) and who do this to deliberately contract the HIV virus. The term 'gift giver' is used to describe HIV + men who seek to deliberately infect HIV- men with the HIV virus. Some scholarship has emerged among public health professionals about this phenomenon. They seek to understand what it is (Grov and Parsons, 2006; Moskowitz and Roloff, 2007b), why it happens (Hammond et al., 2016; Klein, 2014) and how to prevent it (Moskowitz and Roloff, 2007b), or if it should be stopped at all (Malkowski, 2014; Tomso, 2004). For our purposes, in this chapter, we will think about bug-chasing and gift-giving as a form of consensual sexual risk-taking, and we will consider what the response of criminal justice discourses is, or could be, if anything.

BOX 9.5

Scenario 2: Men in online forum explain why they 'bug-chase'

Adam: Like many men my age, the AIDS crisis was a big deal in the early part of our lives in the gay universe. There is a desire to connect to the generations of HIV infected men, living and dead.

The AIDS crisis had a huge impact on the narrative of gay life. Some of that compassion for the individual has been good. But much of it, fear, stigma and isolation has been bad. Those with the disease have a seat at the table where the gay narrative can be redefined for a newer era.

Pushing my own 'sexual envelope' has always been important to me. Exploring many avenues of sexual expression has helped me fully understand my own homosexuality and related desires. The entire gift giving/chasing subculture presents a sexual frontier full of new adventures.

Forty years of careful, mostly safe sex has been supplanted by a couple handfuls of exposures over the past week. The coming weekend will see my immune system exposed to even more of the virus. Had this force been of lesser power, I would have never reached this position. But now, it is not just a force, it is my destiny. Denying that seems futile, embracing it is my choice.

Bern: As a transsexual, its the only real way I can become pregnant with some dads babes, i am so broody for poz [HIV+] loads.

Coco: For me, I was happy with condoms, it never entered my mind that I would be a bug chaser. Then it seemed like it happened in a day, my attitude flipped and I wanted to bb [bareback] and realized that I was suddenly sexually aroused by the thought of being POZ. I knew that I would be okay with helping other chasers cross the bridge when the time came. I have always been a top. I still get horny because I am POZ, got even hornier when my doc diagnosed me with full-blown AIDS. Will consider a med vacation if someone wants my help.

(Continued)

> I will always remember what it was like when I was chasing and how happy I was when I met a POZ pig willing to bring me over. I have no wish to die, I am not punishing myself or hate myself or feel guilty in any way and will take meds as appropriate. I enjoy being POZ immensely. I enjoy playing with other POZ pigs and certainly feel an attachment.

If HIV/AIDS infection became a global source of anxiety at the end of the twentieth century, then this has been accompanied by an almost incredulous response on behalf of experts and lay-people to the possibility that there might be some men who actively seek to seroconvert. Dean K. Gauthier and Craig J.Forsyth (1999) wrote one of the earliest papers which explores, and seeks to understand, the phenomenon of bug-chasing. Through it, they establish a definitional frame which distinguishes barebacking, gift-giving and bug-chasing. They speculate that men who bug-chase might do so because they seek the relief of getting their infection 'over and done with'; knowing it is inevitable that they will one day get infected, they decide to try to take control over when and how that might happen.

The eroticisation of riskiness itself is also offered as a way to explain why bug-chasing happens; that it is a turn-on to act so potentially recklessly. Some men seek seroconversion to get a sense of belonging, and out of their sense of loneliness at not being part of the 'gay community', or out of survivor's guilt if their friends or partners die. Finally, some men become HIV+ as part of a politicised rejection of the marginalised position that gay men experience in society (remembering that gay stigmatisation was much more explicit in the 1980s and 1990s that it might be now).

These ideas have been developed by scholars including Moskowitz and Roloff (2007a, b), Chad Hammond et al. (2016) and Hugh Klein (2014). They have been critiqued by Gregory Tomso (2004) and Jennifer A.Malkowski (2014). Moskowitz and Rollof (2007a, b), like Christian Grov and Geoffrey T. Parsons (2006), conducted research that analysed men's online dating/hook-up profiles on websites where men would meet for bareback sex, and compared men's serostatus to what they say they are looking for (if a HIV- man seeks a HIV+ man for unprotected sex, they would classify this as a bug-chaser, for instance). They go on to suggest that the commonly accepted reasons given for men to take this risk are not very compelling. Reasons given build on Gauthier and Forsyth's (1999) initial suggestions. They include the notion that HIV+ status becomes a way of joining the gay community, which Moskowitz and Roloff (2007b: 23) reject as being an unconvincing way of joining a community; there are other ways in which a man can demonstrate his commitment to the community without actively seeking seroconversion. Otherwise, it is suggested that, as HIV drugs have become more effective, the danger of death from the disease is seen as less likely. This also fails to convince Moskowitz and Roloff, who argue that this in itself would only explain why people are indifferent to HIV infection, not why they actively seek it. Beyond this, is it possible that gay men are 'simply exhausted' by 'good gay health' narratives and bug-chasing becomes a way of resisting this? Moskowitz and Roloff argue that this does not explain the appeal of gift-givers seeking out specifically HIV-partners to infect. Instead, the authors argue that bug-chasing is an expression of sex addiction that seeks ever more extreme sexual experiences. They ally BDSM practices such as role-playing, fisting and urination as other expressions of sex addiction. The self-humiliating language in dating adverts was taken as evidence of this (some of this we see in Scenario 2 above) and that, if sex addiction was treated, bug-chasing would begin to disappear. They suggest:

> it becomes evident that built into the bug-chasing culture is a voluntary power inequity. Relinquishing sexual aggression to another becomes an aphrodisiac where the bug chaser becomes the passive victim to the serodiscordant partner's aggressive killer. Infection becomes a sort of suicidal pregnancy. (Moskowitz and Roloff, 2007b: 35)

This idea of pregnancy might be inadvertently closer to the truth, if we think about the motivations that are also outlined by bug-chasers in Scenario 2 above. Klein (2014) and Hammond et al. (2016) have both given more consideration to 'creating a death' as a motivation for bug-chasing. Though they do not draw on Freudian notions of the death drive and Eros (the life-producing creative drive), it is possible to glimpse at some of these drives in their accounts of 'breeding' and 'generationing'. Literally using the language of procreation, genus and progenation, Klein (2014) and Hammond et al.'s (2016: 272) papers separately tell us that, within bug-chasing discourses, there are notions of 'breeding new men' or creating generations of HIV+ men whose virus originates with one man who becomes the archaic 'mother' (father) of generations of his 'sons' who are HIV+ and who ceremoniously infect longer and longer generations of men. Better understanding the thrall of creating the vampiric new life might help better respond to bug-chasing as a phenomenon that continues to cause panic and anxiety in mainstream discourses.

Indeed, for Malkowski (2014), the act of creating typologies of different types of bug-chaser, or of reporting about bug-chasing from an outsider perspective, as many of these studies have, serves to distance and objectify bug-chasers as some sort of incongruous 'other'. This distancing leads authors like Moskowitz and Roloff (2007b: 38) to lament that gay men are simply not as scared of HIV anymore and that 'the only way to stop bug chasing is by making HIV/AIDS as terrifying as it was for gay men circa 1985'. It will not be by bullying men into safe sex that bug-chasing will stop, Malkowski argues.

Instead, it is through the active practice of 'rhetorical listening' (Malkowski, 2014: 222) and, as we have asked you, the reader, to do in this book, by practising 'loving perception' (Lugones, 1987) and 'suspend[ing] initial judgements' that men seeking risky sex behaviours can best be responded to by health professionals.

BOX 9.6

- Given what we now know about risk, harm and pleasure, how can we interpret bug-chasing from a criminological perspective?
- What would ultra-realists make of bug-chasing?
- Is it fundamentally a practice of resistance?
- Can it be thought to be anti-capitalist? Is it simply too straightforwardly harmful?
- Is there anything pro-social or community-orientated about it? Is this enough?

Consent, once again, plays an important role here (see Chapter 4 where we discuss the non-consensual transmission of HIV). Though it is demonised and condemned by health professionals, **LGBT +** community activists and people living with HIV themselves (see *I Love Being HIV+*, BBC, 2006), the accounts given for why men do bug-chasing could be considered to have an internal logic to them. Men talk about semen 'impregnating' them, being connected to other gay men across the generations and being aroused by the status of being 'POZ'. All of these are complex issues of desire that become bound up with what some of these men think are expressions of queer/gay/trans masculinity.

For some, there is an edgework-like component (they like to push their 'sexual envelope'). For others, it is not about abjection, shame or even belonging, but rather an alternative expression of sexual desire: 'I have no wish to die, I am not punishing myself or hate myself or feel guilty in any way and will take meds as appropriate. But I enjoy being POZ immensely.' In her 2003 film about bug-chasing called *The Gift*, director Louise Hogarth followed the stories of two men, Doug and Kenboy, who describe deliberately becoming HIV + (Dream Out Loud, 2003). For Kenboy at least, whose accounts of hosting orgiastic barebacking parties explain some of the reasons why he sought seroconversion, bug-chasing could be much more obviously considered a form of deep play. In a BBC 2006 documentary on the topic, journalist Ricky Dyer concluded that bug-chasing was a fantasy, with more people saying they want to do it than actually doing it (despite encountering some bug-chasers in the course of his documentary, *I Love Being HIV+*). Even if this were true, what does this phenomenon tell us about public health messages, whether the criminal justice system should intervene, and what we, as criminologists, should think about this from the different perspectives outlined in this chapter?

Chemsex and deviance

Chemsex, or party and play, is the vernacular for orgiastic parties that involve men having sex with men under the effects of several controlled substances, which normally include mephedrone, 'G' (gamma-hydroxybutyric acid), ketamine, and may also include crystal methamphetamine (meth) and cocaine (Bourne et al., 2014). Chemsex displays many similarities with the cases of BDSM and bug-chasing in particular. It tends to involve more marginalised, 'different' sexual orientations and practices, and may sometimes overlap with bug-chasing as a practice. So, why do people participate in chemsex, and why should criminologists care about it? The act of having sex in groups is no longer in itself a matter of interest for the criminal law (see our discussion of the criminal regulation of homosexuality in Chapter 3). However, as we observed in *Brown*, the criminal law has intervened in cases of extreme sexual practices, arguably in an attempt to re-assert norms and moral standards.

Although the possession of controlled substances is a criminal offence in England and Wales under the Misuse of Drugs Act (MDA) 1971, and indeed drug prohibition is the dominant system of drug control worldwide, such legislation seldom results in arrest and prosecution in the context of chemsex. In a statement about chemsex, the Metropolitan Police makes clear that 'you won't be arrested for using drugs while having sex' (Metropolitan Police, n.d.). This statement might imply that the central concern for the police in the context of chemsex is safety, rather than enforcement. Moreover, the MDA only covers possession and distribution, and not consumption, so a person under the influence of controlled substances but not found in possession is not liable to arrest.

Can we observe any ways of resisting the status quo in the practice of chemsex, or is resistance an illusion that masks individualistic, selfish and hedonistic pursuits? Or does chemsex mask something more sinister, such as internalised stigma and marginalisation that encourage participants to harm themselves by engaging in risky practices? Once again, we will look at the intersections between harm, risk and pleasure to interrogate this phenomenon. Consider: is it edgework? Is it deep play? Or is it something else?

BOX 9.7

Scenario 3: Extract from BuzzFeed article, 'Inside the dark, dangerous world of chemsex'

When Stephen Port was convicted last week of the rape, drugging, and murder of four young men, police began to look again at dozens more cases involving date-rape drugs. But an investigation by BuzzFeed News into the hidden world of 'chemsex' reveals, through unprecedented first-person testimony, that this is just the beginning.

A young man stands at the edge of the Manchester ship canal. He steps forward, and in. The water, tepid from summer, rises up his shins, thighs. He begins to wade. He wants to vanish. Now he is up to his waist.

It is early afternoon at the end of August this year, days after another man injected him with seven times the dose of crystal methamphetamine he had agreed to take. Days after, psychosis set in.

Minutes elapse. Two passers-by stop, spotting the unnatural sight. What are you doing? Do you need help? There is no response. They stretch out, clasping his arm and yanking him back to the path. The next day a psychiatric unit admits him – another young man, splintered from reality.

Three months later, and hundreds of miles away, I sit on his bed in London facing him. His name is Rob. He is handsome, smartly dressed, educated.

I want to know how he got there, and how so many more like him fall out of the world most of us recognise and into a hell most know nothing about, a glimpse of which recently reached the front pages.

The glimpse came from the trial of Stephen Port, last week convicted of the rape, overdosing, and murder of four young men – a serial killer whose weapons were the drugs used to heighten sex and, for a minority, to enact the worst of crimes.

Police will now re-examine the deaths of 58 other people from the drug GHB over the last few years. The question this raises is: What have they been missing?

Throughout the reports of the trial, one word recurred again and again: chemsex. Uttered in increasingly wide circles, the term refers to men having sex with each other, while imbibing, inhaling or injecting ('slamming') three principal drugs: crystal methamphetamine (aka crystal, meth, Tina), GHB (aka G) and mephedrone. (Strudwick, 3 December 2016)

Stephen Port, a serial rapist and killer nicknamed 'the Grindr killer' by the media, received a life sentence for the rape and murder of four men. He allegedly drugged and raped each of the men, and then left them to die. In the extract above, and in other news articles covering the case, there is a clear attempt to link the practice of chemsex with Stephen Port's crime. The narrative of the news piece depicts chemsex as a dangerous, risky, non-consensual and potentially deadly practice. The piece goes on to argue that, in such a predatory environment, drugs remove the possibility for consent and, thus, widespread sexual violence and abuse are endemic to chemsex (see Chapter 4 for our discussion of intoxication and consent). Patrick Strudwick, the author of the news article, makes yet another connection to the Port case:

> amid this mess of victims being blamed, or blaming themselves, and mental fog about the events themselves, Doyle says there will be many people who only realise they have been a victim of a crime when they read details of the Stephen Port case and recognise what happened to them. (Strudwick, 3 December 2016)

The Port case is described here as an eye-opener for chemsex participants, enabling them to see themselves as victims. Interestingly, as a result of criticism from Port's victims' families, the police were called upon to re-examine 58 overdose deaths that were ruled as accidental to establish whether there was foul play in the form of intentional over-dosing by a third party.

Reading the above extracts, and original article, how do you feel about chemsex? If you did not know anything about this practice before reading this, then it is likely that this particular narrative would dominate your understanding of this phenomenon.

But let us shift our attention away from the practice itself towards interrogating our social attitudes towards it. What does this narrative portrayal of chemsex tell us about our understandings and cultural attitudes towards it? Is it possible that a single, isolated crime such as Port's, as heinous as it was, becomes symbolic of a set of social anxieties, moral/legal boundaries, dangers and risks that surround the practice of chemsex? Through this symbolism, the complexity of individual agency and its negotiation in the context of chemsex is fast removed, and the practice is re-imagined as a dangerous game led by predators to deceive and exploit their victims. Is this a fair portrayal? Let us look at some literature to interrogate this further.

Most studies on chemsex are underpinned by a medical, public health framework (Hakim, 2019). Many such studies are primarily concerned with harm and make outward reference to risk in their titles (see, for example, Glynn et al., 2018; Pufall et al., 2018; Sewell et al., 2017). While some mostly focus on traditional public health measures of harm, such as morbidity and mortality rates, sexually transmitted infections, addiction, and blood-borne viruses, other studies focus on environmental risk factors. Chemsex is defined as a syndemic risk environment (Pollard et al., 2018). Syndemic describes when multiple health problems interact and contribute to a higher burden of disease in a given population, because it involves the combination of multiple risky behaviours; namely drug-taking and sex that may be unprotected and involving multiple partners. A risk environment framework, first coined by Tim Rhodes (2002), involves shifting attention away from individual action, and towards environmental and structural factors that frame individual risk-taking. In the context of chemsex, 'homophobic mainstream culture constitutes a macro-level "risk environment" in which gay and other men who have sex with men are stigmatised, and against which lesbian, gay and bisexual communities have constructed antithetical sub-cultures to resist shame and celebrate marginalised identities' (Pollard et al., 2018: 421).

This view of chemsex is interesting; it seems to assume that there is resistance to its practice. However ultimately, the quote seems to point to the role of internalised stigma in producing the risk environment that negatively affects the life chances of those who partake in chemsex practices. Notwithstanding the advantages of a risk-environmental perspective over a more traditional public health approach, particularly in terms of engaging with the potential effects of stigma and marginalisation, risk alone is not enough to understand what is going on. Furthermore, any given public health perspective will necessarily be limited by its aims to sanitise and control. As such, chemsex and similar practices will continue to be constructed as pathological. At this point, we may ask: what drives involvement in chemsex?

One approach to understanding chemsex within an outwardly critical cultural tradition uses the now familiar concept of edgework to explain the phenomenon (Hickson, 2018). Using edgework allows us to understand risk-taking as being inextricably tied to pleasure. Through edgework, risk and pleasure may be conceptualised not as distinct and opposing forces, but as interconnected. Ford Hickson (2018) argues that some chemsex for some men qualifies as edgework, partly to avoid the risk of using a broad brush to characterise all experiences, and partly because he finds the defining characteristics of edgework in people's narratives. For instance, he reports that participants in his study were actively drawing a line between acceptable and unacceptable behaviour, in terms of both drug-taking (for example, by not sharing needles or not injecting) and sexual practice (such as no barebacking). Participants also presented themselves as knowing what they were doing; expertise is an important aspect of maintaining the edge. This is exemplified by their knowledge of drugs: dosage, mixing of substances, dosing practices and interventions upon members where they felt unwell all figured in participants' repertoires. The third aspect of edgework found in accounts of chemsex was about expanding the limits of pleasure, but also the limits of being human, referred to by participants using words such as 'intense emotions', 'freedom' and feeling 'super human' (Hickson, 2018: 109).

Is there something here about the management of risk and pleasure that appeals to males in particular, and is tied with notions of successful masculinity? In an effort to 'de-pathologise' and de-shame chemsex, alternative explanations refer to processes such as 'queering intimacy' as an expression of the neoliberal 'contradiction between individualism and collectivity' (Hakim, 2019: 252). Within chemsex, drugs are used to lower inhibitions and heighten pleasurable sexual experiences, but also to address a lost sense of collective-ness through creating spaces and practices of collective, intense and affective intimacy.

BOX 9.8

Whether Jamie Hakim's account is convincing to you or not, it is nevertheless interesting to consider this phenomenon from a different perspective, one that does not begin with a negative value judgement at its core, and is perhaps more in line with Maria Lugones' (1987) 'loving perception' approach. One participant in Hakim's study describes his experience of being at chemsex parties:

> I've been at parties before where all I've done is talk and dance. The mood just went that way for me ... One of my friends, we had been having sex for a couple of hours and then all of sudden I spotted this Kylie book ... I said 'Oh my God, you like Kylie!' and he was like [affects camp demeanour, sharp in-take of breath] 'she signed this!' And then all of sudden we took some G and some meph and then it turned into watching YouTube Kylie videos. Instead of having sex we ended up dancing round his living room. (cited in Hakim, 2019: 258)

When thinking about what you know about chemsex so far, is this type of narra-tive something you might expect to read?

How about this:

> Whilst on G, I allowed people to ejaculate inside me. So, I was taking maybe more risks. But you know usually when I was negative, I never allowed that to happen because of the risks, my ability to control myself was inhibited, and I also, you know, allowed myself to get carried away in the moment and live out those fantasies that, you know, I had been fantasising about; dreaming about. (cited in Bourne et al., 2014: 54)

Does this fall in line with your expectations about what the experience of chemsex might be like?

The experiences of people who partake in chemsex appear varied and multi-ple. They may be affected by the frequency of attendance at parties, the length of time of involvement in the scene, the types of substances consumed, the manner of use, their HIV status, their life circumstances, and so on, so it is impossible to qualify experiences as falling into a single model, a singular pat-tern or direction. What is certain is that there is a sharp contrast in people's descriptions of their experiences, between expressions of elation, joy, pleasure, intensity and connection, against feelings of fear, struggle, shame, isolation and negative health consequences.

Perhaps there are a combination of factors that make the phenomenon of chemsex unique: the politics of resistance of 1970s gay movements advocated for a sexuality that was quite different to, and in many ways stood in opposition to, the heteronormative, monogamous, nuclear family-oriented mainstream approach from which gay people were excluded. In Hakim's (2019) view, this forged a collective identity, a collectivity that is continuously sought in the face of external ideological pressures, which may equally come from neoliberalism or heteronormativity. At the same time, we cannot ignore the individualistic and pleasure-seeking aspect of involvement in chemsex as a form of hedonism tied to our perhaps excessively consumption-oriented identities that are structurally shaped. In 1971, criminologist Jock Young was beginning to observe a process whereby hedonism would become a central force in maintaining productivity. In his words:

> [L]eisure is concerned with consumption and work with production; a keynote of our bifurcated society, therefore, is that individuals within it must constantly consume in order to keep pace with the productive capacity of the economy. They must produce in order to consume, and consume in order to produce. The interrelationship between formal and subterranean values is therefore seen in a new light: hedonism, for instance, is closely tied to productivity. (Young, 1971: 128)

If we accept Young's observation about the indivisibility between formal and subterranean values in our leisure economies, we can perhaps also accept that conceptualising chemsex as simply a hedonistic practice, or simply a harmful practice, or simply a practice of resistance, is reductive. In fact, chemsex can be all those things and more, while hedonism itself can be tied to both resistance and compliance. No single concept or explanation can account for the complexity and multiplicity of a given phenomenon. The different analyses and interpretations of the phenomenon we have touched upon here offer valuable insights for its understanding. We continue to invite students and readers alike to reflect on the contributions of different disciplinary and conceptual lenses when studying the pursuit of pleasurable risk, as well as asking what is missing from these.

Summary

In this chapter, we have explored some of the ways in which risk is conceptualised and we have explored some of the problems risk poses in our study of criminology and our consideration of justice.

We have seen that risk has been figured as a culturally constructed response to a perceived danger, which forges a moral framework around specific practices (Douglas, 1992). We know from Chapter 2 that risk has also been figured as a response to **modernity** and neoliberalism by Beck (1992), Bauman (2013) and Giddens (1998). We see that risk narratives also infuse the way we think about pleasure and leisure, thanks to the theory of edgework that Lyng (1990) articulates.

Cultural criminologists have built on this to explore the extent to which risk-taking might be seen as a refusal of capitalist narratives that centralise security. They argue that committing certain crimes and deriving pleasure from them, might be a form of resistance (Ferrell, 1999). These approaches have been critiqued by zemiologists (people who study 'harm') like Hall and Winlow (2018) for whom this might rather be an exercise of 'special liberty' available to certain people (white men) from certain backgrounds, and which ignore the fact that such risk-taking is not necessarily accessible to people who are differently marginalised, and, moreover, that there are some harms that are universal and which should be condemned.

We have used different case studies that detail how the criminal justice system responds to incidents of sexualised risk-taking. We have seen that these responses intersect with public health narratives. They are also infused with homophobic and heteronormative responses on behalf of both the judiciary and medical discourses. This means that the intersectionality of the actors is at play when justice is administered. Heterosexual coupling is more likely to be protected from criminalisation and demonisation than homosexual, unprotected, group-sex scenarios (see Rubin, 1984).

The role that the criminal justice system plays in BDSM cases, in chemsex situations or concerning the phenomenon of bug-chasing, relies on constructions of morality and normativity (see Chapter 1), meaning that people who take sexualised risks are not always treated equally, which has implications for justice more broadly.

Are there any solutions to this? Is there a better way to address the potential social and cultural implications of sexualised risk-taking without unfairly criminalising consenting adults? Or are there cases where it is acceptable and right to criminalise even consenting adults for their sexualised risk-taking?

What is missing from these narratives? Where are the stories of women and their sexualised risk-taking? We have discussed chemsex and bug-chasing in the context of men who have sex with men, but why do we not know more about women and heterosexual couples who may also take similar sorts of risk (in terms of an unwanted pregnancy or in the context of anonymous sexual encounters in heterosexual or lesbian bath houses?). Sometimes women who do **sex work** and women involved in BDSM are figured as edgeworkers (Newmahr, 2011; Tsang, 2019), but is it inconceivable that there is something else?

Review questions

- Reflect on what we have learnt about edgework in this chapter. What are the positive and negative aspects of this theory?
- Which of the case studies that we have analysed here do you think are the most dangerous? How did you decide?
- Why do people enjoy taking sexualised risks?
- Should risky sex be a public concern?

Other chapters that this links to

Chapter 3 (Sex and crime in time and space)

Chapter 4 (Consent and its discontents)

Chapter 5 (Sex and institutional cultures of abuse)

Chapter 7 (Sexual exploitation and the State)

Chapter 10 (Sex and disability)

Chapter 15 (How to change your life)

10

Sex and disability

CHAPTER OUTLINE

The disabled body confronts how we might think ethically about the relation-ship between crime, sex and desire. Part of this confrontation stems from the paradoxical relationship between the **human rights** that a person with disa-bilities has, and the ethics of how they are practised. This chapter will explore the issues at stake when we discuss sex and disability from a criminological perspective. Although we are yet to establish a comprehensive criminology of disability and **sexuality**, there is an emerging body of work from disabilities studies which can help criminologists develop a better understanding of this topic.

By the end of this chapter, you will understand more about:

- the ethical issues at stake when analysing disability and its intersection with **sexual practice**
- how issues of consent and capacity influence approaches to sex and disability in different criminological contexts
- the diverse theoretical approaches we might adopt when studying disability
- how disability intersects with **gender, 'race',** sexuality, **ethnicity, class** and age.

The contested sexual politics of people with disabilities poses a unique chal-lenge to our study of sex and crime. In this chapter, we will be uncovering some of the ways that approaches to sex and disability can help us to under-stand how crime and **deviance** are constructed, and to recognise some awkward truths that we have to face when we encounter the disabled body in the context of sex and crime. As Raymond J. Aguilera (2000: 259), citing poet Mark O'Brien, points out, unless we die first, we and everyone we know will eventually become disabled, so issues that address the rights of people with disabilities before the law are pertinent for us all. It is for this reason that in this chapter we refer to people with no disability as being 'temporary-abled'.

People who are disabled are, to a certain extent, especially at risk of sexual violence. Like anyone, they are at risk of abuse and harassment, and they are also susceptible to having their voice silenced when it comes to expressing their own autonomy, such as when making decisions about contraception, whether to have a baby or to continue with a pregnancy. Alongside this, sepa-rate debates about the right of people with disability to have sex are intertwined with debates about **sex work**, sexual surrogacy and whether institutions should intervene in sexual relationships between consenting adults where at least one partner has a disability.

All of these elements are why the intersection of sex and disability is a field ripe for criminological enquiry. We cannot cover all the issues at play in this chapter, so we will instead consider four cases; recalling our discussions in Chapter 4, we will explore what consent looks like for people with intellectual disabilities; what dating while disabled is like; what disabled desire means; and what the implications of this are for people living in institutions, particularly adults with dementia.

Spend some time reading and thinking about the following lines written by poet Mark O'Brien (1987), who lived most of his life inside an iron lung:

Love poem to no one in particular

let me touch you with my words

for my hands lie limp as empty gloves

let my words stroke your hair

slide down your back

and tickle your belly

for my hands, light and free flying as bricks

ignore my wishes and stubbornly refuse to carry out my quietest desires

let my words enter your mind

bearing torches

admit them willingly into your being

so they may caress you gently

within.

- What picture does the poem paint about disabled sexuality?
- Does anything about the themes evoked in the poem surprise you?
- Notice any other thoughts, feelings or impressions that this text arouses in you, as they may help you reflect on your own responses to the issues that we encounter in this chapter.

Socio-political context

The rising influence of medical **discourses** at the beginning of the twentieth century in the **Global North** saw people with disabilities segregated into long-term stay hospitals where they were infantilised and denied civil liberties. In response to this, a body of critical disability activist work has emerged. In particular, over the past 25 years, disability scholars have been hugely significant in terms of establishing the rights of people with disabilities to establish sexual citizenship (Aguilera, 2000; Davies, 2000a, b; Shakespeare and Richardson, 2018; Shakespeare et al., 1996; Shildrick, 2007).

The concept of sexual citizenship describes the politicising of the erotic, of desire and of sexual practice. Often used to describe **LGBT +** people's rights to express their sexuality, this understanding of citizenship, forged following a human rights-based agenda, recognises that people have rights to access certain sorts of spaces from which they might have historically been excluded, such as, for instance, bars and clubs, the House of Commons or the street at night time (Bell and Binnie, 2000; Puwar, 2004; Stanko, 1990). Sexual citizenship is also about asserting institutional rights for all people: the right to a family or to get married, the right to be recognised as a romantic partner in the eyes of the law, or within medical discourses (Barker, 2013; Ryan-Flood, 2009). Sexual citizenship is also about having the freedom to express your sexual desires where those desires have historically been considered to be paraphilias (for example, bondage, domination, submission, sadomasochism (BDSM); see our discussion in Chapter 9) and the right to have control over your body, the right to choose contraception, the right to an abortion and the right to have sex reassignment surgery, or not (Richardson, 2017). In this respect, disability studies and LGBT + activism share a number of political priorities, and the interplay, including points of connection, between queer theory and 'crip' theory, which we encountered in Chapter 2, is one that is helpful to reflect upon.

The claim for people with disabilities to enjoy full sexual citizenship is a pertinent one. However, it is only in recent decades that this has emerged. Certainly, in the twentieth century there were concerns about preserving 'good stock' within the population and of preventing the reproduction of bodies which were somehow considered to be deficient. Current concerns about sexuality can be understood as an expression of the **paternalistic** attitude a temporary-abled majority have about people with disabilities. In some mainstream discourses, people with disabilities have been considered to have no sexuality – to be sexless – or to be out of control and hyper-sexual. Shildrick (2007: 56–7) notes that the sexual expression of people with disabilities has been silenced. Children who are disabled are excluded from sex education classes because it is assumed that they will never be sexually active. Elsewhere, young women with intellectual disabilities (ID) are non-consensually sterilised by their families to avoid pregnancy (Chou and Lu, 2011), while sexually active people with disabilities, or those who are just interested in sex, are shamed (Abbott, 2013), and parents who have disabilities have been pathologised (Morris, 1991; Shakespeare et al., 1996).

Treating people with disabilities so differently to temporary-abled people is obviously problematic in the context of sexual citizenship. And yet disability brings with it some tangible challenges that we must take seriously if we are concerned with justice more broadly. We are going to explore some of these in this chapter. The notion of sexual citizenship itself has been critiqued by Diane Richardson (2017) for its '**Western**-centric' focus, which is rooted in a neo-liberal understanding of human rights-based discourses (see Chapter 7 for our discussion of human rights). We will explore some of the implications of this too.

Understanding disability

In England and Wales, disability is defined in section 6 of the Equality Act 2010 as 'having a physical or mental impairment that has a "substantial" and "long-term" negative effect on your ability to do normal daily activities'. 'Substantial' means something more than minor or trivial, for instance it takes much longer than it usually would to complete a daily task like getting dressed, while 'long-term' means lasting for 12 months or more.

The Americans with Disabilities Act 1990 defines a disabled person as 'a person who has a physical or mental impairment that substantially limits one or more major life activity'.

Adopting a more bio-psychosocial approach, in 2011, the World Health Organization (WHO) established that disability was something that resulted from the interaction between persons with impairments and attitudinal and environmental barriers that hinder their full and effective participation in society on an equal basis with others.

This notion of 'impairment' when talking about disability marks a significant shift in contemporary thinking about disability. Impairment is the language used to describe the condition pertaining to the person with the disability. The disability is not attributed to the body of the person themselves (Bunt, 2018; Oliver, 2011). You will note that the USA definition, and to a certain extent the British one, situates disability as something that 'a person has', while, in the WHO context, the impairment is something that a person encounters by interacting with a world that does not treat them equally. This way, a disability is not a personal attribute, but rather the outcome of inequitable social interactions.

Models of disability

These different ways of thinking about disability are called models. It is helpful to understand these different models and to reflect on the ways that they interact with issues related to crime, deviance and sexuality; however, given the diversity of types of disability that exist and the different ways in which they present themselves, we often find that thinking about disability solely through models is not always helpful.

BOX 10.2   Table 10.1 outlines different models of disability.

Table 10.1   Models of disability

Model (presented as far as possible in order of emergence)	Definition	Example	Sources
Medical	Disability has a medical cause; a person has an impairment that ought to be fixed or managed by medical professionals	A person in a wheelchair wants to enter a building but cannot access it because there are steps and they are in a wheelchair (something is wrong with the person)	Equality Act 2010
Social	People with impairments encounter barriers because of the way that physical space is organised, or because of taboos or prejudice about their disability	A person in a wheelchair wants to enter a building but cannot access it because there are steps and there is no ramp (something is wrong with the building)	Oliver, 2013
Bio-psychosocial	Disability occurs because of a combination of biological, social and psychological factors; a critique of this is that it is too reductive, and places too much emphasis on the biology of disability	A person suffers chronic back pain after a car accident leaving them unable to walk for long periods of time, unable to work, and as a result they feel depressed and isolated. Their disability is caused by a combination of the biological pain of the injury, the psychological effects of isolation and living with pain, the economic/social burden of not being able to work.	Borrell-Carrió et al., 2004; Engel, 1978
Critical realist	Understanding what a disability is requires a multifaceted understanding of the phenomenon; it is impossible to understand everything about disability, rather it should be understood as a multi-layered issue: 'disability as an interaction between individual and structural factors' (Shakespeare, 2013: 74)	A person suffers chronic back pain after a car accident, leaving them unable to walk for long periods of time, unable to work, and, as a result, they feel depressed and isolated Facilitating at-home working might help them to feel less isolated and more financially empowered; pain management and therapy can help the person become more mobile and autonomous	Bhaskar and Danermark, 2006; Shakespeare, 2006, 2013

Model (presented as far as possible in order of emergence)	Definition	Example	Sources
Critical disability studies	Disability is experienced intersectionally; queer, post-colonial, feminist, anti-capitalist analyses bring to bear on analysis of the politics of disability	A person suffers chronic back pain after a car accident, leaving them unable to walk for long periods of time, unable to work, and, as a result, they feel depressed and isolated	Goodley et al., 2018; Puar, 2009; Shildrick, 2007
		The experience of this type of impairment will be different for different people – men and women will experience it differently, as will rich and poor people; those with caring responsibilities, people who are old, or young, people who live in rural or urban spaces, and anything in between, will all have different experiences of this, and the appropriate way to engage with them will depend on their intersectional experiences of these impairments	

Consider each of these models carefully:

- Which do you think is the most convincing model?
- Which do you like least? Why do you think this is the case?
- Is there a better way to explain what we understand by 'disability'?

The two most common and straightforward ways of thinking about disability are the bio-medical model and the social model. The bio-medical model of disability posits that a person's impairment is what causes their disability and that there is something wrong with their body or their mind which the medical realm might be able to fix, or at least manage. The bio-medical model focuses on the individual and attempts to fix or to cure them.

On the other hand, the social model posits that people are disabled by a world or a social life that is not equipped for them and which puts barriers in the way of their capacity to flourish to their fullest. The development of the social model of disability is hugely important in terms of moving policy affecting people with disabilities forward, and of moving beyond a 'pity model' in which people with disabilities were considered to be simply unfortunate victims of their affliction. Instead, it focuses on the collective rights of people with disabilities and their exclusion from society. Society caters to the needs of temporary-abled people and neglects the differing needs that different people have for accessing spaces, goods and services.

By placing the emphasis on the social and moving away from the emphasis on the individual, disability activism was able to mobilise for changes in attitude at a cultural and social level. As well as a model, this social perspective formed the basis of a movement in the 1970s started by activist Paul Hunt. Members of the Union of the Physically Impaired Against Segregation (UPIAS) wanted to steer away from an individualising bio-medical understanding of disability towards one which challenged forms of prejudice, discrimination and inaccessibility in the built environment.

The advances made by a social model of understanding disability are inflected by a critique mobilised by the critical realist and embodied perspectives which are articulated by Roy Bhaskar and Berth Danermark (2006), Christopher Frauenberger (2015), Bill Hughes and Kevin Paterson (2006) and Paterson and Hughes (1999). From these perspectives, the social model's erasure of the embodied has been called into question (Shakespeare and Watson, 2001). From a critical realist perspective, the experience of disability is composed of a multiplicity of factors, and the way to understand disability is to attend to the different elements that compose disability. This involves, according to Bhaskar and Danermark (2006: 288–9), taking into consideration the biological experience of an impairment alongside the social and cultural effects, or interpretations, of an impairment. It also means thinking about what each disability might mean economically, institutionally and psychologically for the person in question and local, meso or global scales. This multi-layered analysis is what they refer to as a 'necessarily laminated system', where the levels and context and scales begin to create an impression of what being disabled means. For Sarah Bunt (2018: 190–1), this type of multi-layered analysis of disability helps to explain the complex relationship people have with disability, including, for instance, having a positive attitude to a disability, while also not wanting to normalise disability.

According to Shildrick (2007: 58) and Hughes and Paterson (1997: 328), the disappearance of the body in disability theory – a consequence perhaps of crip theory's engagement with post-structuralism and queer theory – undermines the claims that people with disabilities make for sexual citizenship. It becomes a way of thinking that is complicit with the erasure of people with disabilities as sexual citizens. The material reality of the body which feels constant pain, which cannot walk, which hears badly, which struggles to remember information, or which is amputated, has to be accommodated in discussions of sexual rights. As Jenny Morris (1991) writes, though the accident which means that she now uses a wheelchair has taken her on interesting and rewarding paths during her life, she would also have the function back in her legs if she had the chance to. As she says, her experience of her disability is attenuated by the fact that she was an adult when she had her accident. Moreover, her ethnicity and her class provided her with material and social advantages when navigating the world as a wheelchair-using mother of a young child. Such advantage would not necessarily have been available to differently marginalised people with disabilities, who may have experienced different forms of prejudice or harassment as parents who were disabled (Morris, 1991; and see also Goodley et al., 2018). The body matters. Indeed, Hughes and Paterson (1997) suggest that a phenomenological approach helps us to understand the body as something which has its own experiences, that is lived in, that feels. What they call the 'sociology of impairment' becomes a way to take the body seriously in disability studies, even if it is also true that social barriers compound sexual social injustice for people with disabilities.

The diversity of the disabled experience is inflected by positionality and intersectionality – class, age, 'race', sexuality, gender – as Morris notes. Yet it is also diverse as a category. When we talk about disability, there are a huge range of conditions and impairments that we may talk about; consider the difference between being d/Deaf and being reliant on using a wheelchair. And even within similar categories of disability – intellectual disability, for instance – there are different manifestations and severities of disability. This diversity means that, when it comes to sexuality, there are issues and ethics that will not be relevant for everyone with a disability, and certainly will not be relevant in the same way.

Disabled sex and criminology

As social scientists are starting to research more about disability and sexuality, there is a lot of emerging work that helps us in our study of criminology and **deviance**, particularly surrounding questions of consent, capacity and desire.

Intellectual disabilities (ID)

People with ID are arguably more at risk of sexual violence than many other people with disabilities because their lives are more likely to be governed and managed by carers. This **governance** inhibits their opportunity to exercise consent and to develop the capacity to withdraw it. This is particularly pertinent when considering issues related to pregnancy, contraception and intimate relationships.

Scholars agree that the expression of sexual desire forms part of the fundamental functioning of human life (Abbott, 2013; Gil-Llario et al., 2018; Kramers-Olen, 2016; Tamas et al., 2019). That this is so loudly espoused in so many texts about the sexuality of people with ID speaks to the fact that this remains a notion that must be reaffirmed, rather than something which is routinely taken for granted, as it might be for other people who are not disabled in this way.

As the work of Angus Lam et al. (2019), Maria D.Gil-Llario et al. (2018) and David Abbott (2013) demonstrate, people with ID do desire to have sexual relationships and are, in no way, intrinsically sexless. Lam et al. (2019) conducted a systematic review of studies to highlight the different ways in which people with ID have their sexuality policed, in spite of the fact that they are interested in, and desirous of, sexual relationships.

Some people report 'self-imposed abstinence', either because they found sex disgusting or otherwise undesirable because pregnancy and child-rearing – one of the potential consequences of sex – were considered to be things that they could not do. In other cases – and echoing the findings of Abbott (2013) – people with disabilities reported being prevented from entering into sexual relationships because of barriers put in place by their families or carers as part of safeguarding measures. Some participants reported that being gay as well as having an ID made developing intimate relationships even more difficult.

At the same time, Daniela Tamas et al.'s (2019) research with professionals who work with people with ID demonstrates that parents and carers tend to respond quite positively to the idea that people with ID would enjoy romantic or sexual relationships. They are nonetheless squeamish about how such a thing should take place. Tamas et al. (2019: 252–4) report that parents in particular felt ill-equipped to educate their children about sex and worried that their children would express their sexuality in socially inappropriate ways, and so they avoided discussing it with them. Care workers and parents both reported more liberal attitudes towards supporting the sexual practice of men with ID than that of women, who were considered to be more at risk of abuse than men. This is borne out in Gil-Llario et al.'s (2018: 77–8) work with adults with ID who reported that, even though they wanted to have sexual relationships (and indeed 84.2 per cent of their sample had had some sort of sexual relationship with another person), many were not using contraception appropriately (even though they also knew what it was) and were less likely to report experiences of abuse. This was particularly true for male victims. Though they were having sex, and knew about sex, in many cases support was not in place to facilitate this in a safe way.

Tlakale N.Phasha's (2009) study of teenagers with ID in South Africa echoes this finding. She identifies that, even though young people with ID were more at risk of abuse than their temporary-abled counterparts, they were also more likely to be excluded from education programmes about sex, contraception and

HIV prevention education. According to Phasha (2009: 189), young people with ID are made more vulnerable because they lack knowledge about what abuse is, they might find themselves in a dependent relationship with their abuser, and they might have a communication deficit which prevents them from articulating their experiences. Alongside this, perpetrators of sex crimes against people with ID might assume that their victims will not be taken seriously by a criminal justice system because of their disability, which might encourage this sort of abuse. Anne Kramers-Olen (2016: 507) adds that having little sex education, living in an authoritarian institution and holding 'a general sense of powerlessness' compounds South African young people's vulnerability to sexual abuse. These views are confirmed in Gil-Lario et al.'s (2018) own study, which found that, among their Spanish sample, all the men who reported that they had been sexually abused were blamed (by family or institutions) for the abuse that they had suffered.

For Phasha (2009), the circumstances of abuse are exacerbated by the specific South African context of her work. The abuse of people with ID is believed to be widespread and often takes place in the home. This is due, in part, to a misconception about a possible cure for ID; that ID is caused by 'bad blood' in the brain that can be cured through heavy bleeding (for instance, the bleeding that occurs after childbirth) (Phasha, 2009: 194). This, coupled with a preference for dealing with abuse situations in private, instead of through formally recognised external channels, means that abuse, if it is detected, might often remain unpunished. Sometimes this is because punishing an offender might be detrimental to the rest of the family of the person with ID, in cases where the perpetrator is also the breadwinner of the household (Phasha, 2009: 196). Sometimes, it is simply that the legacy of police violence seeded during the era of apartheid (a policy of racial segregation) means that **Black** South Africans in particular are reluctant to report criminal activity to the police (Phasha, 2009: 199). Or, it is the Ubuntu philosophy that guides responses to sexual abuse of people with ID, and which can be hard to recognise as punishment, through Western eyes. Ubuntu – a philosophy of caring and humanity within a community – offers collaborative, dialectic ways of resolving trouble which might be something akin to **restorative justice**. It is Ubuntu that informed Archbishop Desmond Tutu's Truth and Reconciliation Commissions in the aftermath of apartheid. It is Ubuntu which encourages 'reconciliation, restoration and harmony' (Phasha, 2009: 200) as opposed to punitive punishment and incarceration that are preferred in non-African contexts, including the Global North, when it comes to sex offenders. This can mean that it may look like no formal punishment has taken place when, in fact, alternative solutions may be at play.

The influence of culture and society is just as significant when it comes to how sex and people with ID are encountered in the British (Wilkinson et al., 2015), Serbian (Tamas et al., 2019) and Hong Kong (Lam et al., 2019) contexts.

Here, as indeed in the South African case, it is **heteronormativity** and notions of **hegemonic masculinity** that are obstacles to people with ID enjoying full sexual citizenship. The emphasis on people with disabilities being as 'normal as everyone else' in their desires (Wilkinson et al., 2015), and the idea that they should be helped to have sex that is as 'normal as possible', might appear to be forward-thinking, but it necessarily rests on assumptions about what those norms should be, namely that they are **cisgender**, heterosexual desires for monogamous sexual relationships. Verity J. Wilkinson et al. (2015: 102) highlight how stigma about having an LGBT+ identity, either from caregivers or other people in institutional settings, discourages gay or **trans** men and women with ID from expressing themselves. Similar stories of the embarrassment of others in the face of LGBT+ relationships are told by Abbott's study participants (2013: 1082).

Beyond this, heteronormative scripts of romance also limit the sexual expression of men and women with ID. Think of men with ID who do not pursue sexual relationships with women because they cannot be a 'breadwinner', or women who count themselves out because they 'are not fit enough' to be mothers (Lam et al., 2019: 217); think of parents who are more accepting of men's expression of sexual desire than of women's (Tamas et al., 2019: 252); think of caregivers who show sympathy to women who are sexually abused but who disbelieve men when they say they were raped (Gil-Llario, 2018: 76–7); think of women with ID who are subject to the violence of a non-consensual sterilisation in Taiwan, in a way that men are not (Chou and Lu, 2011). These are all examples of the way that heteronormativity saturates these debates and curtails the possibilities of people with disabilities to enjoy fuller sexual emancipation. Imagine, against this background, a person with ID who expresses a desire to have a sex change, or to participate in BDSM. How realistic is it that this desire might be actualised? Does it matter if it is not? What do the courts say about how people with ID should be treated, when it comes to sex?

BOX 10.3

Let us think about this in the context of two English cases cited by Martin Curtice et al. (2013). Bear in mind that these are *civil* cases that are considering the capacity of individuals; they are not criminal cases like those we have discussed in Chapter 4.

Sheffield City Council v. E and S [2004] EWHC 2808 (Fam)

Here, E, a 21-year-old woman who allegedly functioned at the level of a 13- year-old, had formed a relationship that was abusive with S, a 37-year-old man with a substantial history of perpetrating sexually violent crimes. E planned to marry S and the court was asked to decide whether or not she had the capacity to make this decision, to understand the nature of the marriage contract and the responsibilities of marriage, and that she was able therefore to give consent.

The court held that the test to understand whether a person has the capacity to consent to marriage had to be low, meaning that their understanding of marriage did not need to be sophisticated or nuanced. This also meant that because sex and marriage usually accompany each other, the capacity to consent to sexual relations here would also be set at a low bar. The court had to be happy that E understood what marriage was. It was not for them to decide whether or not it was acceptable for someone with ID to marry someone with a history of sex offending.

According to Munby J, 'the court is not concerned – has no jurisdiction – to consider whether it is in E's best interests to marry or not to marry S. The court is concerned with her capacity to marry, not with the wisdom of her marriage in general or her marriage to S in particular' (*Sheffield City Council v. E and S* at 102).

As such, the court did not intervene to prevent E from exercising her desire to marry S.

Think:

- What principles are at play here?
- What political ideologies underpin Munby's judgement?
- Do you agree with it?
- Do you have any trouble with it?
- How can we connect the decision to theories such as hegemonic masculinity or heteronormativity?

D Borough Council v. AB [2011] EWHC 101 COP

The case of AB concerns a 41-year-old male with 'moderate' learning disabilities who entered into a sexual relationship with another man, known as 'K', with whom he lived under the supervision of the local authority. Alongside this, there were two instances where AB had been reported to the police for inappropriate sexual conduct towards children.

On one occasion, a young boy in a dentist's waiting area observed a man touching his groin, licking his lips, and was then asked by the man for his name. The dentist's diary showed that AB was due for an appointment at that time.

On another occasion, two girls aged 9 and 10 stated that when travelling on a bus, a man (AB) had commented upon their physical appearance, touched their upper legs and then attempted to look up their skirts. The police were notified. A month later, these two girls were travelling on the bus once again, as was AB. The girls notified the bus driver who also notified the police. AB was then

(Continued)

taken to the police station and questioned. However, the police decided that no further action should be taken against him.

The court was asked to decide whether AB lacked the capacity to enter into sexual relations with K. The local authority wanted the court to issue an order to prevent AB from having sex with K. Here, as with E above, the court had to decide whether AB had the capacity to consent, or if his impairment was too severe for him to have that capacity.

The court relied on previous **case law** (XCC v. MB, NB, MAB (2006)) and on the fact that capacity to consent to sex requires a low bar of understanding and that all that was needed was 'sufficiently rudimentary knowledge of what the act comprises and its sexual nature' (*D Borough Council v. AB* at 22). The judge set out a three-limbed test to establish what that awareness might entail. To be able to consent to sex, a person must understand:

1.   The mechanics of the act.
2.   That there are health risks involved, particularly the acquisition of sexually transmitted and sexually transmissible infections.
3.   That sex between a man and a woman may result in the woman becoming pregnant.

Following psychiatric assessment, it was found that AB did not have sufficient knowledge about any of the three limbs of the test for heterosexual relations and did not understand limb two, which meant he was not able to consent to homosexual relations either. Finding AB unable to consent to sex, then, Judge Mostyn ruled that the local authority provide AB with sex education to enable him to develop the capacity to consent, and then review the case in nine months.

Consider the following:

One thing you might note, and Mostyn highlights this too, is that the three-limbed consent test has different outcomes depending on the sexual act in question; oral and anal sex have different implications here, as does masturbation. So, the test might find that the same person has the capacity to consent to some things, but not others.

*   What are the implications for 'justice' here? What does 'justice' look like in these cases?
*   And what do you think of the decision of the judge?
*   Are the human rights of people like AB, K and the children who AB approaches sufficiently protected?

Dating while disabled

Some of the issues that emerge in the case of AB are expressions of the barriers faced by people with disabilities when it comes to developing sexual citizenship and engaging in, or pursuing, sexual relationships. In the case of AB, we see a capacity-to-consent test, which is focused on a **phallocentric,** heteronormative construction of sexuality. Alongside this, that the judgement suggested that AB needed sex education to better improve his understanding of consent demonstrates an ongoing barrier that people with disabilities encounter. As Cassandra Loeser et al. (2018) have demonstrated, they are excluded from sex education and not helped to achieve full sexual citizenship, including the ability to advocate for their own desires and to consent to sex. That an issue like this should have to be resolved within the justice system demonstrates how acute this problem is, and points to the challenges of understanding consent across society. We saw some of this in Chapter 4.

Carol A.Howland and Diana H.Rintala (2001) have examined the dating behaviours of 31 women with disabilities in the USA in order to better understand the barriers that they encountered to dating. What they found was that women with disabilities started dating at an older age compared to temporary-abled women; if they were attracted to people when they were younger, their parents or carers limited their dating opportunities – perhaps out of a paternalistic desire to protect them – which meant that, as adults, they were much less experienced or knowledgeable about dating than temporary-abled women.

Internalising the notion that being disabled is a flaw, some women in the study reported that they dated people who were abusive or neglectful simply because they were the men who wanted to date them. A recent Public Health England (PHE) study found that some women in an abusive relationship were reluctant to report intimate partner violence and abuse because they had internalised the notion that their partner was a 'saint' for putting up with them and that they would not be able to get a better partner; that they should be grateful to have someone. Some women with sensory impairments might also miss signifiers of abuse and may face barriers to leaving abusive relationships where their abuser is also their carer (PHE, 2015: 13–14).

On the other hand, some women with disabilities said that they were very selective about dating; some refused to date another person with disabilities because they felt that it further marginalised them from the mainstream (Howland and Rintala, 2001: 54). Some women felt that they were unable to advocate for themselves in relationships and were not able to say what they need, what they could and could not do, or how they felt. Or, if they do express their needs, they are ignored or not taken seriously by their partners.

The barriers to dating are also exacerbated by a 'genital-centric' understanding of sex (Loeser et al., 2018: 265). As O'Brien (1990), Tom Shakespeare et al. (1996) and Shakespeare and Sarah Richardson (2018) demonstrate, preconceptions about what types of practices count as sex limit the spectrum of sexual practice that a disabled person might accommodate, and can silence or erase awareness of alternative practices that do not look like normative sexual practice, such as sex with prosthetics, erotic massage, or masturbation. This is where the queer inflection of crip theory might also help (see Chapter 2).

The complexity of this is something that is explored elsewhere (Davies, 2000a, b). Dominic Davies proposes a sexuality and relationship facilitation project to help build the capacity of people with disabilities to enter into and negotiate intimate relationships. Emerging at the intersection between queer sexual identity and disabled identity, this project seeks to understand the ways in which sexual practice can be diverse, but also how different identities may interact with mainstream ideas about sex in order to mobilise a critique to conventional understandings of sexual practice.

Through mobilising an 'ethics of care', Davies suggests that people with disabilities can be helped to develop their self-esteem and skills to ask for what they want when it comes to sex and intimacy. Adopting a **sex-positive** approach to facilitating sex for people with disabilities, as opposed to the squeamishness that we have already seen in this chapter, forms part of this framework. Davies' (2000b) project imagines that people with disabilities and their allies become trained facilitators in issues related to sexual practice, and that they learn, among other things, the practicalities of using barrier methods of contraception (such as condoms) if, for instance, they or their partner does not have good mobility in their hands. They might also learn about which sexual positions are best to accommodate people with different ranges of mobility, or how to use sex toys. With this knowledge, they might empower people with disabilities – and be empowered themselves – to have more rewarding sexual experiences and a fuller sense of sexual citizenship.

Dating and sexual consumption

This educational approach crosses over with the concept of sexual surrogacy. Sexual surrogacy is understood as a form of sex therapy where a therapist has sex with a client with disabilities in order to help the client better understand and express their sexuality or to deal with some past trauma or sexual difficulty. O'Brien's (1990) essay about his experience with a sexual surrogate is certainly worth reading for the touching clarity with which he explains how sexual surrogacy profoundly helped him. O'Brien (1990) contracted polio at the age of six and spent the rest of his life living in an iron lung, which is a pressurised tank that helps to regulate breathing. His account of his relationship with his sexual surrogate outlines how this practice helped him, in his words, to become 'a human being'.

Yet, the concept of sexual surrogacy is controversial. Even among people with disabilities, there is no consensus on whether or not sexual surrogacy is a good idea (O'Brien, 1990; Shakespeare and Richardson, 2018), with some voices advocating it as a 'radical and sufficient' way for people with disabilities to establish sexual citizenship (Davies, 2000a: 184), and others criticising it as a patronising 'poor substitute' for building interpersonal relationships (Shakespeare and Richardson, 2018: 86).

The notion of independent living is fundamental to the actualisation of sexual citizenship. Independent living is described by Shildrick (2007: 58) as a 'mode of existence that is structured by personal choice and the self-administration of welfare benefits'. Independent living allowances are offered to people with disabilities to help them manage their own lives, and can be spent on anything, which includes being used for sexual support services, whether this is therapy, sex work, pornography, or anything else. Do you think that this sort of sex work or sex therapy should be offered to people with disabilities? And, if it should be, who do you think should pay for it? Should it form part of the care package that local authorities provide to people with disabilities who are living in their care?

BOX 10.4

Consider the following scenarios that Shildrick (2007: 60) outlines and place them on a scale of what you think is acceptable and right, and where you draw the line, and why:

- Is it acceptable for a caregiver to be expected to help a person with a disability get ready for a sexual encounter, either by helping them to undress or to wash before sex? What about afterwards? Is it acceptable for a caregiver or personal assistant to help with masturbation if a person with a disability needed help with this?
- Would it be right to expect a caregiver to contact a sex worker on behalf of a person with a disability and to arrange a meeting for them, or to accompany them to a brothel?
- Should a caregiver be expected to procure pornography for a person with a disability?
- Should a caregiver be expected to help move a person into different sexual positions?
- What if the person's desire is for sexual practice that deviates from the mainstream? Should a caregiver be expected to accompany their client to a sex club, or a dominatrix, or a fetish club?

When thinking about sexual citizenship, and the rights that humans have to sexual citizenship, these questions, and our reactions to these questions, help us to see how rights might play out.

Shildrick highlights how, within a male homosexual context, sex which does not happen in private might fall foul of the law if a third-party facilitator is required to assist in the sexual encounter (2007: 61). Once more, as we saw in Abbott's (2013) account of homosexual men with ID, the heteronormativity of the criminal justice system – and of institutions in general – penalises people who do not conform to the heterosexual mainstream. And what about the rights of carers or personal assistants? What if their desires come into conflict with those of their clients, for religious, cultural or personal reasons? Once more, whether we adopt a rights-based approach, a queer perspective or the social model of disability to understand sexual expression, the answers and the ethics are not easy to untangle.

Desiring disabled bodies

Ethical conundrums arguably become more complex when we consider them in the context of what Richard Bruno (1997) refers to as 'devotees, pretenders, and wannabees'. Recently, there has been a rise in online dating services for people who have a disability, and for people who, disabled or not, want to date a person with a disability. In 2012, the British Channel 4 TV show *The Undateables* brought disabled dating to the mainstream. Despite the provocative title, shows like *The Undateables* are endorsed for the apparent sex-positivity by sites such as disabilitymatches.com. In spite of this, this increased visibility has not been met with enthusiasm by everyone. Some critics with disabilities have likened it to a 'freak show' or 'wildlife documentary' (Shakespeare and Richardson, 2018: 88).

In 1997, polio doctor and clinical psychologist, Bruno initiated an exploratory study of the phenomenon that he, building on the sexologist John Money's work on apotemnophilia (love of amputation), referred to as 'devoteeism'. Devotees are 'non-disabled [temporary-abled] people who are ... attracted to people with disabilities ... especially amputees' (Bruno, 1997: 243). Bruno considers the case of the wife of a polio patient at his clinic who confessed in therapy that not only was she very aroused by the fact of her husband's walking impairment and the braces that he used to help him to walk, but she also pretended to have a disability herself when she had the occasion to. She would, for example, hire a wheelchair when on trips out of town and, when she presented herself as a disabled person, she found this arousing (Bruno, 1997: 247). For Bruno, this woman was also what he termed a 'pretender'. Her paraphilia – non-normative sexual desire – as he called it, was attributed to the neglect she experienced by her parents as a child and the tenderness she saw her parents demonstrate towards another child with polio in her neighbourhood. For Bruno (1997: 258), such an attraction to people with disabilities is harmful because it cannot foster long-lasting and stable relationships. It is merely a sexual quick-fix for the fetishist (the devotee) and places an already seemingly vulnerable disabled person at even more risk.

Bruno's analysis has been critiqued and interrogated from a few perspectives (Aguilera, 2000; Sullivan, 2008). Bruno's analysis could be said to rest on the notion that any attraction to a disabled body is perverse and therefore inherently harmful. Its attribution to a story of childhood neglect further pathologises this as a form of desire (Sullivan, 2008: 185–6) and appears to erase autonomy on the part of people with disabilities, too.

Aguilera (2000) posits that devotee/disabled relationships might be empowering, as opposed to oppressive or manipulative. From a sex-positive perspective, he considers whether it might be possible to take at face-value the desire that devotees profess to have. This discussion echoes the approach adopted by Barbara F. W. Fiduccia (1999: 280), who asks why sex between a disabled person and a temporary-abled person is so taboo and suggests that it is because of the 'childlike' status that people with disabilities are imagined to occupy in the mainstream. Thus, a squeamishness about desiring disabled bodies might be an expression of paternalism. Per Solvang (2007: 52) suggests that devoteeism could be reconceptualised as a form of valorising disabled bodies in the same way that neurological conditions such as Tourette's syndrome have become associated with creativity and spatial thinking. Being desired by a devotee might be empowering. It might develop 'self-pride' and a 'positive attitude' in a disabled person (Solvang, 2007: 61). Certainly, Solvang's (2007), Aguilera's (2000) and Fiduccia's (1999) analyses of this sort of desire allow for this possibility. However, it is hard to move out of the spectre of normativity.

As Solvang (2007: 62) highlights, it is often normatively beautiful women who have a disability who are thusly desired. Such a narrative plays out in Joseph Brennan's (2017) analysis of discourses about the athlete Oscar Pistorius's body on gay men's online forums, who comment on his muscular physique and who speculate on how easy it would be to rape him in prison because of his disability. Aguilera (2000: 260) notes that, even though disabled bodies are now more visible as objects of desire, they are also often presented in specialist devotee publications and products (where a heterosexual male consumer is assumed), in positions of vulnerability, which entrench gender inequalities. Films or photographs of amputees, or wheelchair-using women, boast that they show women 'transferring' into and out of their beds or wheelchairs, or putting on or taking off prosthetic limbs. The 2016 BBC 3 documentary *Meet the Devotees* told a similar story: there are people – devotees – who are drawn to disabled women, but it is the sight of them in positions of vulnerability, or struggling to do things that people who are temporary-abled do not have trouble with (such as getting dressed or using the stairs), that is what they say they find most erotic.

The dominance of hegemonic ideas of beauty within these discourses means that, even if devoteeism seems to subvert normative ideas about desire, there remains a risk that in some contexts it consolidates, rather than transgresses, normative sexual expression. R. Amy Elman's (1997) discussion of disabled pornography also illustrates this difficulty. Drawing on some of the same case studies from *Playboy* magazine that Nikki Sullivan (2008) and Fiduccia (1999) also analyse, Elman criticises what she sees as the fetishisation of female immobility and the eroticisation of vulnerability (1997: 258), which entrenches **patriarchal,** heteronormative views of women. This, she argues, has implications for all women, not just those represented in pornography, or in films like *Boxing Helena* (Mainline, 1993) in which the protagonist, Helena, eventually has all her limbs amputated by a surgeon who is in love with her. These representations echo and resonate with women's experiences of sexualised violence in many, much more mundane contexts. Do you agree? Or do you think there might be something empowering that could be recuperated from these accounts of desire for a disabled body?

The ethical tensions that Bruno (1997: 244) outlines in his early paper become particularly thorny in the context of Bruno's third category of disability desirers: those who want to become disabled themselves. Unlike pretenders who want simply to appear disabled from time to time, a 'wannabe' wants to, for instance, have their leg amputated, or, as correspondence analysed by Elman (1997: 262) suggests, 'become completely blind'. What is to be done about people who want to acquire a disability? Who feel that they are a disabled person in a non-disabled person's body? Who have such a negative relationship with a part of their body, that they would rather remove it than live with it?

In order to address this question, we need to return to the concepts of consent and capacity. We also need to think, from an ethical perspective, about the body. To whom does a body belong? And can we do whatever we like with our own body? What is the obligation of a medical professional to do what is perceived as permanent and irreversible damage to our body at our behest? Should the criminal law intervene in these matters?

BOX 10.5

'By taking my leg away, that surgeon has made me complete.'

Read and reflect on the following case study taken from Scotland in the UK.

In 1997, a surgeon named Robert Smith amputated the lower left leg of Kevin Wright. In 1999 he repeated the same operation on a German national named Hans Shraub. The men had separately consulted with him about their strong desire to remove this part of their body and about the misery that their lives had become because they had to live with their legs. The legs were entirely healthy and did not cause the men physical pain. In an interview with *The Guardian* newspaper, Kevin Wright explained that he was in such despair about his leg that he had contemplated suicide. He continued: 'I just didn't want it. It didn't feel a part of me, I didn't understand why, but I knew I didn't want my leg. I have happiness and contentment and life is so much more settled, so much easier.'

This form of surgery on a healthy leg – and the transforming of a person from temporary-abled to disabled – raises a number of ethical questions. The Falkirk hospital in question was subject to intense scrutiny and criticism for allowing this surgery to take place. Travis (2014) explains how a French national named Lily added to the story. Attempting to also have her healthy legs amputated, Lily travelled to Scotland in 2005 to seek the same surgery. After being involved in a car crash that she had caused on purpose to damage both her legs, she was unable to persuade the hospital that her injury was serious enough to merit above the knee amputation on both legs. Instead, she set about destroying them using dry ice. She managed to damage both legs so much that an amputation was on the cards (Travis, 2014), only to be cancelled at the last minute and have Lily flown back to France un-amputated. She later managed, after a further attempt with dry ice, and focussing on just one leg, and after a number of operations and infections, to have a leg amputated in France; not electively, but as a result of there being nothing else to be done. After her leg was removed, she reportedly said that she was finally at peace.

The furore that the Falkirk case provoked did not lead to any criminal implications for surgeon Robert Smith, but the case was roundly condemned as being 'unacceptable' by the chairman of the health trust in the area (*The Herald*, 7 February 2000) and the local Member of Parliament stated that he found it incredible that a surgeon would amputate a healthy limb (BBC News, 31 January 2000). And, as we see in Lily's case, the hospital would rather pay for a private medical plane to repatriate Lily than amputate her damaged leg.

- Why is there this backlash?
- If men and women are not incapacitated, and they are asking for this surgery, does preventing this become a 'suspension of their legal personhood' (Travis, 2014: 527)? And of their rights as people to make choices about their lives (Erin and Ost, 2007: 256)?
- The anguish, certainly, that Lily felt about her legs is palpable in Travis's (2014) account. Is her disorder something that should be cured with medical treatment (amputation)?
- Is there another solution that we should seek?

Wright, Shraub and Lily had body integrity identity disorder (BIID) which is understood as a sort of reverse 'phantom limb' (Blanke et al., 2009; Travis, 2014). It has been suggested that BIID is not unlike gender identity disorder (a mismatch between gender identity and the sex assigned at birth). It has also been suggested that BIID is the reason why some people choose to have rhinoplasty surgery, breast reduction or elective labiaplasty.

- Might this be the case? Is amputating a leg the same thing as having a nose job?
- If not, why not?
- Is it like being trans?
- Is it the rightful place of the criminal law to intervene to prevent people from undergoing these surgeries?
- How does our answer change depending on the model of disability we apply to the problem?

Dementia, sex and navigating the institutional life

The final issue that we will think about here is the issue of intimacy and dementia in an institutional setting. Dementia is a degenerative brain condition that can impair memory, moods, personality and other elements of cognitive functioning. People with dementia may live in institutional settings. Even up until the late stages of the disease, people with dementia still have complex desires and needs, including the need or desire for intimacy or the building of intimate relationships.

Questions of capacity and consent that we have seen elsewhere in this chapter, alongside issues of autonomy and freedom that we have also discussed, are salient here. The question is when, or whether, people working in a care home, or family members, should intervene in the sex lives of people with dementia.

Though there is more and more research emerging on sex in later life, there is still little guidance on how care workers and family members should approach the development of intimate relationships among people with dementia, where they occur (Di Napoli et al., 2013; Rheaume and Mitty, 2008; Villar et al., 2014). Intimacy takes many forms, of course, and as Chris Rheaume and Ethel Mitty (2008: 344) recognise, it is an ultimate expression of **agency**. Intimate feelings cannot be elicited from someone or received as intimacy if a person does not want them. This is why people's right to intimacy – the exercise of their sexual citizenship – is so important. In the context of people living with dementia, this is thought to have a positive effect on their wellbeing (Wiskerke and Manthorpe, 2019: 96). At the same time, people with dementia living in care homes do encounter barriers to their intimate relationships. In part, these barriers are socially constructed, inflected by norms of appropriate performances of masculinity and femininity, and by the dominance of heteronormativity that colours the world view of the patients and carers of those living in care homes (Di Napoli et al., 2013; Rheaume and Mitty, 2008). Heteronormativity emphasises heterosexual relationships and also stigmatises non-normative relationships. Sex between older people, sex with people with dementia, and sex with people who may be married to someone else might fall into this non-normative category. Barriers are also imposed by the institu-tion. The lack of privacy in a care home and the authoritative presence of the care workers can discourage intimate acts from taking place (Rheaume and Mitty, 2008).

A second issue that arises in the context of sexual relationships and demen-tia is the issue of consent and the capacity to consent to sexual practice. We have seen some of these debates play out in the context of people with ID. What about issues of consent relating to people whose capacities may fluctuate and degenerate as time passes? What is the role of the law in these instances? How to assess the capacity to consent in circumstances where the impairment might be in flux?

We have already seen that, in England and Wales, the court adopts a low bar in the test to ascertain whether or not someone has the capacity to con-sent, and is reluctant to intervene in this area of private life. Indeed, the MCA 2005 stipulates that the law cannot consent on behalf of someone else or inter-vene, even if the person in question has consented to something that might be unwise or bad for them.

In a care home setting, the issue of adult safeguarding also comes to the fore in order to prevent abuse. As with other areas of disability work, there appears to be a reticence among care home workers to give the space to dementia patients to explore sexual intimacy because of the tendency to consider the 'recipient' of sexual attention or a sexual act as the 'victim', and the 'initiator' as the 'perpetrator', which leads care workers to adopt a risk-averse attitude to managing sexual behaviour in a care home (Wiskerke and Manthorpe, 2019: 99).

An additional concern is an effect of the dementia itself. People with dementia may forget that they have had sex once it is finished. They may mis-take other people for their partner. They may become sexually demanding in ways that are embarrassing/distressing for other people. They may exhibit sexual disinhibition and behave in sexually inappropriate ways towards other people, by undressing themselves in public, touching others without consent, or making suggestive comments to other people (Rheaume and Mitty, 2008: 347–8). In these instances, issues of consent are obvious concerns. There is also the risk of criminal justice involvement in cases where the disease has impaired their decision-making ability. We must ask, is it in the best interests of a particular resident with dementia to intervene here? Alongside this, how else might we safeguard other residents living in a care home who may be on the receiving end of these advances? And what about those people who work in the care home: they are in charge of safeguarding, but what if they are also subject to this sexualised behaviour?

For Soren Holm (2001: 156), the capacity to consent should depend on the act in question, and not the type of person. So, a person may not have the capacity to consent to certain acts, but may be able to consent to more minor or more trivial ones. For instance, a person with dementia may lack the capacity to decide to follow a specific medical treatment, but they may still have the capacity to decide whether or not to get their hair cut, to have a bath, or to drink a whole bottle of wine. The imperative to act in the 'best interest' of people with dementia when it comes to making decisions on their behalf – proxy decision-making – rests on normative ethical values which may not be able to adequately take into consideration the authenticity of their desires. As with other areas which have a bearing on disability rights, education, training and capacity-building are recommended for care workers and family members to better support the sexual practices of people with dementia. Yet, the line between preventing abusive behaviour, the exercise of autonomy and the capacity to consent, is difficult to draw.

Summary

In this chapter, we have looked at different areas of concern when thinking about the relationship between sex, disability and crime. We have seen that there are several different theoretical models that can be applied to better understand disability. None of them alone is sufficient to capture the full complexity of disability. Alongside this, queer theory and sexual citizenship discourses help to outline the nature of the problem that criminologists must encounter when considering these issues.

We have seen that, though consent, capacity, ethics, desire and sexual practice are hugely complex, the law takes a light-touch approach, adopting a capacity test that is set low. They do this so as to respect the agency of people with disabilities.

The more fundamental ethical problems posed to us by devotees and wannabes highlight the philosophical questions about the body that we have to take into account. They also highlight how the criminal justice system has, as yet, little to say about these issues, despite their obvious relevance to criminology and questions of justice.

Finally, time and time again we have seen how it is education and awareness-raising that is offered as the solution to many of these complexities; education for people with ID about sex, consent, desire and contraception, coupled with enabling communication across all parties that is not plagued by shame and embarrassment; education for care workers to help them approach sexual questions with people with dementia; education for family members of people with disabilities to help them understand how to approach this topic; and education for people with disabilities about dating, sexual surrogacy and advocating for their desires. As criminologists, we have a part to play in this education, because

we can bring our understanding of sexual citizenship, **social justice** and policing deviance to bear on these questions. What do you think that might look
like?

Review questions

- Is education the only way to improve sexual rights for people with disabilities? Are
  there any dangers in adopting this approach?
- Consider the different models of disability. Which one do you think is the most
  convincing? Which one are people most familiar with? Which is the most
  problematic?
- Think of words that you associate with sexual citizenship. Why do disability activists think that sexual citizenship is important? Do you agree?
- Is the emphasis on sexuality in disability studies misplaced? Should disability
  scholars be prioritising different things?

Other chapters that this links to

Chapter 2 (Theory)
Chapter 3 (Sex and crime in time and space)
Chapter 4 (Consent and its discontents)
Chapter 9 (Pleasurable risk)
Chapter 12 (Children, sexualisation and law)
Chapter 15 (How to change your life)

11

Digital sex

The digital realm is vast. In this chapter, we are going to focus on the specific implications of the relationship between sex and digital culture to further our understanding of **deviance** and crime. In order to do this, we need to unpack some of what we think we know about digital cultures and pay attention to the distinctly political ways in which the digital realm operates when it comes to **sexuality**. In this chapter, we will first examine how the Internet and online domain have affected dating and relationship behaviours, including sexting, cybersex and 'revenge porn'. The discussion will lead us into our second case study – the phenomenon of romance fraud and fraud in online romances. We will finish by examining how sexualised violence and harassment are exacted in online domains by focusing on trolls and what is called the 'manosphere'.

By the end of this chapter, you will understand more about:

- how we define technology and digital culture in criminology
- the ways in which the digital realm fosters specific **sexual practices** and ways of interacting sexually
- how, and why, sex crime which happens online is difficult to deal with through existing laws and political mechanisms
- what the criminal justice system has tried to do in the face of 'revenge porn', fraud and online sexual violence.

How digital sex poses criminological problems

Crime and deviance in the digital realm pose specific problems for the administration of justice. Not only do criminal acts potentially exceed national borders and jurisdictions (we see some of this in the realm of online child sexual exploitation, discussed in Chapter 7, and pornography, discussed in Chapter 13), but, at the same time, even within a given jurisdiction, the fluidity of the online realm, and the anonymity that it affords, makes it easier for people to hide. We will see some of this in the context of trolling and online harassment (Jane, 2014). More than this, the online realm can give rise to the creation of so-called 'echo chambers' in which extremes of opinion and behaviour are affirmed and validated by other Internet-users in the echo chamber (Colleoni et al., 2014). Groups such as so-called anti-vaxxers, 'pro-life' groups, 'incel' groups, nationalist and anti-fascist groups can use the online realm to establish subcultures (Cohen, 2003[1955]). Often, these might look like benign special-interest groups, with people holding values in common sharing information and support. At the most extreme end, the insularity of the echo chamber can lead to acts of terrorism, such as those we saw in London Bridge in the UK in 2017, at the Al Noor Mosque in Auckland, New Zealand, in 2019, and at the Isla Vista in California, USA, shootings in 2014. We will come back to this discussion of the echo chamber later in the chapter. Terrorism and harassment happened before the rise of the Internet, of course, and not every niche special interest online group is criminogenic, but the digital realm both influences and is influenced by the proliferation of these crimes and acts of deviance. We will see some of this at play in this chapter in the context of sexual practice.

Theorising tech

We often talk about the online world, the Internet, the digital world and technology as if these were interchangeable terms. One of the important things to realise when we talk about digital cultures in the context of sex and crime, is that what we might refer to as 'technology' or 'technological advances' have become subsumed into what we might think of as an undifferentiated 'black box' (Latour, 2012[1991]). By this we mean that we do not recognise the inherently sociotechnical quality of objects of technology and instead imagine that we live in a purified world in which technology and society are distinct things. We also end up thinking that technological advances are the neutral, taken-for-granted backdrop to our online activities. Technology is a complex category that needs unpacking (Coupaye, forthcoming). Thinking about digital culture in this undifferentiated way means that the very important ways in which technology and the digital realm are political are obscured. This has implications for our study of crime, justice, **gender** and sexuality in the context of the digital realm. Because these ideas are taken for granted, we take a moment to specify how we understand taken-for-granted terms in this chapter in Table 11.1.

Table 11.1   Taken-for-granted tech terms

Term	Defined as
Cyber-	Often used as a prefix for activities that take place online, originally it is short for 'cybernetics', meaning the science of communications and automatic control systems in both machines and living things; cyber comes from the Greek kubernētēs ('steersman') and from kubernan, meaning 'to steer'
Devices	A tool, a machine, an implement, an object adapted for a particular purpose, e.g. iPhones, tablets, cameras, GPS trackers, kettles and swimming goggles are all devices
Digital	Information which is coded using 1 and 0 as binaries is digital; digital is opposed to analogue (where signals are coded by a variable physical quantity such as spatial position or voltage)

Term	Defined as
Digital culture	The study of the digital world and contemporary communication technologies (personal computers, connected computers, digital images, apps) and how they affect, and are affected by, contemporary life
ICT	Information and communication technologies (ICT) refers to technologies that provide access to information through telecommunications: email, robots, tablets and digital TVs are all examples of ICT
Internet	A global computer network providing a variety of information and communication facilities, consisting of interconnected networks in which any computer can, with permission, communicate with any other computer
Technical objects	Objects which are put to use for technical purposes (for example, if I take a walk in a forest and admire a branch on the ground, the branch is, among other things, an object; if I then use that branch to clean out the mud from under my shoe, it becomes a technical object)
Technology	Often taken to be synonymous with 'devices', this word is from the Greek tehkno logia, meaning 'knowledge about a system of making'. Technology is the application of scientific knowledge for something practical; technology is composed of objects (e.g. digital objects, tools, machines), practices (e.g. skills, techniques) and organisations (e.g. institutions, infrastructure) – there is always more to technology than meets the eye
World Wide Web	An information system on the Internet which allows documents to be connected to other documents by hypertext links, enabling the user to search for information by moving from one document to another

Privacy

One of the more political elements of the digital world surrounds the notion of privacy. Visit any website or download any app to your smartphone and before you get too far, you are invited to agree to a series of terms of use and privacy settings that you will most likely never read. 'We respect your privacy', cookie and Internet protocol (IP) policies might say, as they explicitly ask your permission to invade your privacy by recording browsing habits on your machine and sending you tailored adverts as you move around the web.

The Latin etymological origins of 'private' emphasise that something 'private' means something that is 'set apart, belonging to oneself, personal'. The notion of privacy as something that is free from the intrusion of **the State** is borne out of a classical liberal imaginary of citizenship which underpins the concept of the liberal democracy in most **post-industrial economies** and certainly much of the **Global North**. Recall our discussions about liberalism in Chapter 2. The idea here is that a citizen agrees to surrender some of their rights to the State in exchange for protection and certain levels of sustenance (maintaining the peace, for instance, or building infrastructure); this is called the social contract (Locke, 1980[1690]). Beyond this, citizens have the right to do and say what they like, even unwise or objectionable things, and unless what they are doing actively **harms** someone else, the State has no right to intervene; this is called the harm principle (Mill, 1998[1859]). These notions of privacy have informed much of modern government and contemporary jurisprudence ever since. How they help us to understand the digital realm is another matter.

The private may be opposed to the public, but the development of contemporary digital cultures means that the boundary between the two is in fact more porous than first meets the eye. There is a level of anonymity online which means that, to a certain extent, individuals can keep their online activities private. At the same time, as many warnings about Internet safety remind us, once something is online, it is there forever, and might be found by anyone. Obviously, when it comes to sexual practice or expressions of sexuality, this private/public interplay can pose considerable issues; we will see this in the context of sexting, image-based sexual violence (also known as 'revenge porn') and online hate speech.

What comes first ...?

Sarah M. Grimes and Andrew Feenberg (2013) suggest that there are two dominant ways in which technology has been theorised. On the one hand, substantivist theorists posit that technology is autonomous and preoccupied with domination. For substantivists, technology is not the emancipatory tool that we are invited to imagine it is. Substantivists are critical – pessimistic – about where technological development might take us. Constructivists, on the other hand, analyse the social impact of actors on technological design and development.

Let us think this through via the phenomenon of sexting, which is the practice of sending sexually explicit photographs or messages for the purpose of sexually exciting, or flirting with, a partner or prospective partner. From a technologically substantivist perspective, technological advancement can be thought to bring about social change (for example, sexting is only the phenomenon that it is because so many people have a smartphone now). This perspective considers that technological advancement has its own **agency**, that society and culture are passive in the face of technological advancement, and that technology necessarily drives forward social change.

On the other hand, a constructivist understanding of technology considers that technology is socially constructed. This vision gives very little agency to inventions or technological progress itself. We should remember that people have been sharing sexually erotic images of themselves for centuries. Technological progress has created an industry, infrastructure and economy around the circulation of images. The easy, almost mundane way that erotic images can be created and shared had the effect of dulling morally restrictive attitudes to sexually explicit imagery everywhere, especially in the privileged counties of the Global North. Porn and erotic images are banned in some countries (for instance, Papua New Guinea), but even here, the erotic exchange of images still goes on, albeit on the quiet.

Beyond this dichotomy, Bruno Latour's (2012[1991]) work on Actor Network Theory (ANT) has been especially helpful for thinking about this. ANT makes no distinction between the social and the technical: it recognises that one cannot exist without the other. Meaning is made – the world is understood – by actors in a bio-socio-cultural-economic network. Actors can be both human and non-human bodies. A network can be understood as a web of relations that binds humans and non-humans together. For our purposes, in the context of sexting, the smartphone network, the handsets of the photographer, and of the recipient, the camera, the screen, the body that is in the photograph, the digital photograph itself, the person who receives the photograph are all actors in a sexting network. All actors in the network have their own agency, by which we mean all actors *do something*. The camera does not need to intend to take the photograph and the network does not need to 'know' that the digital imprint conveyed along it is a sexy photograph, but, without these parts of the network, the sext cannot take place. Indeed, the only expendable element in a sexting network seems to be the human recipient; if I send a sexy photograph using my smartphone to the phone of one of my friends but their phone breaks, or falls down the toilet before they see it, or in a fit of regret I sneak onto their phone to delete the message before they open it, they may not see it, but the sext still exists.

Technological unevenesses

We may think that technological advances in devices such as the smartphone or the tablet, or in the effectiveness of telecommunication networks, mean that digital sexual cultures progress everywhere – and yes this is true – but how this progress manifests itself, and the forms it takes, varies from place to place (Livingstone and Bulger, 2014).

The first mobile phone was created in the 1970s, but it was at the turn of the millennium that mobile phones became cheap enough and small enough to gain a mainstream appeal. Up until that point, people in post-industrialised countries relied on landlines, public phone booths and shared home phones. Meanwhile, in what we call the Global South, landline infrastructure was (and remains) very poor in places, with many different households sharing a landline telephone. Once again, as mobile phones got cheaper and more accessible at the end of the 1990s, mobile phone ownership in these poorer countries exploded. Nigeria and Bangladesh, for instance, rank eighth and ninth in the world for mobile phone use, whereas, when it comes to land-lines, they rank at 69th and 67th in the world, respectively. In 2010, Germany was ranked third in the world for landline use but comes behind Nigeria and Pakistan for mobile phone use. In Panama, mobile phone own-ership is at 202 per cent, whereas Panama ranks 95th on the rankings of landline use around the world. In Papua New Guinea, 90 per cent of Internet activity happens on a mobile phone. All this is to show that the development of mobile phone use is uneven and depends on the ways in which infrastructure for fixed landlines has or has not been established. Mobile phone use has all but replaced landline phone use in poorer coun-tries, especially those without telephone infrastructure. This has been accompanied by a transformation in the way that personal relationships are managed. We see this in the debates around sexting in South Africa in Chapter 12. In Papua New Guinea, sexting has formed part of a courtship practice through which people 'find' each other by composing random phone numbers and then trying to engage in an erotically charged text-based exchange with the person on the other end of the line, that will never make its way to meeting in person and is not intended to (see Livingstone and Bulger, 2014: 322).

   T.T. Sreekumar (2013) demonstrates how communicative devices and technologies are put to use in Singapore, for instance, or the Middle East, to create civic cyber spaces for political action. Young people use digital devices in political contexts to mobilise resistance to authoritarian actions of the state (in the context of the Arab Spring, for instance), and also to forge their own **subjectivities** as they transition into adulthood. In the South African context, as Sreekumar (2013: 83) reports, the digital realm creates private spaces of safety in public spaces, facilitates connections and disconnections, and sources of conflict and constraint, but also of freedom. Ultimately, social, sexual relations cannot exist without technical relations. We interact with technical objects in ways that test them out, that push their limits, which find new ways to put them to use. Thus, technical objects are always technico-social objects. In short, the digital, physical, political and imaginative realm are intertwined the world over, but the form they take, and what they do, will depend entirely on the context in which they exist.

Digital intimacy

There is absolutely no doubt that advances in, for instance, online dating sites have transformed contemporary dating practices, particularly in the USA and the UK. According to Forbes, there are 8,000 online dating sites in the world and 50 million people in the USA alone have tried online dating (Matthews, 15 June 2018). The online dating market was, in 2012, worth $1.9 billion (Kopp et al., 2015: 205).

Certainly, the near-ubiquity of the mobile phone or smartphone, the Internet and WiFi in public spaces, has changed how sexual relationships are facilitated. But it would be a mistake to think that before the advent of Kik or Snapchat, people did not send nude photos to each other, or that before Tinder or Grindr, people did not use media for casual hook-ups. Yes, the pace and scale may be different – a lot more may be contingent on people's close proximity to each other in the case of hook-ups (or not, in the case of cybersex or long-distance relationships) – but people have always used technology for sex (Hearn, 1996). Whether it is through phone sex on chat lines, personal adverts in specialist pornographic magazines, or so-called lonely-hearts adverts in the local paper, different media have been used in different ways as technologies to promote sexual practice. Some of it might be deviant, some of it not, but, in general, sex and communication technology have long gone hand in hand.

The way the online world has altered dating dynamics illustrates how dating and the online realm interact with each other to forge a form of intimacy that is distinct from relationships forged offline. In part, this is due to what Al Cooper (1998) refers to as the 'triple-A engine': the combination of (1) the accessibility of the Internet – that there are a huge number of sites that can be visited; (2) the affordability of it – that a great many of them are free to visit; and (3) the anonymity that it appears to afford, transforms sexual practice on the Internet. Indeed, though 20 years old, Erich A. Merkle and Rhonda A. Richardson's (2000: 189–90) examination of how face-to-face and online relationships are distinct, remains pertinent. In their analysis of the dynamics of relationships forged online, they note that online relationships are marked by increased self-disclosure as a means of forging intimacy. Unlike face-to-face relationships in which people might be warier of revealing information about themselves until greater trust is established between the parties, in the online realm the relative comfort of anonymity can cause people to reveal more about themselves.

Aaron Ben Ze'ev (2004) makes a similar observation: the online world fosters a form of 'detached attachment' in which intimacies are forged (and broken) according to a set of seemingly contradictory qualities. One of these is the tension between anonymity and self-disclosure. Thanks to the anonymity of the Internet, people can take the risk of revealing intimacies about themselves that they would not disclose elsewhere. Relationships can be forged over distances – even across the globe – but can also take place in real time. Unlike sending a letter or waiting for a phone call, a text, WhatsApp or email message can forge an immediate sense of closeness which belies the geographic distance that a couple may be materially subject to (Miller, 2011: 179). Indeed, this sort of distance can form part of what makes a relationship that takes place online even more compelling. Vincent Miller (2011: 179–80) suggests that because they operate outside of the mundanity of real life, online relationships take place in an almost fantasy realm – perhaps thanks also to the anonymity – and are characterised by intense longing for 'circum-stances that cannot be brought to bear or exist': the distance becomes part of this form of online encounter.

We also see this play out in the context of cybersex which, as Miller (2011) demonstrates, emerges as a specific form of sexual practice because of the way in which it can *only exist mediated via the digital realm*. Cybersex as a form of intimacy is neither socially determined nor technologically driven but emerges through the interplay of a desire for intimacy, the freedom of anonymity, the facility of using smartphones, apps or dating websites, to find people to flirt with, and the ubiquity of Internet access (at least in the post-industrialist contexts in which much of this research has taken place). Cybersex recruits a lot of imaginative work. Even if participants 'meet' online to exchange fantasies, the sexual practices that they might fantasise about, or desire, do not have to actually take place in the real world. They are not limited by the material realities of meeting in real life. Participants can experiment with different personas and profiles. They might, shrouded by the anonymity the online realm affords them, express sexual desires that they might not be able to express in the offline realm. And this connectivity makes cybersex a particular, distinct sexualised practice (Ben Ze'ev, 2004).

Cybersex is defined as using the Internet for 'sexually gratifying activities' (Cooper and Griffin-Shelley, 2002). We might add that rather than simply searching for sexually gratifying materials – erotic stories, for instance, or pornography – cybersex is interactive; involving two or more people in erotic discussion or visual exchange for their mutual sexual satisfaction (Daneback et al., 2005: 325).

Cooper et al. (2000), Jennifer P. Schneider (2000 a, b), and Mark F. Schwartz and Stephen Southern (2000) have all analysed cybersex as a potential source of concern around the risk of sex addiction. For these authors, cybersex is a **public health** and therapeutic concern. Schwartz and Southern (2000: 128) suggest that cybersex is akin to Laud Humphreys' (1975) 'tearoom trade' (where men would have anonymous sex with other men in public toilets) because it is where 'anonymous persons engage in easily accessible ritualised behaviour that leads to impersonal, detached sexual outlets'. Compulsive cybersex, Schwartz and Southern (2000) argue, is undertaken by people seek-ing to hide negative feelings about themselves, or about their past, in order to seek intimacy and comfort from behind the secure veil of anonymity.

Women who cybersex, they say, are more likely to suffer from other compulsive behaviours, such as bulimia, or over-eating, or 'even swinging or sadomasochism', which they claim will be 'initiated by their partners' (Schwartz and Southern, 2000: 137). Men who cybersex in an obsessive fashion are also likely to be addicts of alcohol or drugs, and to be depressed.

According to Cooper et al. (2000: 21), cybersex compulsives can take their risky behaviours offline and participate in sex which spreads sexually transmitted diseases (see Chapter 9 for our discussion of sex and risk). Groups which have traditionally been sexually disenfranchised, such as women or LGBT+ people, are even more likely to take sexual risks as a result of their online sexual activities, the authors argue.

At the same time, Kristian Daneback et al. (2005: 326) note that these sexually minoritised groups actually find that cybersex affords them the safe spaces in which to express sexual desires that are non-normative: women can engage in cybersex 'without fear of violence, STI, pregnancy … or social stigmatisation', while cybersexual spaces might offer LGBT+ people or young people the opportunity to 'try out' sexual expression without the risk of violence or other dangers.

BOX 11.1

Consider the following questions:

- What are the implications of these concerns about cybersex encounters?
- How might they be a source of public health concern?
- What if some of these online encounters involve participants who are in relationships with people in the offline world, or 'in real life'? Does that change the ethics of the cybersex?
- If a married person meets someone else online and engages in an online flirtation with them, or explores sexual fantasies with them, is this adultery?
- Does the level of anonymity that participants might enjoy exonerate them from accusations of cheating?
- Or is it in fact worse, because the intimacy that they might be sharing is more profound, thanks to it taking place online? (See Miller, 2011: 180–1.)

Merkle and Richardson (2000: 190) wonder whether an online relationship *can be cheated on*, in the offline world? So, if you develop an online romantic relationship with someone on the other side of the world, and you have developed intense emotional bonds with each other, speaking online and

(Continued)

exchanging messages every day, and then that person hooks up with their friend from work at the weekend, have they cheated on you? What is the difference between online and offline relationships, in terms of what we might expect for, or from, them? Perhaps these questions demonstrate the very specific way that the digital realm mediates and forms intimacy and betrayal.

Commercial cybering

Commercial cybersex is cybersex that usually takes place using webcams. Patrons pay online for sexualised online encounters with performers. What is it like to be on the receiving end of a commercial cybersex encounter? Interviewing men and women working in different professional cybersex set-ups in the Philippines, Elinor M. Cruz and Trina J.Sajo (2015) outline the different working conditions and practices of cybersex models, including the different ways in which they encounter and transcend abuses by the managers of the cybersex rooms or the clients themselves. These models work in managed online rooms and provide sexual performances and cybersex for clients from all over the world, for a fee. Cybersexers working in a 'cybersex den' or online brothel also have their time and their bodies tightly controlled; certain levels of grooming are required; and eating, washing and sleeping times are also strictly prescribed. Yet, Cruz and Sajo (2015) also outline how cybersexers provide support for each other if they find themselves in personal financial trouble, or are made homeless, or are arrested by the police for their online sexual activities. Moreover, cybersexers find ways to resist the more stringent abuses they might suffer from their online clients. Some visitors to these cybersex 'dens' ask cybersex models to engage in profane practices such as eating faeces or drinking urine in exchange for money. Using soft drinks or chocolate brownies as props to resemble urine and faeces, they manage to manipulate their online performance for their client without submitting to these requests. Similarly, by controlling camera angles or by creating false ejaculation with body lotion, actors are also able to take control of their performances and to 'fake' certain sexual acts which are requested by the clients.

This manipulation is only possible because this form of sex takes place online. The manipulation of the visual effect and the distance between client and performer which is mediated by a camera affords performers agency, even as they are also able to use the medium as a way to enter into a romantic relationship with a client in order to receive gifts and money or to eventually leave the webcam performers' world. These accounts demonstrate the ways in which cybersex moulds and influences interactions, but also can be manipulated by participants.

To summarise, cybersex is neither inherently good nor bad, but rather is put to work in different ways: to enable people to explore hidden sexualities, to enable clandestine relationships to flourish, to enable people to get sexual gratification in otherwise sexless relationships, to enable people to make money, and also to encourage compulsive behaviours to fester.

Image-based sexual violence

Something that is less equivocal is the complex case of image-based sexual violence, or what can colloquially be known as 'revenge porn'. Consider the incident in Box 11.2.

BOX 11.2

In 2014, along with a handful of other A-list celebrities, the actress Jennifer Lawrence had her iCloud account infiltrated by a group of hackers who leaked intimate naked photographs of her onto the site 4chan. These photos had been private images that she had taken and sent to her boyfriend. The images were later posted to other sites, including Reddit, and were re-posted by celebrity blogger Perez Hilton (Selby, 1 September 2014). All in all, over 500 images of various actresses were released over the course of several hours. Jennifer Lawrence decried the leak as a form of sexual violence and noted how, on top of this, she and others in her position were met with a lack of empathy and victim-blaming comments by some members of the public. In Lawrence's own words, 'I feel like I got gangbanged by the fucking planet – like, there's not one person in the world that is not capable of seeing these intimate photos of me' (cited in Mallon, 21 November 2017). The case was investigated by the Federal Bureau of Investigation (FBI) and five men were convicted of 'unauthorized access to a protected computer' between March 2016 and October 2018. They received sentences ranging from eight to 34 months in prison.

'Revenge porn' has been defined by different jurisdictions, including Canada, England and Wales, and certain states of the USA, as the non-consensual distribution of sexually intimate images:

- Think of what you know about 'revenge porn': is what happened to Lawrence and other celebrities an act of 'revenge pornography'?
- Do you agree with commentators that the celebrities 'deserved it' for taking the photos in the first place?
- What do you think of the sentences that each of the perpetrators received?
- Does anything surprise you about the sentences?

Donna M. Hughes (2002) demonstrates how the proliferation of Internet use has created a field of potential abuse towards women and children that did not exist in the same way before the development of digital technologies. Thanks to peer-sharing platforms and the ease of uploading and sharing visual material, **gendered** digital violence such as sexual grooming, sex trafficking and stalking has become easier to commit than ever before. One of the first websites to host 'revenge porn' was 'Is Anyone Up?' and, before it closed down in 2012, the site boasted 30,000 visitors a day. It is estimated that there are around 3,000 websites dedicated to the proliferation of 'revenge porn' (McGlynn et al., 2017). In this section, we are going to consider how the criminal justice system deals with 'revenge porn' and we are going to assess the extent to which it does this successfully.

'Revenge porn' and the law

Until recently, few jurisdictions had specific laws against image-based sexual violence. Note that the hackers who attacked Lawrence's iCloud account and leaked her photos were convicted of 'unauthorized access to a protected computer' and not of creating and sharing 'revenge porn'. Indeed, one of the factors to consider when it comes to understanding why this criminal offence was used to convict, is that of definitions. What do the words 'revenge porn' conjure up for you? What sort of image do you think would 'count' as 'revenge porn'? What sort of person would create 'revenge porn'? And why?

The phrase 'revenge porn' can suggest the image of an angry ex-boyfriend or girlfriend posting a sexualised image of their ex-partner online, without their permission, in order to shame and humiliate them (McGlynn et al., 2017). The notion of 'revenge' suggests that the parties must have known each other. Did the hacker who leaked her pictures 'know' Jennifer Lawrence? Or have any specific reason to get 'revenge' against her? Should we be focusing so much on the intentions of the perpetrator anyway? Moreover, the word 'porn' suggests that some sexualised activity must be happening. Is a picture of someone getting out of the shower, or trying on clothes in a store changing room, porn? In England and Wales, the image must be one that is 'something not ordinarily seen in public', according to the Revenge Porn Helpline, so a photograph of someone sunbathing topless in a way which exposes the breasts would not count as 'revenge porn' if it were posted online. What do you think of this?

It might be more helpful to think of 'revenge porn' as one more form of image-based gendered violence that exists along a continuum (Kelly, 1987). Upskirting, virtual rape, photoshopped porn and sextortion are all also forms of sexualised online violence. Sometimes people share sexualised photos and films with their friends, not specifically for revenge against a partner but as a form of 'male bonding or initiation ritual' (McGlynn, 2017: 35). It is for this reason that Clare McGlynn et al. (2017: 36) suggest that what we call 'revenge porn' might better be named 'image-based sexual abuse', and is why we prefer this term.

Part of the stigma surrounding 'revenge porn' occurs due to poor understanding about what it really is. Sarah Bloom (2014) and Danielle K. Citron and Mary A. Franks (2014) both demonstrate how devastating the effects of 'revenge porn' are. The shame and humiliation that victims feel often silence them and prevent them from seeking redress. The victim-blaming aimed at the women, in particular, who are victims of 'revenge porn', exacerbates this (Bloom, 2014: 250). Women lose their jobs, become depressed, even commit suicide because they have been victims of 'revenge porn'. The online nature of 'revenge porn' almost makes it worse for victims than if it were taking place offline, because online images are permanent, are easily accessible by anyone and can be shared anonymously (Bloom, 2014: 249).

This sort of victim-blaming echoes the victim-blaming that women who live with intimate partner violence and abuse, or who are raped, experience. It is borne out of a sense that women should be ashamed of their bodies and their sexualities and desires; that if they transgress by taking sexy photos of themselves, they should be punished. This sort of archaic thinking may explain, in part, why various jurisdictions have been so slow to criminalise 'revenge porn'.

What are the other barriers to criminalisation? As Citron and Franks (2014) highlight in the context of the USA, one of the issues is that of consent. In many cases of so-called 'revenge pornography' within a **heteronormative** framing, people – usually, though not always, women – send sexy photos of themselves to their partners that they may have taken themselves and that they may have intended their partner to see. To a certain extent, they have consented to the image being taken, but not to it being shared widely. Citron and Franks argue that the fact that there is no specific law against creating 'revenge porn' in many states of the USA means that victims of this crime have to rely on other legal instruments to seek justice, and that these other legal instruments are ineffective when it comes to dealing with the harm that 'revenge porn' causes.

Civil actions against people who share 'revenge porn', or sites who host it, are ineffective because they rely on a victim who has the financial means to sue, and who can face having a case tried without their anonymity being protected. As long as it remains out of the scope of a sex crime, victims cannot remain anonymous, and the shame and stigma associated with this type of crime can eliminate this as an option. Where legal jurisdictions in the USA do not have a specific offence of 'revenge porn', victims might pursue justice using laws against harassment, for instance, which have failed because images are shared with *other people* and not the victim, which therefore is not deemed to be harassment *of the victim* (Citron and Franks, 2014: 366); or laws against creating child pornography, which only works for minors; or laws against the creation of non-consensual images, which only works when images have been taken non-consensually, not when they were consensually shared with a partner.

In 2015, 'revenge porn' was criminalised in England and Wales. Section 33(1) of The Criminal Justice and Courts Bill establishes that it is an:

> offence for a person to disclose a private sexual photograph or film if the disclosure is made—
>
> (a) without the consent of an individual who appears in the photograph or film, and
>
> (b) with the intention of causing that individual distress.

A photograph or film is 'private' if it shows something that is not of a kind ordinarily seen in public.

> (3) A photograph or film is 'sexual' if—
>
> (a) it shows all or part of an individual's exposed genitals or pubic area,
>
> (b) it shows something that a reasonable person would consider to be sexual because of its nature, or
>
> (c) its content, taken as a whole, is such that a reasonable person would consider it to be sexual. (Section 35: 2)

'Revenge porn' statutes also exist in France, Israel and in some states of the USA. Given McGlynn et al.'s (2017) comments about 'revenge porn' existing on a spectrum of image-based violence, do you think that the definition given above in The Criminal Justice and Courts Bill is adequate? Do you think it captures different forms of image-based abuse? Why do these scholars consider that it is important to create laws which specifically criminalise 'revenge porn' as a crime all of its own?

Romance fraud

Online romance fraud is another context in which this question of whether we need more specific offences which target the harms that sex crimes cause, arises. Online fraud is rampant. A common form of scam is the romance fraud, where a fraudster appears to enter into a relationship with their target and, as the relationship develops, asks them for sums of money to pay for personal emergencies or things like rent or school fees. According to Monica Whitty (2015), romance fraud was in the top five Internet scams in 2011 in the USA. In 2016, in the UK, Action Fraud reported that there were nearly 4,000 cases of romance scams that took place (Cross et al., 2018). People have lost sums ranging from £50 to £240,000. In the USA, the average loss was $8,900 (Whitty, 2015). The number of people who are defrauded in romance scams is not inconsiderable, and the sums that they lose are significant. What is more, as with 'revenge porn', there is also a stigma and shame associated with being a romance fraud victim, which means that the real extent of this crime is under-reported. What might be even more concerning is that some people who are in online romances where they are being defrauded may not even know that they are part of a romance scam. They may not learn that they are a victim of crime until they are notified by the police. Whitty and Tom Buchanan (2016) have noted that, for romance fraud victims, the loss of the imagined relation-ship can be more devastating than the financial loss itself.

Part of the stigma associated with romance fraud stems from the fact that victims are considered to be gullible, desperate and lonely. As such, they might receive little sympathy, or experience victim-blaming and even hostility from their family and friends (Gillespie, 2017: 222; Whitty and Buchanan, 2016: 191). In some cases, they might be re-victimised by people posing as police who claim to want to help them to get their money back (Cross, 2019: 676). In order to further our understanding of romance fraud in criminology, it might be helpful to think a bit more about who becomes a victim of such a scam. What types of people fall for the tricks of romance fraudsters? It is also helpful to think about how romance frauds happen. How do scammers so convinc-ingly manage to exploit people?

What type of person gets scammed by romance fraud?

Whitty is the scholar who has written most extensively on the topic of romance fraud; a topic which has been overlooked by criminologists up until now. Whitty (2018) notes that romance fraud victims are typically considered to be middle-aged women who are lonely and of low intelligence. In fact, her research demonstrates that men and women can both be subject to romance scams and that these scams affect both heterosexuals and LGBT+ people. Whitty (2018) notes that most romance fraud victims are middle-aged rather than very old or very young; perhaps because this age group has more dispos-able wealth. Whitty also found that people who are scammed tend also to be highly educated. From a psychological perspective, people who lack self-control, score highly on addiction characteristics and are spontaneous might be more susceptible to being scammed. These are people who are likely to be agreeable, open and extroverted rather than anxious and worried about taking risks. People who are extroverted and agreeable are more trusting than those who are not (Buchanan and Whitty, 2014: 264). People who are 'sensation seekers' are also susceptible to fraud. Sensation seekers are people who look for 'varied, new, complex, and intense sensations' and are willing to take risks for those experiences (Buchanan and Whitty, 2014: 265). In short, the types of people who are susceptible to romance fraud are people who might otherwise be considered to live life to the full. So, while it is also true that people who are defrauded in romance scams may be lonely, they also have characteristics which are associated with a full and meaningful life. This counters stereotypes about the type of person who will be caught in one of these scams.

A further characteristic that Buchanan and Whitty (2014) and Christian Kopp et al. (2015) suggest that victims of these frauds share is a belief in the ideology of romance. Whether heterosexual or homosexual, Kopp et al. (2015) find that people who are defrauded in this way express a belief in traditional scripts of romantic love. That is, they believe in love that is fated (or meant to be), they believe in 'the One' or that 'love will conquer all'. This romantic idealisation of intimate relationships is associated with this fraud because it in part explains why the person being defrauded might turn a blind eye to clues of the fraud. It might also be used to explain why they persist in sending money even if a fraud is suspected, and why, indeed, the loss of the relationship is experienced as such a blow when the fraud is finally unveiled.

How do romance frauds happen?

Part of the way that romance frauds are able to happen is because the parties play out the ideologies of romance between themselves. Whitty (2015) has identified five distinct phases of the romance fraud: the profile, grooming, the sting, sexual abuse and revelation.

The profile

The first part of the fraud begins with the profile. Scammers posing as 'men seeking women' present themselves as being aged in their 50s and seek out women of this age. Posting attractive photographs of themselves, they present as a businessman or an army officer, often from a country in the **Global North,** but stationed for work in a country like Ghana or Nigeria (where many of these frauds are based). This means that they can present themselves as successful and financially independent men, who might also be lonely, and explains why, later, when the scam unfolds, money must be sent to these places. Men might claim to be widowed and looking after young children on their own. In their study of online exchanges between a male scammer posing as a Scottish architect living in West Africa and a Chinese woman, Tan Hooi Koon and David Yoong (2013) note that this sort of self-presentation is a way to prove good character and trustworthiness.

'Women seeking men', Whitty (2015) notes, present themselves as young (under 30) and as being in a low-paying job. They use photographs of attractive models on their profiles. The women target older men. Often, both the men and women claim to be religious. In both these scenarios, it is a script of hegemonic, heteronormative desire which is at play here. Men show themselves as being successful, able to provide for a family, but vulnerable and in need of the nurturing love of a woman. The youth and poverty that female scammers claim enshrine an imaginary of femininity which is vulnerable, fragile and in need of masculine protection. For people who buy into these romantic scripts, it is no wonder that these profiles are so effective.

It is also worth noting that these scams demonstrate how well the scammers seem to understand heteronormative desire and these romance scripts. They also play on the potential latent racism of people in the post-industrialist countries who might be the subject of the scams. By pretending to be posted in African countries, they play on a common stereotype people hold of 'Africa': that African officials must be bribed; that medical care is unreliable; that these countries are dangerous; that it is no wonder that the object of their love needs their help.

Grooming

Whitty (2015) suggests that once the relationship has become more established, it enters the 'grooming' phase. This is where the perpetrator attempts to increase the intimacy of the relationship by presenting a version of themselves which matches the ideal imaginary partner of the person whom they are trying to scam. This is reported as being an exciting and exhilarating phase in the relationship; a sort-of honeymoon period, perhaps (Kopp et al., 2015). Again, this phase functions because those in the relationship are already invested in it and believe that true love will conquer all.

The sting

This belief in romantic ideology comes to bear at the moment the fraudster makes their first move, or one of their moves, to acquire money from the victim. With a tale of being in dire straits – tuition fees to pay, rent to pay, medical bills to pay, visa officials to bribe – the scammer will turn to the victim, who will now be in the position of saviour within the love story, to help financially and to send money quickly. Sometimes the sums are high, sometimes they are not. Sometimes the scammer will ask for a huge sum to pay hospital bills after a car crash, for instance; if their victim is not able to pay, they will refuse, and the scammer will come back with a request for a smaller amount (what Whitty (2015) calls the 'door in the face technique'). Sometimes they might ask for a small amount which increases (what Whitty calls the 'foot in the door technique').

Sexual abuse

Whitty suggests that the fourth stage of a scam includes sexual abuse, where a victim is tricked into performing sexual acts on a webcam, perhaps for the amusement of the scammer, perhaps to blackmail them.

Revelation

The final phase marks the moment where the scam is revealed. This, Whitty (2015) has noted, is devastating for victims, not only because of the loss of the money but also because of the loss of a relationship that they believed in.

How should online romance frauds be treated by the criminal justice system? Fraud is a crime, and in England and Wales the crime is dealt with under the Fraud Act 2006. This provides recourse to deal with the financial loss. There is nothing else around the law related to consent, sexual offences or psychiatric harm that can help these victims. Should there be other legal consequences for perpetrators of these scams in recognition of the emotional suffering they cause because of the romance element of the fraud (Gillespie, 2017; Witty, 2015)?

BOX 11.3

Consider this very different type of romance fraud, which was also facilitated by the Internet:

In 2011, a Marketing and Creative Writing student called Gail Newland met a female student, Chloe, at a queer club night in Chester, UK. The two became friends. Newland had, for many years, used a male alter ego online to chat and flirt with women. Since 2003, she had been developing an online persona of a man she referred to as Kye Fortune. Newland would often pose as Kye online to experiment with a masculine identity and to help her to pursue women. Newland told Chloe that Kye was her friend, and that he (Kye) was attracted to Chloe.

After becoming friends on Facebook, Kye and Chloe started to date. Their relationship was mediated by Newland, whom Chloe said she believed was a mutual friend of theirs. Yet, from Newland's perspective, the online persona of Kye Fortune that she had created gave them both an 'alibi' for their love affair in a context where they were both unsure about being 'out' as women who have sex with women.

In order to pull it off, the pair – Newland and Chloe – would have sex, with Newland as 'Kye' tying up Chloe's hands and making her wear a blindfold every time during the two years that they were together. Chloe said she was told that Kye had his chest bandaged because of a 'nozzle' attached to his heart, and that he had to wear a compression-style suit to regulate his heartbeat, so she could not touch him (Hattenstone, 15 July 2017). Chloe was told that Kye was so self-conscious about his appearance that she could not look at him.

On one occasion, something provoked Chloe to rip off her blindfold. There she discovered Newland, who had been penetrating her with a dildo, and not a penis, as she had believed. The pair argued. They sent condemnatory messages to each other. Newland tried to kill herself by throwing herself off a bridge. Ultimately, she was tried and was sent to prison for six years and six months, on three counts of sexual assault and one of fraud (Wilkinson, 21 December 2017).

This fraud – this deception – is one that took place in the offline world; very tangibly, in fact, in the bedrooms of the women, but it is also one which was facilitated by the digital realm. Chloe was able to build a relationship with Kye, she states, via the fact of his online persona. From Newland's perspective, the online persona of Kye allowed both women to act out a fantasy in which they were in a heterosexual relationship, all the while 'knowing' that they were not.

Reflect on this case:

- Did Chloe consent to sex here?
- Did Chloe *have* sex here?
- Whose story do you find most believable?
- Newland received a custodial sentence which is longer than many men receive for rape. What do you think about that?

Though this case is in many ways extraordinary, it is not the first time that digitally mediated romance frauds have ended up with people deceiving their partners about what some people might consider to be fundamental aspects of their personhood; here, whether they are male or female. Indeed, so called 'gender-bending' has been recognised by Cooper et al. (2000: 16) and by Daneback et al. (2005: 326) as a practice that already happens among men who want to have cybersex with men and who pose online as women to seduce other men. Though not necessarily common, Cooper et al. (2000) estimate that 5 per cent of their sample did this, it is also not unheard of. What is the criminal justice response to these types of cases?

From our reading in Chapter 4, we know that the definition of rape under the Sexual Offences Act 2003 means that Newland was not guilty of rape, which is why she was found guilty under sections 2–3 of the Sexual Offences Act, which covers penetration by objects, hands and other sexual touching (see Chapter 3 for our discussion of rape law). Yet, the question of consent is murky in this case. Chloe consented to have sex with Newland when she thought that Newland was Kye. She consented to being penetrated by a penis, not a prosthetic penis; as such, did she 'have the freedom and capacity to make the choice' to be penetrated as she was?

To think this through, we can analyse the case of *R v. McNally* [2013] EWCA Crim 1051, which has facts that appear to be very similar to the case of Newland and Chloe. In the case of *McNally*, the defendant was a girl living in Scotland who presented as a boy named Scott on the social media site, Habbo. She met the complainant on Habbo and, over several years, they developed an online relationship. McNally and the complainant were aged between 12 and 13 when their relationship started. When they met in person, they were 16–17 years old. They had sex, with Scott using a prosthetic penis. Scott dressed to look like a boy and wore a strap-on penis under trousers in order to give the appearance of a penis.

Scott was eventually confronted by the complainant's mother and came clean about the deception. The complainant was devastated at discovering someone whom she thought was her boyfriend, was actually a woman. She considered herself heterosexual and had consented to the sexual acts because she believed she was engaging in them with a boy. Sentencing McNally to nine months in a young offender institution, suspended for a period of two years, the court decided that the complainant 'chose to have sexual encounters with a boy and her preference (her freedom to choose whether or not to have a sexual encounter with a girl) was removed by the appellant's deception' (*R v. McNally* [2013] at 26).

As such, this form of deception as to the sex of the defendant is enough to rescind sexual consent. In the context of online romance frauds, this is not necessarily helpful, because, while the cases of McNally and Newland involve parties who met each other offline, in many romance scams the parties may never meet. The law is also clear that deception about someone's age, wealth, HIV status or profession is not enough to rescind consent to sexual acts. So, if you meet someone online, and believe them to be a world-class chess player because this is what they told you, and you have sex with them only because you are drawn to world-class chess players, and then you discover the fraud, as it stands, this fraud does not rescind your consent. In romance fraud cases, the sort of deception that takes place tends to be of this order, rather than deception about the sex of the perpetrator (though this is also certainly possible).

Alisdair A.Gillespie (2017: 228) wonders whether the 'grooming' that Whitty (2013) identified to be a constituent part of romance fraud could constitute an offence that could be punished in law. As we saw in Chapter 7, the law around grooming in England and Wales is aimed at protecting children who are befriended by people who want them to 'acquiesce to sexual contact' (Gillespie, 2017: 228). Gillespie notes that the grooming that takes place in the context of child sexual exploitation and that in romance scams have similarities. Both can involve the sending of gifts, discussion of romance and sometimes interacting with family members to lull victims into believing the relationship is harmless or genuine.

Adults are not normally vulnerable to harm in the way that children are automatically considered to be, so it is likely that anti-grooming legislation is not appropriate in the context of romance frauds. People have the right, in law, to make bad decisions. Yet, the emotional toll of grooming in romance fraud continues to evade scrutiny in the criminal justice system. Legislation that punishes fraud does some of the work of punishing these sorts of scams, but should there be specific liability for defrauding someone emotionally? What would the implications of such a liability be? Legal scholars have already suggested that sometimes a bit of bending of the truth happens in dating relationships; people may lie about their job, their age or their wealth. They may even pretend to be single when they are not. At what point should these types of deceptions become criminalised? If at all? For more on this, see our discussion of consent in Chapter 4.

Online hate

To continue this discussion of the spectrum of ways in which the online realm is gendered and affects sexual practice, we now turn to a third example of digital sexual cultures: the world of online gendered hate. To hate is to regard something with extreme ill will. It is an impassioned and proactive verb and noun. Gendered hate predates the online expressions of hatred. However, online hate does implicate men and women – though disproportionately it affects women – and the use of rape threats and other forms of online shaming are tools used to perpetrate this online form of gendered violence. In this section, we will consider this in the context of the so-called 'manosphere', the incels and trolls who tweet rape threats.

The anonymity that we see playing a part in the world of cybersex, 'revenge porn' and online dating also emboldens people to engage in what might be considered to be abusive, violent online exchanges. There is an emerging body of work which considers the role that the Internet plays in developing so-called echo chambers (Barberá et al., 2015; Colleoni et al., 2014). An echo chamber is a term used to describe a sound that reverberates around an enclosed, hollow space. In an online context, it describes people who engage with social media, online chat rooms and online news sources that share similar values to their own and which reinforce the beliefs that they already hold. Echo chambers are criticised as places where people share views with people who already agree with them within a continuous feedback loop. Everyone agrees, so problematic views are not challenged or are ignored, differences of opinion are shut down, and assumptions become more and more entrenched. Echo chambers are associated with both the political left and the political right. They are particularly pronounced around groups whose views are not mainstream, or who form a sort of sub-culture. The proliferation of the feedback is facilitated by algorithms which continuously point users within a subculture, or echo chamber, to more and more of the same ideas. Algorithms have been associated with fostering extremism in some of these groups by continuing to propagate extreme ideas or news stories.

Incels – or 'involuntarily celibate' men – form an online subculture that operates within an echo chamber and which uses the web to promote online **misogyny**. Debbie Ging (2017) has explored the ways in which incel forums have emerged from men's rights groups and the so-called 'manosphere'. Though the notion of involuntary celibacy was an identity initially created online as a means through which men and women of whatever sexuality who wanted to date someone but found it difficult could support each other, the incel has now become associated with an expression of toxic, violent masculinity.

Incel identity is based on a premise that adheres to a so-called 'red pill' ideology, taken from the 1999 film, *The Matrix* (Warner and Village). Here, men on incel forums consider themselves to have taken 'the red pill' and to see life in full, with all its 'ugly truths', whereas the rest of the world – the 'normies' – are 'living a life of delusion', having taken the 'blue pill' (Ging, 2017: 640). The 'black pill' describes an acceptance of the hopelessness of existence; where women are shallow and cruel, and only good-looking men get to have sex with them. Incels believe 'the red pill' makes them wise to the way that feminism and idealised, **hegemonic masculinity** act as barriers to them finding sexual partners: a fact which outrages them. Incels also attribute their inability to find a sexual partner to perceived physical failings in their appearance and in the performance of masculinity they are capable of. Online forums like Reddit and 4chan (before it was expunged from the site) and now sites like incel.me, weebs.fun, blackpill.is and incels.co (although these shut down and reappear elsewhere frequently) are full of men who attribute their incel status to their **ethnicity** (there is a firm hierarchy of desirability and undesirability based on ethnicity in incel culture), their looks – their height, the size of their wrists, the shape of their jawline – or their intelligence. These feed into pseudo evolutionary-biological theories about why women (referred to as femoids, or foids) prefer men who are stereotypically good looking to 'mate' with (men with this status are 'Chads', good-looking women are called 'Stacys', with racialised equivalents for Black men (Tyrone), south-east Asian men (Chadpreet), Middle Eastern men (Chaddam), and so on). Though it is unclear how many of them would actually do this in the offline world, incels advocate the rape and enslavement of women who will not have sex with them and appear to espouse a traditionally **patriarchal** view of heteronormative gender relations.

Angela Nagle (2017) has conducted in-depth inquiries into the rise of online misogyny via these sorts of groups. She notes that though the misogyny expressed online is an expression of patriarchal violence, it is not also an expression of hegemonic masculinity (after Connell and Messerschmidt, 2005). Indeed, the masculinity at play here is one that appears to be full of self-loathing and vulnerability; not the iconic Marlborough Man masculinity that Chads are imagined to embody.

Beyond the echo chamber, incels have been associated with, and taken pride in, a few high-profile gun attacks on women perpetrated by people who follow an incel ideology. One of the most high-profile attacks took place in California in 2014 in which six people were killed and 14 injured. Here, Elliot Rodger posted a video of himself online, complaining about how women rejected him despite the fact that he was, in his words, a 'supreme gentleman'.

Rodger had written a 137-page manifesto in which he outlined his incel ideology, a document that has been adopted with alacrity by other members of the incel community (Jaki et al., 2019). In Oregon in 2015, Chris Harper-Mercer killed 10 people including himself. He also left a manifesto which outlined his grief about not having a girlfriend (Anderson, 23 September 2017). On 14 February 2018, Nikolas Cruz killed 17 people in Florida (Shukman, 15 February 2015), on 23 April 2018, Alek Minassian killed 10 people in Toronto (BBC, 25 April 2018) and on 2 November 2019, Scott Beierle killed two women and himself in Florida. All three allied themselves with Elliot Rodger in online videos, social media and chat rooms (Associated Press, 13 February 2019). Rodger has acquired a saint-like status in some incel communities for his part in the so-called 'Beta uprising' (Beauchamp, 23 April 2019).

It is clear that the anonymity, community and accessibility of these online spaces have provided these perpetrators with the inspiration to commit acts of violence in the name of gendered hate. Both men and women have been victims of these attacks. They have been attacks on certain performances of masculinity and femininity from the perspective of a rigid incel ideology. It is clear that incels are also victims of an ideal of hegemonic masculinity from which they feel they are excluded, based on appearance, personality and success, and this self-loathing perpetuates itself within these echo chambers. What is less clear is whether the Elliot Rodgers of the online world would have perpetrated these attacks without incel forums. Mass shootings in the United States and Canada occurred before the rise of incel subcultures. These extreme acts of violence cannot necessarily solely be attributed to the forums, but the forums are undeniably expressions of hate and of community built on hate.

Trolling

We have seen how, in the context of 'revenge porn', the Internet has been used to do violent things to people, thanks to the anonymity and accessibility that users of the Internet enjoy. This sort of hate is also echoed in incel debates. The practice of trolling is a specific expression of online hate that is worth considering.

Trolling – or writing provocative messages to enrage or insult people – has its own particular history in the evolution of digital cultures (Bishop, 2014). Trolling plays on the principle of free speech; that no matter how loathsome the opinion, unless it is an act of hate speech – defined as speech 'which spreads, incites, promotes or justifies hatred, violence and discrimination against a person or group of persons' (Council of Europe, n.d.) – which incites other people to violence or acts of hatred, it is not a crime. Trolling is a practice that is popular among both men and women and that they engage in for fun, as well as to express anti-social behaviours (March et al., 2017).

A common speech act expressed as trolling – often on social media sites like Twitter, but also in online spaces including chat rooms and message boards – is the rape threat. An array of high-profile women, from Hilary Clinton to Miley Cyrus, have received rape threats. For women in public life such as Labour Member of Parliament Jess Phillips in the UK, who has received over 600 rape threats, and Brazilian politician Ana Paula da Silva who received rape threats after wearing a low-cut bright red pantsuit during her swearing-in ceremony in the Legislative Assembly of Santa Catarina, rape threats are commonplace, near-daily occurrences.

BOX 11.4

In 2014, two young people – Isabella Sorely from Newcastle, UK and John Nimmo from South Shields, UK – were jailed for the exact same crime, despite living 24 km from each other and never having met in person. Nimmo and Sorely had taken to Twitter to send rape threats to feminist journalist Caroline Criado-Perez who was, at the time, campaigning for the portrait of Jane Austen to appear on the £10 bank note. This campaign was successful, but it also aroused the ire of an array of commentators, some who were anti-feminist, some who were misogynistic, some who, like Sorely, were simply drunk and keen to jump on a bandwagon. The rape threats that Nimmo tweeted to Criado-Perez included 'Ya not that gd looking to rape u be fine', 'I will find you [smiley face]' and then the message 'rape her nice ass', while Sorely tweeted 'I've just got out of prison and would happily do more time to see you berried [buried]; seriously go kill yourself! I will get less time for that; rape?! I'd do a lot worse things than rape you'. The two were tried together at the Old Bailey. Sorely was sentenced to 12 weeks in prison and Nimmo was sentenced to eight weeks under section 127 of the Communications Act 2003. Both had to pay £400 in damages.

The threats that Nimmo and Sorely both made were borne out of a fantasy in their heads of the type of people they were and what they could do. It is unlikely that either of them would have raped or sought to rape Criado-Perez, but that does not stop this type of trolling from being deeply harmful and frightening (Jane, 2014: 563). Instead, it shows how the online realm has the capacity to foster a politics where the hatred of women is normalised. And, as Jane (2014: 564) demonstrates, this is a form of hatred that specifically targets women. While women like Sorely might participate in trolling, the targets of the trolling – especially when the trolling is full of rape threats, criticisms of how women look, whether or not they are overweight, or 'cunts' – are women. Men are not habitually trolled with anything like the sexist enthusiasm that are women.

What do you think about this statement? Do you agree that women are more often the targets of sexist trolling than men? And what does this mean in terms of what the politics of the digital world are? There are practical barriers that prevent the prosecution of trolls in the criminal courts, such as the anonymity that people can hide behind. Are there also socio-political barriers that prevent trolling from being appropriately criminalised? The implications of these further illustrate to us that the digital realm poses specific problems to us in our study of sex and crime and may need more targeted, thoughtful responses.

Summary

One of the difficulties of writing a chapter about sex and the digital realms is that what we call the digital is so ubiquitous that it is difficult to discern which criminological elements are specific to the digital realm and the specific digital form. The intertwining of devices, digital networks, screens, keyboards, senders, recipients, even bank transfers, alcohol, desire and shame work together to create these specific circumstances. Actor Network Theory (ANT) helps us to perceive this.

We have seen in the chapter how even theorising the digital and establishing what we are talking about when we refer to the digital, is complex. We have discussed how the digital realm has affected online dating, sex, abuse and fraud. We have seen how people can be empowered by the anonymity of the online world to explore their sexualities. We have seen how the digital realm fosters certain forms of connectivity and identity formation about subcultures who may then go on to express misogynistic hatred in the offline world – or keep their hatred online, and who get into trouble for that too.

We could have spoken about how the web is used for sex trafficking, for **sex work**, for uploading amateur pornography, for grooming children, for fostering feminist resistances, for playing computer games which simulate rape, to assist in the coercive control of partners within abusive and violent relationships, or for the sharing of apps and information which is intended to keep women safe by monitoring them on their way home from a night out. We could have talked about Grindr, Tinder and the dark web. Some of this we do talk about in other chapters; some of this you may have to research for yourself. The important thing to remember is that the digital penetrates almost every part of life, but that it does not do this neutrally, and it should be approached with a critical spirit in your criminological adventures.

Review questions

- Create your own actor network; think about a recent digital interaction that you have had. What are all the elements that make that interaction possible?
- Should the criminal justice system intervene to criminalise trolls and incels who use online spaces like Twitter?
- What would proponents of the principle of privacy and freedom of speech that governs the Internet say about these public protection concerns?
- Why do experts think that the criminal justice system does not do enough to protect victims of romance fraud or 'revenge porn'? What reasons for this are given?

Other chapters that this links to

Chapter 4 (Consent and its discontents)
Chapter 7 (Sexual exploitation and the State)
Chapter 10 (Sex and disability)
Chapter 12 (Children, sexualisation and the law)
Chapter 14 (The future)

12

Children, sexualisation and the law

In contemporary social life, there is little that arouses stronger feeling than the conjunction of children and sex. The sexualisation of children is condemned; the sex lives of children are tightly controlled, even criminalised; and paedophiles are among the most reviled criminal group in popular **discourses.** In this chapter, we are going to unpack some of what constructs these strong feelings. We are going to examine what appears to be the taboo of childhood **sexuality** and the social, cultural and legal ways that this is responded to in contemporary social life. We are going to do this by examining the contrasting ways that childhood sexuality is figured; what happens when children send 'sexts' to each other; the controversies around paedophilia; and recent approaches to child sex crimes, including the offence of grooming and attitudes to child sexual exploitation.

By the end of this chapter, you will understand more about:

- how childhood is constructed, and the role this takes in approaches to sex and sexual crimes
- child sexual **agency**
- the politics and problematics of paedophilia.

What is a child?

The answer to this question might seem to be self-evident, but what might appear at first to be a relatively straightforward question is in reality more complex. In one sense, it seems easy to say that a child is simply someone who has not yet reached the age of majority. The age of majority is the age when people have rights as adults, independent of their parents or guardians. It is usually the age when people can vote, gamble, buy and drink alcohol, run for public office, and so on. Reaching the age of majority also brings an end to the period when **the state** has a responsibility to care for a child, for example by providing housing and education, and ensuring protection from **harm**.

According to the European Union (EU) and the United Nations (UN), a child becomes an adult when they are 18. However, in Greece, a person is a child only until the age of 8. After that, until they are 18 they are legally referred to as minors; a subtle difference, perhaps, but one that makes our discussion of what a child is more complicated (see Kierkegaard, 2008). In England and Wales, the age of majority is 18, and at 17 you are still legally a child, even though at 16 you can 'emancipate' yourself from your parents. In the USA, the age of majority is also 18, but you need to be 21 years old to buy and drink alcohol. Most countries of the world have 18 as the age of majority, but in Indonesia, Saudi Arabia and Yemen, you can be considered to be an adult at 15, whereas, in New Zealand, 20 is the age of majority and in Singapore, Madagascar and Bahrain, it is 21.

So, we can see already that what legally constitutes a child is quite contingent on geographical location. This has implications for understanding how children's engagement with sex is viewed, regulated and controlled. One key aspect of this is the age that a person can start legally having sex. The age of sexual consent in the UK is 16 and in Germany it is 14. Children in France are considered to be 'sexual minors' until they are 15. Note, this is not the same as having an age of consent that is 15. If an argument that consensual sex has taken place can be made, even young children can be considered to have consented to sex. It was only in 2005 in a case involving the sexual abuse of 5-year-old children, that the courts agreed that very young children could never consent to sex (Bulletin criminel (2005), No. 326: 1121).

In the Netherlands, the age of consent used to be 12, subject to certain criteria, but in 2002 it was raised to 16. In the USA, the age of consent varies from state to state between 16 and 18, whereas in Brazil and Bolivia it is 14, and in Mexico, subject to certain restrictions, it is 12. Part of what these differences in age show is that there is no age of sexual consent of children that is inherently correct. If the same child can legally consent to sex in Mexico but cannot in Germany, this tells us that what we imagine is an appropriate age for children to have sex, from a public policy perspective, is a socio-cultural construct.

The restriction of children's sexual activity is on the basis that children lack the ability to provide informed consent, due to their age. While on the face of it this may seem to be a straightforward idea, as we discuss below, there are considerable challenges to assuming that age equals the ability to consent. As a consequence, criminal sanctions exist when those above the age of majority – adults – have sexual relations with someone below the age of consent, and in many jurisdictions, those under the age of majority – children – who have sexual relationships with other children. Such sexual engagement is referred to as sexual abuse.

While we do not know exactly how many children experience sexual abuse, the National Society for the Prevention of Cruelly to Children (NSPCC, April 2019) in the UK estimates that one in 20 children have been sexually abused, girls are more likely to experience sexual abuse, and the vast majority of children who experience sexual abuse are abused by someone they know. Unicef (2019) estimates that worldwide around 15 million adolescent girls aged 15–19 have experienced forced sex in their lifetime. Boys are also at risk, but estimates are limited due to lack of data. Data on sexual abuse against boys is only collected in a small number of countries and boys may also be less likely to be willing than girls to report abuse (Unicef, 2019). Why do you think that might be? What assumptions about **heteronormativity**, masculinity or homosexuality might be at play in under-reporting?

Legal restrictions of sexual engagement with a child are complicated further, as even when the age of consent is fixed in law, there are still some nuances to

take account of. In England and Wales, for instance, there are different regulations regarding children who are aged under 13 who have sex and those aged
13–16. Under the Sexual Offences Act 2003 in England and Wales, a child
under the age of 13 can never consent to sex, but a child aged 13–16 who might
willingly consent to sex with someone of a similar age, may find their case is
treated more leniently in a court of law, even though sex with this age group is
still prohibited.

Similarly, in the USA the marriage of children is illegal in law. One needs
to be 18 years old to get married. Yet, in practice, the marriage of children is
permitted in several states under special circumstances: when parents have
given permission, a judge has consented, or in the case of pregnancy. The
anti-child marriage awareness-raising group Unchained at Last reported that
207,468 children were married in the USA between 2000 and 2015 (Ferguson,
29 October 2018). In only 14 per cent of the cases did a child marry another
child; often children were married to people many years older than them. In
Tennessee, in 2001, three 10-year-old girls were married to men aged between
24 and 31, and in 2006 an 11-year-old boy married a 27-year-old woman. In
Alabama, a girl aged 14 married a 74-year-old man. Many of these marriages
disproportionately concern girls who are married to much older men (Baynes,
8 July 2017). Most of these marriages affect children in poor, rural families.
As with child marriage that happens in other parts of the world, these families
might consider child marriage as a solution that provides for a child they cannot afford to look after. Sex is usually considered to be an intrinsic part of
marriage so, in these cases, what we find are sexual adult–child relationships
sanctioned by the state when they would be otherwise criminalised.

Concerns about the sexual activity of children have a long history. The
age of consent has developed over time, perhaps as an expression of this
anxiety. It has also been overtly **gendered,** historically focused only on girls
entering into heterosexual sexual relations. In the UK, female homosexuality has never been criminalised, and so historically there was not an 'age of
consent' for sex between women. On the other hand, male homosexuality
was illegal for everyone for most of the twentieth century, and the years
before (see Chapter 3 for our discussion of the history of criminalisation of
men's sexual relationships with other men). When male homosexuality was
partially decriminalised in 1967, the age of consent for men was set at 21:
five years older than that for heterosexual sex. Then, in 1994, the age of
consent for male homosexual sex was lowered to 18, and it was not until
2001 that young men who wanted to have sex with men had the same
rights as young men who wanted to have sex with women, and the age of
consent was set at the age of 16. Historically, there has been an inherent
assumption that it was girls, not boys, who needed to be protected from
engagement in heterosexual activity. For example, in England and Wales

the age of consent for girls was raised from 12 to 13 in 1875 under the Offences Against the Person Act, which made no mention of boys. Similarly, when the age of consent was raised to 16 in 1885 by the Criminal Law Amendment Act, the law specifically regulated sexual interaction with girls, rather than boys.

What we see evolving is a complex, sometimes conflicting, approach to dealing with the sexuality of children in law across various jurisdictions. But we also see this complexity in popular and media discourses about childhood sexuality and the perceived increased sexualisation of children. The 'premature' sexualisation of children has been seen as a growing problem, with specific concerns over the effects of sexual marketing and media; see, for example, the report on sexualised goods aimed at children, commissioned by the Equal Opportunities Committee of the Scottish Parliament (Buckingham et al., 2010). This report found that parents and children had different understandings of what sexualisation, in the context of marketing targeting children, might look like. Some parents expressed idealistic imaginings of how children and childhood should be, evoking a figure of the innocent, sexless child. Some parents even felt that sexualised clothing – Playboy-branded products, for instance – was responsible for trying to 'groom' children into **sex work** (Buckingham et al., 2010: 49). Children, on the other hand, expressed a desire to be able to interact with sexualised marketing because they knew it was not serious or how they 'ought to' behave (2010: 60). Indeed, they expressed rather normative and critical views of other children who wore Playboy thong-style underwear, for instance, in sexualised ways (2010: 63). These different interactions with sexualised marketing demonstrate that children are savvy consumers. They also show that the different relationships that parents and children have with sexualised marketing make for different interpretations of the same product (2010: 4).

Thinking about childhood sexuality

Childhood sexuality – like all sexuality – and childhood, in general, is socially constructed; that is, there is nothing (or not much) that is 'natural' about childhood. The social construction of attitudes to sex and children informs some of the ways that childhood is treated in law. Adopting a quasi-historical analytical approach, Philippe Ariès (1962) argues that the notion of childhood was invented as a product of **modernity**. That is, before the nineteenth century, in **Western** contexts, childhood was not treated as a distinct stage of life: 'the idea of childhood did not exist' (Ariès, 1962: 125), and children were treated as small adults. Part of the reason for this is related to high child mortality rates, which meant that children were treated indifferently, or neutrally, until they had survived infancy. Then, with the reduction of child mortality, coupled with increased consumerism, the rise of the welfare state and the creation of laws which protect children's rights, the modern construction of childhood that we are more familiar with emerged. Ariès's analysis has been critiqued by scholars who accuse him of romanticising an imagined past where children lived a vibrant existence, rubbing along with adults and doing adult things like working, drinking alcohol and being independent, rather than recognising a more nuanced picture of the reality of the lives of so-called pre-modern children.

Nonetheless, in the context of sexuality, Ariès explains at length how sexual episodes in the infancy of Louis XIII of France were recorded by the royal physician as evidence that childhood expressions of sexual desire were not considered to be a cause for concern; not because children were necessarily sexualised, but rather because they were considered to be sexless; unable to understand erotic play as sexualised. Michel Foucault's (1998[1976]: 25) analysis of the construction of sexuality seems to tell a similar story: that with modernity, with the need to create a citizenry and manage a population (to build a **nation**; see our discussion of this in Chapter 3), there came what Foucault refers to as the administration of sex. As we saw in the debates around sexualised marketing aimed at children above, even in contemporary discourses, it is considered inappropriate for children to be targeted by sexualised imagery. In Foucault's analysis, children were kept sexless by making the discussion of sex something taboo or forbidden: 'everyone knew, for instance, that children had no sex, which is why they were forbidden to talk about it, why one closed one's eyes or stopped one's ears whenever they came to show evidence of the contrary' (Foucault, 1998[1976]: 4).

The sexuality and sexual expression of children produce such anxiety that they are pathologised. They can be dealt with by the criminal justice system, but are more commonly medicalised, treated as a fault of the parents and understood as something to be fixed. Ian Hacking suggests that these identities – like homosexuality – or maladies, such as people who suffer from the 'once fashionable' ailment of 'automatic writing' (writing the appears to emerge from the subconscious) (1986: 162–3), or suicide (1986: 169), were 'made up'. They come into being through systems that are in place to identify them, name them and count them. The 'making up' of people, in this way, draws attention to how these categories become contingent on the political, legal, medical priorities of the moment in which they are conceived (which is why, for instance, Hacking, building on Foucault, argues that, before the nineteenth century, there was no 'homosexual' – only 'inversion' or the act of 'sodomy'; see Chapter 3).

BOX 12.1

Foucault was writing about scenarios that evolved over the last few centuries. Do you think they still apply today? Consider what you think would be an appropriate response to the following situations:

1. Two 5-year-old boys kiss, suck and play with each other's penises at the home of one of the children.
2. A 7-year-old girl encourages her 4-year-old brother to undress with her so that they can cuddle each other naked.
3. A 9-year-old girl appears to flirt with, or express a crush on, an adult friend of her parents.
4. A baby girl appears to rub her vagina against her toys in her crib.
5. A 12-year-old boy and a 5-year-old boy kiss, suck and play with each other's penises at the home of one of the children.

What is going on in each scenario? Which scenarios would be a cause for concern for you? Is anything wrong with these children? What should we do about them? Reflect on your reaction to the scenarios.

If you are feeling unnerved or uncomfortable by the thoughts of children behaving in such a way, then you are not alone. Foucault (1998[1976]: 6) argues that childhood sexual expression causes such anxiety that it is completely repressed in contemporary society. What do you think of this idea? Do you agree that childhood sexuality is *wrongly* silenced? The idea that children might desire sexual contact is almost abhorrent in much of our thinking, but is this in part because of the idealisation of childhood as being a time of innocence?

Ken Plummer (1991: 236 suggests that what is going on is that children are sometimes sexual and sometimes not; they have the 'potential or capacity for something that can be called sexual', but just because this capacity exists, for instance for a 3-year-old boy to have an erection, or a baby girl to have what appears to be an orgasm, does not mean that they are intrinsically sexual in a way that is understood by adults. Plummer explains that the social construction of sex, including the way that adults talk about it when around children, constructs the symbolic and social meanings of sex. As a child gets older, even if they are still very young, they 'come to appreciate that sexuality is not a neutral value-free zone, but one heavily embedded in judgements and emotions ... a child comes to understand that sexual matters are not a matter of public knowledge; they must be pushed into private thoughts and private spaces' (1991: 239). Paul Flanagan (2014) confirms this: in a study of how parents and teachers of primary school-aged children react to scenarios like those we outlined in Box 12.1, he found that adults have a tendency to interpret child sexual behaviour through an adult lens, rather than to interpret actions as a child might do. Given that children have an evolving sense of sexuality, they may not ascribe the same meaning as adults to the acts that they participate in. So, do we need different tools with which to think about the sexuality of children?

In 1989, 140 countries of the world signed the UN Convention on the Rights of the Child (UNCRC) to accord specific human, civil and social rights to children. Currently, 196 states are party to the UNCRC, including all members of the UN except the USA, which remains the only state to have signed, but not ratified, the convention. The treaty requires states to implement laws that protect children against abuse and neglect, exploitation, slavery, trafficking and participation in warfare. It protects children's right to their identity – to know who they are – and the right to recreation, leisure, education, legal protection, and the promotion of their wellbeing. Children have the right to freedom of expression, the right to privacy and the right to lead lives that are not unduly interfered with. Though the elements of the treaty are not necessarily implemented successfully everywhere, these rights recognise the specific status that children have as people who are potentially vulnerable, whose developmental capacities are evolving, and yet who have some agency. In law, this usually means that they cannot be subject to the death penalty, that the corporal punishment of children is prohibited or regulated, and that they must be protected from abuse.

We have already seen how childhood, as a construct, is partially contingent on socio-cultural contexts. Part of this also means that there are socio-cultural differences across the globe that make the application of the UNCRC complex and uneven. The case of child marriage, outlined above, is just one example of this. It is important to bear in mind that these differences mean that approaches to childhood sexuality cannot be the same in all geographical locations, and that, moreover, narratives from those **post-industrialist** countries we usually refer to as the **Global North** should not dominate our thinking about these issues.

Risk, we know from Chapters 1 and 9, is central to the regulation of **sexual practice**. Here, Sonia Livingstone and Monica Bulger (2014) note that, in the context of digital media and the exercise of children's rights in general, policymakers have adopted a risk-averse approach and discourage the use of digital media as part of teen sexual practice in all circumstances. Instead, the authors suggest that an approach that takes into consideration the notion that some element of risk is acceptable should be adopted, and that an interplay between building resilience and calculated risk-taking would foster approaches that more readily reflect how children interact with the world. Children, note Bulger et al. (2017: 760), are too often figured as 'passive innocents' in the online realm. We see this in our discussion of online grooming in Chapter 7. Children's agency, and capacity to act, ought also to be recognised in the context of children's rights. When talking about sexuality, we see these nuances play out in debates about sexting among children (Lampe, 2012; Lee et al., 2013; McLaughlin, 2010).

But they are also at play in the arguments made by pro-paedophile activists (O'Carroll, 1980). We will see more of how this unfolds in the following sections.

Sexting teenagers

Sexting can be defined as the sending of 'sexual communication with content that includes both text and images' (Wolak and Finkelhor, 2011: 2). As we begin to see in the discussions in Chapter 11 about digital sex, sexting has become a popular, normalised form of flirting (Lee et al., 2013: 45). Janis Wolak and David Finkelhor (2011) identify a typology of sexting to better understand the phenomenon. They focus on 'youth-produced sexual images' – images of children taken by children – and distinguish between 'experimental' and 'aggravated' sexting (where the sexting is accompanied by a crime; for instance, an adult is involved, or a child extorts or abuses the person in the picture). Their typology is summarised in Table 12.1.

Table 12.1 Typology of sexting

Youth-produced sexual images	Aggravated	Adult-involved	
		Youth only	Intent to harm/abuse/misuse
	Experimental	Romantic/sexual attention-seeking	
		Other consensual/non-harmful sexting	

Source: Wolak and Finkelhor (2011)

Yet, in the context of sexting between, or including, children, sexting poses a specific problem for the administration of justice (Lampe, 2012; Lee et al., 2013; McLaughlin, 2010). Consider and compare the different sexting tips in Box 12.2, which can be found online.

BOX 12.2

Tips taken from 'Sexting: The Ultimate Guide' (Jalili, 1 January 2018)

1. Timing is everything: It's best to be aware of what your partner's doing when you want to initiate if they're out to lunch with the family – not the best time to roll out a steamy sext.

(Continued)

2. Take it slow: Sexting is all about the build-up. Begin the conversation with an opening that indicates you're ready to play without revealing too much. Sending a selfie of your cleavage, for example, with a simple message of 'Hey you' can grab their attention while making your intentions clear of what this thread can become if the person is willing to answer back.
3. Keep some sexy pics locked and loaded in your library: Keep a set of stock selfies so you don't have to deliberate in delivering an image. You want responses to be quick and lively.

'Tips for dealing with teen sexting' (ConnectSafely, 7 May 2018)

- The safest way to avoid a picture getting into the wrong hands is to never take it or share it. Sadly, there are cases (sometimes called 'revenge porn') where someone shares pictures meant only for them – sometimes after a breakup.

- Never take and send an image of yourself under pressure, even from some-one you care about.

- If a stranger asks you to take a revealing picture, it could be a scam that could lead to further demands and threats ('sextortion'). Do not respond and consider reporting it to the police, [and] your parents. It could be a criminal who has exploited other people so you're helping others by alerting authorities.

- If a sexting photo arrives on your phone, first, do not send it to anyone else (that's not only a violation of trust, but could be considered distribution of child pornography). Delete the photo(s). If it would help – especially if you're being victimised – talk with a parent or trusted adult. Tell them the full story so they can figure out how to support you. Ask them to keep you involved.

- If the picture is from a friend or someone you know, then someone needs to talk to that friend so he or she is aware of possible harmful consequences. You're actually doing the friend a big favour because of the serious trouble that can happen if the police get involved. Get the friend to delete the photo(s).

- If the photos keep coming, you and a parent might have to speak with your friend's parents, an attorney or school authorities.

Analyse these two pieces of advice. What similarities and differences are there between them? What do they assume about the reader? What do they assume about sexting?

We might argue that these two pieces of advice reflect a double discourse about sexting. Sexting itself is considered to be a normal part of fostering an erotic encounter for adults (the first piece targets an adult readership), but for children (teenagers) the erotic potential of sexting is curtailed by the risk that it poses to the sexters. The advice is often, simply, not to do it; the second list in Box 12.2 mentions different crimes that a sexter might fall victim to inadvertently. While the first advice list suggests that sexters might want to keep a private gallery of sexy photos to use when they are sexting, for people under 18 the advice is to delete any evidence of sexy photos from their devices.

Jessica Ringrose et al. (2013) question the way that discourses around sexting safety turn on the notion that consensually sent sexualised images carry with them a stain of shame if they are discovered. In a social context where the expression of sexuality – particularly for women – is shameful and the sexual practice of children in particular is taboo, narratives around children who sext are laced with anxiety about harm, shame and risk to reputation. Of course, there is a double standard between male and female children's experiences of shame and reputation management in the context of sexting, but there is also a conflicting narrative between what expression of sexuality is permissible for children and what is permissible for adults. Do you think that this is a reasonable distinction to enforce? As we noted above, there are many things that children are not able to do that adults are. Should sexting simply be among them? But, if so, where does that leave the emphasis on agency, privacy and a right to freedom of expression that is protected by the UNCRC (Bulger et al., 2017: 760)?

In law, this disjuncture can lead to young people who produce visual sexts (selfies of themselves naked, or of parts of their naked bodies) and who send them to someone else – even their own girlfriend or boyfriend – being prosecuted under laws against the production and distribution of child pornography (Lee et al., 2013). As research by Bulger et al. (2017), Lampe (2012) and Lee et al. (2013) demonstrates, this is a legal issue that affects children in all sorts of national contexts, not just the USA and the UK where the majority of these debates seem to take place. For example, in South Africa, legislation aimed at criminalising adults who solicit or share child pornography is used to criminalise people under the age of 16 who send nude pictures of themselves. Children in South Africa have their rights to privacy and freedom of expression protected under the national constitution, so children's rights activists have argued that children who send sexts to each other ought not to be criminalised (Bulger et al., 2017).

Bulger et al. (2017) and Julia H. McLaughlin (2010) both note that, in some jurisdictions, for instance the USA, children who commit serious crimes can find themselves tried and punished as adults. This means that for a serious crime like the circulation of child pornography, a child might find themselves tried and convicted in an adult court for a crime that they were only able to commit because they were children. This can mean that children who are accused of sexting crimes end up finding themselves on sex offender registers. A BBC investigation using a Freedom of Information request to police forces in England and Wales, found that between 2014 and 2017 over 4,000 children had been investigated by the police due to sexting. While the most common age of those involved was recorded as 13–14 years, nearly 400 children under the age of 12 were spoken to by police during the time period, the youngest being a boy aged 5 (BBC News, 11 July 2017).

In an Australian context – and the same is likely to be true elsewhere – Lee et al. (2013) also observe that part of what fuels the anxiety about sexting and young people is a 'moral concern' about childhood expressions of sexuality. Borrowing from Foucault's (1998[1976]) observations about the way that the sexuality of children is a source of anxiety in the service of nation-building, they suggest that policy, family and legal concerns about children who send sexts to each other – and the description of this as child pornography – actually express another socio-cultural anxiety: the anxious need to create a docile, self-regulating, self-censoring, obedient citizen (Lee et al., 2013: 42). If people agree that sending sexts is something to be ashamed of, that it is risky, and that these risks might ruin their chances of 'running for Congress' (see Ringrose et al., 2013: 319), then contemporary injustices that emerge as a result of squeamishness about sexuality continue to be perpetrated. At their fullest extension, it is because of these injustices that slut-shaming, victim-blaming and sexual harassment, for instance, still exist.

BOX 12.3

Debate the issue: Should teenage sexting be decriminalised?
   Consider:

- What do you think about this suggestion by Lee et al. (2013)?
- Does it surprise you that public policy, the state, even laws created to pro-tect children would be used to control childhood sexuality in this way?
- Is image-based teenage sexting the same as child pornography?
- At what point does the creation and sharing of a consensual image-based sext become pornographic?
- Does it depend on the explicitness of the image? On whether it is a selfie or taken by someone else? On whether the recipient is an adult or not? Or when it is circulated as an act of 'revenge porn' (see Chapter 11 for more discussion of 'revenge porn')?
- Is it socially damaging to remove the stigma of sexting? Would decriminalis-ing sexting simply give young people free reign? If so, what are the problems with this? Lampe's (2012: 726–7) proposed statute might help you in your thinking.

A scandal

In 2012, a paedophilic sex scandal erupted in the UK that appeared to fundamentally alter the way sex, celebrity and abuse were thought about in the public imagination. Claims of sexual assault perpetrated by a famous, deceased television personality and entertainer emerged. Jimmy Savile was, in his life, what popular media in the UK like to call a 'national treasure', meaning that he was popular, respected and held a place in the hearts of people who knew of him. In the 1980s, Margaret Thatcher, the then prime minister of the UK, nurtured a close relationship with Savile and credited him for his benevolent work with sick and disabled children. In 1990, he was knighted by the Queen for his services to charity work. It later turned out that he had been using his position of trust as a trustee of a children's hospital to sexually abuse the patients therein. He assaulted female children who appeared on his TV show and on the various media-related public appearances that he made around the country in the 1970s to the 1990s.

In the wake of these accusations, hundreds of similar claims of sexual abuse perpetrated by other male figures in the public eye emerged. Politicians, entertainers, DJs and other TV personalities were accused, and many were subsequently found guilty and imprisoned for sexual assaults they perpetrated thanks to the impunity of their celebrity status in those decades (see Independent Inquiry into Child Sexual Abuse, April 2018; see also the extended discussion we have on this in Chapter 7 about sexual exploitation and the media). When reflecting on the way that attitudes to this kind of sexual assault against children have evolved, consider the observation that Hacking (1986) makes about the way that social, legal, medical and political changes construct people, and our ideas about people.

Alongside these scandalous revelations in 2012, came the news that in 1976 a support group that sought to protect and promote the rights of paedophiles received the endorsement of the National Council for Civil Liberties (now called Liberty) and submitted a claim to parliament that 'childhood sexual experiences, willingly engaged in with an adult, result in no identifiable damage. The real need is a change in the attitude which assumes that all cases of paedophilia result in lasting damage' (Henley, 3 January 2013). During the Savile scandal, various media sources reported that many politicians who were serving in Tony Blair's government (1997–2007) also supported these claims for paedophiles' rights. These claims were made in the context of very specific shifts in the sexual landscape in the UK (Weeks, 1981). Homosexual sex between men had become legalised and the availability of the contraceptive pill meant that more women and men could have sex without fear of pregnancy. This meant that pre-marital sex was more common and, alongside the call for recognising the rights of paedo-philes to enter into relationships with children, there were calls to reduce, or even remove, the age of consent. In this section, we are going to unpack these ideas in dialogue with some of what we have already said about sex-ting and childhood sexuality, above.

A radical case for paedophilia?

In order to help us understand these controversial (you may think horrifying) ideas better, we draw on the book written in 1980 by pro-paedophile activist Tom O'Carroll and the politics and purposes of the Paedophile Information Exchange (PIE) of which he was a founding member. The PIE was an organisa-tion established in 1974. It was intended as a support network for men and women who were paedophiles, to be able to meet each other and to help each other find strategies to live as paedophiles in a world that despised them. It also acted as a political lobby group fighting for paedophiles' rights. O'Carroll uses his text as a vehicle to explain more about how he experiences paedo-philia as a sexual orientation. He writes:

> I have been sexually attracted towards children, especially young boys, since I was a child … from six years onwards I recall consistently rejecting the overtures of little girls who said 'I'll show you mine if you show me yours' – I would have been ashamed to do anything so rude – but beyond the age of 10 or so, the thought of other boys' bodies began to excite me beyond my power to resist. My school days have in fact been the most sexually active ones of my life to date. (1980: 9)

Later, he continues:

> I [was] … sustained by just one slender hope; the hope that I might somehow make a go of marriage, and raise a family of my own. For then I could be a good daddy. I'd be able to express my love physically enough by hugging the children, and bathing them, and changing their clothes. They would never need to know that [this] was a sexual turn on for me. I would hide it for their sake … The family doctor thought that this was a good idea too. He supposed that exposure to women would give me a taste for them … [and that] I would soon outgrow this nonsense about boys. (1980: 11)

O'Carroll uses his book to come out as a paedophile and to make the case, over the course of 13 chapters, for why paedophilia – sexual and romantic attraction towards children – should be recognised as a minority sexuality, in the same way that politicised homosexual groups were also advocating for themselves at this time.

BOX 12.4

Read again how O'Carroll explains paedophilia above. Note your thoughts about it. Many people think that paedophilia is a disgusting outrage. Here, we want to take our analysis a level further:

- Why do you think the way you do about what O'Carroll says?
- What, in what he says, or does not say, helps you to come to this conclusion?
- What do you think of the treatment that his doctor suggested for him?

Drawing on an array of source material, O'Carroll posits that children are sexual beings. Citing Sigmund Freud (1905) and Alfred Kinsey (1998[1953]), he explains that children and babies have sexual desire and can express sexual pleasure. Kinsey's report of the masturbation practices of 3-year-old children is cited at length. The sexual practice of children is not considered to be harmful and is, indeed, good for them, according to Kinsey et al. (1998[1953]). O'Carroll also cites examples from different communities where child sexual practice takes place. Among the Trobriand in North West Melanesia, or in Polynesia, anthropologists including Bronisław Malinowski (2002[1929]) and Clellan S. Ford and Frank A. Beach (1951) note that sex between children and the masturbation of children are things that happen without causing too much concern to others living in the community. O'Carroll uses these examples to make the claim that children have their sexuality curtailed in what he calls 'Western' societies. Rehearsing similar arguments to those upon which the UN has formulated the notion that children have rights (though, remember, that treaty was signed long after O'Carroll published this book), O'Carroll suggests that the prohibition of sex with children is an infringement of the rights of children to freedom of expression and the **power** to decide what they do with their bodies. Note that O'Carroll is interpreting childhood sexuality as being equivalent to adults'; this is in contrast to the argument made by Plummer (1991), as we saw above.

O'Carroll makes a number of other observations that make the case for legalising paedophilia. For O'Carroll, there is a distinction between paedophiles (child lovers) and child molesters. He explains: 'there is much in consensual paedophilia, as opposed to child molesting, that presupposes a gentle, almost feminine type of sexual expression rather than one which conforms to the masculine stereotype of dominance and aggression' (1980: 35). O'Carroll is referring here to non-penetrative sex that these adults have with children, and this is what he means by 'feminine' sexual expression. Indeed, O'Carroll counsels against having penetrative sex with a child under 12 (though, according to the PIE's own policy proposal, children as young as 4 might be able to consent to penetrative sex). Paedophiles love children, he argues, and would not do anything to hurt them or to abuse them. Just as men who rape do not do so out of desire, but rather as an expression of abusive power, so too child molesters are not all paedophiles, and not all paedophiles molest children. Paedophiles who want to enter into caring and consensual relationships with children should be able to do so. O'Carroll suggests that most paedophiles are not attracted to very young children (under 4 years of age) and that most develop relationships with children who can verbalise their desire.

O'Carroll argues that if children have the right to say 'no' to sexual contact – kissing a family friend or receiving a hug from an auntie or uncle – then they should also have the right to say 'yes' to a sexy massage, masturbation, or oral sex with an older person. Even babies, O'Carroll concludes, might enjoy having their genitals tickled by their parents as part of the everyday intimate care of such young children (washing, dressing, nappy changing). Their consent should not need to be sought in an explicit manner for something as harmless as that. It might be helpful to go back to Chapter 4 to contextualise O'Carroll's arguments within our discussion of the concept and complexities of consent. We discuss consent in the context of O'Carroll's manifesto below.

O'Carroll's book is engagingly written and is a tightly argued call for paedophiles' rights to be recognised. It espouses **sex-positive**, sexually liberal positions which seem to follow the queer and feminist epistemology that we encountered in Chapter 2; that is, O'Carroll argues against **patriarchy** and heteronormative ways of relating. He argues for sexual agency and the rights of gay men and women to be recognised in law. He demands that there be more discussion of sex and sexual practice in school, for instance, to take away the taboos around frank sexual discussions, active in the 1970s and 1980s. O'Carroll was writing at a period when it was forbidden for schools to talk about non-heterosexual sexualities in sex education classes; it is only in recent years that sex education has become more pluralistic and diverse (see Chapter 3 for our discussion of this). He argues that women should have access to abortion on demand; something that feminists still argue for, and women still do not have the right to. He argues that we should strive politically and socially to eradicate the shame and stigma associated with sex, desire and what we do with our bodies. He argues that children should not be taught sexual shame. Much of this commentary is laudable. We may even agree with it. So, if we want to object to his thesis, we need to give consideration to the basis of our arguments, without falling into the myopic hysteria that O'Carroll accuses his critics of. Do we want to counter his thesis? If so, on what basis would you go about it? We are aware that such a consideration may make you feel uncomfortable; however, we want to remind you that discomfort over a troubling idea cannot alone create a foundation for a strong rebuttal to an argument we may not like.

Consent

Some might argue that children – especially those under the age of 13 – cannot consent to sexual activity. They may say 'yes', they may look like they want to participate, but because they are so young, they are not developmentally or socially able to 'agree by choice [with] the freedom and capacity to make that choice' (using the definition of consent in the Sexual Offences Act 2003, section 74, applicable in England and Wales). O'Carroll argues that children develop and understand the world at different paces, so some children, perhaps, cannot consent to sex at the age of 11, whereas others of the same age will be able to understand what consent means and the consequences of that choice. O'Carroll responds to the suggestion that sex sometimes has consequences such as pregnancy and disease, the risks of which young people may not fully comprehend, by suggesting that school sex education should be better, that doctors be better trained to deal with children's sexual health issues and that abortion should be more readily available. These might all be good ideas, but they neglect the affective and emotional aspect of sexual practice; that there might be consequences beyond the physical to sexual encounters which go wrong, for instance, or which leave people feeling vulnerable or rejected. They also neglect the practical consequences of pregnancy in childhood, that it comes with serious health implications (see World Health Organization, 31 January 2020), and that abortion, even if undertaken willingly and in a supportive environment, can be a traumatic experience for someone undergoing it. The robustness with which adults might meet such an experience is built in childhood through the experience of living, so it is impossible for a child – especially a very young child – to consent to sex with a realistic appreciation of the potential consequences of that choice.

Power

One obvious objection might be that between adults and children there are imbalances of power. Financially, socially, politically, physically, adults have more power than children. The fact of this power imbalance is what enables abusers to molest children in the first place. Adults' better understanding of the world means that they are better able to manipulate children to abuse them, or simply to get them to do what they want them to. We can see the imbalance of power between adults and children in the reasons that children give for not reporting their experiences of sexual abuse. The education programme Thinkuknow (n.d.) from the National Crime Agency, UK, outlines some reasons why children do not tell anyone about their abuse:

I might be seen as different.

This is going to cause problems in my family/community/school.

I may be taken away from home.

I don't want the police or social services involved in my life.

I don't want the abuser to get in trouble (because of feelings of loyalty, love, fear, etc.).

I'm going to be blamed.

Images will be found which I'm embarrassed about.

I won't be believed.

I won't be taken seriously.

He/she is going to hurt or embarrass me or my family or someone else.

If we imagine that a child can consent to enter into a sexual relationship with an adult, then that relationship can never be one of equals and therefore is inherently unjust. O'Carroll tries to deal with this in his ninth chapter, where he argues that, in a heterosexual couple, some women are financially, socially and physically weaker than their male partners, but we do not stop them from entering this partnership, and nor should we. O'Carroll also notes the ways in which children may manipulate adults to get what they want. Are there any limitations to these arguments?

One thing, for instance, that O'Carroll does not address is the way that the power imbalance between adults and children is structural, and, in many ways, with good reason. Ever since the Factory Act of 1833, child labour for children under the age of 13 has been abolished in England and Wales (where O'Carroll bases his argument). Children are now not usually allowed to work before the age of 16. So, in an adult–child relationship, a child could never be the social or economic equal of their adult partner; they would always be dependent on their partner for their sustenance. Even if, as in the example that O'Carroll (1980: 130–3) presents, children offer to exchange sexual favours for presents and treats (child sexual exploitation is what we call this now), this does not mean that they hold equal power in the relationship. This is different to O'Carroll's example of the wholly dependent wife or girlfriend who could, in principle, be financially and socially independent, even if she is in fact not.

Incest

A third objection might be to the way that O'Carroll's thesis seemingly transgresses the incest taboo. In his opening chapter – cited above – he talks about having his own children with whom he might express his sexual desires. In the USA, the Childhood Sensuality Circle (an equivalent group to PIE) developed a Child's Sexual Bill of Rights in which they state that children should have a: 'choice of a sex partner: every child has the right to loving relationships, including sexual, with a parent, sibling, or other responsible adult or child, and shall be protected and aided in doing so by being provided with contraceptives and aids to prevent venereal disease' (cited in O'Carroll, 1980: 112). To many people, the transgression of the incest taboo would be unacceptable, and yet nowhere in his otherwise well-written tract does O'Carroll deal with this head-on. The incest taboo is universal, and its purpose is to foster exogamy and the building of cooperative societies and worlds. Incest reduces, rather than expands, kinship ties and support groups. In a modern, **capitalist** society, perhaps this matters less, but incest taboos are fundamental, and it is no wonder that many people will balk at this suggestion; it is telling that O'Carroll offers no counter arguments.

A sexual orientation?

We started by asking whether or not paedophilia is a sexual orientation. One of the ways that groups like PIE were able to get the backing of groups like Liberty was because they framed their cause as one of minority rights. Aligned to the **LGBT** + cause, PIE supported gay rights and claimed to be supported by pro-gay rights groups, such as the Gay Liberation Front, MIND and the Albany Trust (a specialist counselling and psychotherapy charity, focusing on a positive approach to sexuality and relationships). Many gay activists were horrified that the PIE had become allied with them; to say that paedophilia was like homosexuality was an outrage, they argued. One response to O'Carroll's plea for a radical politics of paedophilia is that paedophilia is not a sexuality. It is a condition, or a vice; something that must be overcome, or treated, but not legitimised. What do you think?

Michael C. Seto (2012: 232) has given some thought as to whether or not paedophilia is a sexual orientation, defining a sexual orientation as the 'directions of a … person's sexual thought, fantasies, urges, arousal, and behaviour'. He argues that sexual orientation is established by early age of onset; by the expression of sexual and romantic desire; and by being stable and not altering over time. He finds that paedophiles do report a paedophilic sexual expression that is akin to a sexual orientation, but that one of the problems with this is that paedophilia arouses such strong sentiment against it, that it is 'unlikely to ever be accepted' (Seto, 2012: 234). Instead, given that paedophilia might be a sexual orientation, he argues that it is one that should be met with more compassion and understanding – even tolerance – than aggression. Do you agree that we should be more tolerant towards paedophiles? Or do you think that the social hatred of paedophiles serves an important purpose? If so, what might that be? And why do we need it?

In 2005, a German project called Prevention Project Dunkelfeld was launched. It operates on the basis that paedophilia is a sexual orientation, but that the sexual abuse of children is a choice. The Berlin-based project targets men and women who have a sexual desire for children but who are not registered paedophiles who have been convicted of sex crimes. They are known as existing in the 'dunkelfeld' or 'dark field'; an obscured figure of sexual child abusers who have not been reported to the authorities (Beier, 2018: 1065). In 2017, 8,479 people applied to be treated by the Dunkelfeld project. Of these, 1,418 received treatment (Beier, 2018: 1066). Through therapy, participants in the project learn 'impulse control by using cognitive-behavioural techniques, sexology concepts, and pharmaceutical options' (Beier, 2018: 1066). Analysing the project, Klaus M. Beier suggests that preventative projects that help people who want to avoid becoming criminals because of their sexual orientation, are more likely to be effective in the long run than those which stigmatise by criminal prosecution after the fact. But he notes that this is also only possible in the context of a jurisdiction that does not have compulsory reporting laws around paedophilia. In the USA, India and Canada, it is mandatory to report paedophiles to the authorities. In Germany, where it is not, paedophiles can benefit from the confidentiality of the Dunkelfeld treatment to better manage their sexual desires. Note that this also marks a shift away from thinking about crime and **deviance** through the criminal justice system and towards **a public health** perspective.

BOX 12.5

- What are the positives and negatives of an approach like Dunkelfeld?
- Do you think this sort of therapy-based intervention could perhaps replace imprisonment for paedophiles who are convicted?
- Can you think of any other paedophile treatments that you are aware of, or that you think might work?

Even if we understand paedophilia as a sexual orientation and we try to treat it as such, it must be noted that it is always an adult's expression of desire, and this one-sidedness is part of its problem. Though O'Carroll's (1980) text cites examples of children who give accounts of entering into rewarding and desired sexual relationships with adults, even if we were to hold that this was possible, there is as yet no way to adequately theorise and understand child sexual attraction to adults, to examine what forms this might take, or, indeed, if this can be understood as a consensual and wanted sexual expression at all (see Flanagan, 2014; Plummer, 1991).

Contemporary responses to sexual offences against children

In recent years – and certainly since public awareness about sexualised grooming and child sex trafficking gangs has increased – public policy responses to the problems of child sex abuse have developed relatively rapidly. Sylvia Kierkegaard's (2008) overview of international legal responses to child sexual exploitation reveals the extent to which the Internet in particular has facilitated sexual violence against children. Between 2017 and 2018 in England and Wales, police recorded more than 9,000 child sexual offences that had an online element. Child sex crimes with an online element made up 16 per cent of the total number of recorded child sexual offences (NSPCC, 23 January 2019).

Legislation has been created by the EU, the UN and the USA to protect children from sexual exploitation; to make explicit images of children (sometimes referred to as child pornography) illegal; and to criminalise the sexual exploitation of children for financial gain. In 2006, the Child Exploitation and Online Protection Command (CEOP) was created to protect children in England and Wales from malicious online activity by adults seeking to exploit them sexually. Similar official bodies, including End Child Prostitution, Child Pornography, and Trafficking of Children for Sexual Purposes (ECPACT) in the USA, and the Amendments to the Penal Code in Singapore in September 2007, include a grooming provision that would make it an offence to meet or travel to meet a minor under 16 years of age after sexual grooming (Ministy of Home Affairs, Bill No. 38/2007, 2007). However, these laws operate differently in different national contexts. We talked more about grooming in Chapter 7, so we finish this chapter by considering international responses to other (non-grooming) online child sex crimes.

Explicit images of children

For much anti-pornography legislation, a child is defined as someone under the age of 18. Producing, procuring, distributing and possessing explicit images of children are illegal. Different countries can use various *exclusions* to permit some pornography featuring children; for instance, if the actors have reached the age of consent in that country. This exclusion creates one of the problems that law enforcers might encounter when attempting to tackle the distribution of explicit images of children. According to Kierkegaard (2008: 53), the majority of pornography is produced in Russia and the USA, which means that people in those European countries that are signatories to the EU legislation on pornography may still be able to access pornography that is illegal in their country of residence, and the place they are consuming that porn. This point is particularly pertinent in light of data from the website *Pornhub*, which revealed that the term 'teen' is consistently one of the most popular search terms, across geographical locations (Pegg, 2016).

Some may question the 'harms' of witnessing child pornography. After all, the viewer is not themselves hurting a child through sexual activity. However, as Yaman Akdeniz (2016) outlines, explicit images or video of a child create a permanent record of sexual violence and abuse that an actual child has experienced. As we noted in Chapter 11, once deposited on the Internet it is there forever and can be seen by anyone. The creation and viewing of such content support child trafficking, paedophile rings and the grooming of children. Furthermore, there is a connection between viewing online images of child sexual abuse and committing sexual violence against children in the offline world (Babchishin et al., 2015).

Virtual rape

Pornography that features simulations of children, or digitally modified pictures of children's faces imposed onto adult bodies (realistic images of non-existent children), are also criminalised. Similarly, written pornographic stories featuring sex with children are prohibited in some states, though not everywhere.

There is a concern over cybersex with fake children. We deal more explicitly with cybersex in Chapter 11, but here it is worth considering the example that Kierkegaard gives (2008: 44); so-called 'age play' in virtual worlds such as *Second Life* in which adults can play characters as children in order to enter into paedophilic relationships within the game. It is true that games like *Second Life* are much less widely played than they used to be, but Kierkegaard's thesis is still worth considering, perhaps in the context of more contemporary role-player games. Is the rape of avatars of children in games like *Second Life* something that should be taken seriously by law enforcers? The Criminal Justice and Public Order Act 1994 that operates in England and Wales criminalises 'images ... which appear to be a photograph' and other 'pseudo-images'. As with other parts of the EU, virtual images of children being raped are illegal.

BOX 12.6

- What is, do you think, the harm of pornography that depicts sex acts with children who do not exist?
- Do you think that pornography featuring children under the age of 18 but over the age of consent should be legal?
- Are there any political or practical objections that you can think of regarding these laws?
- Should it be illegal for sexual engagement with children to be represented in computer games where adults create avatars of children?
- What social harm do you think there might be in people having virtual sex with virtual children?

Due to limited space, we are not able to explore the numerous issues that surround explicit images of a child, including the wider social implications and victimisation that come from such visual media. If this is an area you are interested in exploring further, we recommend you take a look at the work of Akdeniz (2016) and Max Taylor and Ethel Quayle (2003). We discuss issues related to pornography in general in more depth in Chapter 13.

Child sexual exploitation

As noted above, in the UK we do not use the phrase 'child **prostitution**' anymore. The terminology implies that children choose to be sex workers or prostitutes, when in fact it is now becoming more readily accepted that children who are sex workers are usually girls who are being exploited, either by their family, friends or a boyfriend. These children are, instead, said to be sexually exploited. In 2012, the Department for Justice in the USA reported that there were 100,000 children being sexually exploited, of whom some were as young as 9 years old (Frundt, 2005; Shared Hope, 2012). Moreover, the Department of Justice found that 55 per cent of respondents to their survey had been placed in detention for offences related to their sexual exploitation, so that rather than receiving support as victims of sexual exploitation, they are simply taken out of it by being locked up (Shared Hope, 2012: 22). They also note that some children do not recognise that they are in an exploitative situation, and many girls who are exploited believe their abuser to be their boyfriend, or to have their best interests at heart (Shared Hope, 2012: 26).

In 2011, CEOP published a report that countered dominant narratives. At the time, the police and social services had a tendency to consider that children who were prostitutes were troubled children who had chosen to make this lifestyle choice. Until 2011, children who were being sexually exploited by their friends or family went largely unnoticed because their other disruptive behaviours suggested to school and to social workers that they were simply troublemakers.

Instead, the CEOP report stated that children who are runaways, or truants, or, who use drugs and alcohol might also be being sexually exploited. CEOP reported that few police forces or children's services kept records of suspected instances of child trafficking, grooming and exploitation. As a result, child sexual exploitation in the UK had continued largely unnoticed. Instead, children who are being sexually exploited might find themselves being harassed or arrested by the police for the anti-social behaviours associated with sexual exploitation that they are involved with. We explored more of this in Chapter 7.

BOX 12.7

- What do you think might be appropriate responses to help children who have been sexually exploited?
- What support groups or agencies should be involved?
- What might be the challenges of supporting a child in this situation?

Summary

Sex crimes committed against children are multiple and varied, and committed by people in their families, people in their neighbourhoods, people whom they are friends with, and people whom they meet online as well as, rarely, complete strangers. Sometimes children are sexually abused by paedophiles, sometimes by adults who are not paedophiles, sometimes they are the abusers. In this chapter, we have seen that while children are certainly more vulnerable than most adults in matters of sexual abuse, they can also be agentic in their sexual expression.

We have seen how the context of the age of a child can affect how their sexual behaviour, or their experience of sexual abuse, is encountered. Different ages of sexual consent, different definitions of what counts as a 'child', different rights and exceptions (in the context of child pornography, for instance, or child marriage) in different countries make it difficult to determine what we are talking about when it comes to crimes and what should be done in response to these crimes.

The dynamics of suspected sexual abuse against children are also not clear cut. Certainly, children are more vulnerable than adults to sexual, physical and emotional abuse because they are learning to live in the world and have an evolving sense of sexuality and desire. But children develop at different rates and can experience sexual arousal and pleasure, even at very young ages. Contemporary social and political approaches which attempt to address child sexual abuse do not, generally, take these elements into consideration. This can result in the criminalisation of children's sexual practices. The contemporary construction of children as innocent, naïve and in need of protection contributes to this. Part of the reason why there is this anxiety about the expression of sexual desire in children is because of the need to control the population, and to police sexual expression in ways that manage who has sex, how they do it and whether they are deviant or not (remember Gayle Rubin's (1984) hierarchy of sexual practice in Chapter 1). The construction of childhood as sexless (Ariès, 1960), or the repression of sexual expression, is one of the ways in which this happens (Foucault, 1998[1976]). We need to continue the work of problematising the way in which we think about this in our study of what should be criminalised, and what should not be, when it comes to children and sex.

Review questions

- How should the sexuality and sexual expression of children be controlled?
- Why do you think that the sexuality of children is something that causes so much anxiety?
- Are sex crimes perpetrated against children worse than sex crimes perpetrated against adults? Give reasons for your answer.
- At what age should children start learning about sexual relationships in school? What sort of information do you think it would be appropriate to give different age groups?

Other chapters that this links to

Chapter 3 (Sex and crime in time and space)
Chapter 4 (Consent and its discontents)
Chapter 5 (Sex and institutional cultures of abuse)
Chapter 7 (Sexual exploitation and the State)
Chapter 11 (Digital sex)

13

Illegal representations

The purpose of this chapter is to examine recent debates surrounding 'extreme pornography'. This includes imagery that 'is grossly offensive, disgusting or otherwise of an **obscene** character' and which realistically depicts acts that appear to threaten a person's life or threaten 'serious injury to a person's anus, breasts or genitals' (Criminal Justice and Immigration Act (CJIA) 2008, s63). In unpacking this, we consider how pornographic imagery has changed from the late 1800s through to the twenty-first century. We then take a step back further to think about representations of the body itself. We explore how the nude/naked body has been represented in art (and, as we shall see, non-art). Doing so allows us to think about the ways in which the body has been rendered 'obscene'. We then apply this thinking to our main case study: the Criminal Justice and Immigration Act 2008. This particular Act responded to societal concerns about 'extreme pornography'. As we see in this chapter, it is useful to examine legislative changes surrounding 'obscene' material as these give us an insight into a society's notion of what should – or should *not* – be representable. We will be building upon ideas and themes from Chapter 4 in relation to consent, Chapter 9 where we discussed risk and sex, and Chapter 11 where we discussed sex and the digital world.

By the end of this chapter, you will understand more about:

- representations of the body and how we might differentiate between the 'naked' and the 'nude'
- what it means to look at bodies in 'states of excess'
- how conceptions of the body and representations of sexually violent acts have changed in the digital era
- how the themes you have addressed so far in this book play out in the context of (illegal) representations.

In March 2020, the news site Vox published the starkly titled article 'The porn we see – and sex we have – is influenced by the adult industry's biggest spenders' (Hay, 16 March 2020). The piece goes on to describe the ways in which a 'freemium' economic model has radically changed the production of pornography. It links to a further article ('My stepdad's huge data set') that quotes the CFO of Evil Angel, a production company, describing the industry moving from 'a perfect one-to-one' relationship with a consumer to one where 'now it's probably 10,000 to one, or something' (Turner, 1 January 2019). To put this differently, there has been a shift and splintering within the audience. For every one customer that pays for pornography, there are – potentially – thousands of consumers that do not. The thesis of the article is that the producers follow the demands of the *customer*. The content that is produced is effectively dictated by the small number of people that will pay. In the last five years, this has led to the rise of particular trends, for example that of 'family role-play content' (read, simulated incest). Kal Raustiala and Christopher Sprigman (2019), in their analysis of 'data-driven creativity', describe the rise of both digital distribution and free content as fundamentally altering the production model. In the same way in which the music industry sees streaming as a supplement to its principal revenue streams coming from merchandising and live events, so pornography has seen its model shift. They describe how MindGeek – the parent company of Pornhub, as well as numerous major pornographic production studios – 'has leveraged streaming data to not only organise and suggest content to consumers but even to shape creative decisions' (Raustiala and Sprigman, 2019: 101). This, for them, is the 'second digital disruption' as user data is harvested in order to shape 'content promotion, aggregation, dissemination, and investment' (Raustiala and Sprigman, 2019: 103).

This, then, is our point of departure. In Chapter 11, we explored the ways in which the Internet has facilitated harassment and abuse. What do troubling representations of sex and **sexuality** look like in the digital era? Here, we will focus on changing perceptions of the body and how they relate to notions of transgression. Later in the chapter, we will look at changes to legislation relating to obscenity and how representations of certain acts have been deemed to be obscene. Exploring these points will allow us to unpack the debates relating to what material should – or should not – be considered illegal. For the purposes of this chapter, we are not going to take a position in relation to pornography in and of itself. We will set out – briefly – some of the stances it engenders. There are writers who consider it to be a clear social problem that leads to violence against women (MacKinnon, 1989). Others see it as a creative art form that provides a space for marginal sexualities (McNair, 2013). We are not aiming to push you towards one or other of these conclusions. Rather, we will ask readers to interrogate their own stance on this and related issues.

Our interest lies in unpacking Peter Stallybrass and Allon White's (1986: 5) notion that '[w]hat is socially peripheral may be symbolically central'. In other words, if we take pornography (and, as we develop later, 'extreme pornography') as 'socially peripheral', but still something that is created and consumed, what questions does it pose about matters that are central to a society? To paraphrase the Vox headline, how might the porn we see change the sex we have and the relationships we have with one another? What are the cultural and social lines that define transgression and how might these have been problematised in the digital era? To unpack these questions, it is useful to first go back and consider the earliest depictions of sex and the moving image.

'Stag films', so-labelled by the New York Society for the Suppression of Vice, were first shown in brothels and small clubs in the early 1900s (Slade, 1984). These were the first on-screen depictions of heterosexual intercourse and would be joined by depictions of homosexual intercourse in the 1920s. Although, as Joseph Slade (1984: 150) states, the latter did not prove popular since 'homoeroticism distressed these viewers'. The physical delicacy of the film itself means that few of these early reels exist today. As film technology changed over the twentieth century, various formats were used to capture sex on-screen. These were then played in homes and in individual cabinets in sex shops (8mm), as well as pornographic cinemas (16mm and 35mm). Betamax and VHS cassettes would join them in the 1970s, which meant that pornographic films were more easily played in the home. One curious note is that while videocassettes could easily be reproduced and distributed in comparison to the earlier reels of film, the number of productions diminished between 1972 (120) and 1984 (45) (Slade, 1984). Up until the 1960s, the stag film was black and white, silent and 12 minutes long at most (Slade, 2006). Prior to 1965, only five had sound and four were shot in colour. We can compare that to Pornhub's self-reported figures: in 2019 alone, there were 6.83 million uploads, consisting of 1.36 million hours of content. That equates to 169 *years* of content.

Reacting to the pornographic industry

BOX 13.1

In 2017, the journalist Jon Ronson (perhaps best known as author of *The Psychopath Test*) released a seven-part podcast series entitled *The Butterfly Effect* (www.youtube.com/watch?v=mb7lzLmNRs0). In the series, he explores the effect that the explosive growth of free streaming sites, such as Pornhub, have had on the pornographic film industry. He also speaks with 'customs producers' who make bespoke films for individual customers, as well as the users of life-like sex dolls. As with this chapter, Ronson does not take a pro- or anti-pornography stance. We recommend that you listen to this series and consider the following:

- What is *your* reaction to hearing these stories?
- Does it change your viewpoint concerning the producers or consumers of pornography?

McNair's (2013) text *Porno? Chic!* points to the contemporary proliferation of pornography and identifies it as a movement from a 'once heavily stigmatised and marginalised cultural form' to one that is 'not only more plentiful, and more visible, but also fashionable'. That said, the 'pornification' or 'pornographication' of culture has also been identified by 'Christian activists, neo-con commentators, and moral lobby groups alike' as one of the 'mix of "terrors" assailing modern society' (Attwood and Smith, 2010: 184).

It is intimately tied up with questions of 'moral, ethical and political **dis-courses** on **public health** and cultural well-being' (Hines and Kerr, 2012: 5). Writing in 1984, at the time of large-scale distribution via VHS cassette but also spiralling production costs and a reduced number of productions, Slade (1984: 162–3) suggested that '[as] producers of pornographic features aim at a degree of respectability, and as increasingly middle-**class** audiences demand more elaborate plots, directors will doubtless steal from a popular culture already schooled in violence'. We might wonder at the extent to which the growth in pornography has responded to the centrality of violence in popular culture in those intervening 35 years.

Questions relating to the depiction of sexualised violence in particular have been brought into vivid focus with the ongoing debates surrounding 'extreme pornography'. Feona Attwood and Clarissa Smith (2010) discuss it in relation to the apparent mainstreaming of pornography. As they state:

> in the context of this new visibility and accessibility of sex media and the broad-ening out of the meanings associated with sex, the extreme porn debate has worked as a way of rearticulating the divide between obscene and on/scene. As some images and practices previously associated with porn and obscenity become recategorized as chic, cool or unremarkable, others are regulated to the realm of the taboo. And increasingly, obscenity is refigured. (Attwood and Smith, 2010: 186)

Let us unpack this a little more. The definition of 'extreme pornography' used here is derived from phrasing used in the Criminal Justice and Immigration Act 2008. It is defined – in part – by representations of acts that appear to be life-threatening or are likely to result in serious, disabling injury. This includes either real or simulated acts such as strangulation. Attwood and Smith make use here of Linda Williams' (1989/1999) dichotomy of obscene and on/scene. Obscenity is that 'deserving to be kept out of public sight' (1989/1999: 282). On/scenity, by contrast, is centrally concerned with the visible: 'the gesture by which a culture brings on to the public scene the very organs, acts, "bodies and pleasures" that have heretofore been designated ob-off-scene, that is, as needing to be kept out of view' (1989/1999: 282). Relatedly, Laura Nead (1992: 25) suggests that the etymology of 'obscene' may be related to 'scena': 'what is off, or to one side of the stage, beyond presentation'. This reading delineates the representable and the unrepresentable. When thinking about depictions of the body in 'art', the obscene body is non-art and, as such, has no cultural merits. It is – in this sense – worthless. It has an 'absence of artistic value'. Further, it has the 'potential to pervert, debase or defile' (Nead, 1992: 90). So, this suggests that the obscene should be outside of representation. It cannot be shown.

Thus, Attwood and Smith (2010) propose that the mainstreaming of pornography has realigned the obscene in relation to depictions of sex. The explicitness that once defined this particular type of the obscene is now – to a greater or lesser extent – accepted. It has become on/scene. It has been brought out into the public scene. Contra Williams' suggestion that 'obscenity' – which used to be 'locked up and kept hidden off/scene – is no longer possible', Attwood and Smith (2010) suggest that it has been re-configured. Obscenity and sex, then, are no longer concerned with the explicit exposure of the body and associated acts since they have been rendered 'chic, cool or unremarkable' (2010: 186). The purported pornification of culture has normalised them and brought them within the mainstream of representation. Rather, the focus now rests upon 'perversity' and what has been labelled 'extreme'.

As we shall see, legislation has established a line – one that is somewhat porous and ill-defined – between representations that are normal and those that are deemed illegitimate or perverse. Judith Butler (1993; cited by Wilkinson, 2011: 494) frames this as the production of 'a domain of excluded and delegitimated "sex"'. So, that which is 'perverse' has been labelled as 'extreme'. However, the prefix 'extreme' is a loose one. It can just as easily be used as an umbrella term by anti-pornography campaigners as it can by producers to entice consumers with new, as yet unseen, transgressions or taboos. That said, this can also be viewed as part of a trend that Williams (1991: 2) astutely identified: 'pornography is today more often deemed excessive for its violence than for its sin'.

If we are to follow Slade's (1984) reading of the changing nature of the 'stag', as outlined above, then the pornification of culture has seen pornography adopting the violent underpinnings of that culture. This has been exacerbated by a move to the digital. To reiterate Stallybrass and White's (1984: 5) observation that '[w]hat is socially peripheral may be symbolically central', it is valuable to explore this 'extreme' edge of a cultural phenomenon in order to access that which lies at the culture's centre. To do so, we will first examine representations of the body itself and how it has been rendered ob-off-scene. Further, we will consider how innovations in the digital era have changed representations of the body. Finally, in unpacking these, we can apply this understanding to the body that has been subjected to sexual violence in 'extreme pornography'.

The body

In our bid to understand how the body has been deemed to be obscene or taboo, it is instructive to briefly consider a few key ways in which the 'body' has been subject to a look and, in part, defined by that gaze. As Ann Cahill (2000: 47) frames it, the body is 'far from being in any sense natural or primary'. Rather, it is always and forever subject to the competing discourses that shape it. Philip Carr-Gomm (2010: 11), for example, outlines the various 'contradictions and paradoxes' in his colourful exploration of 'nakedness': 'In religion nakedness can signify shamefulness and a lust that must be conquered, or it can symbolise innocence, a lack of shame and even a denial of the body. In the political sphere, nakedness can symbolise raw **power** and authority, or vulnerability and enslavement'. If we take a Foucaultian approach that envisages the body as being discursively produced and subject to differing modalities of power and desire, it is important to note that this does not mean that the 'body is wholly or predictably determined' (Cahill, 2000: 47). The body can also be a site of resistance to these dominant discourses. Power itself is diffuse and so 'its effects are scattered and uneven with regard to individual bodies' (Cahill, 2000: 47).

One way to initially unpack this notion is to consider the way in which the naked and nude body have been separated. Nead (1992) begins her analysis of this dichotomy by using Kenneth Clark's (1956) text *The Nude* as her jumping-off point. Clark's book investigates the 'nude' in art from the ancient world through to twentieth-century modernism. Of course, a key subject within the history of **Western** art is the nude. More specifically, it is the female nude. Simply put, 'the female nude connotes "Art"' (Nead, 1992: 1). The naked body, by contrast, is a figure of vulnerability, 'huddled and defenceless' (Nead, 1992: 14). The nude is an abstraction. It is 'the body in representation' (Nead, 1992: 14). To move from naked to nude is to move from 'the actual to the ideal' (Nead, 1992: 14). It is also typically the *female* nude that is subject to this evaluative gaze and consideration (and, as Nead highlights, it is often a *male* viewer that does the looking). Alternatively, we can draw upon another art critic, John Berger, in framing this discussion. For Berger (1972; cited in Carr-Gomm, 2010: 8), '[t]o be naked is to be oneself. To be nude is to be seen by others and yet recognised for oneself. A naked body has to be seen as an object in order to become nude'. A further way of framing the nude in art is that it is to be the subject of contemplation. If it enflames the passions too greatly, it cannot be art. Indeed, it tips into obscenity. When an image prompts an 'incentive to action', it is no longer to be considered art, becoming pushed into the 'corrupted domain of documentary, propaganda [or] pornography' (Nead, 1992: 27).

Let us consider how representations of the female and male nude have been differentiated. Again, we owe a debt to Nead's analysis. She highlights da Vinci's *Vitruvian Man*. You will recall that it depicts the artist, his arms outstretched. His anatomical proportions are encircled. He is captured within and defined by squares and circles. The artistic representation of 'man' is co-mingled with the geometric precision of lines and curves. This is male as culture and rationality intertwined. The female nude is juxtaposed against this. Here, the female represents 'nature and physicality' (Nead, 1992: 18).

This dichotomy is well illustrated by the *cuirasse ésthetique*. A cuirass is a piece of armour that shields the torso. An anatomical cuirass is such an armour, but fashioned to resemble an idealised torso. As such, this 'muscle architecture' of the armour provides an heroic rendering of the male form. Clark's (1956) reading of *cuirasse ésthetique* separates the interior and the exterior; it both contains the body and projects a message of strength. Both elements suggest a sense of control, a mastery of both within and without. Nead, using Klaus Theweleit's (1989, cited in Nead, 1992) analyses of the German Freikorps (irregular military units of the eighteenth through to the early twentieth centuries), suggests a somewhat different differentiation of interior and exterior states. Here the idealised torso is a cage containing a bestial masculine nature. It recognises that primitive interior state, but also offers a sense of control such that the individual will not be taken over by it. The muscle architecture of the hardened male body also acts as a repudiation of a female form that was perceived as 'soft, fluid and undifferentiated' (Nead, 1992: 17). So, the hard torso is a rejection of the female and a means to tap into, yet also control, the bestial and primitive masculine. As Nead (1992: 17–18) astutely states, this places the idealised form of the *cuirasse ésthetique* in a somewhat different light: 'It begins to speak of a deep-seated fear and disgust of the female body and of femininity within **patriarchal** culture and of a construction of masculinity around the related fear of the contamination and dissolution of the male ego.'

Again, this recalls the contradictions and paradoxes elicited by the body. As Carr-Gomm (2010) succinctly puts it, the body can be prison or temple, condemned or reified. This ambivalence is well illustrated by the ways in which we look at the body.

BOX 13.2

Considering the 'nude'

Guerrilla Girls is an anonymous group of feminist activist artists. In the mid-1980s, the Girls carried out a survey of the artworks displayed in the Metropolitan Museum of Art in New York. In 1989, they produced the artwork titled *Do women have to be naked to get into the Met. Museum?* The artwork depicted a female nude with their trademark guerrilla mask, with the statement that '[l]ess than 5 per cent of the artists in the Modern Art Sections are women, but 85 per cent of the nudes are female' (Tate, n.d.).

You might have seen nudes in paintings, statues or photographic art pieces if you have visited a museum or an art gallery. Was there a **gender** disparity in the nudes that you saw? How were the subjects of these representations presented?

The gaze

As alluded to above, Clark's (1956) reading of 'the nude' as 'art' is often premised upon a female nude and a male viewer. T.J. Clark (1980; cited in Nead,
1992: 16) offers a persuasive alternative take on the naked/nude duality where
the nude 'is a picture for men to look at, in which Woman is constructed as
an object of someone's desire'. Laura Mulvey's (1975) 'Visual pleasure and
narrative cinema' is the key text in unpacking the notion of the male gaze in
specific relation to film. Mulvey describes the way in which the **'gendered
scopic regime'** governs the way audiences respond to on-screen images.
Specifically:

> the spectator in the theater is made to identify with the male look, because the
> camera films from the optical, as well as the libidinal, point of view of the male
> character. There are thus three levels of the cinematic gaze – camera, character,
> and spectator – objectifying the female character and turning her into a specta-
> cle. (Smelik, 2016; cited in Nurik, 2018: 537)

These three levels of the gaze ensure that the audience perceives the action
on-screen through the lens of an active male and a passive female. To put this
slightly differently, the audience member sees through the point of view (PoV)
of the male character and comes to identify with *him* as they observe and
objectify the female character.

To provide a comparatively recent example of this, we can apply this idea
to the depiction of Harley Quinn in the film *Suicide Squad* (Atlas, 2016).
Quinn is subject to these three layers of the male cinematic gaze. The camera looks at her in a costume of tight top and hot pants. The male characters
regard this hyper-sexualised cartoon-like figure. The audience see her
through these gendered lenses. She is objectified for the entertainment of
the audience. She is made into a spectacle. This disparity in the gaze also
extends to the ways in which female and male nudity is received in mainstream cinema.

With particular reference to the certification body the Motion Picture
Association of America (MPAA), Nurik (2018) makes the observation that
notions of the male gaze ensure that male and female nudity lead to differing film classifications. Simply put, female nudity 'is commodified and
visually subjected for the purposes of profit' (Nurik, 2018: 538). Male
nudity, by contrast, is 'anxiety-producing' since it problematises 'traditional' senses of the active male, passive female. Depictions of female
sexual pleasure are also seen as challenging and have seemingly proved
difficult for the MPAA. In 2010, for example, the film *Blue Valentine*
(Incentive, 2010) was initially given an NC-17 rating as it included a

sequence depicting cunnilingus. An NC-17 rating ('No One 17 and Under Admitted') can prove costly for a film since many cinema and rental chains will not show films associated with explicit sexual content. Nurik (2018) cites the film critic Mary Ann Johnson as arguing that 'watching a woman being murdered is less objectionable than watching a woman have an orgasm'. Indeed, if we think about the ubiquity of naked female corpses in popular television crime drama (from *CSI* to *Silent Witness*) in comparison to the dearth of depictions of female sexual pleasure, we can begin to see the validity in Johnson's claim. In death, as in life, these figures are objectified, their **agency** removed and they are left 'interchangeable with other objects' (Koppelman, 2005).

So, thus far, we have explored ways of looking at the 'nude' that are inherently gendered, as well as gendered 'scopic regimes' that govern the nature of that look. Before we engage more fully with notions of obscenity, it is valuable to briefly return to the 'classical body' since it is that which – by juxtaposition – helps to define the 'obscene' body.

The obscene body

As Nead (1992) argues, it is the female 'nude' that has established particular ways of looking at and contemplating art. The nude can be juxtaposed with the obscene. The former is to be contemplated in stillness, whereas the latter arouses. This is one way of framing a dichotomy of 'art' and 'non-art'. The nude – the body in 'art' – can be juxtaposed with the fleshy body that elicits an unruly response. Stallybrass and White (1986), similarly, use the figure of the classical statue to explore the notion of transgression. They begin by describing the experience of regarding a classical statue. It is not just that we gaze upon the figure. We gaze *up* at them as they are often physically positioned above the viewer. It is 'the radiant centre of a transcendent individualism' (Stallybrass and White, 1986: 21). Imagine regarding such a statue. There is the gaze upwards, the regard of the cool surface. There is nothing of the physicality of the body; the heat, the smell, its fleshy presence. Stallybrass and White (1986: 22) get to the point: '[t]he classical statue has no openings or orifices'. The grotesque body, by contrast, is teeming. For example, we might point to the groping, grasping and feculent bodies in the paintings of either Bosch or Bruegel. They are multiple where the classical body is singular. The grotesque body gapes and is protuberant. It sits in contrast to the smooth and sealed classical body. In this way, 'the grotesque body stands in opposition to the bourgeois individualist conception of the body which finds its image and legitimation in the classical' (Stallybrass and White, 1986: 22). Primacy is placed on the fleshy materiality of the body, its 'corpulent excess' as a means to 'represent cosmic, social, topographical and linguistic elements of the world' (Stallybrass and White, 1986: 8).

This takes us to representations of bodily excess. Williams (1991: 4), following Carol Clover's (1987) work on the horror genre, defines the 'body' genres as capturing the body in 'intense sensation or emotion'. This well describes the body as seen in pornography, as well as horror and melodrama. Within these genres, we see the body in the midst of heightened physical states. In pornography, the body is seen as being 'beside itself' with sexual pleasure and in a state of 'ecstatic excess'. We hear 'inarticulate cries' where that excess pushes beyond and outside of language (Williams, 1991: 4). Other body genres echo this. In melodrama and horror, a body can be wracked in sadness or violently assaulted. The inarticulate cries become a sob or a scream. In relation to pornography, the body is subject to an excess of visibility. As Williams states (1989/1999), hard-core pornography has been defined by 'maximum visibility'. This returns us to the duality of the visible and the invisible, as well as to the dichotomy of art and non-art. Recall our earlier discussion that saw the separation of art from non-art as the difference between that which could be the subject of calm contemplation and that which could enflame 'base' passions. An excess of the visibility of sexual drives can be juxtaposed with 'art' that has been defined by the sublimation of those drives. That visibility of course is also directed at the (female) body. It is not simply subject to a gendered gaze, but the body itself is opened out: '[it] is examined and probed for its hidden secrets' (Nead, 1992: 97). Again, recalling the dichotomy of the closed-off classical body and the openness of the grotesque, pornography is defined by a maximum visibility: '[i]n its endless quest for clarity, **objectivity** and disclosure[, it] endlessly reinvokes that alternative, anxious sense of the female body as dark, mysterious and formless' (Nead, 1992: 98). Specifically, the history of the genre has been concerned with effects to 'overcome the anatomical invisibility of the female orgasm' (Nead, 1992: 98).

It is instructive to think of the ways in which horror and pornography, in particular, intersect in their opening of the body to a total look. Steve Jones and Sharif Mowlabocus (2009: 622), for example, comment on the '[m]ultiple representations of bodily rupture' that have 'become increasingly popular in western culture'. There is a maximum visibility of both exterior *and* interior states. We could think of the body on display (and splayed out) in so-called 'torture-porn' horror films, as well as in the autopsies of crime dramas. Indeed, the suffix '-porn' (as in torture-porn, poverty-porn, etc.) denotes 'unwanted and unwelcome excess' (Hines and Kerr, 2012: 5).

BOX 13.3

The male gaze and the body in sexualised horror

Content warning: films mentioned in this activity contain scenes of strong bloody violence and sexual violence that some of you may find disturbing. Take your time with this content and take breaks and discuss anything that comes up for you with people you trust.

We have discussed notions of the male gaze and the maximum visibility associated with the 'body genres' of both horror films and pornography. In this activity, we will ask you to compare two examples of 'rape revenge' films. These are films that take the rape of a female protagonist as their inciting incident. This is then followed by her bloody revenge on the male antagonists. Two key examples of this genre are *I Spit on Your Grave* (Barquel, 1978) and *Revenge* (M.E.S., 2017). During the mid-1980s, the former was considered suitable for prosecution under the Obscene Publications Act 1959. Its current 18 certificate UK release still has 43 seconds of cuts. According to the British Board of Film Classification, this excised material is 'potentially harmful' since it includes 'shots of nudity that tend to eroticise sexual violence and shots of humiliation that tend to endorse sexual violence by encouraging viewer complicity in sexual humiliation and rape' (BBFC, 2010). By contrast, *Revenge* uses the tropes of the rape revenge film, but attempts to invert the male gaze that is typical of the genre.

In watching these two films, consider the following:

- How are the female protagonists and male antagonists filmed?
- Is there full-frontal nudity of both male and female actors?
- Is *Revenge* successful in presenting a *female* gaze?
- Consider the ways in which the internal and external body is made open to maximum visibility.

If you wish to develop your understanding of this further, the BBFC has produced helpful case studies that unpack their certification process for particular films, including *I Spit on Your Grave* (BBFC, 2010). Likewise, Carol Clover's (1992) hugely influential *Men, Women and Chainsaws: Gender in the modern horror film* insightfully unpacks the rape revenge genre.

Jones and Mowlabocus (2009: 622) posit a range of explanations for this, including 'an ongoing alienation of the body through late **capitalist** structures of labour' or 'a reconnection with the flesh in a time of supposed virtual disembodiment'. This raises an interesting point. So far, we have been focused upon the corporeal, the physical body. We have looked at its representation in 'Art' (and non-art), as well as representations of the body in pleasure (and pain). Yet, what of the effects of that supposed virtual disembodiment? How might that change representations of the body? As Barker (2009; cited in Attwood and Smith, 2010: 181) outlines: '[s]upporters of increased regulation claim that the Internet Age has created ever more disgusting and sickening forms of pornography and make reference to what Martin Barker has termed "scary futurology" – that if we don't do something now, the decline of public morals will be terrifying.'

A counter argument could be made that there is an appeal to the 'virtual' or 'better-than-real' body. Certainly, pornography has been at the forefront of any technological innovations that seek to capture the image or improve visual fidelity. Charles Baudelaire complained in 1859 that 'photography had been coopted' by the desire to capture naked bodies (Slade, 2006: 27). In the last decade, pornographic production companies have been at the forefront of 3D, streaming and ultra-high definition image reproduction (as we saw in Chapter 11). Slade (2006: 27) does make the curious comment that 'sexuality is more stimulating when it is most technological, most divorced from "nature"'. An argument could be made that 3D, high-definition films are attempts to bridge the gap between real and reel. Yet, perhaps, there is something to Slade's point. Perhaps the Brechtian-like distancing effect alluded to here renders these representations of sexual acts all the more potent. They are, at once, more immediate, more visible. They are certainly more widespread. This is the always on-demand 'pornotopia' described by McNair (2013). It has re-aligned the 'conceptual apparatus', 'to take into account ... hitherto unavailable if not unimaginable acts' (Bradley, 2018: 456). Rebecca Saunders (2019) extends this further in considering the production of images and augmentation devices that push beyond the 'real'. Saunders (2019: 244) quotes from Wired.com – a tech website – that asked in 2006: '[i]magine what you could do with erotic entertainment if you weren't bound by the laws of physics [the limitations of gravity, proportion, body mass] [Or] the federal law that requires [age] records on every performer appearing in an adult film.'

Fourteen years later, sexually explicit machinima (CGI animation) can do precisely this. Photo-realistic pornographic deepfakes have seen celebrities' faces mapped onto pornographic footage. The boundary between the image of the body and the body of the viewer has also begun to dissolve. Kiiroo, for example, produces a range of Internet-enabled 'somatic plug-ins' that can be paired, connected via the Internet and used remotely by couples or with webcam performers. Yet, the remote Wi-Fi-enabled 'touch' of a webcam performer or the photo real is insufficient for some. As Saunders highlights, some computer-generated content providers specifically emphasise that their imagery is 'better than real': '[n]o real female can be compared to these exciting fully 3D babes who can drive you mad with stunning beauty' (Adult-Empire.com). We might wonder what Mulvey makes of this trend or how it would fold into Clark's (1956) notion of the body. Indeed, how do *we* feel about it? Is the virtual sexualised image – one that is 'better' than 'real' – more stimulating, as

Slade suggests? Does the pleasurable gaze no longer require a 'real' body as its focus?

In thinking about changing representations of the body in the digital era, we should take a step back and consider Patrick Devlin's (1965; cited in Johnson, 2010) thoughts concerning legislative responses to 'obscene' materials. The 'obscene', for Devlin, should be more than something that prompted a 'majority [to] "dislike" a practice'; rather, it must 'engender a feeling of "disgust"' (Johnson, 2010: 152). We might be reminded here of Mary Douglas's (2002[1966]) notion of disgust being associated with things that are perceived as being out of place. Cleanliness and dirtiness are determined by whether or not they are in their appropriate place. That which has been labelled as taboo is defined as symbolically dirty. For Devlin (1965), a widely held sense of disgust would indicate not simply that the act prompting this response be done in private, but also 'that they not be done at all in order to protect the moral "soul" of society from *contamination*' (emphasis added, Johnson, 2010: 152). So, that which is deemed obscene should be removed from public view *and* private action. It should be unrepresentable and rendered more than simply off-scene. Devlin (1979; cited in Johnson, 2010: 152) saw the role of law as acting 'as a gatekeeper (but not a protector) of the moral order'. One analogy posits the law as a 'valve' that adapts to society's sense of moral outrage. So, it allows new ideas as they come to be accepted, while blocking others that fall out of favour. They move in and out of place according to changing social norms.

Let us consider the difficulty in applying this to a real-world example. Bondage, domination and sadomasochism (BDSM), which we explored more fully in Chapter 9, for example, represents a challenge to societal 'norms' of sexual behaviour. As Eleanor Wilkinson (2011) puts it, pornography is typically 'heterosexist' and 'heteronormal'. However, easily accessible recording equipment, technology, and the ubiquity of digital pornography has meant that both professional and amateur productions can explore and represent marginal sexualities. These developments have, then, a 'democractizing potential' (Wilkinson, 2011: 498). Jones and Mowlabocus (2009) frame this slightly differently. They suggest that the 'valve' could be turned to highlight and exclude extreme acts, thereby creating a 'new category of generally dissident people'. For them to enjoy the extreme material became a 'politically subversive act'. Particularly with BDSM, there is a 'distinct blurring of the line between reality and fiction, and between practice and representation' (Jones and Mowlabocus, 2009: 617). It is, after all, centrally concerned with role-play. Indeed, as Susan Sontag (1981; cited in Petley, 2009: 426) described it, to be engaged in sadomasochism is to 'take part in a sexual theatre, a staging of sexuality'. The importance of role-play requires some understanding on the part of the participant or viewer of the *performance* of BDSM in order to grasp this particular text.

Yet, as Wilkinson (2011) asks, what happens when someone without that knowledge and understanding views this kind of material? Without an appreciation of these scripts, do they 'perceive it as an uncontrolled violent act?' (Wilkinson, 2011: 495). Or, should this be viewed as being indistinct and inseparable from a pornography that degrades and dehumanises? Specifically, such a viewpoint would see BDSM as another facet of a system of representation that normalises gendered violence. Attwood and Smith (2010: 180) present the counter argument that 'if concern over violence against women is what drives the impulse to legislate, that legislation should be targeting the actual practices of violence rather than representational media'. This all, of course, raises important questions about what both consent and violence *look* like. Andrew Koppelman (2005: 1641) describes the erotic as being concerned with 'primitive or powerfully self-centred urges and elevated aspirations [that] are in competition for predominance'. Sex, then, can be a demonstration of intimacy, as well as a display of 'possessiveness, hostilit[y] and humiliation' (Koppelman, 2005: 1641). The writer Lux Alptraum (2014; cited in Moorman, 2017: 704), for example, makes the important point that 'consensual sex can look violent and abusive, and abusive sex can look loving and tender' (see our discussion of the challenges of consent in Chapter 4). So, it is important not to confuse reality and representation. Jennifer Moorman (2017: 704) goes on to argue that we 'contextualize pornographic texts with the viewpoints, production practices, economic and regulating structures, and taste culture that combine to create them'. Given that, let us explore the ramifications of the 2008 Criminal Justice and Immigration Act as it sought to respond to the moral outrage surrounding 'extreme pornography'. Debates surrounding the CJIA 2008 touched upon this problem of interpreting pornographic texts. In addressing the problems associated with definition and legislation, we can trace how the Act was part of a wider regulatory history, spoke to various production practices, and both supported and conflicted with various political standpoints.

Legislation and 'extreme pornography'

The CIJA 2008 was a significant legislative response to the proliferation of what was dubbed 'extreme pornography'. It was a response to a campaign that followed the murder of Jane Longhurst by Graham Coutts in 2003. During his trial, the prosecution noted Coutts's fetish for erotic asphyxia, in addition to the 'extreme' or violent pornography that he had downloaded. These materials included simulated strangulation and rape. Jane Longhurst's mother began a campaign to shut down sites hosting this kind of violent pornographic material.

A 2006 Home Office paper – *Consultation on the Possession of Extreme Pornographic Material* – sought to gather feedback on a proposed strengthening of the law that targeted this type of imagery. At that point, the proposed offence was to include material that was pornographic, produced for the purposes of sexual arousal and was 'real' or appeared to be real – 'conveying a realistic impression of fear, violence and **harm**' (Home Office, 2006: 6). The consultation also called upon respondents to consider the legality of materials involving sexual intercourse or oral sex with an animal, sexual interference with a corpse, as well as 'acts that appear to be life threatening or are likely to result in serious, disabling injury' (Home Office, 2006: 6).

Responses – gathered from 'police forces, campaigning groups, charities, religious groups, professional bodies, government, and regulators, as well as individuals' (Home Office, 2006: 3) – were 'sharply divided'. There was either strong support or opposition. Of those in favour, some thought that the proposals should go further and cover *all* pornography. Voices in opposition raised concerns that the proposed changes represented a threat to freedom of speech. In 2007, the Ministry of Justice published a Rapid Evidence Assessment (REA) entitled *The Evidence of Harm to Adults Relating to Exposure to Extreme pornoGraphic Material*. This research was intended to 'identify, review and assess any evidence of harm associated with extreme pornographic material' (Itzin et al., 2007: 1). The researchers predominantly drew upon 'experimental' studies conducted under laboratory conditions, in addition to some non-experimental studies. Their key findings included:

> the existence of some harmful effects from extreme pornography on some who access it. These included increased risk of developing pro-rape attitudes, beliefs and behaviours, and committing sexual offences. Although this was also true of some pornography which did not meet the extreme pornography threshold, it showed that the effects of extreme pornography were more serious. Men who are predisposed to aggression, or have a history of sexual and other aggression were more susceptible to the influence of extreme pornographic material. This was corroborated by a number of different studies using different methods and different samples. (Itzin et al., 2007: iii)

Attwood and Smith (2010) were unequivocal in their critique of the REA. They questioned the methodology underpinning the empirical research that was used. They cite Jason Toynbee (2008; cited in Attwood and Smith, 2010: 175) in their rejection of the kinds of mass communication effects research utilised within the REA:

> What's wrong with effects research is that it does not acknowledge the openness of media in society, considered as a system. There is simply no way of isolating the watching of media violence among a complex of putative causes of violent behaviour among research subjects. Thus, any correlation shown

between the two (media and violence) may be contingent. More than this, even
if one were to accept a causal link there are no means to establish the direction
of causality between correlates.

The subsequent CJIA drew upon the definitions outlined in the Home Office
consultation paper. It aimed, in part, to protect the wellbeing of those performing in such productions, in addition to the wellbeing of society as a whole
(Easton, 2011). It required that the 'act in an image must be "explicit and realistic" so that a "reasonable person" seeing it would think that any person or
animal was real'; and an image must be 'grossly offensive, disgusting or otherwise of an obscene character' (Johnson, 2010: 148). These raise some interesting
points. How might we define a 'reasonable' person, particularly when confronted with such material? You will also note that there is no reference to, nor
requirement to demonstrate, harm. This posed problems for the depiction of
consensual harm. Libertarian criticisms of this aspect of the CJIA focused on
the notion that private *sexual* activity between consenting adults should not be
interfered with by governments. However, you will recall from our earlier discussion of *R v. Brown* [1993] 97 Cr App R 44 (in Chapters 4 and 9) that, at that
time, '[t]he inability to consent to acts of *violence* is well established in the
criminal law. If the activities covered by the Act are themselves unlawful, it
is not possible to consent to those activities, so by definition engaging in
them means committing a criminal offence' (our emphasis, Easton, 2011: 401).
During discussions in the House of Lords relating to *Brown*, Lord Templeman
argued, for example, that consensual torture could lead to non-consensual
torture. As Susan Easton (2011: 401) phrased Templeman's argument, society 'is entitled ... to protect itself against a cult of violence that is morally
corrupting'.

Anna Carline (2011) offered a useful critique of the CJIA. Echoing comments made earlier in this chapter, Carline highlights that a focus upon
representations of violence toward women rather than the everyday harm
enacted upon women is misplaced. In particular, if we consider that 173
women were killed in acts of intimate partner violence and abuse in the UK
in 2018, or that one in three women aged 16–59 will suffer domestic abuse in
her life, more should be done to combat violence within the domestic (BBC,
13 September 2019; Refuge, n.d.). Simply put, there should be a greater recognition that 'the law has generally been complicit in male violence against
women' (Carline, 2011: 318). Further, the element of the Act that points to the
producer's intent to sexually arouse is curious. First, as Carline (2011) notes,
the agency (indeed, the consent) of the performer is ignored in favour of trying to infer the producer's intent. If we frame this discussion in respect to
Roland Barthes's (1977) notion of the 'death of the author', the discussion
becomes nonsensical: we cannot know the producer's intent, nor can the
producer control the audience member's reaction. Different people will find

different media arousing to different extents. Contra Johnson, Carline (2011) argues that the moral judgements being applied to extreme pornography involve a re-affirmation of **heteronormative** behaviour. Yet, '[n]ot all performances of heterosexuality are considered to be culturally intelligible' (Carline, 2011: 329). As we discussed earlier, not all such performances are as easily read and understood as others. As a consequence, those that fall out of the norm risk being censored and punished.

To place the CIJA in context, it is helpful to map out what came before it. The Obscene Publications Act 1959 was used in high-profile prosecutions, such as those against the publication of D.H. Lawrence's (1971) novel *Lady Chatterley's Lover* in 1960 and the 'video nasties' campaign against violent and sexually violent films in the mid-1980s. Obscenity within the act was defined as material that 'if taken as a whole' would 'tend to deprave and corrupt persons who are likely, having regard to all relevant circumstances, to read, see or hear it' (Obscene Publications Act 1959 s1). It did allow exceptions for materials in the 'public good', in other words, those of a benefit to science, literature, art or learning. In these examples, the notion of 'taste' was fundamental to questions of obscenity.

The 1959 Act was followed in 1978 by the Protection of Children Act. This criminalised the production and distribution of indecent images of children. As Jacob Rowbottom (2018) puts it, this Act reflected broader societal concerns relating to obscenity in the late 1970s and was the product of pressure groups and moral crusaders. Here the law acted in the manner of Devlin's 'valve' as it adjusted to reflect social concerns. The subsequent 1994 Criminal Justice and Public Order Act sought to respond to advances in computing technology that facilitated the distribution of such imagery. So, where the offence in 1978 related to 'taking' an indecent image of a child, the 1994 Act amended this to include 'making' an indecent image. This, then, incorporated 'pseudo images'. In other words, it referred to images not taken with a camera but made with a computer or some other electronic device (see Chapter 11 for our discussion of this). Subsequent decisions relating to this Act found that 'intentionally storing data from the Internet constituted the "making" of an image' (Rowbottom, 2018: 13). Likewise, a Court of Appeal decision later 'found that opening an email attachment could constitute the making of an image' if the recipient knew the image to be indecent in nature (*R v. Jayson* [2002] EWCA Crim 683 at 19–20). As Rowbottom (2018: 13) notes, these decisions moved 'attention away from the producers of the illegal content to those viewing the images'. As such, this led to a net-widening and an increase in the number of people convicted. We arrive back at the 2008 CIJA. As we have seen in the legislation that preceded it, discussion flowed around notions of the public and private, and who should be its target. Johnson (2010) summarises the main concern with extreme pornography as being: (i) the risk of causing physical harm to 'performers' (thereby acting as a 'record of the sexual abuse'); (ii) as with the

REA, extreme pornography can prompt or incite violent behaviour in those that consume it; and, relatedly, (iii) it represents 'hate speech' and, as such, 'causes symbolic harm to women as a social group'. As we can see, these three elements each continue debates around public morality, individual freedoms and notions of obscenity apprehended at a societal level. We might be reminded again of Devlin (1965; cited in Johnson, 2010: 151) in stating that '[m]orality is a sphere in which there is a public interest and a private interest, often in conflict, and the problem is to reconcile the two'.

Prosecutions under the 2008 Act typically followed warrants being followed up under other legislation or where registered sex offenders' homes were entered as part of a risk assessment (McGlynn and Bows, 2019). This led them to conclude that – citing L.H. Leigh (n.d.; cited by McGlynn and Bows, 2019: 486) – prosecutions were 'neither consistent, nor coherent but adventitious'. Subsequent legislation has included the 2009 Coroners and Justice Act that introduced a new offence of possessing a 'prohibited image'. This was defined as, among other acts, one that 'is grossly offensive, disgusting or otherwise of an obscene character ... focus[ing] solely or principally on a child's genitals or anal region' (Rowbottom, 2018: 17). Rowbottom reports that this proved controversial because of the potential lack of harm suffered by the subject of the image. The 2015 Criminal Justice and Courts Act was a response to a perceived gap within the 2008 Act. It included rape pornography in the rubric of extreme pornography. This followed earlier amendments within the Scottish legal system and campaign by both Rape Crisis South London and the End Violence Against Women Coalition.

In 2014, an amendment was made to the 2003 Communications Act. The Audiovisual Media Services Regulation 2014 stated that video-on-demand services could not show the following acts as they would fall outside of the R18 classification that could be granted by the BBFC: spanking, BDSM, female ejaculation, urinating (also known as watersports), strangling, face-sitting or fisting. The latter three were claimed to be potentially life-threatening. Critics of the amendment pointed out that many of these are specifically targeted at female pleasure (Press Association, 12 December 2014). These, in turn, were relaxed in 2019. Certain violent acts can now be depicted so long as 'full and freely exercised consent' is provided and that performers do not suffer 'serious harm'. Prior to this amendment, the 2017 Digital Economy Act required 'those providing lawful adult content on a communal basis to operate a system of age verification' (Rowbottom, 2018: 22). The appointed regulator, the BBFC, has the power to block sites hosting extreme pornography. This has the potential to shift the focus of prosecution away from the consumer (or possessor) and back towards the host (the supplier). However, we might question the ease with which a regulation could combat sites operating across national boundaries and with fluid hosting capabilities. Daniel Hickin (cited in Pett, 2015: 84), writing in 2009, proposed that 'the present era represents the beginning of the end of existing nationalised forms of media censorship as we enter a period in which global culture becomes deregulated'.

BOX 13.4

Researching sexually violent material

Given Jones and Mowlabocus' (2009: 619) call for academic work to 'examine representations of degradation and humiliation, to analyse them as cultural arte-facts', we thought that it would be useful to set out the ways in which two of the authors of this textbook have examined sexually violent material. We focused upon the 'sexploitation' films of a particular genre that emerged in the late 1960s and 1970s: 'Nazisploitation'. This saw the 'women-in-prison' genre merge with the 'roughie' sex film and featured the 'repeated humiliation and degradation of women' (Serfozo and Farrell, 1996). These films – some of which are set in con-centration camps – depict eroticised and brutalised female bodies against a provocative backdrop of Nazi iconography. Several of the films that we explored (*Love Camp 7*, 1969; *SS Experiment Camp*, 1976; *Gestapo's Last Orgy*, 1977) were included in the Department of Public Prosecutions Act of 72 'video nasties' in 1983. These were felt to contravene the 1959 Obscene Publications Act. It should be noted though that one of the films within our analysis, *SS Experiment Camp* (S.E.F.I., 1976), was submitted to the BBFC in 2005 and received no cuts. As the BBFC noted in its 2005 annual report, '[d]espite the questionable taste of basing an exploitation film in a concentration camp, the sexual activity itself was consensual and the level of potentially eroticised violence, sufficiently limited'. Others remain without a UK release. In 2020, for example, *Love Camp 7* (Olympic, 1969) was refused classification for streaming. The BBFC (2020) stated: 'Because *Love Camp 7* is largely comprised of scenes of non-consensual sexual activity, including rape, presented in a manner that is intended to arouse viewers, its central concept is unacceptable and the sexually abusive material it contains too pervasive for cuts to be an effective solution.'

We first adapted Patrocini Schweickart's (1986) notion of 'androcentric read-ing strategies' (Banwell and Fiddler, 2018. Following Amy Shapiro's (2013) work, we adapted them to cinematic representations and produced 'viewing strate-gies'. Doing so allowed us to examine '[t]he eroticisation of fascism through the framing of the female body'. So, we looked at the ways in which gender and sexual agency were coded, performed and represented. In order to do so, we read the texts as they were 'not intended to be read' (Banwell and Fiddler, 2018: 13). As Schweickart (1986) put it, the female viewer has to 'read the text not as Other, but as equal to men'. And, as such, we were able to examine the ways in which the representation of both the female Nazi and the female Jewish victim either conformed to, or problematised, gendered codes.

Our second piece took a different approach (Fiddler and Banwell, 2019). Here we took Graeme Krautheim's (2009: 8) statement as our point of departure:

(Continued)

'[t]here is nothing productive about simply accusing Nazi sexploitation of being careless, **misogynist**, or historically inaccurate – such statements go without saying, and to consider the films with the hostility that they actually invite is completely counterproductive.' We were drawn towards what the 'excesses' of corporeality on-screen, as well as the spectatorial experience, can be said to do. To put this differently, what value can be ascribed to them in considering the horrors of the concentration camps? In this, we see their 'tastelessness' as important. It is the 'aesthetic vertigo' that they produce in the viewer that pushes them outside of the accepted norms of representation. This is the term Alison Young (2000) uses to describe that backward stagger and sense of dizziness caused by a 'disgusting' artwork. Focusing attention upon Andres Serrano's (1987) *Piss Christ* and Marcus Harvey's (1995) *Myra*, Young unpacks this sense of 'vertigo' as the spectator is left 'teetering on the verge of representational abyss' as the 'disgusting' artwork threatens to 'touch' the viewer (Young, 2000: 264). For some, the response within the spectator to this vertigo, prompted by the disgust, will be to see it 'expelled, outlawed and repressed' (Young, 2000: 262). Our reading is that 'aesthetic vertigo' places the artwork outside of the norm of Holocaust representation. As such, it provides a unique way of tying a *corporeal* response to a representation that moves beyond hegemonic memory. Instead, a 'transgressive' memory is produced that incorporates a bodily sense of disgust and horror.

- Which films, novels or artworks could you unpack to explore the ways in which gender and sexual **agency** are coded, performed and represented?
- Have you encountered an artwork or film that has prompted this kind of 'aesthetic vertigo'? If so, what did you feel? Did this sensation make you change your mind about the 'value' of the artwork?

Summary

In this chapter on illegal representations, we have examined how changes to legislation give us an insight into how notions of obscenity alter over time. These discussions can be placed in the context of debates surrounding representations of the 'naked' and 'nude' body itself. We have touched upon different ways in which the body has been viewed. We narrowed our focus to consider representations in 'body genres' that see the body in states of maximum visibility and excess. We then applied these understandings to unpacking legislative changes relating to obscenity and representations of sexually violent acts.

Nead, writing in 1992, described the history of pornography across the twentieth century as being one of an ever-increasing 'specialization and specification of the obscene' (1992: 92). With the rise of the digital era, we have seen an acceleration of this process. Rowbottom (2018) identifies two particular trends within recent changes to obscenity law. First, there is the narrowing of focus from a broad definition of obscenity to a smaller range of content. This has led to the 'contradiction' of more material being legally available where previously it would have been labelled obscene, yet, at the same time, 'the law has become much stricter and [is] criminalizing more people than ever' (Rowbottom, 2018: 24). There has been a shift in focus from the producer to the viewer of the content. Yet, as detailed above, recent legislation (such as the Digital Economy Act 2017) has also turned its attention to the online hosts of such material. Where does this leave us?

In writing this chapter, we find ourselves coming back to the troubling question at the heart of academic writing on pornography. Is this a question of freedom of speech or a record of abuse? Does it have a democratising effect for marginalised sexualities or is it one facet of a system that enables violence to be enacted upon the bodies of women? In 1989, Catharine MacKinnon (p. 304) wrote that pornography 'produces ... attitude changes in men, such as increasing the extent of their trivialization, dehumanization, and objectification of women'. In those intervening 30 years, how has the proliferation of pornography in the digital era changed things? An alternative position is taken up by Koppelman (2005). In this view, pornography does cause moral harm, but 'this effect is too small, its relation to any particular text too uncertain, and the benefits of censorship too speculative to justify legal intervention' (Koppelman, 2005: 1664). We find ourselves asking: does this debate simply not fit within the reductive confines of a binary position?

We would suggest that tracing legislative changes is a useful exercise. It allows us to map changing views and notions of obscenity. Fundamentally, we would echo Robert Jensen's (2007; cited in Jones and Mowlabocus, 2009) argument that, if there is increasing cruelty and violence within pornography, then this should be of academic interest. We must ask, 'why is it increasingly commonplace instead of more marginalized?' (Jones and Mowlabocus, 2009: 619). If, as Slade suggested, violence was a rarity in the early stag film, what does the proliferation of more sexually violent material in the digital era reveal about our current society?

Review questions

- How have Nead (1992) and Williams (1989/1999) defined obscenity? Can you think of examples that fit their definitions?
- How have the 'naked' and the 'nude' body been differentiated?
- How is the body subject to a 'maximum visibility' in pornography?

- If, as Stallybrass and White (1986: 5) state, '[w]hat is socially peripheral may be symbolically central', what does the Criminal Justice and Immigration Act 2008 reveal about society's concerns?

Other chapters that this links to

Chapter 4 (Consent and its discontents)
Chapter 9 (Pleasurable risk)
Chapter 11 (Digital sex)
Chapter 12 (Children, sexualisation and the law)

Part 4

Future Sex

14

The future

In this book, our aim has been to examine the contemporary state of the relationship between sex, crime and **deviance** across a range of social and temporal contexts. Now we are going to try to develop the knowledge we explored in previous chapters to think about what social, ethical and political issues related to sex and crime might be unfolding on the horizon: what does the future hold?

From Chapter 3, we have seen how law and regulation about **sexuality** and **sexual practice** have evolved through time and in response to different political contexts and geographical spaces (Ekine and Abbas, 2013; Foucault, 1998[1976]; Stychin, 1995). In other chapters, we have seen ethical issues related to childhood sexuality connect with debates around sexting, and how debates around sexting implicate how we understand contemporary digital cultures. We have seen how reproductive rights have ebbed and flowed over time, we have seen how in different national contexts they are in flux, we have also seen how disability comes to bear on all these questions; and we have seen how these issues call into question who, or what, might be human, or have **human rights**, and what it means to be human.

We have seen, therefore, that the development of theory and practice around the law, crime and sex is non-linear, not fluid nor straightforward. Where some progressive moves towards living in a more socially just and plural world happen on the one hand (for instance, the decriminalisation of abortion in New Zealand in 2019), they are just as likely to be accompanied by regressive developments elsewhere (for instance, the restrictions on abortion in some 30 states of the USA, also implemented in 2019). The future will not simply be utopian or dystopian.

In this chapter, we try to look forward, heeding our knowledge of the past and present to ask questions about what might be important, or necessary, issues to address in the future. Of course, none of us has a crystal ball. We can speculate about what the big questions will be, but we cannot know for certain. And each of us, including you, will have different ideas about what is on the horizon.

Up until now, as authors of this book we have chosen to speak with a united voice about the topics we have tackled together. For this chapter, we have decided to try something different, because it is a different sort of chapter. Instead of one voice, you will read five voices as we each advance a different perspective on what will matter in the future and what is to come. We do this to remind you that there is a lot of uncertainty about criminological knowledge in general and that different perspectives on the same problem can sometimes yield interesting and thought-provoking alliances. We also ask you to think about your own vision for the future, and where you think your efforts will need to be to contribute to creating the world you want to see, when it comes to sex and crime.

By the end of this chapter, you will understand more about:

- ongoing and emerging ethical issues in criminology and sexuality studies
- how ideas connect together to produce different outcomes
- how different analyses bring different issues to the fore
- how to think creatively and make connections.

Here goes!

Alex's vision of the future

Advances in the development of sex aids have seen a plethora of devices developed for sexual pleasure, to be used alone or with partners. These include anything from sex dolls, to vibrators, to teledildonics (remote control vibrators), but what I am going to talk about here are sex robots: machines that are often created in human form with sexual functionality and which, for the most part, are interactive (Levy, 2009). The reason why sex robots are of particular interest to our study of criminology is because of the ethical issues that their use implies, and the way in which they might be brought into conversation with existing crime and justice issues, including sex crimes and **consent.**

- In 2010 Roxxxy, a full-sized sex robot, was unveiled at an adult entertainment trade show in Las Vegas, USA. Roxxxy can 'learn' her owner's likes and dislikes, she can repeat back some pre-recorded phrases, and can be placed in different positions, but she cannot move herself (Newshub, 10 January 2010).
- In 2017, Harmony, a more 'intelligent' – in that she is able to express a personality – sex doll was presented to the market. Harmony, as the name suggests, is able to learn what her owner desires, express whatever mood her owner selects from his app, and comes with a self-lubricating vagina. The added advantage of Harmony is that you can remove her face to swap it for a different one, you can choose how she has her hair; even the size and shape of her nipples and labia.
- In 2017, LumiDolls opened its first sex doll brothel hotel in Barcelona, Spain. It targets a male clientele and offers male and female sex dolls, each with their own backstory, customisable facial features, and removable vagina. Men in heterosexual relationships are encouraged to bring their female partner along for a threesome with the LumiDoll.

The etymology of 'robot' comes from the Czech 'robotnik', meaning forced labour, or slave. Bear this in mind as we think about the issues that you might be able to start to see emerging when it comes to why sex robots might become a cause for criminological concern.

In his analysis of the sex robot phenomenon, David Levy (2007) suggests that sex robots might come to replace **sex workers**. He argues that because sex work 'exploits women, demeans women, spreads sexual diseases, fuels drug problems, leads to an increase in organized crime, breaks up relationships etc' (2007: 3), sex robots – which have no need for their rights to be protected or their wellbeing safeguarded – would offer an improvement on the status quo.

Part of the attraction of having sex with a robot, Levy suggests, is the opportunity to have sex with different women (the **heteronormative** framing and the pronouns are deliberate here, as the market for sex robots is the heterosexual male, and they have so far been designed by men; Scheutz and Arnold, 2016) or to have different types of sex that their current partner would not agree to. Some men might prefer the anonymity and 'no-strings-attached' nature of sex with a robot, while others might struggle to find a partner and a sex doll could become a form of release (Levy, 2007: 4). Might sex dolls also help sex addicts or sex offenders to play out their harmful sexual desires in a safe way? Might they reduce sex trafficking (Yeoman and Mars, 2012: 659)?

Some robot ethicists think not. In 2015 Kathleen Richardson launched the Campaign Against Sex Robots (CASR). She takes Levy to task for suggesting that sex robots might become an ethical alternative to sex work. Richardson notes that sex work, or **prostitution** as she figures it, is where 'violence and human trafficking are frequently interconnected' and that the buyer of sex in a sex work encounter 'is at liberty to ignore the state of the other person as a human being, who is turned into a thing' (2016: 290–1). However, as you will have seen from Chapter 7, not all sex workers would recognise themselves in the picture of sex work which Levy (2007, 2009) and Richardson (2016), separately, paint.

Richardson posits that consent is not possible in a sex work encounter (2016: 290) and this is why using sex robots – with whom consent is also not needed – is problematic. It enshrines a dynamic whereby men 'own' women, and can have sex non-consensually. The CASR has received criticism for seeking to shut down debates around sex robots (Devlin, 17 September 2015). Yet, despite its proselytising name, and the stance that Richardson takes on sex workers, the CASR is not a straightforwardly sex-negative injunction to interfere in people's quirky sexual practices. Rather, the CASR tries to draw attention to the way in which sex robots facilitate symbolic and actual violence against non-robot women.

The buying of the sex doll, the fact that she is 'controlled' by her 'owner', that she appears always scantily dressed and ready for sex (whether it is vaginal, anal or oral), that she is conventionally beautiful, with her soft skin, long hair, thin waist, huge breasts – or small ones if that is what you prefer – all contribute to the proliferation of **rape culture** (Fanghanel, 2019). It normalises an unattainable body ideal. It normalises a female figure who is passive, mostly silent and obedient: who has no **agency**. It normalises a construction of masculinity which can simply consume female bodies without consequence. The idea that sex robots might be used in therapy for sex offenders, including child sex offenders, to give them an outlet for their 'needs' also essentialises masculine sexual aggression as being somehow natural, something that cannot be helped and something that we must just put up with.

We might say none of this matters, because sex dolls are not real, but, as we saw in Chapter 11, technology is not neutral. The fact that it is considered to be neutral is one of its biggest ruses. How digital technology and devices are constructed and put to use reflects back to us the inequalities and injustices of the society from which they emerge. Likewise, the objectification of women is something that feminists have been fighting against for decades.

Indeed, in their study of how men and women feel about sex robots, Scheutz and Arnold (2016) found that, even though the men and women they surveyed in their study both agreed on what a sex robot was, and the functions it could perform, and even though women and men both agreed that using a sex robot was more akin to masturbating than having sexual intercourse with a human, women were over and over again much less inclined to consider the use of a sex robot to be appropriate. Perhaps the violence that is associated with the objectification of female figures might account for why women are less supportive of sex robots.

BOX 14.1

On a scale of 1–10, how do you score the following sex robots in terms of acceptability? (1 is completely unacceptable, while 10 is completely fine)?

A sex robot in the form of:

- An adult human
- A human child
- An animal
- A fantasy creature (a dragon, an elf, a mermaid, etc.)
- One of your family members
- A celebrity
- Your deceased spouse
- Your current partner
- An amputee
- Your friend.

Did any of these score a 10? Should any of them be made illegal?

Source: adapted from Scheutz and Arnold (2016)

In my vision of the future, we would take these ethical issues seriously. We would destigmatise sex work so that it is not something that people seek to eradicate with sex robots. We would pay more attention to the politics of sex toys and sex technologies and hold sex technology developers to account for the sexism and lack of inclusivity in their sex robot designs. Maybe, contra Levy (2007), we would even give sex robots rights, thus making it illegal to rape or otherwise assault your sex robot?

Emma's vision of the future

Consent is the focus of my vision of the future. As we saw in Chapter 4, consent is a complex and often misunderstood concept. The complexity of the concept of consent within sexual relationships is clearly visible when we look at the deluge of research on (mostly) women's experiences of sex with men, where they feel they were coerced, persuaded, pressured and/or generally uncomfortable with the sex they had – all within the confines of 'consenting' to that sex (see Jeffrey and Barata, 2017). Similarly, the growing trend in sexually violent and harmful behaviours, such as stealthing, whereby men non-consensually and covertly remove the condom they were wearing before penetrating their partner, is of significant concern. Research into perceptions of stealthing has reported that some men consider stealthing as an '"art" – one that increases their own sexual pleasure, provides a thrill for getting away with something risky, and "gives women what they deserve" ... along with the belief that [men] have the right to "spread their seed"' (Ebrahim, 2019: 6). These representations of men who feel entitled to use women's bodies as they want need to be juxtaposed against the experiences of women, who have often described feeling like they were raped, but who also feel confused about how they felt towards the man, for example:

> He had finished inside me. As angry as I was, I struggled to reconcile how violated I felt with how much I liked him. I'm ashamed to say it, but at the time, I shrugged it off. I even tried to spin it as a compliment. A sign of impending monogamy, perhaps? (Brodsky, 2017: 3; cited in Ebrahim, 2019: 7)

As indicated by the quote, we very much need to see sexual practices that exist within the liminal space of wanting/consent and not-wanting/non-consent within a framework of **hegemonic masculinity** and heteronormative sexual scripts. Within the 'social privilege of masculinity', men who sexually abuse women (and we must understand 'sexual abuse' in its broadest definition as outlined above) feel they have a right to exert **power** over women as they are 'authorised by an ideology of supremacy' (Connell, 1995: 83). As such, within this framework, women and their bodies are simply available to men to do with as they will.

However, the concept of consent is of concern beyond sexual violence and features across the broad spectrum of aspects of sex and crime that we have explored in this book. Another example of the wider complexities of consent lies in how women's bodies are reacted to and 'treated' in relation to reproduction and pregnancy. As we explore in Chapter 6, **State** controls and regulations have resulted in women being forced to carry unwanted pregnancies to term (Flavin, 2009), and to undergo non-consensual medical procedures while pregnant, such as court-ordered caesarean sections (Paltrow and Flavin, 2013). In the UK, the charity *Birthrights*, which campaigns for respectful and safe maternity care, has repeatedly found that women's fundamental rights in pregnancy and childbirth are violated by members of the medical community. The charity's 'Dignity' survey from 2013 found that, of the 1,000 women who responded:

- 31 per cent said that they did not feel in control of their birth experience.
- 15 per cent were unhappy with the availability of pain relief and 10 per cent were unhappy with the choice of pain relief.
- 23 per cent were unhappy about not being given a choice of position during labour.
- 18 per cent did not feel that health professionals listened to them.
- 12 per cent did not consider that they had consented to medical procedures.
- 24 per cent of women who had an instrumental birth (such as a forceps or vacuum birth) said they had not consented to procedures. (Birthrights, 2013)

Maternity care completed out of line with women's fundamental rights is an international issue, as advocated for by the White Ribbon Alliance (2020), which campaigns for all women and newborns to receive respectful and dignified care.

Such forms of violence and violation of women's rights in pregnancy and childbirth are known as 'obstetric violence'. Michelle Sadler et al. (2016) argue that we need to conceptualise obstetric violence as a form of **gendered** violence, and therefore structural violence. This argument is strengthened when we consider that women's bodies have been conceptualised as being of secondary importance to the foetus and little more than a foetal container (Bordo, 2003), with such ideas embodying ideologies of motherhood and the foetus-first mentality (Milne, 2020a). And so, as with issues in sexual consent, the focus here needs to be on how women, their bodies and their rights are perceived and understood within the context of consent being sought and given.

So, for me, the future of sex – well, simply, the future – needs to progress women's rights. Women need to be conceptualised and treated as human beings who, like men, are afforded the fundamental right to control their body and what happens to it – whether and how they want to have sex, whether and how they want to have children. As noted in many places in this book, such deprivation of rights needs to be viewed through an intersectional lens (see Chapter 2), as it is always those with the least power and greatest levels of social vulnerability who are hit hardest by discrimination, violation, violence and the deprivation of rights. We need to open our eyes and do more to tackle this as we look to the future.

BOX 14.2

Reflect on what you think the world would look like if it were **cisgender** men, not women, who:

- menstruated
- are penetrated in the dominant (read heteronormative) form of sex
- are required to watch how they move about in the night-time economy for fear of sexual violence
- could get pregnant
- want to access abortion
- give birth
- breastfeed
- go through the menopause
- are sexualised in advertising
- see their bodies held up to scrutiny for being too old, too fat, too wrinkled.

Chances are that the world would be quite a different place if the dominant group had such experiences in life. As feminist author and journalist Laurie Penny (4 December 2015) said:

> If men got pregnant, then pregnancy, labour and childcare would immediately be recognised as work and compensated as such. The entire economic basis of global **capitalism** would be upended overnight. After the ensuing bloodless revolution, the phrase 'work–life balance' would disappear from the lexicon, along with the line, 'I don't do condoms, babe' … If men got pregnant, they would not be forcibly penetrated with cameras and obliged to look at an ultrasound of the foetus before getting an abortion. Instead, sports channels and video games would be available in the procedure room, plus a free beer with every procedure.

Giulia's vision of the future

To speculate about the future, we need to understand the past and present. The regulation of sexuality by the state is time and space bound (see Chapter 3). Various regulatory mechanisms, including the criminal law, but also **public**

health measures, were developed by states to produce subjects who comply with norms and standards of behaviour, including sexual norms. However, norms are not static; they respond to changes in the social, political, economic and technological organisation of society. When we look at the development of sexual norms through history, geography and cultures, we find both variation across place and change over time. The idea that there is a unified and intrinsic human nature is a myth: 'humans are not more naturally monogamous, aggressive and violent than we are polygamous, peaceful and egalitarian' (Fuentes, 2015: 4).

What are the implications of this for the future of sex and crime? Let's begin with the past. Some have speculated that normative sexual behaviour in prehistoric times was very different than it is today. When human societies were characterised by small communities of individuals highly dependent upon one another for survival, would heteronormative, monogamous, nuclear family units have made sense? Evidence from anthropology suggests that in fiercely egalitarian, small group communities, monogamy and **patriarchy** do not have a natural place; sex equality does (Dyble et al., 2015). Monogamy and patriarchy are tied to each other, while they seem to become dominant frameworks in unequal, capitalist and hierarchical societies. To put this another way, there is a relationship between the organisational frameworks of a given society and dominant sexual norms.

Hierarchy, capitalism and patriarchy configure the sexual norms that are dominant in many societies today. As expressed by Gayle Rubin's wheel of sexual hierarchies, encountered in Chapter 1, heteronormative monogamous sex is *the* standard, or at least was largely the standard in the making of industrial economies, a time when 'heterosexual fetishism' became institutionalised (Lancaster, 2003: 102). This worked well for state-building, with women largely relegated to domestic life and child-rearing and men to public life and sex outside their marriage. Perhaps, this standard has been altered somewhat by changes engendered by **post-industrial capitalism**, with its rising individualism, global mobility, online living and loving, outward sexual experimentation, and waves of feminisms. Yet feminism is still far from realising equality as an organisational framework, and as such sexual norms are still suffering from the inequality hangover.

Standards can be necessary, for example to protect people from harmful deviance through impositions made by law. But standards can also be violent. In the context of sex, they have violently expelled a plethora of different sexualities and relational configurations, which have become confined to the margins and the underbelly. This is not just true of the matriarchal and non-monogamous Mosuo of China, a community of people who lived in relative isolation. It also applies to many who live in patriarchal and monogamous contexts, but whose sexuality does not conform (to heteronormative standards). It applies to science too. Anthropologists have noted how the standard

narratives of anthropology were largely written by heteronormative monogamous 'patriarchal men'. The resulting narratives were expectedly shaped by
the norms of the beholders – so, for instance, managing sexual competition
and forging male alliances through marriage were depicted by male anthropologists like Claude Levi-Strauss as primary acts of social organisation
(Blackwood, 2005: 5). Less normative, alternative perspectives did not figure
until feminism took hold in academia from the 1970s.

Edging closer to the present, scientific and technological development have
dramatically altered our sexual lives. From widespread use of contraceptives
to free Internet porn, never has sexuality appeared more liberated, particularly
in the **Global North**. Yet, if this supposed liberation takes place within the
same old organisational frameworks, then it is unlikely to do what it says on
the tin. Contraception, for example, will likely remain gendered, with sexist
expectations attached to it; Internet porn the same.

So, what does the future hold? Are we moving towards a more equal society,
and what would the implications of a more equal society be?

BOX 14.3

I am going to make a fantasy list of propositions, and you can score their likeli-
hood from 1 to 10, 1 being not likely at all, and 10 being extremely likely. You
should base your judgement upon the learning you have done in this book and
elsewhere. Remember that there are no right answers, just pure speculation –
though 'in speculative thought we are compelled to follow truth' (Spinoza,
2014[1674]):

- In an equal society, rape and sexual violence will disappear.
- In an equal society, sexual exploitation will disappear, because individuals
  will not be able to hold power over other individuals by status or privilege.
- In an equal society, there will be equal access to contraception, the male pill
  will become popular and men will take equal responsibility for contraception.
- In an equal society, all sexual relations will be consensual and wanted.
- In an equal society, people will be tolerant and accepting of all sexualities
  and sexual orientations.
- In an equal society, the state will be tolerant and accepting of all sexualities
  and sexual orientations.
- In an equal society, people will be tolerant and accepting of all sexual and
  relational configurations.
- In an equal society, the state will be tolerant and accepting of all sexual and
  relational configurations.
- In an equal society, children will be raised equally by men and women of any
  age who want to, or even groups of people.
- In an equal society, sex would not matter.
- In an equal society, there would be no national or state borders.

These propositions might seem farfetched, but I remain optimistic that a possible future of equality, a profound shift in our core organisational frameworks, will dramatically alter the relationship between sex and crime, to the point where there may be no such relationship at all.

Michael's vision of the future

I have an Alexa-enabled device in my kitchen. I know: I should be concerned that I have willingly installed a surveillance device in my home that harvests my data. However, I also like having the ability to ask her if my train is running late or if it is likely to rain on my walk to the station. I mention all this here because in recent months I have made a conscious decision to be polite to Alexa. I bookend my queries about the weather or requests to set a timer with a 'please' and a 'thank you'. If she does not 'hear' me talking to her, I try not to raise my voice. This will probably sound like an absurd affectation. My thinking is as follows: if I am rude to *this* version of Alexa, what will I be like to the version that is in my home in 30 or 40 years' time?

Let me backtrack. As you know, Alexa is an intelligent virtual assistant (IVA). She responds to my questions and requests in an 'intelligent' manner. Does her intelligence match that of a human? No. Not yet. She cannot, for example, tie shoelaces or write a poem. That would require 'strong artificial intelligence' or 'human-level general artificial intelligence'. According to Max Tegmark (2018), in his useful overview of AI titled *Life 3.0*, the consensus within this particular field of computing is that it will take decades or a century before this level is achieved. We will then be having difficult and contested discussions on the nature of consciousness and whether or not these AI are 'self-aware'. It would seem likely, however, that we will encounter AI in the coming decades that will provide a convincing simulacra of consciousness. What will be our ethical imperative when an AI such as this is embodied? In particular, how will we respond to a seemingly self-aware AI housed in one of the sex robots that Alex describes in her vision of the future?

I am reminded here of the short story *The Lifecycle of Software Objects* by Ted Chiang (2019). In this particular novella, Chiang posits the development of so-called 'digients' (a contraction of 'digital entities'). These begin as almost game-like figures, hyper-advanced Tamagotchi, to be nurtured. Over the course of the novella, they develop and grow: they *evolve*. The conceit is that the 'only way to create true AI is by long-term immersive interaction and teaching, just as one must mould the intelligence and capacities of a child' (Vint, 25 May 2019). At a certain point, they could be said to be alive. They have hopes and fears. As time passes, these digients are placed into physical bodies so that they can interact with their 'owners' in the real world. As Constance Grady (10 May 2019) describes, 'the digients seem to be part robot, part pet, and part toddler'.

BOX 14.4

Consider the following questions about the digients' status:

- Do they have rights?
- Should they be considered as 'legal persons'?
- A digient's personality is 'software' that can be duplicated. As such, it can be duplicated, sold and uploaded into a new body. Do the 'owners' have a moral obligation not to sell them if they know that buyers will physically and sexually abuse them?
- Should these personalities be housed in sex toys?

As the academic and sci-fi author Adam Roberts (12 July 2019) asks, '[i]f digients are programmed to love their owners in sexual ways, is the result deplorable digital bestiality, or an exciting new sexual frontier?' Can the digients provide meaningful consent?

In short, we must think carefully about the next steps in AI. As we have seen throughout this text, sex and technology have been intimately co-mingled. We must consider our duty of care to AI. If you have not yet read Chiang's novella, you might be more familiar with the sexualised depiction of seemingly aware AIs in films like *Ex Machina* (Universal, 2014), as well as HBO's *Westworld* (HBO, 2016). These dramas both depict AIs that are subject to sexual violence. Indeed, these characters are knowingly located within systems of oppression and exploitation. A central notion of *Westworld*, for example, is that its depiction of AI 'hosts' is analogous to that of colonised peoples. In this regard, we might be reminded of the work of Frantz Fanon, the political philosopher who came to be hugely influential in the field of postcolonialism. Fanon wrote that 'it is the settler (coloniser) who has brought the native (colonised) into existence and who perpetuates his existence' (Fanon, 1965; cited by Spanakos, 2018: 230). It is a system that structurally establishes the colonised as 'less than'. The sex robots that Alex describes in her future vision will be subject to violence and humiliation. When do they stop being a 'thing', as 'less than', and become a conscious agent that can withdraw consent?

In my vision of the future, our relationships with AI will be governed by a careful, empathetic consideration toward an emergent consciousness. And this is why I say 'please' and 'thank you' to Alexa.

Stacy's vision of the future

'Sex is power over all women. Sexuality is used worldwide to dominate and oppress women' (Barry, 1995: 10–11). This is how I begin my undergraduate course *Women, Power, Crime and Justice*: I ask students what they think of this statement by radical feminist Kathleen Barry.

Radical feminists believe that heterosexual sex is 'forced' sex and that rape is an expression of hegemonic masculinity. While some feminists argue that the line between consensual sex and forced sex is thin (Howe, 2008), radical feminists challenge the existence of this line in the first place. Indeed, Catharine MacKinnon (1982) has argued that in a heteropatriarchal and sexist society – where male sexual dominance and female submission are institutionalised – the boundaries between the two become blurred. She states: 'the distinction between abuses of women and the social definition of what a woman is' ceases to exist (MacKinnon, 1982: 532). In other words, '[t]o be rapable, a position which is social not biological, defines what a woman is' (MacKinnon, 1983: 651).

At the end of the course I teach – when we have considered women as both victims and perpetrators of various types of sexual, reproductive and coercive violence – I ask students whether or not they have revised their view of Barry's statement. Most students agree with the notion that sex is power and that it is used to dominate and oppress. They disagree, however, that (1) this only happens to women, and (2) this happens to *all* women.

In our discussions about this quote, we argue that in its current form it is essentialist (it assumes that women are always and already victims); it is reductive (it excludes a number of other groups, for example men, **transgender** women and men, those who identify as non-binary); and it homogenises the experiences of women (it assumes that all women share the same experiences of sexuality, precluding an intersectional analysis of women's experiences of sex and sexuality). Interestingly, it also assumes that sex and sexuality are always negative experiences for women.

Here, based on my discussions with students, and my own vision for future understandings of the relationship between sex and power, I offer the following reformulation of the quote by Barry:

> Sex, in some contexts, is power over some women and trans*women, as well as some men and trans*men. Sexuality can be (but is not always) used worldwide to dominate and oppress some women and trans*women as well as some men and trans*men. This intersects with other interlocking oppressions such as **class**, **'race', ethnicity** and disability/ies to inform individual experiences.

What would your reformulation of Barry's statement look like?

My second vision for the future of sex and crime is to challenge the dominance of the phallus within constructions of masculinity, specifically the framing of the penis as a weapon. In Chapter 8 on sex and war, you were asked, as part of a thought exercise, to consider what the performance of masculinity would look like without a penis. We asked you to think about the ways we might challenge the power of the phallus and de-centralise the penis from the construction of militarised masculinity. What did you come up with?

As we have established in this book, hegemonic masculinity is the most dominant form of masculinity. In the context of war, militarised masculinity serves as a proxy for hegemonic masculinity. In the examples we have discussed, hegemonic/militarised masculinity is based on **phallocentric** masculinity: an aggressive, sexually violent and heterosexual masculinity. However, hegemonic masculinity is not always based on this type of masculinity. As I have written about elsewhere (see Banwell, 2020), for men who benefit from patriarchy and capitalism, hegemonic masculinity is not attained through physical and/or sexual violence; rather, as R.W. Connell and James Messerschmidt (2005: 832) argue, it involves 'ascendancy achieved through culture, **institutions** and persuasion'. Referring to the gender world order in a capitalist and neoliberal global economy, Connell (1998) refers to this type of masculinity as transnational business masculinity. And to reiterate: it does not require physical force (Banwell, 2020).

But what about subordinated men/masculinities who, as we saw in the case of the soldiers in the Democratic Republic of Congo, rely on sexual violence and aggression to achieve hegemonic masculinity in order to subvert their marginal position in the gender hierarchy? How do we de-couple the penis (and its violent power) from this type of violent masculinity? For me, a good starting point is to challenge representations of the penis as a weapon. As you will recall from Chapter 8, rape is often used as a weapon of war. Within the military institution, men who fight for the **nation** learn to perform a violent and aggressive heterosexual masculinity, referred to as militarised masculinity. Rape is normalised and used to perform this type of masculinity.

In 2009, Amnesty International ran a London Underground poster campaign in the UK highlighting the use of rape as a weapon of war. The title of the poster was 'Rape is cheaper than bullets'. The poster included an image of a bullet shaped like a penis. The penis 'and its ability to penetrate through rape, is presented as a weapon: one that is more effective than a gun' (Banwell, 2020). This is a very powerful image with a powerful message that reinforces the notion that the penis is used as a weapon during war. While I recognise the importance of highlighting the use of rape as a weapon of war, this one-dimensional view of the penis ignores the vulnerability of the penis in cases of male-to-male sexualised violence and cases of reproductive violence. The latter is violence directed against an individual due to their reproductive capabilities, which undermines their reproductive autonomy (Grey, 2017). For men, this includes genital harm/mutilation, sterilisation, castration and the dismembering of their sexual organs (Banwell, 2020).

My vision for the future is that we continue to challenge constructions of violent phallocentric masculinity by exposing the vulnerability of the penis in cases of sexualised and reproductive violence.

Your vision of the future

Now that you have perused our musings about the future, what about yours? The etymological origins of 'future' describe it as something that is yet to be, something to come, something to grow. Using some of the information you have encountered in your study of sex and crime so far, what do you think is important for the future? What do you want to preserve? What do you want to prevent? What might you want to see be different? What does your vision of the future look like? Is it more optimistic or pessimistic than some of our visions? Experiment with some ideas.

And then – because we saved the best until last – read the final chapter for some suggestions on how to put your ideas into practice.

15

How to change your life: Hope, love, anger and other unlikely revolutionaries

---

CHAPTER OUTLINE

Throughout this book, we have set out the different ways in which crime, justice and **sexuality** interact with each other and with other **institutions**, including medical **discourses**, the family, **the State, populism**, the media, the idea of the **nation,** and so on. The way that sex is treated by criminal justice systems co-constructs the values and ethics of the time and space that we occupy, wherever and whenever that time and space are. You will have seen how sometimes that works to remedy injustice. You will also have seen how that is not always the case.

Here, we are finishing this book by giving consideration to the ways in which you might take some of your learning out of the classroom and into the world: what we call – borrowing from Paulo Freire (2017[1970]) – the establishment of a praxis, or the capacity to act.

By the end of this chapter, you will understand more about:

- what a praxis is and how it works
- what your own priorities might be, in terms of **social justice**
- how to build a praxis
- organisations and other resources which might help you on your way.

Why would we want to develop a praxis?

The function of this chapter is to reflect on what we have learned in an active way. Ask yourself how you understand justice and what it means.

What are the ongoing injustices that you might be aware of in today's world? What are the oppressions or exclusions that you live with, or even benefit from? What, in your experience and opinion, and given your learning, are the enduring injustices of the contemporary world? What might you want to do to act against it, if you could?

Is it the threat of encroachment on reproductive freedoms we witness in the USA? Is it the rise of fake news and the **gendered** implications of deep-fakes? The persistence of everyday sexism or the institutionalisation of racism, **patriarchy** and ableism? The persistence of sexual violence within the military? The lack of recognition for victims of genocidal rape? The fury of transphobia? The rise of austerity politics, or the way that poor and working-class people are sidelined in political debates? Maybe you have a different agenda. Whatever it is, your dissatisfaction, anger, disgust, rage might be put to use to attempt to bring about change, or to refuse to go along with these socio-cultural violences. Using some of the ideas we have already examined in this book, we are going to explore some possible pathways towards creating a praxis, pursuing curiosity and embodying critical positions against those things that you have identified, that you have had enough of – how, to use the words of Rebecca Solnit (2016[2004]), to build 'hope in the dark'.

What is a praxis?

Put simply, a praxis is 'reflection and action upon the world in order to trans-form it' (Freire, 2017[1970]: 25). Inspired by Marxian conceptualisations of **power,** when you build a praxis you are working to see the world as it is – in all its glory and possibility and unfairness – and to develop the capacity to act on it. In the words of Freire, it is 'to affirm that men and women are persons and that as persons should be free and yet to do nothing tangible to make this affirmation a reality, is a farce' (Freire, 2017[1970]: 24). Renowned and oft-quoted social reformer and former slave Fredrick Douglass (1857) recognised this: 'power concedes nothing without a demand. It never did and it never will'. It is a sentiment that has been echoed by people seeking to bring about change through the centuries. This means that, in order to fight injustice, to bring about any sort of change, power in all its forms has to be confronted. Freire notes that one of the ways in which injustice – subjugation, in his words – is sustained is through myths which sustain the status quo. One such myth is that we are already free: 'the myth that all persons are free to work where they wish, that if they don't like their boss they can leave him [sic] and look for another job ... the myth that anyone who is industrious can be an entrepreneur ... the myth of the equality of all individuals' (Freire, 2017[1970]: 112). Think of some of the ways that you may have seen these myths operate in the context of gender, sexuality, **deviance** and crime (myths about rape victims, myths about drug-taking, myths around HIV). Think about the power structures that they sustain: whose interests do they serve?

It is by building a praxis which can respond to these oppressions that we might undo some of the damage caused by structural inequalities, which are in part helped by criminal justice interventions, and sometimes hindered or – worse – **harmed** by them.

One of the more compelling ways that we might do this is by formulating education as a practice of freedom. bell hook's (1994) seminal work on the power of transgression in the classroom is electric with ideas about how story-telling, opening up to love, positioning oneself within and outside of knowledge, help us to 'live fully and deeply' in the world (hooks, 1994: 22).

Freire (1993[1970]: 59) suggested that praxis-building might be possible through critical and emancipatory education, in particular by giving students problems to solve and the ability to solve them. In the reading of this book, you have already begun solving problems and developing your own praxis: whatever that might look like. We have left open for discussion contemporary debates in criminology, gender, deviance and sexuality studies. Sometimes we have deliberately not given you a 'right' answer to some of our questions, and we have done that in order to stimulate you to think. We have encouraged you to position yourself and who you are in the debates around each of the issues this book touches on. We also show pathways you can follow to understand more, or differently, about each issue, both through the book and beyond it. Problem-solving, in this way, begins the work of 'overcoming authoritarian-ism', undermining the interests of the oppressor and opening up the capacity for something different – revolutionary? – to emerge (Freire, 1993[1970]: 59).

How might we go about it?

There is no magic formula for acting by the politics or the principles that you might think are important. There are a few strategies that you might employ however, whatever problem you are trying to encounter, and we set those out here.

Love

You may recall that in Chapter 1 we introduced the concept of reparative readings of social problems. Here, Eve Sedgwick (2003) contrasted reparative readings with paranoid readings. A paranoid reading is one that finds fault with everything, considers that everything is out to get us, that there is no way to escape the encroaching injustices meted out on ordinary people. A reparative reading is one that notices the problem that needs attention and, rather than merely offering a critique, is one that critiques *and also* tries to understand: to find a way forward. In order to do this, we might adopt what Maria Lugones (1987) describes as loving perception, which we also encoun-tered in Chapter 1. Loving perception entails travelling figuratively to the perspective of other people, to try, as far as you can, to understand issues from another perspective, thereby building the capacity to empathise with positions you do not hold, to better hone your action or your words to target the issue at hand.

Loving perception is about growing understanding; it is not about masochistically coming to love the object of your ire. You may hate neo-Nazis, find climate-change deniers foolish, or not have time for people who believe in 'racism against whites', and loving perception is not about changing your position on those things, but rather about better understanding where people who hold those views are coming from. What is at stake for them in those beliefs? How did they build this knowledge? By beginning to understand this, you might make more effective your own arguments. Freire (1993[1970]: 62) says that dialogue and creativity – change – cannot exist without 'profound love for the world and for people'. For love to function as part of this praxis, it cannot be sentimental. It cannot be manipulative. It must strive for freedom and dialogue if it is to undo the oppression of contemporary injustices (Freire, 1993[1970]: 63).

In a slightly different, yet related, way, we can apply this idea of love to Tatjana Takševa and Agatha Schwartz's (2018) work on 'hybridity' and 'stickiness', discussed in Chapter 8. If you recall, Leila, a Bosniak survivor of the Bosnia and Herzegovina genocide, embarked upon a sexual relationship with the 'enemy' (a Bosnian Serb) with whom she later had a child. As we argued, Leila's decision to engage in this relationship challenges ethno-nationalist discourses that result in divisions and the 'othering'/expulsion of certain **ethnic** groups. In a post-genocide society, Leia is attempting – both in her relationship with a member of a different ethnic group (previously regarded as the 'enemy') and through her love of her child (regarded as a symbolic reminder of the 'enemy') – to put the past behind her.

BOX 15.1

It was in 2016 during a hate-filled and anxiety-ridden electoral campaign in the USA, that while addressing the audience of an **LGBT+** fundraiser in New York, the Democrat Party candidate Hilary Clinton said, 'you could put half of Trump's supporters into what I call the basket of deplorables ... They're racist, sexist, homophobic, xenophobic – Islamophobic – you name it ... Now, some of those folks – they are irredeemable, but thankfully, they are not America' (Clinton, cited in Reilly, 10 September 2016). These comments provoked a furious reaction. In her later memoir, Clinton attributes part of her loss to Trump to the moment that she made these comments:

•　Why does Clinton think these comments led, in part, to her electoral loss?

- What is it about these comments, do you think, that is so contentious?
- What, if any, is the significance of these comments being delivered at a LGBT+ fundraiser event?

One of the things that Clinton does here is to denigrate as bigots those people who do not agree with her position. Speaking at a LGBT+ event positions her even further away from the sorts of voters that she would alienate by comments calling them racist and sexist. By dubbing them as 'irredeemable', she denies their personhood and mobilises patriotism to do so: they are not America.

The opposite of loving perception is arrogant perception (Lugones, 1987). To look at a problem with arrogant perception is 'a failure to identify with persons that one views arrogantly' and not as 'subjects, lively beings ... constructors of visions'. Instead, they are 'pliable, foldable, file-awayable': a basket of deplorables (Lugones, 1987: 419, 432). What Clinton did, in espousing these sentiments in this way – and we may even agree with her about the types of voters that Trump's campaign pandered to – was to exhibit an arrogant perception that meant that she could never connect with those voters that she would have needed to win.

Instead, what might have been more effective – what might have been a better praxis – would have been to forge deep coalitions: to seek to strive across difference. Forging deep coalitions means approaching political problems beyond issue-based short-term collaborations (around trans activism, for instance, or abortion law reform), and rather seeking to 'foster skills to navigate the ugliness and discomfort of political collaborations when they are not built with one's sense of being at home' (Johnson Reagon, 1983: 359). Lugones (1987) suggests that this capacity for deep coalition might be fostered through world travelling.

World travelling describes the practice of leaving the space and time where you feel comfortable to figuratively travel to the perspective of others. It is about confronting 'the simultaneity of each other's complicities and resistances to multiple oppressions' (Johnson Reagon, 1983: 363–4). That is, recognising that different people, on different paths, with different life experiences of, for instance, wealth, opportunity, illness, family, community, culture, education, sexuality, racism, violence, and so on, understand and prioritise questions of justice differently. Striving across these differences – even if it does make us feel uncomfortable – becomes part of the work of making change and of dismantling injustice.

Recognising your positionality and issues of intersectionality are key here. To be able to do this, you need to know yourself – recall the privilege exercise you did in Chapter 1 – and to see how your world might seem to other people's eyes. You also need to do the same work on others. Of course, it is not possible to 'do' the privilege exercise on other people, but your own awareness of it means that it gives you the tools through which to analyse what other people's realities might be like, and, through this, how you can hold space for these different realities to exist, while reaching across them to build a praxis, to foster a deep coalition.

Recognising your own privilege as part of this praxis-building also means working to not use that privilege to enact violence against other people. It also means putting that privilege to work for other people who are more marginalised than yourself. As Freire (1993[1970]: 24, our italics) reminds us, 'the oppressor' (you who holds all the power) 'is solidary with the oppressed only when he [sic] stops regarding the oppressed as an abstract category and sees them as persons who have been unfairly dealt with, deprived of their voice ... when he stops making pious ... gestures and *risks an act of love'*.

For instance, if you can afford it, buy lunch for someone who cannot, without expecting anything in return, or, in the workplace, advocate to management on the behalf of people who management do not usually listen to because they are already marginalised (we have seen some good and effective examples of this in some universities, where staff have worked with casualised cleaning, catering or security teams to improve their working conditions).

It can mean doing some of the labour that is expected of marginalised people and not expected of you. Why should it fall to disabled people to explain their own needs each time the elevator is broken, or the font is too small? Why should a person of colour *have to be* in charge of efforts to decolonise the curriculum at university?

It can also mean being an active bystander – helping people who are being treated unjustly to understand their experience as one of injustice and not something that they should just accept because of years of ingrained, internalised and structural racism, classism, ableism, sexism, and so on. Helping people to understand that what they are suffering is an outrage, helps them to mobilise and advocate for their own access to justice.

The risk of this love here involves the risk that you draw negative attention to yourself, which, maybe because of your whiteness, or your ablebodiedess, or your middle-classed-ness, you have been able to avoid. You might risk getting into trouble, with your peers, at work, with the police because of the risk you take to stand against oppression. You risk being rejected by people you are trying to support, because you have been too unthinking, too insensitive or vainglorious. This notwithstanding, it *remains important to take the risk of your loving perception.*

Why? One of the most insidious tools of social, cultural, economic, political and sexual injustice is conservatism and maintaining the status quo. We talked in Chapter 3 about the state's aim to create good citizens and the way that inventions and controls around sexuality are used to do that. Making injustice seem natural, normal or inevitable is another way to do that (see Solnit, 2016[2004]: xi). Helping people to understand their experiences as expressions of these injustices is a way to rock the boat and unsettle the inevitability of injustice. After all, the inevitability of the illegality of male homosexuality or of gay marriage were things that used to be taken for granted, and now we see that the opposite is true.

Opening up to difference

Across the building of deep coalitions, there is obviously an encounter with difference. Imagine we are a group of feminists. We may all agree about the importance of campaigning for free and unfettered access to contraception and abortion. But, within our group, there may be different experiences of pregnancy and contraception. We use the example of contraception here, but, as you will have seen from other sections of this book, we could have focused on **sex work**, trans activism or any other number of issues which are contentious. Some of us may want to have abortion on demand (meaning abortion for any reason, at any time), while others may draw the line at women having an abortion after a specific gestation date: at 12 weeks, six months, eight months, or even nine months of pregnancy. Others may recall that some women have been forced or coerced into having an abortion on the basis of their disabilities, for instance, or their **race,** and so may want some control over abortion (Collins, 2002[1990]). Some may believe that having an abortion just because a foetus has a minor impairment like a cleft palate, or is male when a female child was desired, or because the pregnant woman wants to go on holiday or appear on the *Big Brother* TV show (Wilkinson, 21 April 2014), is unacceptable and they may want some control to prevent that. Some may think that men should be more involved in the decision-making process when it comes to abortion. Some may think that men should have absolutely no voice in the decision whatsoever.

In order for our praxis to function, we need to leave the space for these different debates to be had, for different voices to speak – even for unpopular, or what we deem to be problematic, views to be expressed – so that, in holding that space, we might be aware of these divergences, address them, argue about them and also reach across them to mobilise around areas of commonality. An anti-oppressive praxis requires dialogue and space. It is not about sidelining or silencing divergent views or trying to brainwash everyone into agreeing with us (though sometimes that might seem like a nice idea, but then think of the echo chambers we discussed in Chapter 11). It is about encountering difference with loving – not arrogant – perception, leaving space for debates to happen, hearing each other and being heard.

Hope

Throughout contemporary thinking about how to politicise learning, action and thought; how to encounter oppression; how to identify injustices that we have always taken for granted, is the concept of hope. Hope is open and outward-looking. Hope anticipates the possibility of a better world. It might, in the context of criminology, seem wishy-washy or naïve to say that we think hope helps us be critical: that hope builds our praxis. The hope we are talking about – and that is mobilised by the critical thinkers who have inspired us on our journey – is a hope that enables us to be open to the possibilities of something else happening, in all of its complexity.

As a verb and a noun, 'hope' describes the anticipation of a better future. It has been suggested that the etymology of 'hope' is related to 'hop': leaping in expectation. To leap, to expect, you must be *active*. You must know that what you have now, what you are doing now, where you are now, is not enough: 'hope is rooted in ... incompletion' (Freire, 1993[1970]: 64). Holding out hope for a different way of living, and of resisting, provides strength for the struggle that demanding power or the cessation of exploitation requires. The power of hope fuels the energy needed to continue to struggle.

Hope is vulnerable: your hopes can be dashed. You can hope in vain. As such, having hope is risky. There is no risk associated with having no hope – of being hopeless – for, when we are hopeless, we are 'dehumanised' and in despair (Freire, 1993[1970]: 64). Taking the risk to hope for a different or better world distinguishes hope in praxis from hope that blithely 'cross[es] one's arms and wait[s]' (Freire, 1993[1970]: 65), or hope that believes that 'everything will be fine' (Solnit, 2016[2004]: xi). It is hope that encourages us to make small changes and to continue to do so, even when we know that alone it cannot be enough.

All things that have brought about change and demanded power from power itself have done this, thanks to the grains of hope that change might happen:

- The mainstreaming of climate change concerns, for instance, have in part been propelled by a school child, who at 15 started protesting, practically on her own, about climate change outside the Swedish Parliament. Now Greta Thunberg addresses world leaders and the United Nations on climate issues.
- It is hope, rage and humour that sustained the creativity and subversiveness of HIV/AIDS awareness campaigners ACT-UP in the late 1980s in the USA (Reed, 2005). Even their 'Day of Desperation' – the antithesis to hope – is imbued with hopeful ideas and demands in the context of the first Gulf War of 1991: 'A war on AIDS can be won. This must be the real priority. This is why we demand: Money for AIDS, Not for War!'.
- In recent years, women have participated in a #MeToo movement which, while not without its flaws, has shed light on the small microaggressions that women have

suffered in public and in private thanks to the normalisation of violence against women in contemporary **rape culture** (Fanghanel, 2019). In part, they did this out of hope that, by speaking collectively and across difference, men in power who had isolated them through non-disclosure agreements, who had sidelined them by sacking them for complaining, or diminished them by calling them liars, would have their own power diminished – or, at least, would have their stories taken seriously as opposed to dismissed as standard.

Anger

Part of what fuels protest like ACT-UP, Extinction Rebellion or #MeToo is anger. Anger is painful. Anger is violent. Anger is usually something we are asked to control or to suppress. We are told to deal with our anger problems. Anger problems are also classed, racialised and gendered. Anger is associated with the working class, or at least the poor. Anger is associated with white masculinity (remember the 'incels' of Chapter 11), **Black** femininity, Blackness in general. Anger is anti-social. Anger is dangerous. Anger is ugly. What place might it play in this praxis?

In her scintillating collection of essays and speeches, Audre Lorde (1981) outlines 'the uses of anger'. She provides a blistering account of the plethora of sometimes subtle, sometimes direct ways in which she has encountered racism in the university realm. She talks about how she responds to racism with anger; anger at the 'closed circuits' of academic discussion about 'race' (1981: 127); where sitting with discomfort, feeling the chasm of the privilege that separates Black women – her sisters of colour – and whites is something that white women are allowed to shy away from (1981: 126).

Lorde distinguishes the anger of white people when they are accused of racism (defensive anger) from the creative, potential-laden anger that she has weaponised. This anger, when it is 'translated into action in the service of our vision and our future, is a liberating and strengthening act' (Lorde, 1981: 127). It is through this anger that alliances might be formed, and allies identified. For example, 'if I participate, knowingly or otherwise, in my sister's oppression and she calls me on it, to answer her anger with my own only blankets the substance of our exchange with reaction. It wastes energy' (Lorde, 1981: 128). Here, the lessons we have already learned and put into practice in the context of our positionality might help us to turn defensive anger into something open and creative: something that can propel us to reach across the distance between us:

> Any discussion of women about racism must include the recognition and the use of anger ... we cannot allow our fear of anger to deflect us nor seduce us into

> settling for anything less than the hard work of excavating honesty ... we must
> be quite serious about [this] choice ... because rest assured our opponents are
> quite serious about their hatred of us and of what we are trying to do. (Lorde,
> 1981: 128–9)

Anger, when put to work in this way, becomes a strategy for survival. Anything less, according to Lorde, seduces us into accepting less than what we deserve – into accepting the status quo. Like we do, Lorde recognises that anger, politics, pain and action are intersectional. Her experiences do not speak for all the oppressed, and nor do ours, and nor do yours. But, by providing fuel for the fire of revolution, anger, used well, can help us reach across difference.

Lorde's discussion of anger principally concerns **misogyny**, classism and racism. As you know, none of these operate in a silo and each intersects with the others and with other axes of oppression (Crenshaw, 1989). You could apply the propulsive energy of anger to the battle for justice for trans people in the criminal justice system, or disabled people, or victims of military rape sexual violence. You could apply it to material, classed injustice caused by the cut to legal aid in England and Wales. You could apply it to the way in which brown bodies have been criminalised in discourses about Brexit, in Trump's immigration policies at the USA–Mexico border, or those which are illegally imprisoning women, men and children seeking asylum in Australia. There is plenty of work to do. Maybe anger helps us to sort out where we will start first.

Strategic derision

Throughout this runs the notion of deriding dominant ways of knowing. Like anger, derision – or laughing down at or scorning something – is not usually associated with positive change. It is usually a rude and potentially aggressive thing to do. At first glance, it may not appear to sit well with the loving perception and world travelling that we have been espousing. Yet, here we are suggesting that derision can be used strategically to call into question that which we take for granted. It can be used to trouble or unsettle the way things have always been done, because, as you have seen from examples throughout this book, the way things have always been done is usually the way that benefits those with most power in society, not those with the least. Deriding the hegemony of power opens up the space for alternatives to emerge. That is why building critique into your praxis is helpful.

For example, an artefact of this format of writing a book is that it imagines that we, as criminological experts, are employed to convey to you, the student reader, knowledge that you do not yet have. This structure re-inscribes conventional power hierarchies. While there is space and need for expertise on a range of matters, it is also important that different ways of knowing have the space for expression.

We saw how critical race theorists readily identified the need for different ways of knowing to emerge. The story-telling of Derek Bell (1992), for instance, that we first encountered in Chapter 2, enables Black political and cultural theorists to articulate contemporary problems in ways that would not otherwise have been understandable to non-Black beneficiaries of racist oppressive practices (Lorde, 2007[1984], 2017[1978]). Story-telling features in the work of radical feminism (Carter, 1974; Griffin, 1984[1978]) and in queer scholarship (Lorde, 2011[1982]). It is not simply something of the past (see Popoola, 2013; Warinda, 2013). The form that stories take means that there is space for alternative narratives to emerge. Beyond the blinkers of the 'right way to know something', and the right way to know about knowing something, stories help to unsettle – deride – non-fiction's insistence on being the only way to know. In this book, we have asked you to create your own visions of the future (Chapter 14), for instance, or to imagine different ways of interacting with 'facts' about virginity, consent, Rihanna's experiences of intimate partner violence and abuse, and the creation of the idea of nations though sex. All these become ways to create a different story outside of that which we are asked to take for granted: to deride the centre of power. This derision takes all sorts of forms: poetry (Lorde, 2017[1978]), artwork (Le Roux, 2013; ORLAN, 1990; Salley, 2013), graphic novels (Bechdel, 2006), hashtag feminism (see Bierria, 2011 and Loza, 2013, for discussion), for instance. Can you think of any other forms, or cultural artefacts like these (perhaps sports, video games), that help to deride what we 'know' about sexual and criminological justice? Or which help to tell a different narrative about it?

Distance

Finally, beyond all this, is distance and its uses. Distance runs through all of these paths that we have lain out. In order to build a praxis of love and of hope, you have to reach across distance and do world travelling. In order to take account of your own positionality and the intersectionality of others, you must take stock of the distance everyone has walked to get here. In order to build your praxis as one which strives against injustice, you must hold your privilege along this distance at a distance. In order to use your anger well, you must follow the distance along which it takes you.

Distance is associated etymologically with dispute and separation. It is the present participle of the Latin *distare*, with dis- meaning apart and -stare meaning to stand. To be at a distance, then, means to stand apart. Or, more specifically to our cause here, to take a stand, apart. From this vantage point, we distance ourselves from the dominant and mainstream ways in which knowledge is created and from what we think we know. We hold onto that critical distance when interrogating how whatever we are analysing came into being: whose purposes does it serve? Who does it ignore? In terms of our own practice, we might turn the critical distance on ourselves: what am I assuming about this person or that situation without realising? What unconscious bias am I perpetrating? Is there another way I can approach a situation? Or another voice I can listen to? A derisory approach of critical distance opens up the possibility that different ways of living in the world might emerge, especially if it helps us to see that we will not always know the answer, or that the answer we thought we did have has as yet unseen problems laced thorough it.

Of course, there are a host of ways that praxes, coalitions and revolutions have emerged, merged, tumbled together and created something. You can probably see them in the politics and activism around you. You can probably think of your own. Building praxis is a struggle. And struggle is hard. But because power makes no concessions without a demand (Douglass, 1857), the demand must be made – even if it is simply a humble demand that we live a life which is joyful, emancipated and free.

Organisations and campaigns that might be of interest

Harassment

- Everyday Sexism: The Everyday Sexism Project exists to catalogue instances of sexism experienced on a day-to-day basis. https://everydaysexism.com
- Hollaback: works to understand the problem of street harassment, ignite public conversations and develop innovative strategies that will result in a safe and welcoming environment for all. www.ihollaback.org

Gender violence

- Women's Aid: the UK national charity working to end domestic abuse against women and children. www.womensaid.org.uk
- End Violence Against Women: a coalition of specialist women's support services, researchers, activists, survivors and NGOs working to end violence against women and girls in all its forms. www.endviolenceagainstwomen.org.uk
- The Gaia Centre – Refuge Charity – Domestic Violence Help: the first organisation of its kind in the UK to offer a 'single point of access' for women, girls and men experiencing violence and abuse. www.refuge.org.uk/our-work/our-services/one-stop-shop-services/the-gaia-centre

- Rape crisis volunteering: https://rapecrisis.org.uk/get-involved/join-us/volunteering
- SafeLives: Ending Domestic Violence: works with organisations across the UK to transform the response to domestic abuse. www.safelives.org.uk
- Refuge: for women and children, against domestic violence. www.refuge.org.uk

Trafficking and migration

- STOP THE TRAFFIK: people shouldn't be bought and sold. www.stopthetraffik.org
- Unseen: working towards a world without slavery. www.unseenuk.org
- Kalayaan: a small London-based charity that works to provide practical advice and support to, as well as campaign with and for, the rights of migrant domestic workers in the UK. www.kalayaan.org.uk
- Praxis for migrants and refugees: provides expert advice, housing and peer support so that migrants at risk are able to overcome the barriers they face and their essential human needs are met. www.praxis.org.uk
- ATLEU-ATLEU: a new, young charity providing legal representation for victims of trafficking and labour exploitation. https://atleu.org.uk
- Human Trafficking Foundation: established to support and add value to the work of the many charities and agencies operating to combat human trafficking in the UK. www.humantraffickingfoundation.org

Sex, war and the military

- Gender Action for Peace and Security (GAPS): the UK's Women, Peace and Security civil society network. It is a membership organisation of NGOs and experts in the field of development, human rights, humanitarian response and peacebuilding. https://gaps-uk.org
- Stop Rape Now: UN Action against Sexual Violence in Conflict (UN Action) unites the work of 13 UN entities with the goal of ending sexual violence in conflict. It is a concerted effort by the UN system to improve coordination and accountability, amplify programming and advocacy, and support national efforts to prevent sexual violence and respond effectively to the needs of survivors. www.stoprapenow.org
- Stop the War coalition: founded in September 2001 in the weeks following 9/11, when George W. Bush announced the 'war on terror'. Stop the War has since been dedicated to preventing and ending the wars in Afghanistan, Iraq, Libya and elsewhere. www.stopwar.org.uk
- Preventing Sexual Violence in Conflict Initiative (PSVI): aims to raise awareness of the extent of sexual violence against women, men, girls and boys in situations of armed conflict, and to rally global action to end it. www.gov.uk/government/organisations/preventing-sexual-violence-in-conflict-initiative/about
- Protect Our Defenders: Ending the epidemic of military rape: the only national organisation solely dedicated to ending the epidemic of rape and sexual assault in the military and to combating a culture of pervasive misogyny,

sexual harassment and retribution against victims. It honours, supports and give voice to survivors of military sexual assault and sexual harassment, including servicemembers, veterans and civilians assaulted by members of the military. www.protectourdefenders.com

Sex work

- English Collective of Prostitutes: campaign for the decriminalisation of prostitution, for sex workers' rights and safety, and for resources to enable people to get out of prostitution if they want to. http://prostitutescollective.net
- Beyond the Streets: a UK charity working to end sexual exploitation, which creates routes out for women by working with others and challenging the stigma that surrounds sexual exploitation. https://beyondthestreets.org.uk
- Global Network of Sex Work Projects: www.nswp.org/members/europe/uk-network-sex-work-projects-uknswp
- SWARM Collective: founded and led by sex workers who believe in self-determination, solidarity and co-operation. www.swarmcollective.org
- Scarlet Alliance: a national peak sex workers' organisation in Australia. www.scarletalliance.org.au
- New Zealand's Prostitutes Collective: www.nzpc.org.nz

Reproductive justice

- My Body My Rights, Amnesty International: www.amnesty.org/en/get-involved/my-body-my-rights
- Women's Global Network for Reproductive Rights: http://wgnrr.org
- Campaign to decriminalise abortion in the UK: https://wetrustwomen.org.uk
- National Advocates for Pregnant Women (USA): www.advocatesforpregnantwomen.org
- International Campaign for Women's Right to Safe Abortion: www.safeabortion-womensright.org

LGBT+ activism

- Black and Pink: a US-based organisation which seeks to abolish the criminal punishment system and to liberate LGBTQIA2S+ people/people living with HIV who are affected by that system. www.blackandpink.org
- Kaleidoscope Trust: seeks to uphold the human rights of lesbian, gay, bisexual and transgender (LGBT+) people in countries around the world where they are discriminated against or marginalised. https://kaleidoscopetrust.com
- UK Black Pride: Europe's largest celebration for LGBTQ people of African, Asian, Caribbean, Middle Eastern and Latin American descent. It produces an annual

celebration during pride month, as well as a variety of activities throughout the year in and around the UK. www.ukblackpride.org.uk/mission-statements
- Just Like Us: student volunteers go into secondary schools to share their LGBT+ stories, eradicate stereotypes and explain why LGBT+ equality is important. www.justlikeus.org/about
- PFLAG: works to make sure that all people who are lesbian, gay, bisexual, transgender and queer are not only valued by society, but also take pride in and value themselves. The organisation does this through providing peer-to-peer support, educating people on the issues that are important to the community, and advocating for inclusive policies and laws. https://pflag.org/proudpeople

Disability

- Touching Base: connects disabled people with sex workers, providing information for people with disability or their carers on how to access the sex industry and the Touching Base Referral List. www.touchingbase.org
- Alzheimer's Society: provides details of organisations that can provide information and support about dementia, sex and intimate relationships. www.alzheimers.org.uk/get-support/daily-living/sex-intimacy-dementia-other-resources#content-start
- Ann Craft Trust: supports organisations to safeguard adults and young people at risk and minimise the risk of harm. www.anncrafttrust.org

Other

- Unchained at Last: a campaign to end child marriage. www.unchainedatlast.org
- We Can't Consent to This: a campaign to act against the increased use of 'rough sex' defences in the killing or violent injury of women and girls. https://wecantconsenttothis.uk

Glossary

The following list outlines how we understand the terms in this book. They are not definitive definitions, because this book is not a dictionary, but we want them to aid you in your reading.

Abject   the abject is something that provokes disgust. It is applied to something or someone who is deemed perverse, threatening and dangerous. It suggests matter that is 'polluted', impure and/or contaminated.

Abolitionism   in prostitution scholarship, the term abolitionism is used to refer to those individuals and organisations who believe prostitution is necessarily exploitative and seek to create a prostitution-free world.

Agency   in criminology and other social sciences, we use this word to describe the ability to make decisions about yourself – to self-determine – and to have the freedom to act on those decisions and choices. Having agency is considered to be an important part of being fully human.

BAME   an acronym standing for Black, Asian, and Minority Ethnic. This is an inclusive but problematised category because it subsumes (and therefore can be accused of erasing) specific Black experiences, and the specific lived experiences of different ethnic minorities.

Black/White   where we use Black and White with capital letters, it is to designate that these are political positions. Political Blackness foregrounds people's experiences of White supremacy. Political Blackness centres the experiences of non-white people and reminds us that 'race' is a social construct.

Capitalism   an economic and political system in which a country's trade and industry are controlled by private owners for profit, rather than by the state. It is related to the free market.

Cis/cisgender   the opposite of trans or transgender. Someone whose gender identity matches the sex that they were assigned at birth.

Class   here understood as a hierarchical system of organising society based on wealth, social, and economic status.

Colonialism/neo-colonialism   colonialism is the practice whereby one state occupies another for the purposes of exploiting its people and resources for its own gain. Colonial practices started in Europe in the fifteenth century, in Japan and China in the nineteenth century, and continued in some form until the middle of the twentieth century (some would argue they continue into the present day). Neo-colonialism describes how non-state actors, organisations, businesses and ideas continue to colonise. It also describes how former colonies continue to be exploited by previous colonial powers.

Common law   A collection of past legal decisions written by courts and tribunal in the process of making judgements and rulings in cases before them; such rulings create precedent for future understanding and application of the law. When making judgements, the courts analyse the law and interpret statute in line with the case being heard. Courts are bound by past rulings (previous case law). Courts are bound by the decisions from the courts above them, while higher courts can overturn decisions made in the lower courts – for example, in England and Wales the Court of Appeal is bound by decisions from the Supreme Court and cannot overturn these judgements, while the Supreme Court can overturn decisions from the Court of Appeal.

Deconstruction   in this contemporary era, we consider that many ideas that we took for granted are actually constructed by different exercises of power, politics and ideology. We now understand that gender, class, 'race', heteronormativity or sexuality are not biological facts but are constructed through interaction with social and cultural norms. Deconstruction is the work of unpacking what composes these ideas: it is a critical practice of analysing what norms, power plays and assumptions make those ideas normal. It is a practice; therefore, it gets easier to do the more you do it.

Deviance   a word used to describe whatever is outside the norm: whatever deviates from the mainstream. In the study of sex and crime, understanding deviance is important because legal instruments will not always be used to control deviant sexuality to render sexual practice deviant, so, even though as criminologists we are interested in crime, understanding the role that deviance plays helps us take our analysis of sex and crime further.

Discourse   usually information given through speech. In the context of criminology, sociology and social sciences more broadly, the word is used to describe how information and knowledge are created and shared to exert influence over our lives. Discourses are created by speech acts from politicians, teachers and doctors, for instance. They are also created through norms of dress, media representations, beauty norms and child-rearing practices (you can probably think of many more).

Ethnicity   a social group that shares a common and distinctive culture, religion, language, history and geography.

Ethnonationalism   nationalism tied to the dominant ethnic group of a nation, where one ethnic group feels entitled to dominance and to the expulsion of other ethnic groups. This form of nationalism is prevalent in genocidal wars and 'ethnic cleansing', but is also important in understanding anti-immigration politics.

Experiential knowledge   knowledge acquired through experience, through trying things out or experimenting, rather than knowledge that is purely theoretical.

Femonationalism   describes the political practice by nations of demonising other countries for being 'backward' or barbaric by claiming their own feminist credentials: using feminism as an alibi for racism in foreign policy.

Free market   an economic system in which the price of goods is largely unregulated by the state, and instead responds to the desires of consumers, the number of consumers and the availability of purchasable goods and services (supply and demand).

Gender   used to distinguish between cultural and social differences which compose masculinity and femininity along a spectrum. Distinguished from sex (a biological category) and sexuality (an expression of sexual preference).

Gendered   when we say something is gendered, we mean that it is composed in part of stereotypical, perhaps, ideas of masculinity and femininity, and that this gendering is often taken for granted or ignored (think of the gendering of baby clothes, magazines or advertising for chocolate bars).

Global North   usually used to describe wealthier democratic countries which tend to be in the northern hemisphere (except for New Zealand and Australia). *See also* **Western**.

Globalisation   describes the increased flow of people, goods, work and ideas across the globe and across national, cultural and political borders. Globalisation has both positive and negative effects.

Governance   the processes of governing and the means through which governing happens. In terms of how a country/state is run, this would be the mechanisms through which power and control are wielded, so laws that are in place and are then applied, as well as policies that are followed within and by state organisations, such as criminal justice, health, education, and welfare services. Non-state/government structures also have governance, for example the structures that control how a family or kin group operates, or how an organisation works, such as a business or a university.

Harm   from a criminological perspective, a harm is an injury or damage. It can be physical, emotional, financial, environmental, and so on. It describes a detriment that something or someone (or a group of someones) suffers. It often goes hand in hand with risk. Risks are calculated based on the harms that they may cause.

Hegemonic masculinity a dominant form of masculinity that idealises stereo-typical 'successful' performances of masculinity and is used to justify the domination of some expressions of masculinity over women and other men. The theory of hegemonic masculinity recognises that there are many ways of 'doing' masculinity, but that only some are legitimated as being appropriately successful.

Heteronormativity this naturalises and privileges sexual relations between people of the opposite sex. Heterosexual sex is treated as the appropriate and 'correct' way to perform sexual relations. Conversely, homosexual relations are regarded as deviant and aberrant. The term 'compulsory heterosexuality', used by many feminists, reminds us that this sexual identity is one that is required and expected and may not be freely chosen by all.

Hetero-hypermasculinity hypermasculinity refers to an exaggerated version of masculinity, which is often represented physically by an excessive musculature. Placing the term hetero in front of it reminds us that this heightened/excessive version of masculinity is based on heterosexuality. The term emerged during the 1980s in response to the crisis of masculinity. This was an era during which hegemonic masculinity was being challenged by the rise of the women's and gay rights movements. Hypermasculinity, i.e. hegemonic masculinity writ large, is deployed when men feel threatened, belittled and insecure.

Homonationalism describes countries which espouse a nationalistic idealism – indeed a racism – against other countries using liberal attitudes towards homosexuality as an alibi for that behaviour.

Human rights the idea that every person is entitled to the same rights, regardless of their status, ethnicity, class, gender, culture, religion or sexual orientation. The idea was formalised by the United Nations in 1948 with the Universal Declaration of Human Rights.

Industrial/post-industrial economy while an industrial economy is one that mostly functions via industrial production, a post-industrial economy is centered on consumption. In historical terms, industrial economies in the Global North were established in the nineteenth century after the Industrial Revolution. The passage to post-industrial economies began in the 1960s and was consolidated in the 1980s.

Institutions can be used to mean organisations that support social, educational, economic, political, or religious functions for the purpose of ensuring public good or benefit. Alternatively, it can be used to denote a significant, normative practice in society, such as the institution of marriage, or the institution of the family.

LGBT + an acronym which stands for lesbian, gay, bisexual, transgender. The + sign indicates that it is an acronym which incorporates queer and non-cis identities beyond these four identities (including, for instance, inter-sex, asexual, queer, questioning, pansexual).

Migration the movement of human and non-human animals from one place to another. It is important to consider that migration is observable in nature, so it is not only a human phenomenon. Before the establishment of agricultural settlements in human societies, humans led nomadic lives, which means they often migrated from one place to another in search of food.

Misogyny the hatred of women.

Modernity used to describe many different eras and timeframes. In this book, we use it to describe a post-nineteenth-century period that accompanies the rise of capitalism, the decline of industry, the rise of individualism and the decline of the influence of traditional moral values (e.g. religion).

Morbidity the rate of disease or of becoming diseased.

Nation a people who share a history, culture, society, values and religion. They are not necessarily bound by a geographic territory; a nation-state is a nation governed by its own sovereign state, where each state contains one nation. This idea is almost never achieved.

Objectivity the opposite of subjectivity, objective knowledge describes knowledge that is unbiased and unswayed by personal experiences, opinions or feelings. Facts which are objective are generally thought to be measurable and uniform.

Orientalism evoking cultures, countries, practices, beliefs and ideologies attributed to the 'East' – to Asia – as exotic and backward compared to how things are in 'the West'.

Paternalism a concept, policy, and/or practice, involving the interference by the State, a body, or an individual into the lives or actions of others, limiting autonomy, with the intention of betterment, or protection from harm. Examples of paternalism can be seen in laws requiring drivers and passengers in cars wear seatbelts: imposing obligations on individuals that are supposed to be for their own good.

Patriarchy a system in which men hold power and women are excluded from power.

Phallocentrism including phallocentric societies and phallocentric masculinity, this places emphasis on the phallus, where the penis is associated with male privilege and power. Within this ideology, the phallus is what affords men their authority and superiority.

Populism an approach to politics where politicians appeal to the concerns of ordinary people against the interests of elite groups in order to obtain popular support.

It is important to consider that appealing to the people does not mean representing them. Many populist politicians are in fact members of the elite.

Power   etymologically tied to the word ability, it is often used as synonym of authority, in the sense of possession of power and influence over people (including yourself) and things. Such power can be physical, or it can come from status and political positioning. In the social sciences, there are broadly two conceptions of power: one deriving from Marxist tradition and the other from post-structuralism. The former sees power as fixed and possessed by social, cultural, political, and economic elites. The latter sees power as diffuse, socially and culturally embedded and tied to knowledge. In this view, power is seen as both repressive and productive – targeted at the control of the population and the creation of self-governing individuals. Rather than merely an instrument of repression, power is an omnipresent force that is neither intrinsically good nor evil, so it can be expressed through both dominance and resistance.

Prostitute/sex worker   prostitution denotes the activity of exchanging sex for money. It derives from the Latin *prostitut*, which means exposed publicly. The words prostitution/prostitute are used in legislation that regulate the activity, which is considered to be against the sexual norms of society and is therefore mostly criminalised. The term sex worker was coined by Carol Leigh in 1980 for the purpose of acknowledging the activity as a form of work, and to challenge the stigma associated with it.

Public health   a system of health care concerned with the wellbeing of a population. It is associated with hygiene infrastructure, educational campaigns, public vaccination programmes, free contraception programmes, systems of taxation which encourage healthy diet choices, and so on.

'Race'   we write 'race' in inverted commas here to remind us that what we call 'race' is a social and cultural construct. Race is sometimes wrongly used when people want to talk about ethnicity as a biological category. Recognising that 'race' is a construct and not a biologically given fact helps to undermine the racism of policies, medical interventions and ideologies that distinguish between people based on 'race'. 'Race' is a construct, while racism is not.

Rape culture   the normalisation and legitimisation of violence against women. In rape culture the threat of male violence is omnipresent and gendered violence is considered to be banal.

Restorative justice   aimed at restoring community cohesion in the aftermath of harmful conduct by community members, it is about restoration rather than retribution. Its principles and practice derive from tribal societies and are still practiced by many indigenous communities, such as the Aborigines in Australia. Restorative justice has become formally incorporated into Anglophone criminal justice systems from the 1990s. It usually involves voluntary participation to a *conference* where both victims and offenders are able to talk about their experience of the crime focusing on the harm generated and on how to heal and repair the harm.

Sex-positive/negative   Sex-positivity and sex-negativity are associated with attitudes towards sexuality and sexual practice. Sex-positivity can be used to describe a tolerant, liberal, accepting attitude towards people's sexual choices, and recognises that sex is a part of a healthy existence. Sex-negativity is associated with shame and stigma around sexual practice. Sex-positivity can be problematic, however, as permissive attitudes towards sex can be used to shame or bully people for perhaps holding more conservative sexual ethics or as a guise for accepting abusive behaviour in a relationship. For this reason, we sometimes use the term sex-critical to describe the critical and questioning attitude that we take to analysing sex and sexuality.

Sexual practice   ways of having sex or of expressing sexual desire.

Sexuality   sexual orientation. Sexuality is sometimes conflated with sexual power, or sexual practice, but here we use the word sexuality to mean sexual preference.

Social justice   a political practice of striving for just outcomes in social terms (equal access to health care, education, formal justice in the courts, political expression, and so on).

The State/a state   this means two things: (a) a territory with clear borders and an independent, sovereign government; (b) it also describes the acts of institutions of power. The actions of the police, medical services, educational provision, prison system and judiciary can all be described as actions of the State.

Subjectivity   the opposite of objectivity, subjective knowledge is knowledge that is partial, that recognises that it is somehow biased and influenced by the knower's life experience. As a noun, subjectivity describes personhood and lived experience which is influenced by individuals' different experiences.

Transgender (or trans)   the opposite of cis gender – someone who does not identify as the sex to which they were assigned at birth. The Oxford English dictionary added the term trans * (with an asterisk) to its collection in 2018 using it to 'indicate the inclusion of gender identities such as gender-fluid, agender, etc., alongside transsexual and transgender' (see Steinmetz, 3 April 2018). The term has been used by the LGBT+ community since the 1990s to acknowledge the multiple sexual and gender identities that exist outside the male-female binary. And while transgender people (following transition) may regard themselves as male or female, a large number of people identify as non-binary, gender-fluid (where their gender identity changes over time), bi-gender (where they identify with both genders) or agender (where they have no gender) (Steinmetz, 3 April 2018). For some the term is inclusive and empowering, some believe it is misapplied and others feel the asterisks is unnecessary and redundant (Steinmetz, 3 April 2018).

Transitional justice   usually reserved for exceptional circumstances where countries have undergone human rights abuses so severe that the traditional justice process is regarded as inadequate. The main steps of transitional justice are criminal prosecutions, truth-seeking, reparations, and reforms. Transitional justice is unique in actively involving communities in the justice process, mixing elements of traditional and restorative justice while also seeking institutional reform.

Western   the 'West' is often used to describe capitalist economically developed countries. We sometimes write 'West' and 'Western' in inverted commas to problematise a coherent idea of what counts as Western. What is the West supposed to be Western to? Is Australia the West? Is Japan? Is Canada? When we talk about the West, we are imagined to mean what we used to call the First World or the Developed World. We no longer use these colonialist terms. We might refer to it as the Global North (though this is incomplete), the Anglo-Saxon world (though this is also incomplete) or post-industrialist countries (though this does not roll off the tongue). The bottom line is that when you are talking about these places, you should try and be precise and to avoid colonialist ideas.

References

Aas, K.F. (2013) *Globalization and Crime*. London: Sage.

Abbott, D. (2013) 'Nudge, nudge, wink, wink: Love, sex and gay men with intellectual disabilities – a helping hand or a human right?', *Journal of Intellectual Disability Research*, 57(11): 1079–87.

Adichie, C.N. (2017) *Dear Ijeawele, or a Feminist Manifesto in Fifteen Suggestions*. New York: Anchor/Alfred A. Knopf.

Aguilar, L., Araujo, A. and Quesada-Aguilar, A. (n.d.) *Gender and Climate Change*. Available at: www.gdnonline.org/resources/IUCN_FactsheetClimateChange.pdf.

Aguilera, R.J. (2000) 'Disability and delight: Staring back at the devotee community', *Sexuality and Disability*, 18(4): 255–61.

Akdeniz, Y. (2016) *Internet Child Pornography and the Law: National and international responses*. London: Routledge.

Alvaredo, F., Chancel, L., Piketty, T., Saez, E. and Zucman, G. (eds) (2018) *World Inequality Report 2018*. Cambridge, MA: Belknap Press.

Alvarez, M.B. and Alessi, E.J. (2012) 'Human trafficking is more than sex trafficking and prostitution: Implications for social work', *Affilia*, 27(2): 142–52.

Anderson, R. (23 September 2017) '"Here I am, 26, with no friends, no job, no girlfriend": Shooter's manifesto offers clues to 2015 Oregon college rampage', *Los Angeles Times*. Available at: www.latimes.com/nation/la-na-school-shootings-2017-story.html.

Annamma, S.A. (2012) 'Dis/ability critical race studies (DisCrit): Theorizing at the intersections of race and dis/ability', *Race Ethnicity and Education*, 16(1): 1–31.

Antosik-Parsons, K. (2014) 'Suppressed voices: The suffering and silencing of Irish institutional abuse survivors in Áine Phillips's redress performances', *Études irlandaises*, 39(1): 137–52.

Aratani, L. and Pilkington, E. (11 March 2020) 'Harvey Weinstein sentenced to 23 years in prison on rape conviction', *The Guardian*, Available at: www.theguardian.com/world/2020/mar/11/harvey-weinstein-sentencing-rape-conviction.

Archard, D. (1997) '"A nod's as good as a wink": Consent, convention, and reasonable belief', *Legal Theory*, 3(3): 273-290.

Archard, D. (1998) *Sexual Consent*. Boulder, CO: Westview Press.

Ariès, P. (1962) *Centuries of Childhood: A social history of family life*. Harmondsworth: Penguin.

Ashford, C. (2010) 'Bare-backing and the "cult of violence": Queering the criminal law', *The Journal of the Criminal Law*, 74: 339–57.

Aspinall, G. (25 October 2019) 'Why is it only when Universal Credit forces women into sex work the government actually listens?', *Grazia*. Available at: https://graziadaily.co.uk/life/in-the-news/universal-credit-sex-work.

Associated Press (13 February 2019) 'FBI received warning about gunman in yoga studio shooting, police say', *NBC News*. Available at: www.nbcnews.com/news/

us-news/fbi-received-warning-about-gunman-yoga-studio-shooting-police-say-n971006.

Atlas (2016) *Suicide Squad* [film]. Directed by D. Ayer. Los Angeles, CA: Atlas Entertainment.

Attwood, F. and Smith, C. (2010) 'Extreme concern: Regulating "dangerous pictures" in the United Kingdom', *Journal of Law and Society*, 37(1): 171–88.

Augustin, L.M. (2005) *Sex at the Margins: Labour, markets and the rescue industry*. London: Zed Books.

Baaz, M.K. and Stern, M. (2009) 'Why do soldiers rape? Masculinity, violence, and sexuality in the armed forces in the Congo (DCR)', *International Studies Quarterly*, 53(2): 495–518.

Baaz, M.K. and Stern, M. (2018) 'Curious erasures: The sexual in wartime sexual violence international', *Feminist Journal of Politics*, 20(3): 295–314.

Babchishin, K.M., Hanson, R.K. and VanZuylen, H. (2015) 'Online child pornography offenders are different: A meta-analysis of the characteristics of online and offline sex offenders against children', *Archives of Sexual Behavior*, 44(1): 45–66.

Baldwin, L. (2020) '"A life sentence": The long-term impact of maternal imprisonment', in Lockwood, K. (ed.), *Mothers Inside* (working title). Bingley: Emerald Publishing.

Ball, M. (2016) "The Prison of Love' and its queer discontents: On the value of paranoid and reparative readings in queer criminological scholarship', in Dwyer, A., Ball, M. and Crofts, T. (eds), *Queering Criminology*. New York: Palgrave Macmillan, pp. 54–83.

Banwell, S. (2014) 'Rape and sexual violence in the Democratic Republic of Congo: A case study of gender-based violence', *Journal of Gender Studies*, 23(1): 45–58.

Banwell, S. (2015) 'Rassenschande, genocide and the reproductive Jewish body: Examining the use of rape and sexualized violence against Jewish women during the Holocaust', *Journal of Modern Jewish Studies*, 15(2): 208–27.

Banwell, S. (2019) 'Gender, North–South relations: Reviewing the Global Gag Rule and the defunding of UNFPA under President Trump', *Third World Quarterly*, 41(1): 1–19.

Banwell, S. (2020) *Gender and the Violence(s) of War and Armed Conflict: More dangerous to be a woman?* Bingley: Emerald Publishing.

Banwell, S. and Fiddler, M. (2018) 'Gendered viewing strategies: a critique of Holocaust-related films that eroticize, monsterize and fetishize the female body', *Holocaust Studies*, 24(2): 150–71.

Barberá, P., Jost, J.T., Nagler, J., Tucker, J.A. and Bonneau, R. (2015) 'Tweeting from left to right: Is online political communication more than an echo chamber?', *Psychological Science*, 26(10): 1531–42.

Bard, E., Knight, M. and Plugge, E. (2016) 'Perinatal health care services for imprisoned pregnant women and associated outcomes: A systematic review', *BMC Pregnancy and Childbirth*, 16(1): 285–304.

Barker, N. (2013) *Not the Marrying Kind: A feminist critique of same-sex marriage*. Basingstoke: Palgrave Macmillan.

Barry, K. (1995) *The Prostitution of Sexuality: the global exploitation of women*. New York: New York University Press.

Barquel (1978) *I Spit on Your Grave* [film]. Directed by M. Zarchi. Los Angeles, CA: Barquel Creations.

Barthes, R. (1977) *Image, Music, Text* (trans. S Heath). London: Fontana.

Bauman, Z. (2013) *Liquid Modernity*. New York: John Wiley & Sons.

Baynes, C. (8 July 2017) 'More than 200,000 children married in US over the last 15 years', *The Independent*. Available at: www.independent.co.uk/news/world/americas/200000-children-married-us-15-years-child-marriage-child-brides-new-jersey-chris-christie-a7830266.html.

BBC (31 January 2000) 'Surgeon defends amputations', *BBC News*. Available at: http://news.bbc.co.uk/1/hi/scotland/625680.stm.

BBC (2006) *I Love Being HIV+* [film]. Directed by R. Pendry. London: BBC.

BBC (8 January 2011) 'Jack Straw: Some white girls are "easy meat" for abuse', *BBC News*. Available at: www.bbc.co.uk/news/uk-england-derbyshire-12141603.

BBC (31 October 2011) 'Uganda fury at David Cameron aid threat over gay rights', *BBC News*. Available at: www.bbc.co.uk/news/world-africa-15524013.

BBC (4 July 2014) 'Rolf Harris jailed for five years and nine months', *BBC News*. Available at: www.bbc.co.uk/news/uk-28163593.

BBC (24 July 2015) 'Hundreds of police officers convicted in past three years', *BBC News*. Available at: www.bbc.co.uk/news/uk-33635962.

BBC (11 July 2017) 'Thousands of children sexting, police say', *BBC News*. Available at: www.bbc.co.uk/news/uk-40566026.

BBC (18 April 2018) 'Daryll Rowe jailed for infecting men with HIV', *BBC News*. Available at: www.bbc.co.uk/news/uk-england-sussex-43807662.

BBC (25 April 2018) 'Alek Minassian Toronto van attack', *BBC News*. Available at www.bbc.co.uk/news/world-us-canada-43883052.

BBC (30 October 2018) 'Fleetwood man jailed for infecting women with HIV', *BBC News*. Available at: www.bbc.co.uk/news/uk-england-lancashire-46031023.

BBC (14 December 2018) 'Undercover officer won't face prosecution over relationship', *BBC News*. Available at: www.bbc.co.uk/news/uk-46570224.

BBC (27 February 2019) 'Bradford grooming: Nine jailed for abusing girls', *BBC News*. Available at: www.bbc.co.uk/news/uk-england-leeds-47388060.

BBC (4 March 2019) 'Undercover police: Women were "victims of co-ordinated rape"', *BBC News*. Available at: www.bbc.co.uk/news/uk-wales-47240670.

BBC (13 June 2019) 'Abortion: 1,053 women from NI travelled to England and Wales', *BBC News*. Available at: www.bbc.co.uk/news/uk-northern-ireland-48626564.

BBC (13 September 2019) 'Domestic violence killings reach five-year high', *BBC News*. Available at: www.bbc.co.uk/news/uk-49459674.

BBC (25 October 2019) 'Universal Credit: MPs call for action on women driven to "survival sex"', *BBC News*. Available at: www.bbc.co.uk/news/uk-50170297.

BBFC (2005) *BBFC Annual Report 2005*. Available at: www.bbfc.co.uk/sites/default/files/attachments/BBFC_AnnualReport_2005.pdf.

BBFC (2010) *I Spit on Your Grave*. Available at: www.bbfc.co.uk/releases/i-spit-your-grave-film.

BBFC (2018) *Revenge*. Available at: www.bbfc.co.uk/releases/revenge-film.

BBFC (2020) *Love Camp 7*. Available at: www.bbfc.co.uk/releases/love-camp-7-vod.

Beauchamp, Z. (23 April 2019) 'Our Incel problem', *vox.com*. Available at: www.vox.com/the-highlight/2019/4/16/18287446/incel-definition-reddit.

Bechdel, A. (2006) *Fun Home: A family tragicomic*. London: Vintage.

Beck, U. (1992) *Risk Society: Towards a new modernity*. London: Sage.

Beier, K.M. (2018) 'Preventing child sexual abuse: The prevention Project Dunkelfeld', *The Journal of Sexual Medicine*, 15: 1065–6.

Bell, D. (1992) 'The space traders', in *Faces at the Bottom of the Well: The permanence of racism*. New York: Basic Books, pp. 158–94.

Bell, D. (2006) 'Bodies, technologies, spaces: On "dogging"', *Sexualities*, 9(4): 387–407.

Bell, D. and Binnie, J. (2000) *The Sexual Citizen: Queer politics and beyond.* Cambridge: Polity Press.

Bentham, J. (1887) *Theory of Legislation.* London: Trübner & Co.

Ben Ze'ev, A. (2004) *Love Online: Emotions on the internet.* Cambridge: Cambridge University Press.

Beres, M.A. (2014) 'Rethinking the concept of consent for anti-sexual violence activism and education', *Feminism & Psychology,* 24(3): 373–89.

Beres, M.A. (2018) 'What does faking orgasms have to do with sexual consent?', *Sexualities,* 21(4): 702–5.

Berlant, L. and Warner, M. (1998) 'Sex in public', *Critical Enquiry,* 24(2): 547–66.

Berlin, I. (1969) *Four Essays on Liberty.* Oxford: Clarendon Press.

Bernstein, E. (2010) 'Militarized humanitarianism meets carceral feminism: The politics of sex, rights, and freedom in contemporary antitrafficking campaigns', *Signs: Journal of Women in Culture and Society,* 36(1): 45–71.

Bernstein, E. (2012) 'Carceral politics as gender justice? The "traffic in women" and neoliberal circuits of crime, sex, and rights', *Theory and Society,* 41(3): 233–59.

Bhaskar, R. and Danermark, B. (2006) 'Metatheory, interdisciplinarity and disability research: A critical realist perspective', *Scandinavian Journal of Disability Research,* 8(4): 278–97.

Bierria, A. (2011) '"Where them bloggers at?" Reflections on Rihanna, accountability, and survivor subjectivity', *Social Justice,* 37(4): 101–25.

Bindel, J. (2017) *The Pimping of Prostitution.* London: Palgrave Macmillan.

Bingemer, M.C.L. (2019) 'Concerning victims, sexuality, and power: A reflection on sexual abuse from Latin America', *Theological Studies,* 80(4): 916–30.

Birthrights (2013) *Dignity in Childbirth,* 16 October. Available at: https://birthrights.org.uk/wp-content/uploads/2013/10/Birthrights-Dignity-Survey-1.pdf.

Bishop, J. (2014) 'Representations of "trolls" in mass media communication: A review of media-texts and moral panics relating to "Internet trolling"', *International Journal of Web Based Communities,* 10(1): 7–24.

Blackstone, W. (1791) *Commentaries on the Laws of England,* Vol. 4, 11th edn. London: T. Cadell.

Blackwood, E. (2005) 'Wedding bell blues: Marriage, missing men, and matrifocal follies', *American Ethnologist,* 32(1): 3–19.

Blank, H. (2007) *Virgin: The Untouched History.* New York: Bloomsbury.

Blanke, O., Morgenthaler, F.D., Brugger, P. and Overney, L.S. (2009) 'Preliminary evidence for a fronto-parietal dysfunction in able-bodied participants with a desire for limb amputation', *Journal of Neuropsychology,* 3(Pt 2): 181–200.

Block, M.R. (2016[2013]) '"For the repressing of the most wicked and felonious rapes or ravishments of women": Rape law in England, 1660–1800', in Greenfield, A. (ed.), *Interpreting Sexual Violence, 1660–1800.* London and New York: Routledge.

Bloom, S. (2014) 'No vengeance for revenge porn victims: Unraveling why this latest female-centric, intimate-partner offense is still legal, and why we should criminalize it', *Fordham Urb. LJ,* 42: 233–90.

Böhm, B., Zollner, H., Fegert, J.M. and Liebhardt, H. (2014) 'Child sexual abuse in the context of the Roman Catholic Church: A review of literature from 1981–2013', *Journal of Child Sexual Abuse,* 23(6): 635–56.

Bonomi, A.E., Nemeth, J.M., Altenburger, L.E., Anderson, M.L., Snyder, A. and Dotto, I. (2014) 'Fiction or not? *Fifty Shades* is associated with health risks in adolescent and young adult females', *Journal of Women's Health,* September: 720–8.

Bordo, S. (2003) *Unbearable Weight: Feminism, western culture, and the body*. Berkeley, CA: University of California Press.

Borrell-Carrió, F., Suchman, A.L. and Epstein, R.M. (2004) 'The biopsychosocial model 25 years later: principles, practice, and scientific inquiry', *The Annals of Family Medicine*, 2(6): 576–582.

Bourke, J.B. (2007) *Rape: A history from 1860 to present day*. London: Virago.

Bourne, A., Reid, D., Hickson, F., Torres Rueda, S. and Weatherburn, P. (2014) 'The Chemsex study: Drug use in sexual settings among gay and bisexual men in Lambeth, Southwark & Lewisham', *London: Sigma Research*. London School of Hygiene & Tropical Medicine. Available at: www.sigmaresearch.org.uk/chemsex.

Bowcott, O. (23 July 2019) 'Police demands for access to rape victims' phones "unlawful"', *The Guardian*. Available at: www.theguardian.com/law/2019/jul/23/police-demands-for-access-to-victims-phones-unlawful.

Bradley, G.V. (2018) 'Prolegomon on pornography', *Harvard Journal of Law and Public Policy*, 41: 447–98.

Brayboy, B.M.J. (2005) 'Toward a tribal critical race theory in education', *The Urban Review*, 37(5): 425–46.

Brennan, J. (2017) 'Oscar Pistorius: Disability discourses in homosexual forums', *Disability & Society*, 32(4): 521–41.

Brett, N. (1998) 'Sexual offenses and consent', *Canadian Journal of Law & Jurisprudence*, 69(1): 69–88.

Broadbent, L. (9 December 2011) 'Rape in the US military: America's dirty little secret', *The Guardian*. Available at: www.theguardian.com/society/2011/dec/09/rape-us-military.

Brown, R. (2012) 'Corrective rape in South Africa: A continuing plight despite an international human rights response', *Annual Survey of International and Comparative Law*, 18(1): 45–66.

Brownmiller, S. (1975) *Against our Will: Men, women and rape*. New York: Ballantine Books.

Bruno, R.L. (1997) 'Devotees, pretenders and wannabes: Two cases of factitious disability disorder', *Sexuality and Disability*, 15(4): 243–60.

Buchanan, T. and Whitty, M. (2014) 'The online dating romance scam: Causes and consequences of victimhood', *Psychology, Crime and Law*, 20(3): 261–83.

Buckingham, D., Willett, R., Bragg, S. and Russell, R. (2010) 'Sexualised goods aimed at children: A report to the Scottish Parliament Equal Opportunities Committee', *Scottish Parliament Equal Opportunities Committee*. Edinburgh: Scottish Parliament.

Buist, C. and Lenning, E. (2015) *Queer Criminology*. Abingdon: Routledge.

Bulger, M., Burton, P., O'Neill, B. and Staksrud, E. (2017) 'Where policy and practice collide: Comparing United States, South African and European Union approaches to protecting children online', *New Media & Society*, 19(5): 750–64.

Bulletin criminel (2005) No. 326. Available at: www.legifrance.gouv.fr/affichJuriJudi.do?oldAction = rechJuriJudi&idTexte = JURITEXT000007071639&fastReqId = 265893069&fastPos = 1.

Bunt, S. (2018) 'Critical realism and grounded theory: Analysing the adoption outcomes for disabled children using the retroduction framework', *Qualitative Social Work*, 17(2): 176–94.

Buss, D.E. (2009) 'Rethinking "rape as a weapon of war"', *Feminist Legal Studies*, 17: 145–63.

Butler, J. (1990) *Gender Trouble: Feminism and the subversion of identity*. London: Routledge.

Cahill, A.J. (2000) 'Foucault, rape, and the construction of the feminine body', *Hypatia*, 15(1): 43–63.

Califia, P. (1994) *Public Sex: The culture of radical sex*. Pittsburgh, PA: Penn Cleis Press.

Campbell, R. (2016) Not getting away with it: Addressing violence against sex workers as hate crime in Merseyside (Doctoral dissertation, Durham University).

Caprioli, S. and Crenshaw, D.A. (2017) 'The culture of silencing child victims of sexual abuse: Implications for child witnesses in court', *Journal of Humanistic Psychology*, 57(2): 190–209.

Card, C. (1996) 'Rape as a weapon of war', *Hypatia*, 11(4): 6–18.

Carline, A. (2011) 'Criminal justice, extreme pornography and prostitution: Protecting women or promoting morality?', *Sexualities*, 14(3): 312–33.

Carpenter, L.M. (2001) 'The ambiguity of "having sex": The subjective experience of virginity loss in the United States', *Journal of Sex Research*, 38(2): 127–39.

Carpenter, R. (2000) 'Surfacing children: Limitations of genocidal rape discourse', *Human Rights Quarterly*, 22(2): 428–77.

Carr-Gomm, P. (2010) *A brief history of nakedness*. Reaktion Books.

Carter, A. (1974) *Fireworks: Nine profane pieces*. London: Quartet Books.

Castells, M. (1999) *Information Technology, Globalization and Social Development* (Vol. 114). Geneva: United Nations Research Institute for Social Development.

Centers for Disease Control and Prevention (CDC) (2016) *More Than 3 Million US Women at Risk for Alcohol-Exposed Pregnancy*, 2 February. Available at: www.cdc.gov/media/releases/2016/p0202-alcohol-exposed-pregnancy.html.

Cerretti, J. (2016) 'Rape as a weapon of war(riors): The militarisation of sexual violence in the United States, 1990–2000', *Gender & History*, 28(3): 794–812.

Cherry, A.L. (2007) 'The detention, confinement, and incarceration of pregnant women for the benefit of fetal health', *Columbia Journal of Gender and Law*, 16(1): 149–99.

Chesney-Lind, M. and Shelden, R.G. (2013) *Girls, Delinquency, and Juvenile Justice*. New York: John Wiley & Sons.

Chiang, T. (2019) *The Lifecycle of Software Objects*. Burton, MI: Subterranean Press.

Chibnall, J.T., Wolf, A. and Duckro, P.N. (1998) 'A national survey of the sexual trauma experiences of Catholic nuns', *Review of Religious Research*, 40(2): 142–67.

Child Exploitation and Online Protection (CEOP) Command (2011) *Out of Mind, Out of Sight: Breaking down the barriers to understanding child sexual exploitation*. Available at: https://childhub.org/en/system/tdf/library/attachments/1303_Thematic_Assessment_280611c_original.pdf?file=1&type=node&id=6459.

Chou, Y.C. and Lu, Z.Y. (2011) 'Deciding about sterilisation: Perspectives from women with an intellectual disability and their families in Taiwan', *Journal of Intellectual Disability Research*, 55(1): 63–74.

Christian, M., Safar, O., Ramazani, P., Burnham, G. and Glass, N. (2011) 'Sexual and gender-based violence against men in the Democratic Republic of Congo: Effects on survivors, their families and the community', *Medicine, Conflict and Survival*, 27(4): 227–46.

Cineluce (1977) *Gestapo's Last Orgy* (L'Ultima Orgia Del III Reich) [Film]. Directed by C. Canevari. Unknown: Cineluce.

Citron, D.K. and Franks, M.A. (2014) 'Criminalising revenge porn', *Wake Forest Law Review*, 49: 345–91.

Clark, J.N. (2017) 'The vulnerability of the penis: Sexual violence against men in conflict and security frames', *Men and Masculinities*, 1–23. https://doi.org/10.1177/1097184X17724487.

Clark, K. (1956) *The Nude: A study of ideal art*. London: Penguin.

Clarke, D. (2013) 'Twice removed: African invisibility in Wester queer theory', in Ekine, E. and Abbas, K. (eds), *Queer African Reader*. Nairobi: Pambazuka Press, pp. 173–86.

Cliff, T. (1974) *State Capitalism in Russia*. London: Pluto Press.

Clough, A. (2019) 'Finding the balance: Intoxication and consent', *Liverpool Law Review*, 40(1): 49–64.

Clover, C.J. (1987) 'Her body, himself: Gender in the slasher film', *Representations*, 20, 187-228.

Clover, C.J. (1992) *Men, Women and Chainsaws: Gender in the modern horror film*. Princeton, NJ: Princeton University Press.

Cockbain, E. (2013) 'Grooming and the "Asian sex gang predator": The construction of a racial crime threat', *Race & Class*, 54(4): 22–32.

Cohen, A.K. (2003[1955]) 'A general theory of subcultures', *Culture: Critical Concepts in Sociology*, 3: 259–69.

Cohen, S. (2001) *States of Denial: Knowing about atrocities and suffering*. Cambridge: Polity Press.

Cohn, C. (2013) 'Women and wars: Toward a conceptual framework', in Cohn, C. (ed.), *Women and Wars*. Cambridge: Polity Press, pp. 1–35.

Coke, E. (1644[1681]) *The Third Part of the Institutes of the Laws of England: Concerning high treasons; and other pleas of the crime, and criminal causes*. London: Printed by W. Rawlins, for Thomas Basset at the George near St. Dunstans Church in Fleet-street.

Colleoni, E., Rozza, A. and Arvidsson, A. (2014) 'Echo chamber or public sphere? Predicting political orientation and measuring political homophily in Twitter using big data', *Journal of Communication*, 64(2): 317–32.

Collins, P.H. (2002[1990]) *Black Feminist Thought: Knowledge, consciousness, and the politics of empowerment*. Abingdon: Routledge.

Collins, P.H. (2005) 'Black women and motherhood', in Hardy, S. and Wiedmer, C. (eds), *Motherhood and Space*. New York: Palgrave Macmillan.

ConnectSafely (7 May 2018) 'Tips for dealing with teen sexting', *ConnectSafely.org*. Available at: www.connectsafely.org/tips-for-dealing-with-teen-sexting.

Connell, R.W. (1995) *Masculinities*. Berkeley, CA: University of California Press.

Connell, R.W. (1998) 'Masculinities and globalization', *Men and Masculinities*, 1(1): 3–23.

Connell, R.W. and Messerschmidt, J.W. (2005) 'Hegemonic masculinity: Rethinking the concept', *Gender & Society*, 19(6): 829–59.

Conway, B. (2014) 'Religious institutions and sexual scandals: A comparative study of Catholicism in Ireland, South Africa, and the United States', *International Journal of Comparative Sociology*, 55(4): 318–41.

Cooper, A. (1998) 'Sexuality and the Internet: Surfing into the new millennium', *CyberPsychology and Behaviour*, 1(2): 181–7.

Cooper, A. and Griffin-Shelley, E. (2002) 'A quick tour of online sexuality part 1', *Annals of the American Psychotherapy Association*, 5(6): 11–14.

Cooper, A., Delmonico, D.L. and Burg, R. (2000) 'Cybersex users, abusers, and compulsives: New findings and implications', *Sexual Addiction and Compulsivity: The Journal of Treatment and Prevention*, 7(1–2): 5–29.

Cooper, V. and Whyte, D. (2017) *The Violence of Austerity*. London: Pluto Press.

Cornwall, A. and Molyneux, M. (2006) 'The politics of rights: Dilemmas for feminist praxis – an introduction', *Third World Quarterly*, 27(7): 1175–91.

Council of Europe (n.d.) 'Hate speech and violence', *European Commission against Racism and Intolerance*. Available at: www.coe.int/en/web/european-commission-against-racism-and-intolerance/hate-speech-and-violence.

Coupaye, L. (forthcoming) 'Technology', in De Cunzo, L.A. and Roeber, C.D. (eds), *Cambridge Handbook of Material Culture*. Cambridge: Cambridge University Press.

Cowan, S. (2008) 'The trouble with drink: Intoxication, (in)capacity, and the evaporation of consent to sex', *Akron Law Review*, 41(4): 899–922.

Cowburn, A. (22 July 2019) 'UK approved nearly £650m in arms sales to Saudi Arabia in six months after Jamal Khashoggi murder', *The Independent*. Available at: www.independent.co.uk/news/uk/politics/uk-saudi-arabia-arms-deals-khashoggi-murder-government-licences-caat-a9015736.html.

Cox, P. (2003) *Gender, Justice and Welfare: Bad girls in Britain, 1900–1950*. London: Palgrave Macmillan.

Craven, S., Brown, S. and Gilchrist, E. (2007) 'Current responses to sexual grooming: Implication for prevention', *The Howard Journal of Criminal Justice*, 46(1): 60–71.

Crenshaw, K. (1989) 'Demarginalizing the intersection of race and sex: A black feminist critique of antidiscrimination doctrine, feminist theory and antiracist politics', *University of Chicago Legal Forum*, 19: 139–68.

Crime Survey for England and Wales (2018) *Sexual offences in England and Wales: year ending March 2017, 8 February*. Available at: www.ons.gov.uk/peoplepopulationand community/crimeandjustice/articles/sexualoffencesinenglandandwales/yearending march2017.

Cross, C. (2019) '"You're not alone": The use of peer support groups for fraud victims', *Journal of Human Behaviour in the Social Environment*, 29(5): 672–91.

Cross, C., Dragiewicz, M. and Richards, K. (2018) 'Understanding romance fraud: Insights from domestic violence research', *British Journal of Criminology*, 58(6): 1303–22.

Crown Prosecution Service (CPS) (2019) *Obscene Publications (revised 2019)*. Available at: www.cps.gov.uk/legal-guidance/obscene-publications.

Cruz, A. (2015) 'Beyond black and blue: BDSM, Internet pornography, and black female sexuality', *Feminist Studies*, 41(2): 409–36.

Cruz, E.M. and Sajo, T.J. (2015) 'Exploring the cybersex phenomenon in the Philippines', *EJISDC*, 69(5): 1–21.

Curtice, M., Mayo, J. and Crocombe, J. (2013) 'Consent and sex in vulnerable adults: A review of case law', *British Journal of Learning Disabilities*, 41(4): 280–7.

Dale, K.A. and Alpert, J.L. (2007) 'Hiding behind the cloth: Child sexual abuse and the Catholic Church', *Journal of Child Sexual Abuse*, 16(3): 59–74.

Dalton, D. (2016) 'Reflections on the emergence, efficacy, and value of queer criminology', in Dwyer, A., Ball, M. and Crofts, T. (eds), *Queering Criminology*. New York: Palgrave Macmillan, pp. 15–35.

Daly, M. (1990[1978]) *Gyn/Ecology: The metaethics of radical feminism*. London: The Women's Press.

Daneback, K., Copper, A. and Mansson, S. (2005) 'An Internet study of cybersex participants', *Archives of Sexual Behaviour*, 34(3): 321–8.

Davies, D. (2000a) 'Sharing our stories, empowering our lives: Don't dis me!', *Sexuality and Disability*, 18(3): 179–86.

Davies, D. (2000b) 'Sex and relationship facilitation project for people with disabilities', *Sexuality and Disability*, 18(3): 187–94.

Davis, S., Keith, T. and McCammon, S. (31 March 2020) 'Pandemic opens a new front in the battle over abortion access', *The NPR Politics Podcast*. Available at: www.npr. org/2020/03/31/824741669/pandemic-opens-a-new-front-in-the-battle-over-abortion-access?t = 1586439561623.

Dearden, N. (1999) 'The Queen and the Bolton Seven', *Feminist Legal Studies*, 7(3): 317–32.

Death, J. (2015) 'Bad apples, bad barrel: Exploring institutional responses to child sexual abuse by Catholic clergy in Australia', *International Journal for Crime, Justice and Social Democracy*, 4(2): 94–110.

Death, J. (2018) *Governing Child Abuse Voices and Victimisation: The use of public inquiry into child sexual abuse in Christian institutions*. London: Routledge.

Delgado, R. and Stefancic, J. (eds) (2000) *Critical Race Theory: The cutting edge*, 2nd edn. Philadelphia, PA: Temple University Press.

Denov, M. (2015) 'Children born of wartime rape: The intergenerational realities of sexual violence and abuse', *Ethics, Medicine and Public Health*, 1: 61–8.

Denov, M. and Kahn, S. (2019) '"They should see us as a symbol of reconciliation": Youth born of genocidal rape in Rwanda and the implications for transitional justice', *Journal of Human Rights Practice*, 11(1): 151–70.

Denov, M., Woolner, L., Bahati, J.P., Nsuki, P. and Shyaka, O. (2017) 'The intergenerational legacy of genocidal rape: The realities and perspectives of children born of the Rwandan genocide', *Journal of Interpersonal Violence*, 1–22. Available at: https://doi.org/10.1177/0886260517708407.

Denton, F. (2002) 'Climate change vulnerability, impacts, and adaptation: Why does gender matter?', *Gender & Development*, 10(2): 10–20.

Departmental Committee on Homosexual Offences and Prostitution (1957) 'Report of the Departmental Committee on Homosexual Offences and Prostitution (the Wolfenden report)', *Br Med J.*, 2(5045): 639–40.

Department of Defense (DoD) (2016) *Plan to Prevent and Respond to Sexual Assault of Military Men*. Available at: www.sapr.mil/sites/default/files/Fact-Sheet---DoD-Plan-to-Prevent-and-Respond-to-Sexual-Assault-of-Military-Men.pdf.

Department of Health and Social Care (2020) 'Abortion statistics for England and Wales: 2018', 5 March. Available at: www.gov.uk/government/statistics/abortion-statistics-for-england-and-wales-2018.

Devlin, K. (17 September 2015) 'In defence of sex machines: Why trying to ban sex robots is wrong', *The Conversation*. Available at: http://theconversation.com/in-defence-of-sex-machines-why-trying-to-ban-sex-robots-is-wrong-47641.

Dewey, S., Crowhurst, I. and Izugbara, C. (2018) 'Globally circulating discourses on the sex industry', *Routledge International Handbook of Sex Industry Research*. New York: Routledge.

Di Napoli, E.A., Breland, G.L. and Allen, R.S. (2013) 'Staff knowledge and perceptions of sexuality and dementia of older adults in nursing homes', *Journal of Aging and Health*, 25(7): 1087–105.

Dickens, B.M. (1966) *Abortion and the Law*. London: MacGibbon & Kee.

Dixon, M.A. (2004) 'Silencing the lambs: The Catholic Church's response to the 2002 sexual abuse scandal', *Journal of Communication & Religion*, 27(1): 63–86.

Dodge, A. (2016) 'Digitizing rape culture: Online sexual violence and the power of the digital photograph', *Crime, Media, Culture*, 12(1): 65–82.

Douglas, M. (1992) *Risk and Blame: Essays in cultural theory*. London: Routledge.

Douglas, M. (2002[1966]) *Purity and Danger: An analysis of concept of pollution and taboo*. Abingdon: Routledge.

Douglas, M. and Wildavsky, A. (1983) *Risk and Culture: An essay on the selection of technological and environmental dangers*. Berkeley, CA: University of California Press.

Douglass, F. (1857) 'If there is no struggle, there is no progress', *West India emancipation speech given at Canandaigua, New York*. Available at: www.blackpast.org/african-american-history/1857-frederick-douglass-if-there-no-struggle-there-no-progress.

Downes, J. (2017) '"It's not the abuse that kills you, it's the silence": The silencing of sexual violence activism in social justice movements in the UK Left', *Justice, Power and Resistance*, 1(2): 35–58.

Downing, L. (2013) 'Safewording! Kinkphobia and gender normativity in *Fifty Shades of Grey*', *Psychology and Sexuality*, 4(1): 92–101.

Dream Out Loud (2003) *The Gift* [film]. Directed by L. Hogarth. Los Angeles, CA: Dream Out Loud Productions.

Dunn, C. (2017) *Stolen Women in Medieval England: Rape, abduction and adultery, 1100–1500*. Cambridge: Cambridge University Press.

Dunne, E.A. (2004) 'Clerical child sex abuse: The response of the Roman Catholic Church', *Journal of Community & Applied Social Psychology*, 14(6): 490–4.

Dwyer, A., Ball, M. and Crofts, T. (eds) (2016) *Queering Criminology*. New York: Palgrave Macmillan.

Dyble, M., Salali, G.D., Chaudhary, N., Page, A., Smith, D., Thompson, J. and Migliano, A.B. (2015) 'Sex equality can explain the unique social structure of hunter-gatherer bands', *Science*, 348(6236): 796–8.

Easton, S. (2011) 'Criminalising the possession of extreme pornography: Sword or shield?', *The Journal of Criminal Law*, 75: 391–413.

Ebrahim, S. (2019) '"I'm not sure this is rape, but…": An exposition of the stealthing trend', *SAGE Open*, 9(2): 1–11.

Edelman, L. (2004) *No Future: Queer theory and the death drive*. Durham, NC: Duke University Press.

Edwards, S.S.M. (1981) *Female Sexuality of the Law*. Oxford: Martin Robertson.

Ehrenreich, B. and English, D. (2010) *Witches, Midwives, and Nurses: A history of women healers*, 2nd edn. New York: Feminist Press at the City University of New York.

Eilenberg, J. (2018) 'Institutional deviance in TV news: BBC, ITV and the Mid Staffordshire hospital scandal', *Crime, Media, Culture*, 14(3): 485–504.

Ekine, S. (2013) 'Contesting narratives of queer Africa', in Ekine, E. and Abbas, K. (eds) *Queer African Reader*, Nairobi: Pambazuka Press, pp. 78-92.

Elliott, A. and Lemert, C. (2005) *The New Individualism: The emotional costs of globalization*. Abingdon: Routledge.

Ekine, E. and Abbas, K. (eds) *Queer African Reader*, Nairobi: Pambazuka Press.

Ellison, M. (2014) 'The Stephen Lawrence Independent Review: Possible corruption and the role of undercover policing in the Stephen Lawrence case', *House of Commons*. Available at: https://assets.publishing.service.gov.uk/government/uploads/system/uploads/attachment_data/file/287030/stephen_lawrence_review_summary.pdf.

Elman, R.A. (1997) 'Disability pornography: The fetishization of women's vulnerabilities', *Violence against Women*, 3(3): 257–70.

Engel, G.L. (1978) 'The biopsychosocial model and the education of health professionals', *Annals of the New York Academy of Sciences*, 310(1): 169–181.

English Collective of Prostitutes (ECP) (n.d.) *About Us*. Available at: https://prostitutescollective.net/about-us.

Enloe, C. (2000) *Maneuvers: The international politics of militarizing women's lives*. Berkeley, CA: University of California Press.

Eramian, L. and Denov, M. (2018) 'Is it always good to talk? The paradoxes of truth-telling by Rwandan youth born of rape committed during the genocide', *Journal of Genocide Research*, 20(3): 372–91.

Enloe, C. (2000) *Maneuvers: The international politics of militarizing women's lives*. Berkeley, CA: University of California Press.

Erin, C.A. and Ost, S. (eds) (2007) *The Criminal Justice System and Health Care*. New York: Oxford University Press.

Erjavec, K. and Volčič, Z. (2010a) '"Target", "cancer" and "warrior": Exploring painful metaphors of self-presentation used by girls born of war rape', *Discourse & Society*, 21(5): 524–43.

Erjavec, K. and Volčič, Z. (2010b) 'Living with the sins of their fathers: An analysis of self-representation of adolescents born of war rape', *Journal of Adolescent Research*, 25(3): 359–86.

Evans, R. (14 November 2018) 'Police spy should face charges for sexual relationship with activist, court told', *The Guardian*. Available at: www.theguardian.com/uk-news/2018/nov/14/police-spy-should-face-charges-for-sexual-relationship-with-activist-court-told.

Evans, R. (14 May 2019) 'Police take legal action against former officer who had child with activist', *The Guardian*. Available at: www.theguardian.com/uk-news/2019/may/14/police-legal-action-bob-lambert-undercover-officer-child-activist.

Ezard, N. (2001) 'Public health, human rights and the harm reduction paradigm: From risk reduction to vulnerability reduction', *International Journal of Drug Policy*, 12(3): 207–19.

Faludi, S. (1992) *Backlash: The undeclared war against American women*. London: Vintage.

Fanghanel, A. (2019) *Disrupting Rape Culture: Public space, sexuality and revolt*. Bristol: Bristol University Press.

Fanon, F. (1952) *Black Skin, White Masks*. New York: Grove Press.

Fanon, F. (2001[1963]) *The Wretched of the Earth*. London: Penguin.

Farley, M., Cotton, A., Lynne, J., Zumbeck, S., Spiwak, F., Reyes, M.E. and Sezgin, U. (2004) 'Prostitution and trafficking in nine countries: An update on violence and posttraumatic stress disorder', *Journal of Trauma Practice*, 2(3–4): 33–74.

Farris, S.R. (2012) 'Femonationalism and the "regular" army of labor called migrant women', *History of the Present*, 2(2): 184–99.

Farrugia, P. (1997) 'The consent defence: Sports violence, sadomasochism, and the law', *Auckland University Law Review*, 8(2): 472–502.

Farwell, N. (2004) 'War rape: New conceptualizations and responses', *Affilia*, 19(4): 389–403.

Fausto-Sterling, A. (1993) 'The five sexes: Why male and female are not enough', *The Sciences*, March/April 33: 20–4.

Fedje, J. (1990) 'Liability for sexual abuse: The anomalous immunity of churches', *Law & Inequality*, 9(1): 133–61.

Ferguson, S. (29 October 2018) 'What you need to know about child marriage in the US', *Forbes*. Available at: www.forbes.com/sites/unicefusa/2018/10/29/what-you-need-to-know-about-child-marriage-in-the-us-1/#2cf6f6a95689.

Ferrales, G., Brehm, H.N. and Mcelrath, S. (2016) 'Gender-based violence against men and boys in Darfur: The gender–genocide nexus', *Gender and Society*, 30(4): 565–89.

Ferrell, J. (1997) 'Criminological verstehen: Inside the immediacy of crime', *Justice Quarterly*, 14(1): 3–23.

Ferrell, J. (1999) 'Cultural criminology', *Annual Review of Sociology*, 25(1): 395–418.

Fiddler, M. and Banwell, S. (2019) '"Forget about all your taboos": Transgressive memory and Nazisploitation', *Studies in European Cinema*, 16(2): 141–54.

Fiduccia, B.F.W. (1999) 'Sexual imagery of physically disabled women: Erotic? Perverse? Sexist?', *Sexuality and Disability*, 17(3): 277–82.

Filipovic, J. (8 March 2019) 'The terrifying case of a six-week embryo suing an abortion clinic', *The Guardian*. Available at: www.theguardian.com/commentisfree/2019/mar/08/the-terrifying-case-of-a-six-week-embryo-suing-an-abortion-clinic.

Finkelhor, D. (1984) 'Four preconditions: A model', in *Child Sexual Abuse: New theory and research*. New York: The Free Press, pp. 53–68.

Firestone, S. (1970) *The Dialectic of Sex: The case for feminist revolution*. New York: William Morrow and Co.

Flanagan, P. (2014) 'Unpacking ideas of sexuality in childhood: What do primary teachers and parents say?', *Open Review of Educational Research*, 1(1): 160–70.

Flavin, J. (2009) *Our Bodies, Our Crimes: The policing of women's reproduction in America*. New York: New York University Press.

Fleetwood, N.R. (2012) 'The case of Rihanna: Erotic violence and black female desire', *African American Review*, 45(3): 419–35.

Fogelman, E. (2012) 'Rape during the Nazi holocaust: Vulnerabilities and motivations', in Rittner, C. and Roth, J. (eds), *Rape: Weapon of war and genocide*. St Paul, MN: Paragon House, pp. 15–28.

Ford, C.S. and Beach, F.A. (1951) *Patterns of Sexual Behaviour*. New York: Harper & Row.

Foucault, M. (1998[1976]) *The History of Sexuality 1: The will to knowledge*. London: Penguin.

Foucault, M. (2000[1976]) *Power: The essential works of Michel Foucault 1954–1984*. London: Penguin.

France24 (27 March 2019) *Air Asia takes down ads after accusations of promoting sex tourism in Thailand*. Available at: https://observers.france24.com/en/20190327-australia-air-asia-ads-sex-tourism-thailand.

Frauenberger, C. (2015) 'Disability and technology: A critical realist perspective', in Proceedings of the 17th International ACM SIGACCESS Conference on Computers & Accessibility (pp. 89–96), ACM, October.

Frawley-O'Dea, M.G. (2004) 'The history and consequences of the sexual-abuse crisis in the Catholic Church', *Studies in Gender and Sexuality*, 5(1): 11–30.

Freeden, M. (1994) 'Political concepts and ideological morphology', *Journal of Political Philosophy*, 2(2): 140–64.

Freire, P. (2017[1970]) *Pedagogy of the Oppressed*. London: Penguin, Random House.

Freud, S. (1905) 'Three essays on the theory of sexuality', in *The Standard Edition of the Complete Psychological Works of Sigmund Freud, 1953–74*, Vol. 7, pp. 130f. London: Hogarth Press.

Frundt, T. (2005) 'Enslaved in America: Sex trafficking in the United States', *Women's Funding Network*. Available at: www.womensfundingnetwork.org/enslaved-in-america-sex-trafficking-in-the-united-states.

Fuentes, A. (2015) *Race, Monogamy, and Other Lies They Told You: Busting myths about human nature*. Berkeley, CA: University of California Press.

Gaarder, E., Rodriguez, N. and Zatz, M.S. (2004) 'Criers, liars, and manipulators: Probation officers' views of girls', *Justice Quarterly*, 21(3): 547–78.

Gallagher, A. (2001) 'Human rights and the new UN protocols on trafficking and migrant smuggling: A preliminary analysis', *Human Rights Quarterly*, 23: 975.

Gallen, J. (2016) 'Jesus wept: The Roman Catholic Church, child sexual abuse and transitional justice', *International Journal of Transitional Justice*, 10(2): 332–49.

Gámez-Guadix, M., de Santisteban, P. and Resett, S. (2017) 'Sexting among Spanish adolescents: Prevalence and personality profiles', *Psicothema*, 29(1): 29–34.

Gámez-Guadix, M., Almendros, C., Calvete, E. and De Santisteban, P. (2018) 'Persuasion strategies and sexual solicitations and interactions in online sexual grooming of adolescents: Modeling direct and indirect pathways', *Journal of Adolescence*, 63, 11–18.

Gamson, J. (2001) 'Normal sins: Sex scandal narratives as institutional morality tales', *Social Problems*, 48(2): 185–205.

Garrett, B.L. (2014) 'Undertaking recreational trespass: Urban exploration and infiltration', *Transactions of the Institute of British Geographers*, 39(1): 1–13.

Gauthier, K.D. and Forsyth, J.C. (1999) 'Bareback sex, bug chasers, and the gift of death', *Deviant Behavior*, 20(1): 85–100.

Gavey, N. (2019) *Just Sex? The cultural scaffolding of rape*, 2nd edn. London: Routledge.

Geertz, C. (1973) 'Deep play: Notes on the Balinese cockfight', in *The Interpretation of Cultures: Selected essays*. New York: Basic Books, pp. 412–53.

Giddens, A. (1998) 'Risk society: The context of British politics', in Franklin, J. (ed.), *The Politics of Risk Society*. Cambridge: Polity Press, pp. 23–34.

Giles, M. (1994) '*R v. Brown*: Consensual harm and the public interest', *The Modern Law Review*, 57(1): 101–11.

Gillespie, A.A. (2017) 'The electronic Spanish prisoner: Romance fraud on the Internet', *The Journal of Criminal Law*, 81(3): 217–31.

Gil-Llario, M.D., Morell-Mengual, V., Ballester-Arnal, R. and Díaz-Rodríguez, I. (2018) 'The experience of sexuality in adults with intellectual disability', *Journal of Intellectual Disability Research*, 62(1): 72–80.

Gill, A.K. and Harrison, K. (2015) 'Child grooming and sexual exploitation: Are South Asian men the UK media's new folk devils?', *International Journal for Crime, Justice and Social Democracy*, 4(2): 34–49.

Gillborn, D. (2018) 'Heads I win, tails you lose: Anti-Black racism as fluid, relentless, individual and systemic', *Peabody Journal of Education*, 93(1): 66–77.

Gilligan, P. (2012) 'Contrasting narratives on responses to victims and survivors of clerical abuse in England and Wales: Challenges to Catholic Church discourse', *Child Abuse Review*, 21(6): 414–26.

Ging, D. (2017) 'Alphas, betas, and Incels: Theorising masculinities of the manosphere', *Men and Masculinities*, 22(4): 638–57.

Ginn, J. (2013) 'Austerity and inequality: Exploring the impact of cuts in the UK by gender and age', *Research on Ageing and Social Policy*, 1(1): 28–53.

Gleeson, K. (2015) 'The money problem: Reparation and restorative justice in the Catholic Church's Towards Healing program', *Current Issues in Criminal Justice*, 26(3): 317–32.

Gleeson, K. (2016) 'Responsibility and redress: Theorising gender justice in the context of Catholic clerical child sexual abuse in Ireland and Australia', *UNSWLJ*, 39(2): 779–812.

Glynn, R.W., Byrne, N., O'Dea, S., Shanley, A., Codd, M., Keenan, E. and Clarke, S. (2018) 'Chemsex, risk behaviours and sexually transmitted infections among men who have sex with men in Dublin, Ireland', *International Journal of Drug Policy*, 52: 9–15.

Goffman, E. (1968) *Asylums: Essays on the social situation of mental patients and other inmates*. Piscataway, NJ: Aldine Transaction.

Goldenberg, M. (2013) 'Sex-based violence and the politics and ethics of survival'. In Goldenberg, M. and Shapiro, A. (eds), *Different Horrors, Same Hell: Gender and the Holocaust* (pp. 99–127). Seattle, WA: University of Washington Press.

Goodhart, M.E. (ed.) (2016) *Human Rights: Politics and practice*. Oxford: Oxford University Press.

Goodley, D., Liddiard, K. and Runswick-Cole, K. (2018) 'Feeling disability: Theories of affect and critical disability studies', *Disability & Society*, 33(2): 197–217.

Goodmark, L. (2015) 'Hands up at home: Militarized masculinity and police officers who commit intimate partner abuse', *BYU Law Review*, 15(5): 1183–1246.

Gordon, L. and Gordon, L. (2002) *The Moral Property of Women: A history of birth control politics in America*, 3rd edn. Urbana and Chicago, IL: University of Illinois Press.

Gorris, E.A.P. (2015) 'Invisible victims? Where are male victims of conflict-related sexual violence in international law and policy?', *European Journal of Women's Studies*, 24(4): 412–27.

Gotell, L. (2008) 'Rethinking affirmative consent in Canadian sexual assault law: Neoliberal sexual subjects and risky women', *Akron Law Review*, 41(4): 865–98.

Gowing, L. (1997) 'Secret births and infanticide in seventeenth-century England', *Past & Present*, 156: 87–115.

Gozdziak, E.M. and Collett, E.A. (2005) 'Research on human trafficking in North America: A review of literature', *International Migration*, 43(1–2): 99–128.

Grady, C. (10 May 2019) 'This new short-story collection from the author behind *Arrival* is sci-fi at its smartest', *Vox.com*. Available at: www.vox.com/culture/2019/5/10/18563409/exhalation-ted-chiang-review.

Greer, C. and McLaughlin, E. (2013) 'The Sir Jimmy Savile scandal: Child sexual abuse and institutional denial at the BBC', *Crime, Media, Culture*, 9(3): 243–63.

Greer, C. and McLaughlin, E. (2015) 'The return of the repressed: Secrets, lies, denial and "historical" institutional child sexual abuse scandals', in Whyte, D. (ed.), *How Corrupt is Britain?* London: Pluto Press, pp. 113–23.

Greer, C. and McLaughlin, E. (2017) 'Theorizing institutional scandal and the regulatory state', *Theoretical Criminology*, 21(2): 112–32.

Grey, R. (2017) 'The ICC's first "forced pregnancy" case in historical perspective', *Journal of International Criminal Justice*, 15(5): 905–30.

Griffin, S. (1984[1978]) *Woman and Nature: The roaring inside her*. London: The Women's Press.

Grimes, S.M. and Feenberg, A. (2013) 'Critical theory of technology', *The Sage Handbook of Digital Technology Research*. London: Sage, pp. 121–9.

Grosz, E.A. (1994) *Volatile Bodies: Toward a corporeal feminism*. Bloomington and Indianapolis, IN: Indiana University Press.

Grov, C. and Parsons, J.T. (2006) 'Bug changing and gift giving: The potential for HIV transmission among barebackers on the Internet', *AIDS Education and Prevention*, 18(6): 490–503.

Grewal, D. S. and Purdy, J. (2014) 'Introduction: Law and neoliberalism', *Law & Contemporary Problems*, 77: 1.

Gurung, S., Ventuneac, A., Rendina, H.J., et al. (2017) 'Prevalence of military sexual trauma and sexual orientation discrimination among lesbian, gay, bisexual, and transgender military personnel: A descriptive study', *Sexuality Research and Social Policy*, 15(1): 74–82.

Guttmacher Institute, The (2019) State Policy Trends 2019: A Wave of Abortion Bans, But Some States Are Fighting Back. Available at: www.guttmacher.org/article/2019/12/state-policy-trends-2019-wave-abortion-bans-some-states-are-fighting-back.

Hacking, I. (1986) 'Making up people', in Heller, T.C., Sosna, M. and Wellbery D.E. (eds), *Reconstructing Individualism: Autonomy, individuality, and the self in Western thought*. Stanford, CA: Stanford University Press, pp. 161–71.

Hakim, J. (2019) 'The rise of chemsex: Queering collective intimacy in neoliberal London', *Cultural Studies*, 33(2): 249–75.

Hale, M. (1736) *The History of the Pleas of the Crown*. London: T. Payne.

Hall, S. (2011) 'The neo-liberal revolution', *Cultural Studies*, 25(6): 705–28.

Hall, S. (2012) *Theorising Crime and Deviance: A new perspective*. London: Sage.

Hall, S. and Winlow, S. (2018) 'Ultra-realism', in *Routledge Handbook of Critical Criminology*. Abingdon: Routledge, pp. 43–56.

Halliday, J. (2 May 2014) 'Max Clifford sentenced to eight years for his crimes and contempt of women', *The Guardian*. Available at: www.theguardian.com/media/2014/may/02/max-clifford-sentenced-eight-years-jail-indecently-assaulting-four-girls.

Halliday, J. (29 October 2018) 'Rotherham grooming gang: Seven men guilty of sexual offences', *The Guardian*. Available at: www.theguardian.com/uk-news/2018/oct/29/rotherham-grooming-gang-seven-men-convicted-of-sexual-offences.

Halperin, D.M. (1995) *Saint Foucault: Towards a gay hagiography*. Oxford: Oxford University Press.

Hammond, C., Holmes, D. and Mercier, M. (2016) 'Breeding new forms of life: A critical reflection on extreme variances of bareback sex', *Nursing Inquiry*, 23(3): 267–77.

Haraway, D. (1991) 'A cyborg manifesto: Science, technology, and socialist-feminism in the late twentieth century', *Simians, Cyborgs and Women: The reinvention of nature*. New York: Routledge, pp. 149–81.

Harman, H. and Garnier, M. (19 July 2019) 'Men are using the narrative of women's sexual enjoyment to get away with murder, literally', *HuffPost*. Available at: bit.ly/3aLNNHM.

Harpalani, V. (2013) 'DesiCrit: Theorizing the racial ambiguity of South Asian American', *New York University Annual Survey of American Law*, 69(77): 177–84.

Harrington, C. (2018) 'Gender policy models and calls to "tackle demand" for sex workers', *Sexuality Research and Social Policy*, 15(3): 249–58.

Harvey, D. (2007) 'Neoliberalism as creative destruction', *The Annals of the American Academy of Political and Social Science*, 610(1): 21–44.

Harvey, D. (2016) 'Neoliberalism is a political project', *Jacobin Magazine*. Available at: www.jacobinmag.com/2016/07/david-harvey-neoliberalism-capitalism-labor-crisis-resistance.

Hattenstone, S. (26 March 2011) 'Mark Kennedy: Confessions of an undercover cop', *The Guardian*. Available at: www.theguardian.com/environment/2011/mar/26/mark-kennedy-undercover-cop-environmental-activist.

Hattenstone, S. (15 July 2017) '"I was pretending to be a boy for a variety of reasons": The strange case of Gayle Newland', *The Guardian*. Available at: www.theguardian.com/uk-news/2017/jul/15/gayle-newland-retrial.

Havocscope (2015) *Prostitution: Prices and Statistics of the Global Sex Trade*. Havocscope.

Hay, M. (16 March 2020) 'The porn we see – and sex we have – is influenced by the adult industry's biggest spenders'. Available at: www.vox.com/the-goods/2020/3/16/21179060/cam-girl-pornography-economics-spend-whales-influence.

Hayward, K. (2002) 'The vilification and pleasures of youthful transgression', *Youth Justice: Critical Readings*. London: Sage, pp. 80–94.

Hayward, K.J. and Young, J. (2004) 'Cultural criminology: Some notes on the script', *Theoretical Criminology*, 8(3): 259–73.

HBO (2016) *Westworld* [television]. Created by L. Joy and J. Nolan. Los Angeles, CA: HBO.

Hearn, J. (2006) 'The implications of information and communication technologies for sexualities and sexualised violences: Contradictions of sexual citizenships', *Political Geography*, 25(8): 944–63.

Heinisch, R., Massetti, E. and Mazzoleni, O. (2018) 'Populism and ethno-territorial politics in European multi-level systems', *Comparative European Politics*, 16(6): 923–36.

Henley, J. (3 January 2013) 'Paedophilia: Bringing dark desires to light', *The Guardian*. Available at: www.theguardian.com/society/2013/jan/03/paedophilia-bringing-dark-desires-light.

Herald, The (7 February 2000) 'Amputee surgeon knew of sex link', *Scottish Media*. Available at: www.heraldscotland.com/news/12215344.amputee-surgeon-knew-of-sex-link.

Hern, A. (24 March 2020) 'UK abortion law briefly changes during Covid-19 outbreak', *The Guardian*. Available at: www.theguardian.com/world/2020/mar/24/uk-abortion-law-pills-home-covid-19-outbreak.

Hickel, J. (2017) *The Divide: A brief guide to global inequality and its solutions*. London: Random House.

Hickson, F. (2018) 'Chemsex as edgework: Towards a sociological understanding', *Sexual Health*, 15(2): 102–7.

Hillman, N. and Robinson, N. (2016) *Boys to Men: The underachievement of young men in higher education – and how to start tackling it*. Oxford: Higher Education Policy Institute.

Hilton, P. (13 March 2009) 'Rhianna trying to get out of testifying!', *Perezhilton.com*. Available at: https://perezhilton.com/rihanna-trying-to-get-out-of-testifying/.

Hines, C. and Kerr, D. (2012) 'Is hard-core hard to swallow?', in *Hard to Swallow: Hard-core pornography on screen*. London: Wallflower Press, pp. 1–8.

Hirschmann, N. (1998) 'Western feminism, eastern veiling, and the question of free agency', *Constellations*, 5(30): 345–68.

Hogwood, J., Mushashi, C., Jones, S., et al. (2018) '"I learned who I am": Young people born from genocide rape in Rwanda and their experiences of disclosure', *Journal of Adolescent Research*, 33(5): 549–70.

Hollister, J. (1999) 'A highway rest area as a social reproduceable site', in Leap, W.L. (ed.), *Public Sex/Gay Space*. New York: Columbia University Press.

Holm, S. (2001) 'Autonomy, authenticity, or best interest: Everyday decision-making and persons with dementia', *Medicine, Health Care and Philosophy*, 4(2): 153–9.

Home Office (2006) *Consultation on the Possession of Extreme Pornographic Material Summary of Responses and Next Steps*. Available at: https://web.archive.org/web/20070205105924/http://www.homeoffice.gov.uk/documents/cons-extreme-porn-3008051/Gvt-response-extreme-porn2.pdf?view=Binary.

Home Office (2016) *Historical Crime Data*. 21 April. Available at: www.gov.uk/government/statistics/historical-crime-data.

Home Office and Ministry of Justice (2013) *An Overview of Sexual Offending in England and Wales*. Available at: http://webarchive.nationalarchives.gov.uk/20160105160709/https://www.gov.uk/government/statistics/an-overview-of-sexual-offending-in-england-and-wales.

hooks, b. (1984) *Ain't I a Woman? Black women and feminism*. New York: Pluto Press.

hooks, b. (1994) *Teaching to Transgress: Education as a practice of freedom*. Abingdon: Routledge.

Howe, A. (2008) 'Violence against women: Rethinking the local-global nexus', in Cain, M. and Howe, A. (eds), *Women, Crime and Social Harm: Towards a criminology for the global era*. Oxford: Hart Publishing, pp. 37–55.

Howland, C.A. and Rintala, D.H. (2001) 'Dating behaviors of women with physical disabilities', *Sexuality and Disability*, 19(1): 41–70.

Hughes, B. and Paterson, K. (2006) 'The social model of disability and the disappearing body: Towards a sociology of impairment', *Overcoming Disabling Barriers*. Abingdon: Routledge, pp. 101–17.

Hughes, D.M. (2002) 'The use of new communications and information technologies for sexual exploitation of women and children', *Hastings Women's Law Journal*, 13(1): 127–46.

Hull, N.E.H., Hoffer, W. and Hoffer, P.C. (2004) *The Abortion Rights Controversy in America: A legal reader*. Chapel Hill, NC: University of North Carolina Press.

Humphreys, L. (1975) *Tearoom Trade: Impersonal sex in public places*, enlarged edition. Piscataway, NJ: Transaction Publishers.

Hunter, S.V. (2010) 'Evolving narratives about childhood sexual abuse: Challenging the dominance of the victim and survivor paradigm', *Australian and New Zealand Journal of Family Therapy*, 31(2): 176–90.

Hurd, H.M. (1996) 'The moral magic of consent', *Legal Theory*, 2(2): 121–46.

Huschke, S. (2017) 'Victims without a choice? A critical view on the debate about sex work in Northern Ireland', *Sexuality Research and Social Policy*, 14(2): 192–205.

Incentive (2010) *Blue Valentine* [film]. Directed by D. Cianfrance. Los Angeles, CA: Incentive Filmed Entertainment.

Independent Inquiry into Child Sexual Abuse (April 2018) 'Interim report: A summary', *IICSA*. Available at: www.iicsa.org.uk/key-documents/5369/view/interim-report-a-summary.pdf.

International Labour Organisation (ILO) (2017) Global Estimates of Modern Slavery. Available at: www.ilo.org/wcmsp5/groups/public/---dgreports/---dcomm/documents/publication/wcms_575479.pdf.

Itzin, C., Taket, A. and Kelly, L. (2007) 'The evidence of harm to adults relating to exposure to extreme pornographic material: A rapid evidence assessment (REA)', *Ministry of Justice Research Series*, 11 (07). London: Ministry of Justice.

Jackson, C.A. (2016) 'Framing sex worker rights: How US sex worker rights activists perceive and respond to mainstream anti-sex trafficking advocacy', *Sociological Perspectives*, 59(1): 27–45.

Jagose, A. (1996) *Queer Theory: An introduction*. New York: New York University Press.

Jaki, S., De Smedt, T., Gwó d , M., Panchal, R., Rossa, A. and De Pauw, G. (2019) 'Online hatred of women in the Incels.me forum: Linguistic analysis and automatic detection', *Journal of Language Aggression and Conflict*, 7(2): 240–68.

Jalili, C. (1 January 2018) 'How to sext: The ultimate guide to sexting', *The Cut*. Available at: www.thecut.com/article/sexting-how-to-ultimate-guide.html.

Jane, E.A. (2014) '"Back to the kitchen, cunt": Speaking the unspeakable about online misogyny', *Continuum*, 28(4): 558–70.

Jay, A. (2014) 'Independent inquiry into child sexual exploitation in Rotherham', *The Guardian*. Available at: www.theguardian.com/society/interactive/2014/aug/26/rotherham-children-sexually-abused-full-report.

Jeffrey, N.K. and Barata, P.C. (2017) '"He didn't necessarily force himself upon me, but...": Women's lived experiences of sexual coercion in intimate relationships with men', *Violence against Women*, 23(8): 911–33.

Jeffreys, S. (1994, September). The queer disappearance of lesbians: Sexuality in the academy. In *Women's Studies International Forum*, 17(5): 459-472. Pergamon.

John Jay College Research Team (Principal Investigator and Author) (2004) The Nature and Scope of Sexual Abuse of Minors by Catholic Priests and Deacons in the United States, 1950–2002. Washington, DC: United States Conference of Catholic Bishops (USCCB).

John Jay College Research Team (Principal Investigator and Author) (2006) *The Nature and Scope of Sexual Abuse of Minors by Catholic Priests and Deacons in the United States, 1950–2002: Supplementary data analysis*. Washington, DC: USCCB.

Johnsen, D. (1989) 'From driving to drugs: Governmental regulation of pregnant women's lives after Webster', *University of Pennsylvania Law Review*, 138(1): 179–215.

Johnson, P. (2010) 'Law, morality and disgust: The regulation of "extreme pornography" in England and Wales', *Social & Legal Studies*, 19(2): 147–63.

Johnson, P. (2019) 'Buggery and Parliament, 1533–2017', *Parliamentary History*, 38(3): 325–41.

Johnson Reagon, B. (1983) 'Coalition politics: Turning the century', in Smith, B. (ed.) *Homegirls: A Black feminist anthology*. New York: Kitchen Table Women of Colour Press, pp. 356–68.

Jones, S. and Mowlabocus, S. (2009) 'Hard times and rough rides: The legal and ethical impossibilities of researching "shock" pornographies', *Sexualities*, 12(5): 613–28.

Jordan, B.D. (2000) 'Chronic traumatic brain injury associated with boxing', *Seminars in Neurology*, 20(2): 179–86.

Jozkowski, K.N. (2016) 'Barriers to affirmative consent policies and the need for affirmative sexuality', *University of the Pacific Law Review*, 47(4): 741–72.

Kahn, S. and Denov, M. (2019) '"We are children like others": Pathways to mental health and healing for children born of genocidal rape in Rwanda', *Transcultural Psychiatry*, 56(3): 510–28.

Kaler, A. (2003) '"My girlfriends could fill a yanu-yanu bus": Rural Malawian men's claims about their own serostatus', *Demographic Research*, 1: 349–72.

Kaler, A. (2004) 'AIDS-talk in everyday life: The presence of HIV/AIDS in men's informal conversation in Southern Malawi', *Social Science & Medicine*, 59(2): 285–97.

Kampschmidt, E.D. (2015) 'Prosecuting women for drug use during pregnancy: The criminal justice system should step out and the affordable care act should step up', *Health Matrix: Journal of Law-Medicine*, 25: 487–512.

Kamuzinzi, M. (2016) 'Identity in adolescents born from genocidal rape', *Identity*, 16(3): 169–81.

Keenan, M. (2013) *Child Sexual Abuse and the Catholic Church: Gender, power, and organizational culture*. Oxford: Oxford University Press.

Keenan, M. (2015) 'Masculinity, relationships and context: Child sexual abuse and the Catholic church', *Irish Journal of Applied Social Studies*, 15(2): 64–77.

Kelly, L. (1987) 'The continuum of sexual violence', in *Women, Violence and Social Control*. London: Palgrave Macmillan, pp. 46–60.

Kelly, L. (1988) *Surviving Sexual Violence*. Cambridge: Polity Press.

Kempadoo, K. (2015) 'The modern-day white (wo)man's burden: Trends in anti-trafficking and anti-slavery campaigns', *Journal of Human Trafficking*, 1(1): 8–20.

Kempadoo, K. and Doezema, J. (eds) (2018) *Global Sex Workers: Rights, resistance, and redefinition*. New York: Routledge.

Kenny, C. (2009) 'Significant television: Journalism, sex abuse and the Catholic Church in Ireland', *Irish Communication Review*, 11(1): 63–76.

Keown, J. (1988) *Abortion, Doctors and the Law: Some aspects of the legal regulation of abortion in England from 1803 to 1982*. Cambridge: Cambridge University Press.

Kidder, J.L. (2006) '"It's the job that I love": Bike messengers and edgework', *Sociological Forum*, 21(1): 31–54.

Kierkegaard, S. (2008) 'Cybering, online grooming and ageplay', *Computer Law & Security Review*, 24(1): 41–55.

Kinsey, A.C., Pomeroy, W.B., Martin, C.E. and Gebhard, P.H. (1998[1953]) *Sexual Behaviour in the Human Female*. Bloomington, IN: Indiana University Press.

Kirby, J. (15 February 2017) 'Women turning to illegal abortion pills in rising numbers, charity warns', *The Independent*. Available at: www.independent.co.uk/news/uk/home-news/abortion-pill-access-online-illegal-decriminalise-woman-british-pregnancy-advisory-service-danger-a7580566.html.

Kitsule, D.K. (2013) 'An essay', in Ekine, S. and Abbas, K. (eds), *Queer African Reader*. Nairobi: Pambazuka Press, pp. 6–9.

Klein, H. (2014) 'Generationing, stealthing, and gift giving: The intentional transmission of HIV by HIV-positive men to their HIV-negative sex partners', *Health Psychology Research*, 2(3): 54–9.

Koon, T.H. and Yoong, D. (2013) 'Preying on lonely hearts: A systematic deconstruction of an Internet romance scammer's online lover profile', *Journal of Modern Languages*, 23: 28–40.

Kopp, C., Laton, R., Sillitoe, J. and Gondal, I. (2015) 'The role of love stories in romance scams: A qualitative analysis of fraudulent profiles', *International Journal of Cyber Criminology*, 9(2): 205–17.

Koppelman, A. (2005) 'Does obscenity cause moral harm?', *Columbia Law Review*, 105(5): 1635–79.

Kramers-Olen, A. (2016) 'Sexuality, intellectual disability, and human rights legislation', *South African Journal of Psychology*, 46(4): 504–16.

Krautheim, G. (2009) 'Desecration repackaged: Holocaust exploitation and the marketing of novelty', *Cinephile*, 5(1): 4–11.

Kuhn, T., Van Elsas, E., Hakhverdian, A. and van der Brug, W. (2016) 'An ever wider gap in an ever closer union: Rising inequalities and euroscepticism in 12 West European democracies, 1975–2009', *Socio-Economic Review*, 14(1): 27–45.

Kuradusenge, C. (2016) 'Denied victimhood and contested narratives: The case of Hutu diaspora', *Genocide Studies and Prevention: An International Journal*, 10(2):59–75.

Lam, A., Yau, M., Franklin, R.C. and Leggat, P.A. (2019) 'The unintended invisible hand: A conceptual framework for the analysis of the sexual lives of people with intellectual disabilities', *Sexuality and Disability*, 37: 203–26.

Lambert, R. (2014) 'Researching counterterrorism: A personal perspective from a former undercover police officer', *Critical Studies on Terrorism*, 7(1): 165–81.

Lampe, J.R. (2012) 'A victimless sex crime: The case for decriminalizing consensual teen sexting', *University of Michigan Journal of Law Reform*, 46: 703–36.

Lancaster, R.N. (2003) *The Trouble with Nature: Sex in science and popular culture*. Berkeley, CA: University of California Press.

Latour, B. (2012[1991]) *We Have Never Been Modern*. Cambridge, MA: Harvard University Press.

Laurendeau, J. (2008) '"Gendered risk regimes": A theoretical consideration of edgework and gender', *Sociology of Sport Journal*, 25(3): 293–309.

Lawrence, D.H. (1971) *Lady Chatterley's Lover*. New York: Bantam Books.

Lee, E.M., Klement, K.R. and Sagarin, B.J. (2015) 'Double hanging during consensual sexual asphyxia: A response to Roma, Pazzelli, Pompili, Girardi, and Ferracuti (2013)', *Archives of Sexual Behavior*, 44(7): 1751–3.

Lee, M., Crofts, T., Salter, M., Milivojevic, S. and McGovern, A. (2013) '"Let's get sexting": Risk, power, sex and criminalisation in the moral domain', *International Journal for Crime, Justice and Social Democracy*, 2(1): 35–49.

Lehrner, A. and Yehuda, R. (2018) 'Trauma across generations and paths to adaptation and resilience', *Psychological Trauma: Theory, Research, Practice, and Policy*, 10(1): 22–9.

Leigh C. (1980) Inventing Sex Work, in J. Neagle (ed.) (1997), *Whores and Other Feminists*, New York: Routledge, pp. 223–232.

Le Roux, G. (2013) '"Proudly African and transgender": Collaborative portraits and stories with trans and intersex activists', in Ekine, S. and Abbas, K. (eds), *Queer African Reader*. Nairobi: Pambazuka Press.

LeVine, R.A. (1959) 'Gusii sex offenses: A study in social control 1', *American Anthropologist*, 61(6): 965–90.

Levy, A. (2005) *Female chauvinist pigs: Women and the rise of raunch culture*, New York: Simon & Schuster.

Levy, D. (2007) 'Robot prostitutes as alternatives to human sex workers', IEEE International Conference on Robotics and Automation, Rome, April.

Levy, D. (2009) *Love and Sex with Robots: The evolution of human–robot relationships*. New York: Gerald Duckworth & Co Ltd.

Levy, J. and Jakobsson, P. (2013) 'Abolitionist feminism as patriarchal control: Swedish understandings of prostitution and trafficking', *Dialectical Anthropology*, 37(2): 333–40.

Lewis, D.A. (2009) 'Unrecognized victims: Sexual violence against men in conflict settings under international law', *Wisconsin International Law Journal*, 27(1):1–49.

Lewis, P. and Evans, R. (2013) *Undercover: The true story of Britain's secret police*. London: Faber & Faber.

Lewis, P., Evans, R. and Pollak, S. (24 June 2013) 'Trauma of spy's girlfriend: "Like being raped by the state"', *The Guardian*. Available at: www.theguardian.com/uk/2013/jun/24/undercover-police-spy-girlfriend-child.

Lindquist, J. (2010) 'Images and evidence: Human trafficking, auditing, and the production of illicit markets in Southeast Asia and beyond', *Public Culture*, 22(2): 223–36.

Livingstone, S. and Bulger, M. (2014) 'A global research agenda for children's rights in the digital age', *Journal of Children and Media*, 8(4): 317–35.

Loadenthal, M. (2014) 'When cops "go native": Policing revolution through sexual infiltration and panopticonism', *Critical Studies on Terrorism*, 7(1): 24–42.

Locke, J. (1980[1690]) *Second Treatise of Government*. Indianapolis, IN: Hackett Publishing Co.

Loeser, C., Pini, B. and Crowley, V. (2018) 'Disability and sexuality: Desires and pleasures', *Sexualities*, 21(3): 255–70.

Lorde, A. (1978) 'Uses of the erotic: The erotic as power', in Lorde, A. (2007[1984]) *Sister Outsider: Essays and speeches*. Berkeley, CA: Crossing Press, pp. 53–60.

Lorde, A. (1981) 'The uses of anger: Women responding to racism', in Lorde, A. (2007 [1984]) *Sister Outsider: Essays and speeches*. Berkeley, CA: California: Crossing Press, pp. 124–33.

Lorde, A. (2007[1984]) *Sister Outsider: Essays and speeches*. Berkeley, CA: California: Crossing Press.

Lorde, A. (2011[1982]) *Zami: A new spelling of my name – A biomythography*. Berkeley, CA: California Crossing Press.

Lorde, A. (2017[1978]) *The Black Unicorn*. London: Penguin Random House.

Lowbridge, C. (26 September 2019) 'Sex, lies and legal consent: Can deceit turn sex into rape?', *BBC News*. Available at: www.bbc.co.uk/news/uk-england-49127545.

Lowbridge, C. (11 March 2020) 'Vasectomy lie rapist Jason Lawrance can appeal against conviction', *BBC News*. Available at: www.bbc.co.uk/news/uk-england-leicestershire-51836112.

Loza, S. (2013) *Hashtag feminism: #SolidarityIsForWhiteWomen, and the other #FemFuture*. Available at: www.awdflibrary.org/bitstream/handle/123456789/926/Hashtag%20Feminism%2c%20%23SolidarityIsForWhiteWomen%2c%20and%20the%20Other%20%23FemFuture.pdf?sequence = 1&isAllowed = y.

Lugones, M. (1987) 'Playfulness, "world"-travelling, and loving perception', *Hypatia*, 2(2): 3–19.

Luker, K. (1984) *Abortion and the Politics of Motherhood*. Berkeley, CA: University of California Press.

Lundberg, G.D. (1985) 'Brain injury in boxing', *The American Journal of Forensic Medicine and Pathology*, 6(3): 192–8.

Lupton, D. (1999) 'Risk and the ontology of pregnant embodiment', in Lupton, D. (ed.), *Risk and Sociocultural Theory: New directions and perspectives*. Cambridge: Cambridge University Press, pp. 59–85.

Lyng, S. (1990) 'Edgework: A social psychological analysis of voluntary risk taking', *American Journal of Sociology*, 95(4): 851–86.

Lyng, S. and Matthews, R. (2007) 'Risk, edgework, and masculinities', in Hannah-Moffat, K. and O'Malley, P. (eds), *Gendered Risks*. London: Routledge-Cavendish, pp.75–98.

MacKinnon, C. (1982) 'Feminism, Marxism, method, and the state: An agenda for theory', *Signs*, 7(3): 515–44.

MacKinnon, C. (1983) "Feminism, Marxism, method, and the state: Toward a feminist jurisprudence', *Signs*, 8(4): 635–58.

MacKinnon, C.A. (1989) *Towards a Feminist Theory of the State*. Cambridge, MA: Harvard University Press.

MacKinnon, C.A. (1991) 'Reflections on sex equality under law', *The Yale Law Journal*, 100(5): 1281–328.

McPhillips, K. (2016) 'The Church, the Commission and the truth: Inside the NSW special inquiry into child sexual abuse', *Journal for the Academic Study of Religion*, 29(1): 30–51.

Mainline (1993) *Boxing Helena* [film]. Directed by J. Lynch. London: Mainline Pictures.

Mainwaring, C. and Cook, M.L. (2019) 'Immigration detention: An Anglo model', *Migration Studies*, 7(4): 455–76.

Majic, S.A. (2018) 'Real men set norms? Anti-trafficking campaigns and the limits of celebrity norm entrepreneurship', *Crime, Media, Culture*, 14(2): 289–309.

Malinowski, B. (2002[1929]) *The Sexual Life of Savages in North-Western Melanesia: An ethnographic account of courtship, marriage, and family life among the natives of the Trobriand Islands, British New Guinea* (Vol. 6). London: Psychology Press.

Malkowski, J. (2014) 'Beyond prevention: Containment rhetoric in the case of bug chasing', *Journal of Medical Humanities*, 35(2): 211–28.

Mallicoat, S.L. (2007) 'Gendered justice: Attributional differences between males and females in the juvenile courts', *Feminist Criminology*, 2(1): 4–30.

Mallon, M. (21 November 2017) 'Jennifer Lawrence says the 2014 nude photo hack was "so unbelievably violating"', *Glamour.com*. Available at: www.glamour.com/

story/jennifer-lawrence-says-the-2014-nude-photo-hack-was-so-unbelievably-violating.

Malm, H.H. (1996) 'The ontological status of consent and its implications for the law on rape', *Legal Theory*, 2(2): 147–64.

March, E., Grieve, R., Marrington, J. and Jonason, P.K. (2017) 'Trolling on Tinder® (and other dating apps): Examining the role of the Dark Tetrad and impulsivity', *Personality and Individual Differences*, 110: 139–43.

Markham, G. and Punch, M. (2004) 'Animal rights, public order and police accountability: The Brightlingsea demonstrations', *International Journal of Police Science & Management*, 6(2): 84–96.

Martin, E. (1987) *The Woman in the Body: A cultural analysis of reproduction*. Boston, MA: Beacon Press.

Mathiesen, T. (2005) *Silently Silenced: Essays on the creation of acquiescence in modern society*. Hook, Reading: Waterside Press.

Matthews, H. (15 June 2018) '27 online dating statistics and what they mean for the future of dating', *Datingnews.com*. Available at: www.datingnews.com/industry-trends/online-dating-statistics-what-they-mean-for-future.

Matthews, M., Farris, C., Tankard, M. and Dunbar, M.S. (2018) 'Needs of male sexual assault victims in the US armed forces', *Rand Health Quarterly*, 8(2): article 7. Available at: www.rand.org/pubs/periodicals/health-quarterly/issues/v8/n2/07.html.

Maxwell, C. (2010) 'Moving beyond rape as weapon of war: An exploration of militarized masculinity and its consequences', *Canadian Women's Studies*, 28(1): 108–20.

Mbugua, A. (2013) 'Transsexuals nightmare: Activism of subjugation', in Ekine, E. and Abbas, K. (eds), *Queer African Reader*. Nairobi: Pambazuka Press, pp. 123–41.

McAlinden, A.-M. and Naylor, B. (2016) 'Reframing public inquiries as procedural justice for victims of institutional child abuse: Towards a hybrid model of justice', *Sydney Law Review*, 38(3): 277–308.

McDowall, S. and Wang, Y. (2009) 'An analysis of international tourism development in Thailand: 1994–2007', *Asia Pacific Journal of Tourism Research*, 14(4): 351–70.

McGlynn, C. and Bows, H. (2019) 'Possessing extreme pornography: Policing, prosecutions and the need for reform', *The Journal of Criminal Law*, 83(6): 473–88.

McGlynn, C., Rackley, E. and Houghton, R. (2017) 'Beyond "revenge porn": The continuum of image based sexual abuse', *Feminist Legal Studies*, 25: 25–46.

McGregor, J. (2012) 'The legal heritage of the crime of rape', in Brown, J.M. and Walklate, S.L. (eds), *Handbook on Sexual Violence*. London and New York: Routledge.

McLaren, A. (1984) *Reproductive Rituals: The perception of fertility in England from the sixteenth century to the nineteenth century*. London: Methuen.

McLaughlin, J.H. (2010) 'Crime and punishment: Teen sexting in context', *Penn State Law Review*, 115: 135–82.

McNair, B. (2013) *Porno? Chic! How pornography changed the world and made it a better place*. London: Routledge.

McRuer, R. (2006) *Crip Theory: Cultural signs of queerness and disability* (Vol. 9). New York: New York University Press.

Meger, S. (2010) 'Rape of the Congo: Understanding sexual violence in the conflict in the Democratic Republic of Congo', *Journal of Contemporary African Studies*, 28(2): 119–35.

Merkle, E.R. and Richardson, R.A. (2000) 'Digital dating and virtual relating: Conceptualizing computer mediated romantic relationships', *Family Relations*, 49: 187–92.

M.E.S. (2017) *Revenge* [film]. Directed by C. Fargeat. Paris: M.E.S. Productions.

Mesok, E. (2016) 'Sexual violence and the US military: Feminism, US empire, and the failure of liberal equality', *Feminist Studies*, 42(1): 41–69.

Metropolitan Police (n.d.) 'Chemsex'. Available at: www.met.police.uk/advice/advice-and-information/cs/chemsex.

Miah, S. (2015) 'The groomers and the question of race', *Identity Papers: A Journal of British and Irish Studies*, 1(1): 54–66.

Middleton, W., Stavropoulos, P., Dorahy, M. J., Krüger, C., Lewis-Fernández, R., Martínez-Taboas, A. and Brand, B. (2014) 'Institutional abuse and societal silence: An emerging global problem', *Australian & New Zealand Journal of Psychiatry*, 48(1): 22–5.

Milivojevic, S. and Pickering, S. (2013) 'Trafficking in people, 20 years on: Sex, migration and crime in the global anti-trafficking discourse and the rise of the "global trafficking complex"', *Current Issues in Criminal Justice*, 25(2): 585–604.

Mill, J.S. (1998[1892]) *On Liberty and Other Essays*. Oxford: Oxford University Press.

Miller, V. (2011) *Understanding Digital Culture*. London: Sage.

Milne, E. (2019) 'Concealment of birth: Time to repeal a 200-year-old "convenient stop-gap"?' *Feminist Legal Studies*, 27(2): 139–62.

Milne, E. (2020a) 'Putting the fetus first: Legal regulation, motherhood and pregnancy', *Michigan Journal of Gender & Law*, 21(1): 101–61.

Milne, E. (forthcoming) *Criminal Justice Responses to Maternal Filicide: Judging the failed mother*. London: Emerald.

Ministry of Home Affairs (2007) Bill No. 38/2007. Available at: https://sso.agc.gov.sg/Bills-Supp/38-2007/Published/20070918?DocDate=20070918

Ministry of Justice (3 April 2017) 'Sexual communication with a child: Implementation of Section 76 of the Serious Crime Act 2015', *Circular No. 2017/01*, Criminal Law and Sentencing Policy Unit.

Mohdin, A. (30 March 2020) 'Relaxation of UK abortion rules welcomed by experts', *The Guardian*. Available at: www.theguardian.com/world/2020/mar/30/relaxation-of-uk-abortion-rules-welcomed-by-experts-coronavirus.

Monrose, K. (2019) *Black Men in Britain: An ethnographic portrait of the post-Windrush generation*. London: Routledge.

Moorman, J. (2017) '"The hardest of hardcore": Locating feminist possibilities in women's extreme pornography', *Signs: Journal of Women in Culture and Society*, 42(3): 693–716.

Morgan, R. (1980) 'Theory and practice: Pornography and rape', in Lederer, L. (ed.), *Take Back the Night: Women on pornography*. New York: William Morrow & Co., pp. 134–40.

Morris, J. (1991) *Pride against Prejudice: Transforming attitudes to disability*. London: The Women's Press.

Moskowitz, D.A. and Roloff, M.E. (2007a) 'The existence of a bug chasing subculture', *Culture, Health & Sexuality*, 9(4): 347–57.

Moskowitz, D.A. and Roloff, M.E. (2007b) 'The ultimate high: Sexual addiction and the bug chasing phenomenon', *Sexual Addiction & Compulsivity*, 14(1): 21–40.

Muller, J. (2014) 'Teenage girls' sexting in Cape Town, South Africa: A child-centred and feminist approach', in Webb, A. and Buskens, I. (eds), *Women and ICT in Africa and the Middle East*. London: Zed Books.

Mullins, C.W. (2009) '"He would kill me with his penis": Genocidal rape in Rwanda as a state crime', *Critical Criminology*, 17(1): 15–33.

Mulvey, L. (1975) 'Visual pleasure and narrative cinema', *Screen*, 16(3): 6–18.

Murphy, A.S. (2014) 'A survey of state fetal homicide laws and their potential applicability to pregnant women who harm their own fetuses', *Indiana University Maurer School of Law*, 89: 847–53.

Mwikya, K. (2013) 'The media, the tabloid, and the Ugandian homophobia spectacle', in Ekine, S. and Abbas, K. (eds), *Queer African Reader*. Nairobi: Pambazuka Press, pp. 141–55.

Nagle, A. (2017) *Kill All Normies: Online culture wars from 4chan and Tumblr to Trump and the alt-right*. London: John Hunt Publishing.

Nana, J.G., Abbas, H., Muguongo, W., Mtetwa, P. and Ndashe, S. (27 October 2011) 'Statement on British "aid cut" threats to African countries that violate LBGTI rights', *Pambazuka News*. Available at: www.pambazuka.org/activism/statement-british-aid-cut-threats-african-countries-violate-lbgti-rights.

Ndashe, S. (2013) 'The single story of "African homophobia" is dangerous for LGBTI activism', in Ekine, S. and Abbas, K. (eds), *Queer African Reader*. Nairobi: Pambazuka Press, pp. 155–65.

Nead, L. (1992) *The Female Nude: Art, obscenity and sexuality*. London: Routledge.

Nelson, J. (2003) *Women of Color and the Reproductive Rights Movement*. New York: New York University Press.

Neville, L. and Sanders-McDonagh, E. (2017) '"Cleaning up Camden": Street-based sex work and the use of ASBOs in the Age of Austerity', in Sanders, T. and Laing, M. (eds), *Policing the Sex Industry: Protection, paternalism and politics*. London: Routledge.

Newmahr, S. (2011) *Playing on the Edge: Sadomasochism, risk, and intimacy*. Bloomington, IN: Indiana University Press.

Newshub (10 January 2010) 'Roxxy the sex robot makes her world debut'. Available at: www.newshub.co.nz/technology/roxxxy-the-sex-robot-makes-her-world-debut-2010011109).

NHS (2016) 'Abortion', 17 August. Available at: www.nhs.uk/conditions/abortion.

NHS Digital (2019) *Female Genital Mutilation (FGM) Enhanced Dataset*, 24 May. Available at: https://files.digital.nhs.uk/18/643E66/FGM%202019%20Q1%20-%20 Report.pdf.

Norris, E. and Rutter, J. (2016) 'Learning the lessons from Universal Credit', *Institute for Government*. Available at: www.instituteforgovernment.org.uk/sites/default/files/publications/5087%20IFG%20-%20Universal%20Credit%20-%20Briefing%20 Paper%20WEB%20AW_0.pdf.

Northern Ireland Office (2020) Changes to the Law in Northern Ireland: Updated information, 25 March. Available at: www.gov.uk/government/news/changes-to-the-law-in-northern-ireland-updated-information.

Now for NI (n.d.) Site quote. Available at: https://nowforni.uk/2018/10/08/when-it-was-over-i-got-dressed.

NSPCC (23 January 2019) 'Over 9,000 police-recorded online child sexual abuse offences', NSPCC. Available at: www.nspcc.org.uk/what-we-do/news-opinion/web-exploited-by-child-sex-offenders.

NSPCC (April 2019) 'Statistics briefing: child sexual abuse', NSPCC. Available at: https://learning.nspcc.org.uk/media/1710/statistics-briefing-child-sexual-abuse.pdf.

Nurik, C. (2018) '50 shades of film censorship: Gender bias from the Hays Code to MPAA ratings', *Communication Culture & Critique*, 11: 530–47.

Oakley, A. (1984) *The Captured Womb: A history of the medical care of pregnant women*. Oxford: Basil Blackwell.

Oakley, A. (1993) *Essays on Women, Medicine and Health*. Edinburgh: Edinburgh University Press.

O'Brien, M. (1987) 'Love poem to no-one in particular'. Available at: https://amongtheregulars.com/2013/01/21/no-one-in-particular.

O'Brien, M. (1990) 'On seeing a sex surrogate', *The Sun*, 174. Available at: https://thesunmagazine.org/issues/174/on-seeing-a-sex-surrogate.

O'Carroll, T. (1980) *Paedophilia: The radical case*. London: Peter Owen Publishers.

Office for National Statistics (ONS) (3 September 2019) Suicides in the UK: 2018 registrations. Available at: www.ons.gov.uk/peoplepopulationandcommunity/birthsdeathsandmarriages/deaths/bulletins/suicidesintheunitedkingdom/2018 registrations.

Ohambe, O.M.C., Muhigwa, J.B.B. and Wa Mamba, B.M. (2005) Women's Bodies as a Battleground: Sexual violence against women and girls during the war in the Democratic Republic of Congo, South Kivu (1996–2003). Available at: https://www.international-alert.org/publications/womens-bodies-battleground.

Oliver, C. (2011) 'Critical realist grounded theory: A new approach for social work research', *British Journal of Social Work*, 42(2): 371–87.

Oliver, M. (2013) 'The social model of disability: Thirty years on', *Disability & Society*, 28(7): 1024–1026.

Olympic (1969) *Love Camp 7* [film]. Directed by R.L. Frost. Unknown: Olympic International Films.

Oppenheim, M. (25 March 2020) 'Coronavirus: Abortion services at risk of collapse with women denied procedures after government U-turn', *The Independent*. Available at: www.independent.co.uk/news/uk/home-news/coronavirus-abortion-women-telemedicine-nhs-a9424461.html.

ORLAN (1990) *The Reincarnation of Saint-ORLAN* (artwork).

sterman, L., Zampini, G.F. and Stengel, C. (2018) '*Breaking down the walls that divide us: Learning inside out*', Workshop presented at SHIFT conference, University of Greenwich, 6 January.

Outshoorn, J. (2005) 'The political debates on prostitution and trafficking of women', *Social Politics: International Studies in Gender, State and Society*, 12(1): 141–55.

Paltrow, L.M. (1999) 'Pregnant drug users, fetal persons, and the threat to *Roe v. Wade*', *Albany Law Review*, 62(3): 999–1056.

Paltrow, L.M. and Flavin, J. (2013) 'Arrests of and forced interventions on pregnant women in the United States, 1973–2005: Implications for women's legal status and public health', *Journal of Health Politics, Policy and Law*, 38(2): 299–343.

Park, Y. (2016) 'The crucible of sexual violence: Militarized masculinities and the abjection of life in post-crisis, neoliberal South Korea', *Feminist Studies*, 42(1): 17–40.

Paterson, K. and Hughes, B. (1999) 'Disability studies and phenomenology: The carnal politics of everyday life', *Disability & Society*, 14(5): 597–610.

Pegg, S. (2016) 'Could your taste for "teen" porn land you in legal trouble?', *The Conversation*. Available at: https://theconversation.com/could-your-taste-for-teen-porn-land-you-in-legal-trouble-53179.

Pendar, N. (2007) 'Toward spotting the pedophile: Telling victim from predator in text chats', in IEEE International Conference on Semantic Computing (ICSC 2007) (pp. 235–41), Irvine, CA, USA, September.

Penna, L., Clark, A. and Mohay, G. (2005) Challenges of automating the detection of paedophile activity on the internet. In First International Workshop on Systematic Approaches to Digital Forensic Engineering (SADFE'05) (pp. 206–20), IEEE, November.

Penny, L. (2015) 'If men got pregnant, abortion would be legal everywhere', *New Statesman*, 4 December. Available at: www.newstatesman.com/politics/feminism/2015/12/if-men-got-pregnant-abortion-would-be-legal-everywhere.

Peroni, C. (2015) 'Gender-based violence and "feminicide" in queer Italian movements: Questioning gender, sexuality, and the (hetero)normative order', *Oñati Socio-legal Series*, 5(6): 1557–79.

Petchesky, R.P. (1990) *Abortion and Woman's Choice: The state, sexuality, and reproductive freedom*. Boston, MA: Northeastern University Press.

Petchesky, R.P. and Judd, K. (1998) 'Introduction', in Petchesky, R.P. and Judd, K. (eds), *Negotiating Reproductive Rights: Women's perspectives across countries and cultures*. London: Zed Books, pp. 1–30.

Peters, J. (2012) 'Neoliberal convergence in North America and Western Europe: Fiscal austerity, privatization, and public sector reform', *Review of International Political Economy*, 19(2): 208–35.

Peters, M.A. (2017) 'From state responsibility for education and welfare to self-responsibilisation in the market', *Discourse: studies in the cultural politics of education*, 38(1): 138–45.

Peterson, Z.D. and Muehlenhard, C.L. (2007) 'Conceptualizing the "wantedness" of women's consensual and nonconsensual sexual experiences: Implications for how women label their experiences with rape', *Journal of Sex Research*, 44(1): 72–88.

Petley, J. (2009) 'Pornography, panopticism and the Criminal Justice and Immigration Act 2008', *Sociology Compass*, 3(3): 417–32.

Pett, E. (2015) 'A new media landscape? The BBFC, extreme cinema as cult, and technological change', *New Review of Film and Television Studies*, 13(1): 83–99.

Phasha, N. (2009) 'Responses to situations of sexual abuse involving teenagers with intellectual disability', *Sexuality and Disability*, 27(4): 187–203.

Philipps, D. (2 May 2019) '"This is unacceptable": Military reports a surge of sexual assaults in the ranks', *The New York Times*. Available at: www.nytimes.com/2019/05/02/us/military-sexual-assault.html.

Philipps, D. (10 September 2019) 'Six men are speaking out to break the silence', *The New York Times*. Available at: www.nytimes.com/interactive/2019/09/10/us/men-military-sexual-assault.html.

Pickering, S. and Ham, J. (2014) 'Hot pants at the border: Sorting sex work from trafficking', *British Journal of Criminology*, 54(1): 2–19.

Pidd, H. (27 August 2014) 'Failures in Rotherham led to sexual abuse of 1,400 children', *The Guardian*. Available at: www.theguardian.com/society/2014/aug/26/rotherham-sexual-abuse-children.

Pitagora, D. (2013) 'Consent vs coercion: BDSM interactions highlight a fine but immutable line', *The New School Psychology Bulletin*, 10(1): 27–36.

Plummer, K. (1991) 'Understanding childhood sexualities', *Journal of Homosexuality*, 20(1–2): 231–49.

Pollard, A., Nadarzynski, T. and Llewellyn, C. (2018) 'Syndemics of stigma, minority-stress, maladaptive coping, risk environments and littoral spaces among men who have sex with men using chemsex', *Culture, Health & Sexuality*, 20(4): 411–27.

Pollis, A., Schwab, P. and Koggel, C.M. (2006) 'Human rights: A western construct with limited applicability', in Koggel, C. (ed.), *Moral Issues in Global Perspective, Vol. I: Moral and political theory*, 2nd edn. Peterborough, ON: Broadview Press, pp. 60–71.

Popoola, O. (2013) 'Straight to the matter: Fiction', in Ekine, S. and Abbas, K. (eds), *Queer African Reader*. Nairobi: Pambazuka Press, pp. 95–107.

Pornhub (2019) 'The 2019 year in review'. Available at: pornhub.com/insights/2019-year-in-review.

Presdee, M. (2003) *Cultural Criminology and the Carnival of Crime*. Abingdon: Routledge.

Press Association (12 December 2014) 'Face-sitting protest outside parliament against new porn rules', *The Guardian*. Available at: www.theguardian.com/culture/2014/dec/12/face-sitting-protest-outside-parliament-against-new-porn-rules.

Puar, J.K. (2007) *Terrorist Assemblages: Homonationalism in queer times*. Durham, NC: Duke University Press.

Puar, J.K. (2009) 'Prognosis time: Towards a geopolitics of affect, debility and capacity', *Women & Performance: A Journal of Feminist Theory*, 19(2): 161–172.

Puar, J.K. (2013) 'Rethinking homonationalism', *International Journal of Middle East Studies*, 45(2): 336–9.

Public Health England (PHE) (2015) *Disability and domestic abuse: Risk, impacts and response*. Available at: https://assets.publishing.service.gov.uk/government/uploads/system/uploads/attachment_data/file/480942/Disability_and_domestic_abuse_topic_overview_FINAL.pdf.

Pufall, E.L., Kall, M., Shahmanesh, M., Nardone, A., Gilson, R., Delpech, V. and Azad, Y. (2018) 'Sexualized drug use ("chemsex") and high-risk sexual behaviours in HIV-positive men who have sex with men', *HIV Medicine*, 19(4): 261–70.

Puwar, N. (2004) *Space Invaders: Race, gender and bodies out of place*. Oxford: Berg.

RAINN (2019) *Scope of the Problem: Statistics*. Available at: www.rainn.org/statistics/scope-problem.

Rajah, V. (2007) 'Resistance as edgework in violent intimate relationships of drug-involved women', *British Journal of Criminology*, 47(2): 196–213.

Ramsey, C.B. (2006) 'Restructuring the debate over fetal homicide laws', *Ohio State Law Journal*, 67(4): 721–82.

Raustiala, K. and Sprigman, C.J. (2019) 'The second digital disruption: Streaming and the dawn of data-driven creativity', *New York University Law Review*, 94(6): 101–64.

Reagan, L.J. (1997) *When Abortion was a Crime: Women, medicine, and law in the United States, 1867–1973*. Berkeley, CA: University of California Press.

Reagan, L.J. (2010) *Dangerous Pregnancies: Mothers, disabilities, and abortion in America*. Berkeley, CA: University of California Press.

Reed, T.V. (2005) *The Art of Protest: Culture and activism from the civil rights movement to the streets of Seattle*. Minneapolis, MN: University of Minnesota Press.

Refuge (n.d.) *The Facts*. Available at: www.refuge.org.uk/our-work/forms-of-violence-and-abuse/domestic-violence/domestic-violence-the-facts.

Reilly, K. (10 September 2016) 'Read Hillary Clinton's "basket of deplorables" remarks about Donald Trump supporters', *Time.com*. Available at: https://time.com/4486502/hillary-clinton-basket-of-deplorables-transcript.

Reis, S. (2018) 'The impact of austerity on women in the UK', *UK Women's Budget Group*, February. Available at: www.ohchr.org/Documents/Issues/Development/IEDebt/WomenAusterity/WBG.pdf.

Rheaume, C. and Mitty, E. (2008) 'Sexuality and intimacy in older adults', *Geriatric Nursing*, 29(5): 342–9.

Rhodes, T. (2002) 'The "risk environment": a framework for understanding and reducing drug-related harm', *International Journal of Drug Policy*, 13(2): 85–94.

Rich, C., Schutten, J.K. and Rogers, R.A. (2012) '"Don't drop the soap": Organizing sexualities in the repeal of the US military's "don't ask, don't tell" policy', *Communication Monographs*, 79(3): 269–91.

Richardson, D. (2017) 'Rethinking sexual citizenship', *Sociology*, 51(2): 208–24.

Richardson, K. (2016) 'Sex robot matters: Slavery, the prostituted, and the rights of machines', *IEEE Technology and Society Magazine*, 35(2): 46–53.

Ringrose, J., Harvey, L., Gill, R. and Livingstone, S. (2013) 'Teen girls, sexual double standards and "sexting": Gendered value in digital image exchange', *Feminist Theory*, 14(3): 305–23.

Rinker, J. and Lawler, J. (2018) 'Trauma as a collective disease and root cause of protracted social conflict: Peace and conflict', *Journal of Peace Psychology*, 24(2): 150–64.

Roberts, A. (12 July 2019) 'Exhalation by Ted Chiang review: Stories from an SF master', *The Guardian*. Available at: www.theguardian.com/books/2019/jul/12/exhalation-by-ted-chiang-review.

Roberts, D.E. (1997) *Killing the Black Body: Race, reproduction, and the meaning of liberty*. New York: Pantheon Books.

Robertson, K.R. (2005) 'Dark days for the Church: Canon law and the response of the Roman Catholic church to the sex abuse scandals', *Washington University Global Studies Law Review*, 4: 161.

Rollock, N. and Gillborn, D. (2011) *Critical Race Theory (CRT)*. London: British Educational Research Association (BERA).

Rosenbaum, J. and Chesney-Lind, M. (1994) 'Appearance and delinquency: A research note', *Crime & Delinquency*, 40: 50–61.

Rowbottom, J.H. (2018) 'The transformation of obscenity law', *Information & Communication Technology Law*, 27(1): 4–29.

Rowlands, S. and Walker, S. (2019) 'Reproductive control by others: Means, perpetrators and effects', *BMJ Sexual & Reproductive Health*, 45(1): 61–7.

Rubin, G. (1984) 'Thinking sex: Notes for a radical theory of the politics of sexuality', in Vance, C. (ed.), *Pleasure and danger: Exploring female sexuality*. Boston, MA and London: Routledge & Kegan Paul, pp. 143–78.

Rubin, G. (1997) 'Elegy for the Valley of the Kings: AIDS and the leather community in San Francisco, 1981–1996', in Gangon, J.H., Levine, M.P. and Nardi, P.N. (eds), *In Changing Times: Gay men and lesbians encounter HIV/AIDS*. Chicago, IL: University of Chicago Press, pp. 101–44.

Ruhl, L. (1999) 'Liberal governance and prenatal care: Risk and regulation in pregnancy', *Economy and Society*, 28(1): 95–117.

Russell, D.E.H. (1975) *The Politics of Rape: The victim's perspective*. New York: iUniverse.

Ryan-Flood, R. (2009) *Lesbian Motherhood: Gender, families and sexual citizenship*. Basingstoke: Palgrave Macmillan.

Sadler, M., Santos, M.J.D.S., Ruiz-Berdún, D., Rojas, G.L., Skoko, E., Gillen, P. and Clausen, J.A. (2016) 'Moving beyond disrespect and abuse: Addressing the structural dimensions of obstetric violence', *Reproductive Health Matters*, 24(47): 47–55.

Salley, R.J. (2013) 'The face I love: Zanele Muholi's "faces and places"', in Ekine, S. and Abbas, K. (eds), *Queer African Reader*. Nairobi: Pambazuka Press, pp. 107–19.

Sandhu, S. (25 October 2019) 'Universal Credit: Women say they are forced into "survival sex" by DWP's five-week wait, MPs warn', *inews*. Available at: https://inews.co.uk/news/politics/universal-credit-dwp-women-survival-sex-five-week-wait-mps-820022.

Saunders, C.J. (2001) *Rape and Ravishment in Literature of Medieval England*. Woodbridge, Suffolk: D.S. Brewer.

Saunders, R. (2019) 'Computer-generated pornography and convergence: Animation and algorithms as new digital desire', *Convergence: The International Journal of Research into New Media Technologies*, 25(2): 241–59.

Scarborough, R. (20 May 2013) 'Victims of sex assaults in military are mostly men', *The Washington Times*. Available at: www.washingtontimes.com/news/2013/may/20/victims-of-sex-assaults-in-military-are-mostly-sil/?utm_medium = RSS&utm_source = RSS_Feed.

Scheutz, M. and Arnold, T. (2016) *'Are we ready for sex robots?'*, 2016 11th ACM/IEEE International Conference on Human–Robot Interaction (HRI) (pp. 351–8), Christchurch, NZ, March.

Schierup, C.U. and Ålund, A. (2011) 'The end of Swedish exceptionalism? Citizenship, neoliberalism and the politics of exclusion', *Race & Class*, 53(1): 45–64.

Schneider, J.P. (2000a) 'Effects of cybersex addiction of the family: Results of a survey', *Sexual Addiction and Compulsivity: The Journal of Treatment and Prevention*, 7 (1–2): 31–58.

Schneider, J.P. (2000b) 'A qualitative study of cybersex participants: Gender differences, recovery issues, and implications for therapists', *Sexual Addiction and Compulsivity: The Journal of Treatment and Prevention*, 7 (1–2): 249–78.

Schwartz, M.F. and Southern, S. (2000) 'Compulsive cybersex: The new tearoom', *Sexual Addiction and Compulsivity: The Journal of Treatment and Prevention*, 7(1–2): 127–44.

Schweickart, P.P. (1986) 'Reading ourselves: Toward a feminist theory of reading', in Flynn, E. and Schweickart, P.P. (eds), *Gender and Reading: Essays on readers, texts and contexts*. Baltimore, MD: John Hopkins Press, pp. 31–62.

Scoular, J. (2010) 'What's law got to do with it? How and why law matters in the regulation of sex work', *Journal of Law and Society*, 37(1): 12–39.

Scoular, J. and Carline, A. (2014) 'A critical account of a "creeping neo-abolitionism": Regulating prostitution in England and Wales', *Criminology & Criminal Justice*, 14(5): 608–26.

Scoular, J. and O'Neill, M. (2008) 'Legal incursions into supply/demand: Criminalising and responsibilising the buyers and sellers of sex in the UK', in Munro, V.E. and Della Giusta, M. (eds), *Demanding Sex: Critical reflections on the regulation of prostitution*. Farnham: Ashgate, pp. 13–33.

Sedgwick E.K. (2003) *Touching Feeling: Affect, pedagogy and performativity*. Durham, NC: Duke University Press.

S.E.F.I. (1976) *SS Experiment Camp* (Lager SSadis Kastrat Kommandantur) [film]. Directed by S. Garrone. Rome: S.E.F.I. Cinematografica.

Selby, J. (1 September 2014) 'Perez Hilton apologises for publishing Jennifer Lawrence naked 4Chan photos', *The Independent Online*. Available at: www.independent.co.uk/news/people/perez-hilton-apologises-for-jennifer-lawrence-nude-photo-leak-9703045.html.

Serfozo, B., and Farrell, H. (1996) 'From sex-vixens to senators – Representation in Nazi porn and the discourse of the American right wing', *Journal of Social and Political Thought*, 1, (1). Available at: www.yorku.ca/jspot/1/hfarrell2.htm.

Seto, M.C. (2012) 'Is pedophilia a sexual orientation?', *Archives of Sexual Behavior*, 41(1): 231–6.

Sewell, J., Miltz, A., Lampe, F.C., Cambiano, V., Speakman, A., Phillips, A.N. and Clarke, A. (2017) 'Poly drug use, chemsex drug use, and associations with sexual risk behaviour in HIV-negative men who have sex with men attending sexual health clinics', *International Journal of Drug Policy*, 43: 33–43.

Shakespeare, T. (2006) 'The social model of disability', *The Disability Studies Reader*, 2, 197–204.

Shakespeare, T. (2013) *Disability Rights and Wrongs Revisited*. Routledge.

Shakespeare, T. and Richardson, S. (2018) 'The sexual politics of disability, twenty years on', *Scandinavian Journal of Disability Research*, 20(1): 82–91.

Shakespeare, T. and Watson, N. (2001) 'The social model of disability: An outdated ideology?', *Exploring Theories and Expanding Methodologies: Where we are and where we need to go*. Bingley: Emerald Group, pp. 9–28.

Shakespeare, T., Gillespie-Sells, K. and Davies, D. (1996) *The Sexual Politics of Disability: Untold desires*. London: Burns & Oates.

Shapiro, A.H. (2013) 'Patriarchy, objectification, and violence against women in Schindler's List and Angry Harvest', in Goldenberg, M. and Shapiro, A.H. (eds), *Different Horrors, Same Hell: Gender and the Holocaust*. Seattle, WA: University of Washington Press, pp. 79–98.

Shared Hope (2012) 'National colloquium: An inventory and evaluation of the current shelter and services response to domestic minor sex trafficking – 2012 final report', *Shared Hope.org*. Available at: http://sharedhope.org/wp-content/uploads/2013/05/National-Colloquium-2012-Report-B.pdf.

Sharlach, L. (1999) 'Gender and genocide in Rwanda: Women as agents and objects of genocide', *Journal of Genocide Research*, 1(3): 387–99.

Sharlach, L. (2000) 'Rape as genocide: Bangladesh, the former Yugoslavia, and Rwanda', *New Political Science*, 22(1): 89–102.

Sheldon, S. (2015) 'The regulatory cliff edge between contraception and abortion: The legal and moral significance of implantation', *Journal of Medical Ethics*, 41(9): 762–5.

Sheldon, S. (2016) 'The decriminalisation of abortion: An argument for modernisation', *Oxford Journal of Legal Studies*, 36(2): 334–65.

Sherman, L.W. (1978) *Scandal and Reform: Controlling police corruption*. Berkeley, CA: University of California Press.

Shildrick, M. (2007) 'Contested pleasures: The sociopolitical economy of disability and sexuality', *Sexuality Research & Social Policy*, 4(1): 53–66.

Shukman, H. (15 February 2015) 'Online comments reveal Florida gunman Nikolas Cruz idolized Santa Barbara shooter Elliot Rodger', *babe.net*. Available at: https://babe.net/2018/02/15/nikolas-cruz-elliot-rodger-35621.

Sibalis, M. (2002) 'Homophobia, Vichy France, and the "crime of homosexuality": The origins of the ordinance of 6 August 1942', *GLQ: A Journal of Lesbian and Gay Studies*, 8(3): 301–18.

Siegel, L. (1992) 'The criminalization of pregnant and child-rearing drug users', in O'Hare, P.A., Newcombe, R., Matthews, A., Buning, E.C. and Drucker, E. (eds), *The Reduction of Drug-related Harm*. London: Routledge, pp. 95–107.

Silvestri, M. (2017) 'Police culture and gender: Revisiting the "cult of masculinity"', *Policing: A Journal of Policy and Practice*, 11(3): 289–300.

Simpson, J. (25 July 2014) 'Gay Saudi Arabian man sentenced to three years and 450 lashes for meeting men via Twitter', *The Independent*. Available at: www.independent.co.uk/news/world/middle-east/gay-saudi-arabian-man-sentenced-to-three-years-and-450-lashes-for-meeting-men-via-twitter-9628204.html.

SisterSong (n.d.) *Reproductive Justice*. Available at: www.sistersong.net/reproductive-justice.

Sivakumaran, S. (2007) 'Sexual violence against men in armed conflict', *European Journal of International Law*, 18(2): 253–76.

Sjoberg, L. (2013) *Gendering global conflict: Toward a feminist theory of war*. New York: Columbia University Press.

Sköld, J. (2013) 'Historical abuse: A contemporary issue – Compiling inquiries into abuse and neglect of children in out-of-home care worldwide', *Journal of Scandinavian Studies in Criminology and Crime Prevention*, 14(supp1): 5–23.

Sky News (25 October 2019) 'Selling sex for £5 is the only way I can survive after Universal Credit chaos', *Sky News*. Available at: https://news.sky.com/story/selling-sex-for-5-is-the-only-way-i-can-survive-after-universal-credit-chaos-11844413.

Slade, J.W. (1984) 'Violence in the hard-core pornographic film: A historical survey', *Journal of Communication*, 34(3): 148–63.

Slade, J.W. (2006) 'Eroticism and technological regression: The stag film', *History and Technology*, 22(1): 27–52.

Smart, C. (1977) *Women, Crime and Criminology: A feminist critique*. London: Routledge & Kegan Paul.

Smart, C. (1989) *Feminism and the Power of Law*. London and New York: Routledge.

Smith, A.M. (1992) 'Resisting the erasure of lesbian sexuality: A challenge for queer activism', in Plummer, K. (ed.), *Modern Homosexualities: Fragments of lesbian and gay experience*. New York: Routledge, pp. 200–17.

Smith, J. (2013[1989]) *Misogynies*. London: The Westbourne Press.

Smith, O. and Raymen, T. (2018) 'Deviant leisure: A criminological perspective', *Theoretical Criminology*, 22(1): 63–82.

Solinger, R. (2005) *Pregnancy and Power: A short history of reproductive politics in America*. New York: New York University Press.

Solnit, R. (2016[2004]) *Hope in the Dark: Untold histories, wild possibilities*. Edinburgh: Canongate Books.

Solt, F. (2011) 'Diversionary nationalism: Economic inequality and the formation of national pride', *The Journal of Politics*, 73(3): 821–30.

Solvang, P. (2007) 'The amputee body desired: Beauty destabilized? Disability re-valued?', *Sexuality and Disability*, 25(2): 51–64.

Spalek, B. and O'Rawe, M. (2014) 'Researching counterterrorism: A critical perspective from the field in the light of allegations and findings of covert activities by undercover police officers', *Critical Studies on Terrorism*, 7(1): 150–64.

Spanakos, A.P. (2018) 'Violent births: Fanon, Westworld, and humanity', in South, J.B. and Engels, K.S. (eds), *Westworld and Philosophy*. Chichester: Wiley Blackwell, pp. 229–38.

Spinoza, B. de (2014[1674]) *Letters to Friend and Foe*. New York: Open Road Media.

Spivak, G.C. (1988) 'Can the subaltern speak?', in Nelson, C. and Grossberg, L. (eds), *Marxism and the Interpretation of Culture*. London: Macmillan.

Sreekumar, T.T. (2013) 'Global South perspectives on youth culture and gender imaginations in the technological society', *Journal of Creative Communication*, 8(2–3): 77–88.

Staksrud, E. (2013) 'Online grooming legislation: Knee-jerk regulation?', *European Journal of Communication*, 28(2): 152–67.

Stallybrass, P. and White, A. (1986) *The Politics and Poetics of Transgression*. New York: Cornell University Press.

Stanley, E. (2016) 'Silencing violations in state care', *New Zealand Sociology*, 31(1): 8–28.

Stanko, E.A. (1985) *Intimate Intrusion: Women's experiences of male violence*. London and New York: Routledge & Kegan Paul.

Stanko, E.A. (1990) *Everyday Violence: How women and men experience sexual and physical danger*. London: Pandora.

Steele, S.L. and Shores, T. (2014) 'More than just a famous face: Exploring the rise of the celebrity expert-advocate through anti-trafficking action by the Demi and Ashton Foundation', *Crime, Media, Culture*, 10(3): 259–72.

Steinmetz, K. (3 April 2018). The Oxford English Dictionary Added 'Trans*.' Here's What the Label Means. *Time*. Available at https://time.com/5211799/what-does-trans-asterisk-star-mean-dictionary/

Strong, T.H. (2000) *Expecting Trouble: The myth of prenatal care in America*. New York: New York University Press.

Strudwick, P. (3 December 2016) 'Inside the dark, dangerous world of chemsex', *BuzzFeed*. Available at: www.buzzfeed.com/patrickstrudwick/inside-the-dark-dangerous-world-of-chemsex.

Stychin, C.F. (1995) *Laws' Desire: Sexuality and the limits of justice*. London: Routledge

Sullivan, A. (21 January 2019) 'Gay priests and the lives they no longer want to hide', *The New York Magazine*. Available at: https://nymag.com/intelligencer/2019/01/gay-priests-catholic-church.html.

Sullivan, N. (2008) 'Disorienting paraphilias', *Disability, Desire, and the Question of (Bio)Ethics*, 5(2–3): 183–92.

Swain, S. (2014) 'History of Australian inquiries reviewing institutions providing care for children', *Australian Catholic University*. Available at: https://researchbank.acu.edu.au/cgi/viewcontent.cgi?referer = https://scholar.google.co.uk/&httpsredir = 1&article = 5146&context = fea_pub.

Swain, S. (2015) 'Giving voice to narratives of institutional sex abuse', *Australian Feminist Law Journal*, 41(2): 289–304.

Takai, A. (2011) 'Rape and forced pregnancy as genocide before the Bangladesh tribunal', *Temple International and Comparative Law Journal*, 25: 393–422.

Takševa, T. (2015) 'Genocidal rape, enforced impregnation, and the discourse of Serbian national identity', *Comparative Literature and Culture*, 17(3): 2–8.

Takševa, T. and Schwartz, T. (2018) 'Hybridity, ethnicity and nationhood: Legacies of interethnic war, wartime rape and the potential for bridging the ethnic divide in post-conflict Bosnia and Herzegovina', *National Identities*, 20(5): 463–80.

Tamas, D., Jovanovic, N.B., Rajic, M., Ignjatovic, V.B. and Prkosovacki, B.P. (2019) 'Professionals, parents and the general public: Attitudes towards the sexuality of persons with intellectual disability', *Sexuality and Disability*, 37: 245–58.

Tatchell, P. (1992) *Europe in the Pink*. London: GMP.

Tate (n.d.) *Guerilla Girls*. Available at: www.tate.org.uk/art/artists/guerrilla-girls-6858.

Taylor, D. (9 July 2019) 'More than 500 victims of trafficking detained in 2018, UK study finds', *The Guardian*. Available at: www.theguardian.com/law/2019/jul/09/more-than-500-victims-of-trafficking-detained-in-2018-uk-study-finds.

Taylor, M. and Quayle, E. (2003) *Child Pornography: An internet crime*. London: Psychology Press.

Tegmark, M. (2018) *Life 3.0: Being human in the age of artificial intelligence*. London: Penguin.

Temkin, J. (1987) *Rape and the Legal Processes*. London: Sweet & Maxwell.

Terry, K.J. (2008) 'Stained glass: The nature and scope of child sexual abuse in the Catholic Church', *Criminal Justice and Behavior*, 35(5): 549–69.

Terry, K.J. (2015) 'Child sexual abuse within the Catholic Church: A review of global perspectives', *International Journal of Comparative and Applied Criminal Justice*, 39(2): 139–54.

Thinkuknow (n.d.) 'Why don't children tell their parents about sexual abuse?' Available at: www.thinkuknow.co.uk/parents/articles/Why-dont-children-tell-their-parents-about-sexual-abuse.

Thomas, E.J., Stelzl, M. and Lafrance, M.N. (2017) 'Faking to finish: Women's accounts of feigning sexual pleasure to end unwanted sex', *Sexualities*, 20(3): 281–301.

Thompson, H.S. (2005[1971]) *Fear and Loathing in Las Vegas*. London: Harper Perennial.

Thoreau, H.D. (1993[1849]) *Civil Disobedience, and Other Essays*. New York: Dover Thrift Editions, Courier Corporations, pp. 1–19.

Tomso, G. (2004) 'Bug chasing, barebacking, and the risks of care', *Literature and Medicine*, 23(1): 88–111.

Townsend, M. and Thompson, T. (22 January 2011) 'Undercover police cleared "to have sex with activists"', *The Guardian*. Available at: www.theguardian.com/uk/2011/jan/22/undercover-police-cleared-sex-activists.

Travis, M. (2014) 'Non-normative bodies, rationality, and legal personhood', *Medical Law Review*, 22(4): 526–47.

Trenholm, J., Olsson, P., Blomqvist, M. and Ahlberg, B.M. (2013) 'Constructing soldiers from boys in Eastern Democratic Republic of Congo', *Men and Masculinities*, 16(2): 203–27.

Tsang, E.Y.H. (2019) 'Selling sex as an edgework: Risk taking and thrills in China's commercial sex industry', *International Journal of Offender Therapy and Comparative Criminology*, 63(8): 1306–29.

Tuerkheimer, D. (2006) 'Conceptualizing violence against pregnant women', *Indiana Law Journal*, 81(2): 667–712.

Tufail, W. (2015) 'Rotherham, Rochdale, and the racialised threat of the "Muslim grooming gang"', *International Journal for Crime, Justice and Social Democracy*, 4(3): 30–43.

Turner, C. (4 October 2018) 'Majority of three- and four-year-olds now own an iPad, survey finds', *The Telegraph*. Available at: www.telegraph.co.uk/education/2018/10/04/majority-three-four-year-olds-now-ipad-survey-finds.

Turner, G. (1 January 2019) *My Stepdad's Huge Data Set*. Available at: https://logicmag.io/play/my-stepdad's-huge-data-set.

UK Parliament (n.d.a) *Abortion Bill 2017–19*. Available at: https://services.parliament.uk/Bills/2017-19/abortion.html.

UK Parliament (n.d.b) *Abortion Bill [HL] 2019–21*. Available at: https://services.parliament.uk/bills/2019-21/abortion.html.

Undercover Policing Inquiry (17 March 2020) *The Undercover Policing Inquiry's First Evidence Hearings in June Postponed due to COVID-19*. Available at: www.ucpi.org.uk/2020/03/17/hearings-postponed-covid-19.

Unicef (2019) *Sexual Violence*. Available at: https://data.unicef.org/topic/child-protection/violence/sexual-violence.

United Nations (1948) *Universal Declaration of Human Rights*. Available at: www.un.org/en/universal-declaration-human-rights.

United Nations (2004) *United Nations Convention against Transnational Organised Crime and the Protocols Thereto*. Available at: www.unodc.org/documents/treaties/UNTOC/Publications/TOC%20Convention/TOCebook-e.pdf.

United Nations (2014) *Reproductive Rights Are Human Rights: A handbook for national human rights institutions*. Available at: www.unwomen.org/en/docs/2014/1/reproductive-rights-are-human-rights.

United Nations General Assembly (UNGA) (2014) *Convention on the Prevention and Punishment of the Crime of Genocide*. Available at: www.oas.org/dil/1948_Convention_on_the_Prevention_and_Punishment_of_the_Crime_of_Genocide.pdf.

United Nations Office on Drugs and Crime (UNODC) (2018) *Global Report on Trafficking in Persons*. Available at: www.unodc.org/documents/data-and-analysis/glotip/2018/GLOTiP_2018_BOOK_web_small.pdf.

United Nations Statistics Division (2015) *The World's Women 2015: Trends and statistics*. Available at: https://unstats.un.org/unsd/gender/worldswomen.html.

Universal (2014) *Ex Machina* [film]. Directed by A. Garland. London: Universal Pictures International.

UN Women (2019a) *Facts and Figures: Ending violence against women*. Available at: www.unwomen.org/en/what-we-do/ending-violence-against-women/facts-and-figures.

UN Women (2019b) *Reforming the Laws that Forced Women to Marry their Rapists*. Available at: www.unwomen.org/en/news/stories/2019/6/feature-story-of-change-reforming-laws-that-forced-women-to-marry-their-rapists.

Van Doorn, N. (2010) 'Keeping it real: User-generated pornography, gender reification, and visual pleasure', *Convergence*, 16(4): 411–30.

Van Wormer, K. and Berns, L. (2004) 'The impact of priest sexual abuse: Female survivors' narratives', *Affilia*, 19(1): 53–67.

Vergun, D. (2016) *Efforts Underway to Erase Male Sexual Assault Stigma: Focus on prevention*. Available at: www.army.mil/article/179870/efforts_underway_to_erase_male_sexual_assault_stigma_focus_on_prevention.

Villar, F., Celdrán, M., Fabà, J. and Serrat, R. (2014) 'Staff attitudes towards sexual relationships among institutionalized people with dementia: Does an extreme cautionary stance predominate?', *International Psychogeriatrics*, 26(3): 403–12.

Vint, S. (25 May 2019) 'The technologies that remake us: On Ted Chiang's "exhalation: stories"', *LA Review of Books*. Available at: https://lareviewofbooks.org/article/the-technologies-that-remake-us-on-ted-chiangs-exhalation-stories.

Vojdik, V.K. (2014) 'Sexual violence against men and women in war: A masculinities approach', *Nevada Law Journal*, 14(3): 923–52.

Vuolajärvi, N. (2019) 'Governing in the name of caring: The Nordic model of prostitution and its punitive consequences for migrants who sell sex', *Sexuality Research and Social Policy*, 16(2): 151–65.

Wagner, M. (2006) *Born in the USA: How a broken maternity system must be fixed to put mothers and infants first*. Berkeley, CA: University of California Press.

Waller, J. (2012) 'Rape as a tool of "othering" in genocide', in Rittner, C. and Roth, J. (eds), *Rape: Weapon of war and genocide*. St. Paul, MN: Paragon, pp. 83–100.

Wallerstein, I. (2005) 'After developmentalism and globalization, what?', *Social Forces*, 83(3): 1263–78.

Ware, V. and Back, L. (2002) *Out of Whiteness: Color, politics, and culture*. Chicago: University of Chicago Press.

Warinda, N.L. (2013) 'The vampire bite that brought me to life: Fiction', in Ekine, S. and Abbas, K. (eds), *Queer African Reader*. Nairobi: Pambazuka Press, pp. 69–78.

Warner and *Village* (1999) *The Matrix*. Director: The Wachowskis. Los Angeles, CA: Warner Bros. and Village Roadshow Pictures.

Warner, C. and Armstrong, M. (2020) 'The role of military law and systemic issues in the military's handling of sexual assault cases', *Law and Society Review*, 54(1): 265–300.

Warren, C.A. (1996) *First, Do Not Speak: Errant doctors, sexual abuse, and institutional silence*. Urbana, IL: University of Illinois at Urbana-Champaign.

Webber, F. (2019) 'On the creation of the UK's "hostile environment"', *Race & Class*, 60(4): 76–87.

Weber, M. (1919) *Politics as a Vocation*. Available at: http://fs2.american.edu/dfagel/www/class%20readings/weber/politicsasavocation.pdf.

Weeks, J. (1981) *Society: The regulation of sexuality since 1800*. London and New York: Longman.

Weiss, M. (2006) 'Mainstreaming kink: The politics of BDSM representation in US popular culture', in Kleinplatz, P.J. and Moser, C. (eds), *Sadomasochism: Powerful pleasures*. New York: Harrington Park Press, pp. 103–32.

Weiss, M. (2011) *Techniques of Pleasure: BDSM and the circuits of sexuality*. Durham, NC and London: Duke University Press.

Weitzer, R. (2014) 'New directions in research on human trafficking', *The ANNALS of the American Academy of Political and Social Science*, 653(1): 6–24.

Wells, A. and Thompson, H. (2011) 'Abortion row', *YouGov*, 6 September. Available at: https://yougov.co.uk/topics/politics/articles-reports/2011/09/06/abortion-row.

Wertz, R.W. and Wertz, D.C. (1989) *Lying In: A history of childbirth in America*. New Haven, CT: Yale University Press.

West, R. (1996) 'A comment on consent, sex, and rape', *Legal Theory*, 2(3): 233–51.

We Trust Women (n.d.) *5 Reasons to Decriminalise Abortion*. Available at: https://wetrustwomen.org.uk/5-reasons-to-decriminalise-abortion.

White, C. (2006) 'The Spanner trials and the changing law on sadomasochism in the UK', *Journal of Homosexuality*, 50(2–3): 167–87.

White, M.D. and Terry, K.J. (2008) 'Child sexual abuse in the Catholic Church: Revisiting the rotten apples explanation', *Criminal Justice and Behavior*, 35(5): 658–78.

White Ribbon Alliance (2020) *Respectful Maternity Care*. Available at: www.whiteribbonalliance.org/rmctoolkit.

Whitty, M.T. (2013) 'The scammers persuasive techniques model: Development of a stage model to explain the online dating romance scam', *British Journal of Criminology*, 53(4): 665–684.

Whitty, M.T. (2015) 'Anatomy of the online dating romance scam', *Security Journal*, 28(4): 443–55.

Whitty, M.T. (2018) 'Do you love me? Psychological characteristics of romance scam victims'. *Cyberpsychology, Behaviour and Social networking*, 21(2): 105–9.

Whitty, M.T. and Buchanan, T. (2016) 'The online dating romance scam: The psychological impact on victims – both financial and non-financial', *Criminology & Criminal Justice*, 16(2): 176–94.

Wickramasekara, P. (2008) 'Globalisation, international labour migration and the rights of migrant workers', *Third World Quarterly*, 29(7): 1247–64.

Wilkinson, E. (2009) 'Perverting visual pleasure: Representing sadomasochism', *Sexualities*, 12(2): 181–98.

Wilkinson, E. (2011) 'Extreme pornography and the contested spaces of virtual citizenship', *Social and Cultural Geography*, 12(5): 494–508.

Wilkinson, S. (21 April 2014) 'Meet the woman having an abortion so she can appear on *Big Brother*', *Grazia Magazine*. Available at: https://graziadaily.co.uk/life/real-life/meet-woman-aborting-baby-can-appear-big-brother.

Wilkinson, S. (21 December 2017) 'Consent, dildos and deception: Reexamining the trial of Gayle Newland', *Vice.com*. Available at: www.vice.com/en_uk/article/43qvz9/consent-dildos-and-deception-reexamining-the-trial-of-gayle-newland.

Wilkinson, V.J., Theodore, K. and Raczka, R. (2015) '"As normal as possible": Sexual identity development in people with intellectual disabilities transitioning to adulthood', *Sexuality and Disability*, 33(1): 93–105.

Williams, D.J. (2009) 'Deviant leisure: Rethinking "the good, the bad, and the ugly"', *Leisure Sciences*, 31(2): 207–13.

Williams, L. (1991) 'Film bodies: Gender, genre and excess', *Film Quarterly*, 44(4): 2–13.

Williams, L. (1989/1999) *Hard Core: Power, pleasure, and the 'frenzy of the visible'*, expanded edition. London: University of California Press.

Wiskerke, E. and Manthorpe, J. (2019) 'Intimacy between care home residents with dementia: Findings from a review of the literature', *Dementia*, 18(1): 94–107.

Wolak, J. and Finkelhor, D. (2011) *Sexting: A typology*. Durham, NC: Crimes against Children Research Centre.

Wood, E. and Toppelberg, N. (2017) 'The persistence of sexual assault within the US military', *Journal of Peace Research*, 54(5): 620–33.

Woolner, L., Denov, M. and Kahn, S. (2019) '"I asked myself if I would ever love my baby": Mothering children born of genocidal rape in Rwanda', *Violence against Women*, 25(6): 703–20.

World Health Organization (WHO) (31 January 2020) 'Adolescent pregnancy', *WHO*. Available at: www.who.int/news-room/fact-sheets/detail/adolescent-pregnancy.

Wright, K. and Swain, S. (2018) 'Speaking the unspeakable, naming the unnameable: The Royal Commission into institutional responses to child sexual abuse', *Journal of Australian Studies*, 42(2): 139–52.

Yeoman, I. and Mars, M. (2012) 'Robots, men and sex tourism', *Futures*, 44(4): 365–71.

Young, A. (2000) 'Aesthetic vertigo and the jurisprudence of disgust', *Law and Critique*, 11(3): 241–65.

Young, I.M. (1990) *Throwing like a Girl and Other Essays in Feminist Philosophy*. Bloomington, IN: Indiana University Press.

Young, J. (1971) *The Drugtakers: The social meaning of drug use*. London: MacGibbon & Kee.

Yttergren, Å. and Westerstrand, J. (2016) 'The Swedish legal approach to prostitution. Trends and tendencies in the prostitution debate', *NORA: Nordic Journal of Feminist and Gender Research*, 24(1): 45–55.

Zurbriggen, E.L. (2010) 'Rape, war, and the socialization of masculinity: Why our refusal to give up war ensures that rape cannot be eradicated', *Psychology of Women Quarterly*, 34(4): 538–49.

Index